A Geography of
19th-Century Britain

A Geography of 19th-Century Britain

P. J. Perry

Reader in Geography, University of Canterbury,
Christchurch, New Zealand

B. T. Batsford Ltd,
London & Sydney

First published 1975

Copyright © P. J. Perry, 1975

Printed and bound in Great Britain by
Redwood Burn Ltd, Trowbridge and Esher
for the publishers,
B. T. Batsford Ltd, 4 Fitzhardinge Street, London W1 and
23 Cross Street, Brookvale, N.S.W. 2100, Australia.

ISBN hardcover 0 7134 3021 4
       paperback 0 7134 3022 2

Contents

List of Figures

List of Photographs

Acknowledgements

No book, least of all an overview, can be written without a great deal of help from a great number of people; that help I am delighted to acknowledge.

Firstly my thanks are due to my colleagues in the University of Canterbury, where the book was conceived and completed, and friends in the University of Cambridge, where it came into existence during a period of leave in 1972-3. The maps were drawn and many of the photographs prepared in the Department of Geography of the University of Canberbury, where too a difficult manuscript was transformed into an immaculate typescript. The origin of particular maps and pictures is acknowledged elsewhere and it remains to thank collectively the many individuals and institutions who helped in this respect. As this book was written in libraries and on the basis of their resources I most gladly acknowledge the expertise and tolerance of the many librarians who have helped me, particularly in Christchurch and Cambridge.

My teachers are now become too numerous to mention; nevertheless they deserve my thanks. Professor Gordon East has proved a most helpful editor, and two colleagues, Dr G. C. Wynn and Dr L. E. Richardson, geographer and historian respectively, undertook the arduous but essential task of reading a preliminary version and providing critical comment. Responsibility for failings and shortcomings is mine alone.

Finally I would wish to thank David Peat who whiled away my lunch hours, the campanologists of Cambridge and elsewhere with whom I enjoyed so many delightful evenings, Rachel-Mary who came as often as she could, and my many friends, relations and helpers who found themselves in some wise caught up with the making of this book.

Peter Perry

Christchurch, N.Z.   1974

For the Perrys and the Armitages

Introduction

The aim of this book is to acquaint students of nineteenth-century British history and twentieth-century British geography with the geography of nineteenth-century Britain. The book may interest my academic peers, but its particular concern is the needs of students in their last two years at school and their first and second years at university or college. With their requirements rather than with those characteristic of the research frontier I have tried to contend.

An assumption that some knowledge of the geography of nineteenth-century Britain is needed by the historian and the geographer makes no claim to originality. Rather it is to share the point of view of a number of notable historians, Macaulay, Trevelyan and Clapham for example, and of the doyen of British geographers, Clifford Darby. Darby has written that 'the foundations of geographical study lie in geomorphology and historical geography', and that these foundations exist to be built upon. My aim is then to underpin the larger structures of nineteenth-century history and twentieth-century geography. My experiences as a university teacher and my reading convince me that the methodological developments of the last quarter-century have neither removed the need for such underpinnings nor done very much to improve students' substantive or methodological grasp of these foundations. And at the risk of appearing arrogant I would thus claim to be taking part in the basic activity of every university, so succinctly expressed by Sir Alan Bullock in the phrase 'grappling with ignorance'.

I make no claim that this book is original scholarship (whatever that phrase may mean), but an organiser and arranger of 'other men's flowers' can scarcely avoid putting forward some of his own ideas, especially when he has hitherto worked in such areas as nineteenth-century population geography, transport geography, and, more recently and more extensively, agricultural geography. My involvement in these areas of research has, I think, facilitated and stimulated the operation of taking an overview which is the essence of this book. In parting company from the many academics who assert, by precept and practice, that the time is never ripe for taking such perspectives I would strongly assert that the research frontier is the proper place from which to view so rich a panorama. Whether or not the reader shares this point of view, or the substantive opinions put forward in the book itself, I can but hope that he enjoys reading it as much as I have enjoyed writing it.

1 Britain in 1800:
A Transitional Geography

Britain in 1800 was in the middle of that transition known to later generations as the Industrial Revolution[1]; a thinly peopled and primarily rural society on the periphery of Europe was becoming densely populated, urban and industrial, soon to occupy a lynch-pin role in the world economy. Many of these changes were conspicuous – canal building, road improvement, new cotton mills by the score in east Lancashire – but it would be a mistake to believe that these were the changes which captured the popular imagination at the start of the nineteenth century. The popular imagination was captured by Napoleon Bonaparte and his military success; a traveller through Britain could not fail to observe his impact on the landscape: army encampments, unusually active naval dockyards, defensive works such as the Royal Military Canal, even a surge of enclosure of open fields and wasteland brought about by wartime inflation and fears for the nation's food supply. Most of these changes were not of lasting importance; even those which were, enclosure for example, commonly extended beyond what could be sustained after the war. The fundamental changes were relatively inconspicuous – the population explosion, the establishment of factories, the widespread adoption of up-to-date farming methods. Moreover in certain sectors it is hard to see fundamental changes when allowance has been made for the effects of war; coalmining and wool manufacturing for example were progressing unspectacularly in established locations, by established methods and for established markets. If the economic, social and military situation favoured change it was not such as to bring about simultaneous or instantaneous

revolution on a broad front. The political institutions of the
period were certainly not such as directly to favour change for
they reflected a vanished geography, rotten boroughs rather
than manufacturing towns, and a traditional view of society in
which the landed interest was pre-eminent over the urban or
industrial. Where property rights were at stake Parliament acted,
in regulating enclosure and canal and railway building for
example; where they were not it was usually unconcerned, an
attitude by no means unfavourable to the interests of the first
generation of factory-building industrialists.

Early nineteenth-century Britain was then an institutionally
conservative — its critics would probably have used stronger
language, corrupt or rotten — society, but not so powerfully or
deliberately so as effectively to restrain the forces of change,
social, economic and geographic.

The methods and motives of those who brought about these
changes were, in essence, the increase of private profit. They
may have limited appeal in the 1970s, and indeed have recently
been described as the 'unacceptable face of capitalism', but
whether or not we approve we live in a world as much of their
making as of ours. A survey of how the geography of Britain
changed during the course of the nineteenth century must then
point to the present; it must necessarily begin with a view of the
geography of 1800. A comprehensive insight into this geography is impossible and like the surveyor's framework of bench
marks any view is necessarily selective, providing nothing more
than the basis from which important and accessible points may
be picked out and described. The latter adjective is as important
as the former, for there remain many lacunae in our knowledge
of Britain at the start of the nineteenth century. Fragmented,
partial and imperfect studies are the raw materials for an
overview and they always will be, thus invalidating the
commonest criticism of any attempt at scholarly synthesis —
the limitations and shortcomings of what has already been
done. The search for a final and authoritative historical
geography of any period or place is sure to be as unending as
the quest of the historical Jesus. The reward is not the finding
but the seeking.

THE INCREASE OF POPULATION

In 1789 England and Wales had a population exceeding eight million, in 1815 exceeding 11 million; the population of Scotland grew from a million and a quarter in 1755 to exceed two million in 1821. These rates of increase are less spectacular than those of the Third World in the twentieth century, but

Figure 1. The population of Britain at the first (1801) census, and Ireland at the first (1821) census. (Persons per thousand acres: 1, 1600 and over; 2, 800-1599; 3, 400-799; 4, 200-399; 5, 100-199; 6, less than 99.) Note (i) axial belt from Thames to Mersey, (ii) high densities in East Anglia and the West of England, (iii) high and relatively uniform densities in Ireland. (Redrawn from Watson, J.W., and Sissons, J.B., *The British Isles: A Systematic Geography*, London, 1964, figure 29.)

prior to the nineteenth century they had rarely been achieved and never sustained. The population geography of Britain at the start of the nineteenth century is not however merely a matter of spectacular numerical increase; geographical redistribution was both part of the phenomenon of increase and one of its causes. In fact much of the increase was concentrated in a few areas. In 1700 the most densely populated county in England, Worcestershire, had 141 persons per square mile; the least, Westmorland, 54 per square mile. Comparable figures in 1801 are 360 for Surrey and 55 for Westmorland. In some localities, notably but not exclusively in Scotland, depopulation on a modest scale had already begun in rural areas.

The general pattern of redistribution which was taking place eventually replaced the dominance of the lowland zone in general, East Anglia, London and the West Country in particular, by an axis of maximum population extending from London through the Midlands to Liverpool (figure 1). In 1800 this axis was very incomplete and interrupted and moreover there were other new areas of high density — the West Riding and central Scotland for example. The most rapid increase of population was to be found on the coalfield margins of the highland zone, where not only coal but also water power was most abundant, conspicuously in Lancashire. Much of this growth was as yet rural rather than urban: Liverpool and Manchester were growing fast, but even the newest cotton mills were as often as not in the countryside.

The increase of population in the cities and in the new industrial communities resulted on the one hand from migration, on the other from natural increase. The former process was, at this period, primarily one of local drift rather than long-distance movement; thus the labour force of Lancashire cotton and Black Country iron came from nearby rural areas, supplemented by a few Irish and Scots already willing to travel long distances in search of a job. These migrants were in turn replaced by people moving in from more remote rural communities. This kind of movement took place despite the existence of a Poor Law which inhibited mobility by providing relief only in the parish of 'settlement', in fact generally of origin. Such a model of population movement in the pre-railway age seems inherently likely and is supported by contemporary evidence; it does, however, leave a problematic loose end in some of the most remote and rural areas unless either a high level of natural increase in rural Britain at large or rural depopulation in distant parts is assumed. By comparison some much publicised movements, southern pauper children to northern mills for example, are unimportant. Early nineteenth-century population movement was in fact an unspectacular process.

The demographic mechanism underlying the increase of population and thus bearing on its redistribution is a more contentious issue, perhaps the most contentiously and continuously debated theme in British economic and social history. Did the large and rapid increase which took place — 14 per cent between 1801 and 1811 for example — result from fewer deaths or more births? In recent years a fall in the death rate has usually been regarded as the more important component, and it has been related by scholars to such diverse circumstances as food supply, clothing, housing, medical knowledge and even the Gin Acts. The issue is made even more difficult by uncertainty as to the timing and character of the increase before the 1801 census. In the 1950s renewed emphasis was given to the possible role of higher fertility in the second half of the eighteenth century as a major cause of increase. This reinterpretation has since been challenged, but it has served to emphasise the possibility of the operation of several spatially distinct mechanisms of increase. Higher fertility in urban areas than rural areas, at least in part a result of a different age-sex structure, has long been recognised as one of these. Secondly from late in the eighteenth century the death rate appears to have fallen faster in agricultural than in manufacturing communities, despite the age-sex structure — a consequence perhaps of a better diet and a healthier environment? An important new phenomenon is the recognition that the solution to the industrial and demographic problem may be largely geographical. Some such possible solutions have been examined: for example the long accepted view that the Speenhamland[2] system (the supplementation of the labourer's wage to subsistence level from the rates) encouraged larger families has been shown to be probably false. Others await attention — the higher wages of the farm labourer in the north by comparision with the south, the effects of 'open' and 'close' villages, the differences between the new manufacturing communities (youthful in their age-sex structure and with a market for child labour) and the old market and provincial towns.

Finally the geographical implications of rather localised population increase must be considered. More people had to be fed, clothed, housed and employed. Whether or not this was done badly or well, whether or not standards of living rose or fell, demands were made on particular resources and on the environment in general. They were answered as far as possible by old and new technologies or by straightforward expansion of existing practice. New mills were built, new mines were sunk, new land was brought into use, new landscapes and new environments were made. In many instances the rate of consumption of irreplaceable resources grew rapidly; coal and iron had been nibbled at in the eighteenth century, now they were gobbled up. It is scale, impact and timing which are the distinctive features of the Industrial Revolution and its demographic counterpart.

AGRICULTURE

A rapidly increasing population had to be fed, neither well fed, nor reliably fed, nor interestingly fed, by present-day standards, but at least kept alive and able to work. Fortunately a number of changes favouring agricultural improvement, particularly higher output per acre and per unit of capital, had been going on since at least the seventeenth century. Economic circumstances had been particularly favourable for these changes since about 1750. Wartime inflation, accompanied by a characteristic concern with the security of the nation's food supply and a run of adverse seasons, brought these changes to something of a climax early in the nineteenth century. This prosperity was for the farmer and landowner and was not shared by the labourer. Moreover a limited technology and wartime conditions generated a degree of distortion in patterns of land-use.

These changes were grafted onto an old established system, a mainly pastoral tradition in the highland north and west, and an arable tradition in the lowland south and east. These were linked by inter-regional movements of livestock (mostly on the hoof) and to some extent of grain. As there was no way of transporting perishable produce more than a few miles, and as bulky goods such as grain could only be moved cheaply over long distances by water, a degree of local and regional autonomy in food supply remained. But there were already well developed regional specialisations: orchards and hop-fields in Kent (handy for London markets); grazing in Leicestershire and the North Riding; store sheep and cattle breeding in Wales and Aberdeenshire respectively. Environmental constraints were as yet scarcely challenged, and thus since drainage techniques were superficial most heavy land was either indifferent permanent pasture or wheat-beans-fallow in rotation.

Enclosure or its absence was, however, of some importance in this respect. For example, where 'red lands' of the Oxfordshire Middle Lias were enclosed in the early nineteenth century the traditional open-field rotation of wheat-beans-barley-fallow gave way to the Norfolk four-course (wheat-turnips-barley-clover) followed by beans and oats.

Enclosure was only one among several determinants of farming practice. It was in its own final phase of efflorescence during the first two decades of the century, the characteristic change in the rural landscape, from open field or common to hedgerow and field. Farming paid well even as rents rose and often one-year tenancies ousted long leases. There was more concern over the nation's food supply than over security of tenure, and the response to these circumstances was to enclose and intensify. In Scotland the process contained a further dimension, the sometimes brutal transformation of peasant township to tenant farm and sheep run, a radical transformation of traditional society and its settlement pattern. The general social impact of enclosure is however debatable and has certainly at times been exaggerated; its impact on the landscape, made as it was over several centuries, remains evident.

Other opportunities for long-term agricultural investment remained limited; the technology of under-drainage barely existed, pedigree livestock were the fancy of the few rather than the mania of the many. The important contemporary development most easily overlooked was the general elevation of standards; thus Arthur Young observed in 1809 'a great change in their [the farmers'] ideas, knowledge and practice', although he went on to add a typical corrective — 'a great deal of ignorance and barbarity remains'[3]. Some of these changes related to the progress of manufacturing industry — grassing down in east Lancashire where there was an expanding market for butter, cheese, milk and meat for example — but they were also reported from remote and rural counties such as Pembrokeshire. The general economic (and military) situation more often favoured the breaking up of old grassland, such as the chalk downs, to provide for the forbears of the arable sheep, the Oxford and Hampshire Downs. Social changes also had their agricultural consequences, as when the Blackface sheep spread over the border from the Pennines to replace breeds suited to the old Scottish peasant townships.

Farm workers remained the largest occupational group in Britain. The labour force of the new industries came essentially from increase rather than from an exodus from the land. Agriculture was in fact intensive, but as yet unmechanised, and thus resembled industry in its demand for labour. However there is evidence of agricultural over-population, and thus individual impoverishment, in the rural south, where farm workers' wages were lower than in the north. Less rational and more localised was the mismatching of residence and workplace inherent in the existence of 'open' and 'close' villages, particularly in East Anglia and the East Midlands. In 'close' villages a single resident landowner restricted the number of houses and resident labourers to keep down the poor rates. Additional labour came from the fewer, often squalid, 'open' villages where landowners were too numerous to act so restrictively. In many cases this system operated at the cost of an exhaustingly long journey to work.

Farming was still Britain's basic industry in 1800 — only one-fifth of the population was urban — and it was prosperous in temporarily very favourable circumstances. On average the country was still just about self-sufficient, although beginning to depend on some imported inputs. How far this self-sufficiency was responsible for high prices, a pauperised labour force and a geographically rather irrational land-use pattern is arguable. These owed at least something to the war, and often served to mask less spectacular developments of more lasting significance.

INDUSTRY

To any traveller in Britain in 1800, particularly from overseas, the pace and scale of industrial growth must have seemed astonishing. His attention would probably been drawn to cotton and iron in particular, to the most spectacular and most basic of industries, but he could scarcely fail to notice more localised examples, non-ferrous metals in the Swansea valley, chemicals at Glasgow, not least for the environmental devastation they were causing. Even industries which were losing ground on a relative scale, wool for example, were generally growing and prosperous in war conditions. Moreover the war brought new industries which were to prove long-lasting to some towns, bootmaking to Leicester for example.

Coal was not the most evidently expanding industry in 1800; it had not attained the importance of its late nineteenth-century Golden Age of steam ships, steam railways, steam-driven machinery and huge export markets. Nevertheless coal was already a common form of domestic heating, integral to iron-making, and exercising a growing locational power over manufacturing industry in general through the steam engine, although it had not yet eliminated water power as a motive force and locational factor. By a fortunate chance coal and water power were often geographically coincident, as on the Pennine margins.

Coal output probably exceeded ten million tons per annum by 1800. Northumberland and Durham produced a third of the nation's coal and the antiquity of the industry in this area and its role as London's supplier of 'sea coal' ensured that it received a great deal of notice. A larger share of output, perhaps two-fifths, came from the pits of Lancashire, Yorkshire and the Midlands, and was destined for less conspicuous local industrial and domestic use. Scotland, Wales, Cumberland and the Somerset-Bristol field were the other main producers.

Technologically the industry was starting to move from the primitive to the sophisticated. Most pits were shallow and in the form of a bell[4], and therefore shortlived; but in Cumberland a depth of nearly 1,000 feet had been reached. There were more and more large enterprises such as the Lowther mine, employing 200 men in 1811, a development owing much to the increased use of underground tramways. These were almost as important to the growth of the industry as the more obvious device of the surface tramway. Coalmining remained a dangerous job, but the tramway and the northward spread of longwall working to replace 'bord and pillar'[5] ensured increased productivity. The typical colliery was a group of several pits together with a larger number of abandoned workings, often in a semi-rural setting and sometimes by 1800 served by a canal. Most coalfields were remote from the established centres of population and were themselves less densely populated than the manufacturing areas. Coalmining was labour-intensive, but the population of Durham and Northumberland in 1801 was less than half that of Lancashire. Salford Hundred (Manchester excluded) had more people than either county. There was however some degree of association with coal-consuming industry: integrated coal and iron industries operated in Wales and Scotland, coalpits were owned by Cheshire salt manufacturers. On the other hand coal remained prohibitively expensive in some inland areas, in the south of England in particular. As the eighteenth century gave place to the nineteenth the adult collier found his work less arduous, his earnings higher and his domestic circumstances more civilised[6]. The industry grew, but its most rapid growth awaited new markets, new technologies, new means of transportation (plate 1).

Cotton was something of a 'boom and bust' industry in the early nineteenth century — expansion was rapid but erratic. Nevertheless its proportionate contribution to the gross national product doubled in the first decade of the century. Like coal it was an industry of the upland margins, not only in and around east Lancashire, already its principal locale, but also in Scotland, the East Midlands and more widely. Water power rather than coal was the principal locational force in the early years of factory cotton spinning between about 1780 and 1810; during this period cotton manufacturers were active in converting old water mills as well as in building new ones. The good fortune of the country around Manchester was its endowment with coal as well as water. By 1800 spinning was well on course to become an exclusively factory activity. Weaving remained largely domestic, widely dispersed within the spinning area, and as yet prosperous. Factory spinning made for cheap and plentiful yarn, but factory weaving was faced with technical problems. The geographical separation of spinning and weaving, south and north of Rossendale, had not yet begun, but more localised specialisation was already evident — fine spinning in Bolton, calicoes in Blackburn, muslin on Clydeside. Raw materials were the particular concern of Liverpool as an importer and of the canals as distributors.

Cotton has always been regarded as the epitome of the early phase of the Industrial Revolution in particular. The rapid growth of a large-scale industry was both spectacular and of major economic significance. Largely as a result the population of Manchester township grew from 22,481 in 1774 to 70,409 in 1801, and of the whole parish from 41,032 to 102,300. New settlements, created by the industry, grew even more rapidly around the water wheels or steam engines of the spinning mills. The evident dynamism of the rising industry attracted further investment, the motive force of its further growth and more extensive geographical impact.

The eighteenth-century iron industry was *par excellence* the industry of transformed technology. Some time in the early eighteenth century Abraham Darby made iron with coke, a relatively slowly adopted innovation; the puddling process[7] for wrought iron manufacture was developed in the 1780s and much more speedily taken up. Moreover the coalfields provided not only the fuel and reducing agent but also the black-band ores, the industry's principal raw material until the second half of the nineteenth century. It is thus no surprise that the Northumberland and Durham coalfield, ill-endowed with such ores, saw the most meagre development of the industry at this date.

New technology was one cause of the rapid growth of the iron industry in the years around 1800. The Napoleonic war boosted one traditional market, the increased popularity of the steam engine another. It appears that there was an approximately fourfold increase in output between the late 1780s and 1806, when about a quarter of a million tons was produced. The West midlands and South Wales accounted for two-thirds of this, already, as has been noted, in some degree of integration with mining. Likewise the characteristic location was as yet semi-rural on the margin of the uplands. Within the West Midlands the main centre of production was already moving to Staffordshire from the relative remoteness and inaccessibility of Shropshire; Scotland and the West Riding were the other main areas of production but as yet they were growing less rapidly than the major centres. At the other extreme the Weald, the traditional centre of English iron-making, ceased to produce at some date between 1796, when 173 tons were made, and 1806. The industry had moved to coal.

It is impossible to go on to examine the impact of the Industrial Revolution on every industry, not least because of the continuing importance of domestic manufacturing. The woollen industry, for several centuries pre-eminent among Britain's manufactures, was still largely domestic in the West Riding, Norfolk and the West of England, its three main centres. So also were the Bridport rope and net industry, pin and needle making at Gloucester and Redditch for example. The pace and extent to which these activities passed to the factory — and net-making remains partly domestic — depended on the chances of location, technical change and entrepreneurial activity. Among the last to fall were some that might be regarded as family activities rather than domestic industry — baking and garment-making for example — and here too an element of home activity has survived. The limited evidence suggests what might be expected, that this domestic, and at times subsistence, element in the economy was more marked and persistent in the highland zone of northern and western Britain than in the lowland south and east, ironically in the same area as the earliest factory triumphs. At the same time there were industries which though small in scale and widely dispersed were, for technical reasons, rarely domestic — flour-milling (albeit the mill was often attached to a house) and paper-making for example.

MOBILITY

For most of the inhabitants of Britain at the start of the nineteenth century transport and movement meant walking. They could afford no other way, and in many instances lived off the beaten track of even the humblest carrier's cart. The technology as well as the finance of mass transportation lay in the future, coastal shipping to some degree excepted. Thus people walked: to work, to seek a wife, to sell their produce or their labour. The chapman or pedlar, his goods on his back or his packhorse, carried on a substantial part of the country's retail trade, while the pedestrian drover managed an important part of its food supply — Welsh cattle[8] and, less spectacularly if more chaotically, poultry from the home counties to London, for example. Pedestrian power was even used to propel narrow boats through canal tunnels.

The roads and lanes used by these walkers, by coach, by cart, and by horseman, were generally in an unsatisfactory state. Neither the problems of road management and finance nor those or road construction had been solved. Most roads were cared for — inasmuch as this took place at all — by the parishes through which they passed; the task was reluctantly undertaken and ineffectively executed. The chances were that the turnpike trusts, responsible for about one-fifth of the mileage, would act more energetically but still with limited expertise. Only Metcalfe among the great trinity of English road builders had carried out much work by 1800; the full fruition of his ideas, and those of Macadam and Telford, belongs to the succeeding generation. The quality of the road surface in 1800 was more likely to reflect available raw materials, a matter of geology, and the energy and affluence of those charged with its care, than technological expertise. Only a few wealthy bodies, the City of London for example, could afford to import exotic durables such as Purbeck stone for mere road making.

Yet despite these problems the roads had improved since 1750. More legislation relating to roads passed through Parliament, including a General Turnpike Act in 1773, and more traffic passed along the roads. Moreover traffic moved faster, the surest sign of better conditions,, not least because of work to ease gradients. Edinburgh had been 10-12 days from London in 1754; it was four days by 1776. The roads were generally at their best near the towns (more money counting for more than more traffic), in the summer, and off the clays; winter traffic was often discouraged and in such areas as the Weald might find it extremely difficult to move anyway. In these circumstances it is scarcely surprising that both road and road improvement were expensive. Indeed some turnpike trusts were financially unsound before the railways were built. The passenger paid a particularly high price for speed: inside fares on fast coaches were of the order of fourpence to fivepence a mile. By comparison with the fast coach, freight haulage by road was a long-established business, although by 1800 canal competition had reduced its role to that of a feeder in some areas. Thus Pickford, one of the major carriers, gradually transferred his London base to the City Wharf from 1806.

The canal network was essentially a late eighteenth-century creation, and by 1800 the Thames, the Severn, the Mersey and the Humber were connected via the Midlands. The Pennines and the Thames-Severn watershed were each crossed by three canals early in the nineteenth century. Quicker and more reliable than road haulage, canal carriage was also very much cheaper; bulky goods of low value such as bricks and grain were carried at one quarter to one half the cost of road transport. Not surprisingly the canals soon handled all traffic of this kind in the areas they served, depending however on the horse and cart for the first and/or last stage of distribution. By comparison passenger traffic was never of much importance; this passed directly from coach or coastal shipping to the railway.

The canal companies provided the waterway and its services; they were rarely carriers. A diversity of canal companies meant a diversity of dimensions, an obstacle to efficient nationwide use. Moreover many canals were built extremely slowly. Only those built cheaply and at an early date were generally profitable, particularly those in industrial districts. Rural canals, the reputedly trunk routes across such watersheds as the Cotswolds, paid poorly if at all. But the canal investor was not always primarily seeking a dividend. He might be wishing to market his produce — as in the case of the Glamorgan Canal for example, to export his coal. Outside the Midlands and the neighbourhood of the four major estuaries the canal network was as fragmentary as it was unprofitable; much of Britain was remote from the canals and their influence. Where they were built they were a conspicuously new and notably persistent feature in landscape and economy.

Britain's maritime trade passed through a very large number of ports, some of them very small and handling no more than two or three cargoes of, say, coal or timber a year. Not only were there numerous small ports but also small vessels; a great deal of coastwise trade was carried on in vessels of no more than ten tons. Even the important Newfoundland trade carried on across the stormy North Atlantic involved numerous vessels of no more than 100 tons. The steamer was still an idea or a toy.

By common consent the coal trade, particularly between London and the Tyne, was the most important part of the coastwise trade, employing a greater tonnage than the whole overseas trade. 'Sea coal' was cheap on the coast but increasingly expensive inland. Much of the overseas trade was 'protected', to the British West Indies and British North America for example, and some of it was still monopolistic and quasi-military such as that of the East India Company. London and Liverpool were the major ports and by 1800 the latter had already begun to build its dock system; London followed in the first decade of the nineteenth century. At the same time remote, ancient, and nationally unimportant harbour works such as the Cobb at Lyme Regis could still look to government aid for major repairs even if at least some of its users were at the same time defrauding the government of revenue by smuggling.

PATTERNS OF SETTLEMENT

Population increase and redistribution necessarily brought about a new geography of settlement, but these were not the only forces for change in this context. Enclosure usually led to some dispersal of settlement in the lowland zone, and the new farmhouses which were built in the process often reflected the wider availability of brick and the decay of vernacular tradition in areas served by the canals. In the highland zone enclosure sometimes meant dispossession and depopulation rather than dispersal. In other respects established patterns survived, the tacit acceptance of a low standard of housing for the mass of the population for example. The one-room cottage was commonplace in Scotland and by no means unknown in England and Wales in 1800.

If rural settlement was to some degree controlled and planned the typical industrial settlement of 1800 sprawled unorganisedly around its parent mill or forge and only occasionally did an owner[9] give form and shape to the domestic part of the new industrial landscape. Sometimes, as at Oldham, the enclosure of waste land was intimately associated with new urban growth. In many instances a rural setting redeemed these communities, at least during their formative years, from the consequences of unplanned and rapid growth, but it could not for ever stave off the effects of poor building methods, non-existent drainage and sewerage, unpaved and unlit roads and lanes. Industrialisation created not only 'scores of little colonies centred on the new mills'[10] but new suburbs or simply a higher density of population in existing towns. These latter provided some of the worst living conditions. Nottingham for one was hemmed in by open fields controlled by intransigent burgesses and by parks owned by noble but inflexible lords. Where 10,000 people had lived in 1739 there were nearly 30,000 in 1801, workers in lace and knitwear manufacture, inhabitants of 'a chequerboard of mean streets, alleyways and courts, and a byeword for filth and misery beyond belief'.[11] Ironically some 'close' villages no more than a few miles from Nottingham were actually losing population during this period. Country towns had their alleyways and courts too but they rarely had to face such pressures as the manufacturing communities, and for a few wartime agricultural prosperity brought about a rebuilding or a face-lift.

The settlement geography of 1800 is then a geography of heightened contrasts, of the emergence of new communities and new forms of settlement on the margins of the uplands, and of an initial and transient phase of urbanisation not repeated until the 1920s. New materials from hitherto inaccessible sources competed with the local and traditional in areas opened up by the canals. A continuance of dispersion characterised the lowland zone, incipient depopulation the heart of highland zone.

ENVIRONMENTAL IMPACT

What kind of impact were the British making — and had they made — on their environment in 1800? Thousands of years of occupation even at low, although slowly increasing, population densities had made demands upon resources and had organised their use. Thus the last wave of enclosure was but one stage in a continuous and continuing process of bringing most of Britain into pastoral or agricultural occupation. Already there was a shortage of timber and demands on non-renewable resources such as coal and iron had increased sharply during the eighteenth century. The methods used to extract these resources were often very damaging to the environment, the shallow 'bell' coalpit for example, where a high risk of subsidence was associated with numerous workings over a wide area to obtain a little coal. This was not only a matter of the rights of property and of limited technology but of a failure fully to apprehend the nature of the resource. New factories were less directly damaging, adding to the already numerous dams and weirs and increasing coal consumption, creating concentrations of houses and their refuse; their most distinctive form of pollution was associated with bleaching and dyeing and appears not to have become a severe problem by 1800.

Atmospheric pollution, the concentration of domestic and industrial chimneys, and river pollution, the use of running water for rubbish disposal, were established situations rather than new problems. Novelty was to be found in the increasing extent and concentration and new locations of such activity. Comment — and opposition — was reserved for the new noxious industries, the Swansea valley copper works for example. There in 1804 'the columns of smoke from the different manufactories contribute to make Swansea if not unwholesome a very disagreeable place of residence'.[1][2] The major problems lay in the future: while Rennie calculated that in 1808 the Thames received 800,000 tons of mud and rubbish a year from London and its inhabitants, a marked deterioration and a public concern culminated only in the 'great stink' of 1858.[1][3]

Early nineteenth-century society took dirt for granted. It was part of the human condition, an inevitable accompaniment of industrialisation and urbanisation, and its role in disease was as yet little understood. Although the water closet was patented in 1775 and 1778, the sanitary revolution is essentially a feature of the nineteenth century. Absence of comment does not imply absence of concern or of problems, but the evidence suggests that mismanagement of the environment had as yet produced problems only for a few people and in a few areas. That a large number of people were poorly housed was to some degree a matter for regret, but as this had always been so, it scarcely called for urgent action. When Blake wrote of 'dark satanic mills'[1][4] early in the nineteenth century he symbolised a likely future rather than an actual present.

REGIONAL PATTERNS

As important a question as that of environmental impact is that of regional patterns, the regional geography of Britain. In 1800 most people were still living out their lives within narrow spatial limits, the farm, the village, the occasional — perhaps annual — visit to the market town. The world of the factory worker — mill, terrace and 'tommy shop'[15] — was if anything even more limited than that of his country cousin. The Napoleonic War, like all wars, had jerked a number of men out of this constrained geographical context, but only temporarily, and most people lived out their lives within narrow spatial limits.

Functional regions on a larger scale existed within the economy, indeed for some purposes, the rearing and fattening of cattle for example, Britain as a whole acted as such. The spatial association and interdigitation of coal, iron and iron-using manufactures in the West Midlands and the existence of a concentration of paper manufacturing around London are examples of more localised functional regions. Each port possessed its hinterland, distorted from geometrical simplicity by such circumstances as topography, turnpike gates, and harbour dues. Likewise the county and the county town provided a functional region and a focus for the social life of the middle and upper classes; a small number of specially or fortuitously favoured towns such as Bath and Brighton fulfilled a similar national role.

Superimposed upon this pattern or system of functional regions was one of broad regional differences. The most basic of these, the highland zone and the lowland zone, is as old as the human occupation of Britain; to some degree it was becoming muted by 1800 as new farming methods spread into the highland zone and such processes as enclosure re-organised settlement patterns. But as these old differences diminished so new dichotomies emerged, in the wages and productivity of agricultural labour between north and south, in the character and forms of urban life between the old provincial towns and the new factory communities, in the relationship between population increase and employment opportunity in town and country. Benjamin Disraeli the novelist and later prime minister used the phrase 'the two nations' to summarise the situation as it had developed by 1845, comparing the rich and the poor;[16]

the geographer may prefer to think of three, juxtaposing the new manufacturing and mining centres of the upland margins — the new Britain of 1800 — with either highland zone and lowland zone, or with town and country (plates 2 and 3), and thus comparing the dynamo and mainspring of nineteenth-century geographical change with sharply contrasted conservative forces.

NOTES

1 The phrase was coined not by contemporary observers but by Arnold Toynbee in his Oxford lectures, published after his death in 1883.

2 So called because it was adopted, though not invented, by the Berkshire magistrates, meeting at the Pelican Inn, Speenhamland, a suburb of Newbury, in 1795. It was widely adopted in the south and regarded by contemporaries as a cause of population increase.

3 Young, A., *General View of the Agriculture of Oxfordshire*, London, (revised edition) 1813, p.35.

4 That is, their cross-section approximated to that of a bell, with a short vertical shaft for access.

5 'Bord and pillar' left coal standing as supports between the workings and thus removed less than half of the available coal; 'longwall' removed all available coal. For detailed descriptions see Ashton, T.S. and Sykes, J., *The Coal Industry of the Eighteenth Century*, Manchester, (2nd edition) 1964, pp. 14-32.

6 Ashton, T.S., and Sykes, J., *The Coal Industry of the Eighteenth Century*, Manchester, (2nd edition) 1964, p. 174.

7 This allowed wrought iron to be made with coal instead of the much more expensive charcoal.

8 An interesting survey of four centuries of this trade is Skeel, C., 'The cattle trade between Wales and England from the fifteenth to the nineteenth centuries', *Transactions of the Royal Historical Society*, series 4, vol. 9, 1926, pp. 135-55.

9 Robert Owen (1771-1858) took over New Lanark mills in 1800 where he built a model village and schools, limiting child labour, and mixing a degree of socialism with a deal of

paternalism.

10 Millward, R., *Lancashire: an illustrated essay on the History of the landscape*, London, 1955, p. 78.

11 Chambers, J.D., *Modern Nottingham in the Making*, Nottingham, 1945, p. 6.

12 Hilton, K.J. (ed.), *The Lower Swansea Valley Project*, London, 1967, p. 26.

13 Ehrlich, B., *London on the Thames*, London, 1968, pp. 32-4. One result of the 'great stink' was the *Report of the Select Committee on the River Thames*, 1858.

14 William Blake in the introductory lines to his poem 'Milton' written between 1800 and 1804. It is often, and incorrectly, referred to as 'Jerusalem'.

15 Because mills and mines were commonly isolated and worked long hours, their owners often ran shops to provide for their employees' needs. To the unscrupulous these 'tommy shops' were a marvellous opportunity for sharp practice and profiteering — see Benjamin Disraeli, *Sybil or the Two Nations*, 1845, ch. 3. The practice was outlawed by the Truck Acts of 1831 and 1887.

16 Benjamin Disraeli, *Sybil or the Two Nations*, 1845. The novel is set in the late 1830s, in part in a mining community. It contains not only brilliant and cogent economic and social criticism, but much sound historical geography.

FURTHER READING

Agriculture, Board of, *The Agricultural State of the Kingdom*, London, 1816 (reprinted, with an introduction by G.E. Mingay, Bath, 1970).

Aiken, J., *A Description of the Country from Thirty to Forty Miles Round Manchester*, London, 1795 (reprinted Newton Abbot, 1968).

Armstrong, W.A., 'La population de l'Angleterre et du pays de Galles, 1789-1815', *Annales de Démographie Historique*, 1965, pp. 31-38.

Ashton, T.S., and Sykes, J., *The Coal Industry of the Eighteenth Century*, Manchester, (2nd edition) 1964.

Clapham, Sir J.H., *An Economic History of Modern Britain:*

Volume 1 The Early Railway Age 1820-1850, Cambridge, 1926 (Book 1, 'Britain on the Eve of the Railway Age')

Crump, W.B., (ed.), *The Leeds woollen industry 1780-1820*, Leeds, Thoresby Society, volume 32, 1931.

Edwards, M.M., *The Growth of the British Cotton Trade 1780-1815*, Manchester, 1967.

Gleave, M.B., 'Dispersed and nucleated settlement in the Yorkshire Wolds 1770-1850', *Institute of British Geographers: Transactions and Papers*, No. 30, 1962, pp. 105-18.

Halfpenny, E., '"Pickfords": expansion and crisis in the early nineteenth century', *Business History*, vol. 1, 1959, pp. 115-25.

Lambert, A.M., 'The agriculture of Oxfordshire at the end of the eighteenth century.' *Agricultural History*, vol. 29(1), 1955, pp. 31-8.

2 People and Place: The Geography of Population and Settlement

Population growth and productivity increase were the essence and the dynamic of Britain's experience in the nineteenth century. The evaluation is that of an historian, Kitson Clark,[1] the topics are as legitimately a workplace for the geographer and are the concern of the greater part of this book. Both population growth and productivity increase were accompanied by geographical redistribution and were subject to geographical constraints. This chapter considers the increase of population and then the resultant reorganisation of patterns of settlement, possibly the more basic and certainly the more closely defined of these two major themes.

Britain's first census took place in 1801 (fig. 1, p. 3) and was repeated, with generally increasing accuracy and detail, every ten years. The relatively bald and simple 1801 enumeration took place in the middle of the population explosion and is thus an inappropriate starting point for discussion of the mechanics and implications of that explosion.[2] More often the period from about 1750 to 1830 is considered as something of a unity, at least in part because better demographic data become available after the latter date, an effective system of registration of births, marriages and deaths in 1837, the census enumerators' books in 1841, and a particularly detailed census in 1851.

Great Britain's population of 10.5 million in 1801 reached 37 million by 1901. The country had also provided large numbers of emigrants, more than 120,000 per annum in peak years as early as mid-century. Population increase was more rapid in earlier decades of the century and in urban areas. The highest rate of overall increase from one census to the next was achieved between 1811 and 1821 and it was also during this decade that rural increase was at a maximum. For the largest towns, those with more than 20,000 people, the maximum rate of increase was reached only in the decade 1831-1841 but their lower rates of increase earlier in the century were still greater than rates of increase in rural areas at this date. As early as the decade 1841-1851 one English, three Welsh, and eight Scottish counties recorded a decrease of population. By 1851 more than half the population lived in towns (boroughs or places with more than 2000 people); by 1901 nearly four-fifths lived in boroughs or urban districts, an almost exact reversal of the 1801 situation. London had one million people in 1801, seven million in 1901; even at the start of the nineteenth century people were moving out from the city centre to rural or surburban Paddington and Poplar, and a 'census' taken in 1866 revealed that the City had twice as many commuters as residents.

Other cities and towns grew as spectacularly, mining and manufacturing centres and ports in particular. Small towns provide the most striking instances: Barry had a population of 100 in 1881, of 13,000 ten years later. Although rural depopulation was widespread in the second half of the century few counties had a smaller population in 1901 than 1801, and over wide areas population density had altered remarkably little. Great changes were confined to certain small — and discontinuous — areas of Britain. The rapid growth of London and Lancashire in the first half of the century so far outstripped the experience of other areas that even relatively rapidly industrialising counties such as Derbyshire, Nottinghamshire, and Leicestershire were increasing in population at a rate less than the national average during this period. In the second half of the century 30 per cent of all registration districts (certainly a smaller proportion of total area) increased in population at a rate faster than the national average. Nevertheless this high degree of localisation was part of a broad redistribution of population away from the ancient pre-eminence of the rural lowland zone towards the dominance of London and the new manufacturing and mining communities of the Midlands, the North of England, Wales and Scotland.

MECHANISMS OF GROWTH

Britain's population increased throughout the nineteenth century because the level of fertility remained higher than the level
of mortality. This situation came into existence before 1800
and was sustained beyond 1900, although during the course of
the century the difference between the two diminished.
Moreover where mortality had been diminishing more rapidly
than fertility, the reverse of this situation came to prevail. In
neither instance did major changes occur early in the century;
the nationwide decline in crude and standardised death rates
first appears in the 1860s, for the very young and the old 20
years later. The control of infant mortality is in fact essentially
a twentieth-century phenomenon: in the 1840s 72 children per
1,000 died in their first five years, in the 1890s 63, by the
1930s 20. The same is true of fertility; there were 137 births
per 1,000 women of childbearing age in the 1840s, 123 in the
1890s – realisation of the socio-economic advantages of a smaller
family had as yet had little effect – less than 80 in the late 1930s.

These changes during the nineteenth century were primarily
the result of an improved environment rather than of better
medical care. The diminishing impact of tuberculosis, responsible for perhaps half the reduction of the death rate between
1851 and 1901, was a matter not of drugs and hospitals but of
diet and housing. Typhoid and cholera retreated in the face of
drains and a safe water supply. More fortuitously the virulence
of scarlet fever sharply diminished from a peak in the 1860s. By
comparison the new antiseptic surgery and the old methods of
smallpox control, effective though they were, had little significance (recent research ranks therapeutic advance only fourth as a
factor in nineteenth-century mortality decline, after food,
sanitation and the lessened virulence of scarlet fever). The
eventual decline in fertility was more a matter of attitude than
of technical progress; crude but effective contraceptive methods
had been known and used, where it was felt they were needed,
for centuries. In the nineteenth-century context some commentators on changing fertility have emphasised a shifting of
the economic balance in favour of smaller families as child
labour was restricted and educational compulsion extended;
others have favoured a broader explanation embracing an
extension of middle class attitudes and aspirations through a

widening sector of the population as well as public, and at times highly publicised, debate on new contraceptive methods late in the century.

All of these circumstances, the virulence of scarlet fever excepted, contained a geographical component. The reliability of sewage disposal, the quality of the water supply, the level of real wages — and thus the quality of clothing, food and housing — varied from place to place even within a single industry or community. Likewise children were outlawed from the mines half a century before the 'part timer'[2] ceased to contribute to the farm labour force and the parental purse. The figures for life expectancy (in 1837) given below are thus scarcely surprising:

	Average age at death	
	Manchester	Rutland
Professions and gentry	38	52
Tradesmen and farmers	20	41
Mechanics and labourers	17	38

What is surprising is that so little work has been done on these differences and their consequences. It seems likely that through most of the century and for most people rural Britain was healthier than urban, bearing in mind however that there was a persistent although diminishing industrial element in the rural economy. The farmworker enjoyed probably a healthier workplace and a lower risk of unemployment, possibly the freshest food but certainly the lowest wages; his children remained an economic asset longer than in any other occupation. How far was this the basis of the ability of rural areas to supply part of the nineteenth-century urban labour force, and what was the complementary role of natural increase in urban growth and eventual urban dominance?

MIGRATION AND INCREASE

The concentration of nineteenth-century population increase, whatever its origins, into a small number of areas — the making of the first conurbations — thus raises the question how far their growth was self-sustaining or continuously dependent on migration? The evident existence of migration, the unhealthy urban environment, and perhaps the intrinsic appeal of the

topic, have tended to create an emphasis on migration: recent
research indicates the pre-eminence of natural increase — the
cities were after all communities of young adults — while
acknowledging the role of population movement.

For the period of 1801-1831, that of the first four censuses,
only estimates of the respective roles of natural increase and
migration are possible. These have been made by Deane and
Cole (figures 2-4) who concluded that the industrial and
commercial counties owed twice as much of their growth to
natural increase as to in-migration. Only London (Surrey and

Figure 2. Estimated natural population increase as a percentage of
total population increase in England (by counties) and Wales
1801-31: 1, more tnan 200%; 2, 150%-200%; 3, 100%-150%; 4,
50%-100%; 5, less than 50%. (Deane, P., and Cole, W.A., *British
Economic Growth 1688-1959*, Cambridge, 1962, drawn from table
25.)

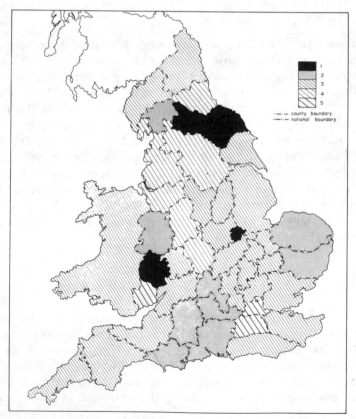

Middlesex) owed more than half its increase to migration, and both its excess of births over deaths and its demographic magnetism were diminishing by comparison with the previous century. Among other major areas of population increase Lancashire owed little more than a quarter of its increase to migration and Warwickshire was in a similar position; in Staffordshire and the West Riding the migrant's role was minimal. This latter contrast may however be a statistical accident, as a serious limitation of census-based migration studies for this period is that they necessarily define migration in terms of crossing a county boundary. The main centrés of population in Lancashire and Warwickshire, Manchester and Birmingham, are, like London, much closer to the county

Figure 3. Migration and natural increase (rates per thousand) in England (by counties) and Wales, 1801-30. (Drawn from same source as figure 2, table 26.)

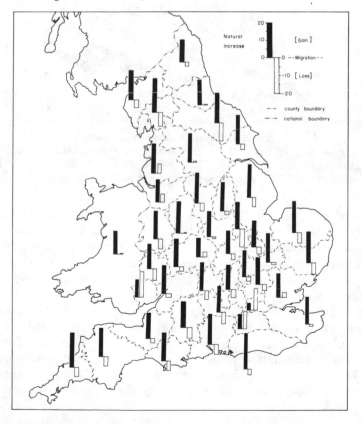

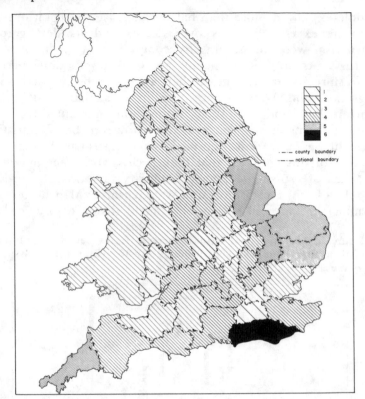

Figure 4. Differences between average birth rates and death rates (b.r. − d.r.) in England (by counties) and Wales, 1801-30: 1, less than 10.0; 2, 10.0-12.5; 3, 12.5-15.0; 4, 15.0-17.5; 5, 17.5-20.0; 6, more than 20.0 (Drawn from same source as figure 2, table 29.)

boundary than their peers in Yorkshire and Staffordshire. But there exists the possibility that earlier urbanisation and a less dispersed industrial population in the first two counties, in fact a closer resemblance to London, accounted for their greater dependence on in-migration. Wide variations in birth and death rates from county to county are generally evident at this period, but on the whole a fall in death rates is apparent in London and rural counties, the cumulative impact of two centuries of agricultural advance. A rise in birth rates accounts for the increasing population of mining and manufacturing counties.

Work on the period after 1831, notably by Cairncross, Lawton, Fiedlander and Welton, rests on a more sophisticated

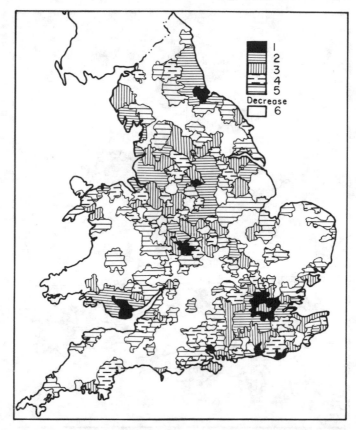

Figure 5. Summations of total percentage population change in each census decade (by registration district), England and Wales, 1851-1911: 1, 200 and over; 2, 100-200; 3, 50-100; 4, 25-50; 5, 0-25; 6, decrease. (Redrawn from Lawton, R., 'Rural depopulation in nineteenth century England', in Steel, R.W., and Lawton, R., *Liverpool Essays in Geography*, Liverpool, 1967, p.236.)

statistical base (figures 5-7). Throughout the middle decades of the century a relatively steady stream of migrants headed for the towns, southern as well as northern. In the 1880s this flow, to the northern towns in particular, was sharply checked, despite the existence of agricultural depression. Reputed, possibly real, industrial depression converted migrants to emigrants and only the south coast resorts retained an internal magnetism. This trend was reversed in the 1890s but was resumed after 1900. The demographic attraction of particular

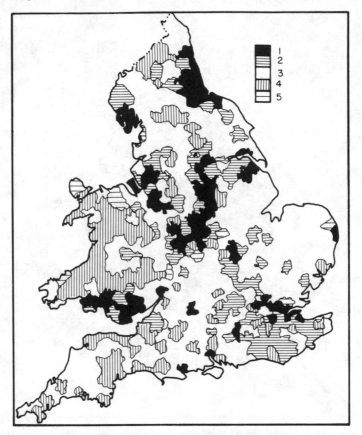

Figure 6. Summations of percentage natural change (i.e. balance of births and deaths) in each census decade (by registration district), England and Wales, 1851-1911: 1, 100 and over; 2, 80-100; 3, 60-80; 4, 40-60; 5, less than 40. (Redrawn from same source as figure 5, p.238.)

coalfields varied from decade to decade, but their overall role was consistently to attract about 100,000 migrants per decade, and to a greater extent than the manufacturing towns they were pre-eminently areas of high natural increase. Dependence on migration for growth was associated particularly with the early stages of rapid industrial urbanisation — Middlesborough and Merthyr Tydfil, boom towns of the middle and early decades of the century respectively, are good examples. In some rural areas out-migration had reduced fertility as early as the 1860s, but

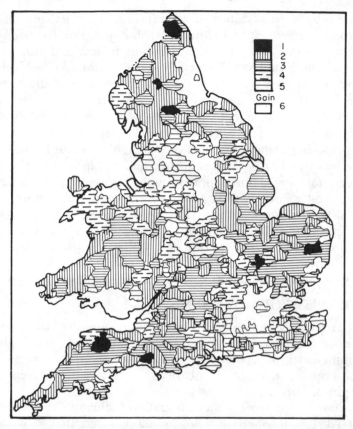

Figure 7. Summations of percentage net migrational loss (i.e. balance of natural and total change) in each census decade (by registration district), England and Wales, 1851-1911: 1, 100 and over; 2, 75-100; 3, 50-75; 4, 25-50; 5, 0-25; 6, gain. (Redrawn from same source as figure 5, p.240.)

relatively low mortality and large families generally sustained a steady outflow with but localised absolute depopulation. Lawton's maps (figures 5-7) for the period 1851-1911 aptly summarise the situation: in Cairncross's words 'the north of England triumphed over the south mainly by superior fertility (and not, as we used to be taught, by attracting migrants). In seventy years the north gained three more inhabitants for every two added to the population of the south'.[3] Marriage triumphed over mobility. A triumph extending back beyond the beginning of the century but barely sustained to its end.

The relative importance of migration and natural increase in the changing geography of the Scottish population has been less thoroughly analysed than the situation in England and Wales. While in the broad sense Scottish socio-economic development in the nineteenth century paralleled that south of the border, three factors suggest that migration was proportionately more important to the north. Not only was there an established tradition of out-migration from densely populated and technically primitive farming districts in the Highlands and Islands, but there was also a rather higher degree of geographical localisation of economic and demographic growth, particularly in the Clyde Valley, and a Poor Law slightly more favourable to movement. Local statisticians were generally convinced of the importance of migration — of late eighteenth-century Greenock it was said that one could 'walk from one end of the town to the other . . . without hearing a word of any language but Gaelic'.[4] It remains for present-day scholars to prove or disprove their contention.

MECHANISMS OF MOVEMENT

The propensity to migrate like the propensity to increase possessed a distinctive geography. Migration is a geographical phenomenon in a second sense — how far? in what direction? — which requires as much attention as the matter of differences in its regional impact.

Ravenstein's work on migration during the decade 1871-1881, published in 1885, demonstrated that movement took place more often in short steps than in large leaps (plate 4), and that a wave or ripple motion of this kind served to bring people from country to city. Such movement took place up the hierarchy of settlement, from farm to hamlet, hamlet to village, village to town, town to city. It was generated on the one hand by the attractive force of the towns and cities — city lights and city wages — and by a degree of rural over-population indicated by very low wages for example. It is also possible that it owed something to the retreat of cultivation — and population — from marginal areas during the prolonged depression after 1815. Ravenstein's model has been substantially confirmed by subsequent scholarship, albeit with strictures relating to differences in county size, and is regarded as the norm not only for the nineteenth but for earlier centuries. It can scarcely be said to have been rigorously tested; this may in fact be impossible, and

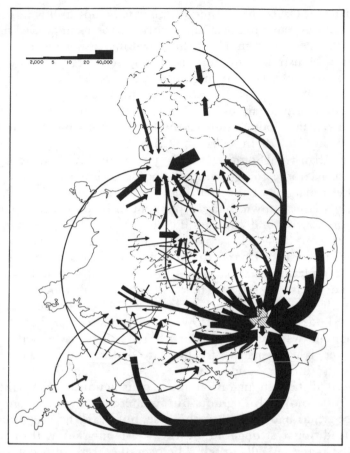

Figure 8. Net numbers of persons migrating between counties, 1861 census. (Redrawn from Smith, C.T., 'The movement of population in England and Wales in 1851 and 1861', *Geographical Journal*, Vol. 117, 1951, p.206.)

local and nationwide studies for the decade 1851-1861 have indicated its limitations (figure 8). Certainly in the second half of the century direct long-distance movement became commonplace for skilled workmen and the direct attractive force of the city extended more widely, just as the industrial north began to lose some of its demographic magnetism. On the whole Ravenstein's model of population movement best fits Lancashire, the West Riding, the West Midlands and London, growing concentrations of population set in areas of fairly dense rural population. Other developing districts were not in this position, South Wales, Northumbria and Scotland for example, which as coalfields generated much of their own increase while as rapidly growing industrial communities in not very densely populated areas they attracted some migrants from afar.

South Wales provides an interesting example, in some respects exceptional, of the migrational component in nineteenth-century population growth. Glamorgan's population grew from 70,879 in 1801 to 231,849 in 1851 (still a lower density than rural Somerset) and more than a million by 1911. The initial force for growth was not coal but the iron on the northern margins of the coalfield. In 1851 Merthyr Tydfil, the county's largest town, had 40 per cent of its population natives of four nearby rural counties, Pembroke, Cardigan, Carmarthen and Brecon. Coalfield expansion, beginning in the east and spreading westwards, and the creation of the coal ports, called forth population increase beyond the possibility of supply from adjacent Welsh counties. Their contribution dropped from 70 per cent of all in-migration in 1861-71 to 40 per cent in 1871-81 as the total inflow rapidly increased. Population movement was no irrational rush to streets paved with gold however; it was sensitive to the state of the coal trade in terms of both numbers and distance — the slump of the 1890s reduced distant in-migration most conspicuously. Nevertheless by 1900 non-Welsh migrants outnumbered natives not only on the coast, as had long been the case, but in the mining interior, the traditional stronghold of the Welsh migrant with a more limited range of skills to sell. The overall pattern thus comprises a long-term trend — more non-Welsh immigrants, a degree of locational choice relating to migrant origins, and a sensitivity to the local economy manifest in the variable level of in-migration from distant parts.

RURAL DEPOPULATION

The converse of urban growth was evidently primarily a matter of out-migration although by the end of the century this had so affected the structure of some rural populations that they were failing to replace losses through death. The implications of rural depopulation were the subject of considerable contemporary discussion (almost as much in Britain as in France, if somewhat less emotionally). It was not a question of absolute and prolonged decline over wide areas but of continuing and widespread relative decline, absolute loss in some counties from mid-century and in some locations from rather earlier, and of the apparent age- and ability-selective character of rural out-migration and thus of its impact on rural social life and the rural economy. As used at this period the term 'rural depopulation' was less a precise statement than a vague complaint of real and imaginary ills. Moreover the geographical basis of rural out-migration lacked the apparent logic of coalfield-based industrial growth; it was a widespread phenomenon showing little correlation, spatial or temporal, with the century's several agricultural crises (save at a very local level and perhaps more widely at the margins of cultivation in the years immediately after 1815). Pull was proving more effective than push, witness the continuance of overpopulation and congestion in remote parts of the highland zone. How far the railways played a part is uncertain. Their influence is unlikely to have been great at the local level, but it was probably indispensable for long-distance movements. Canon Girdlestone[5] could scarcely have moved 600 farm labourers from Devon to the north in the 1860s without its aid. The role of a degree of breakdown in rural isolation towards the end of the century is equally uncertain — whether perhaps it became possible to live in the country and work in the town, likewise the converse.

EMIGRATION AND IMMIGRATION

Movement overseas from Britain has as long a history as internal migration and its characteristic nineteenth-century features are massive increase, widespread interest and improved document-ation. Whereas rural depopulation smacked of decadence, emigration might, at least from mid-century, be seen as a sign of fashionable virtues; self-help, initiative, enterprise and imperial vigour.

Emigration was a highly selective operation. Whether to go? Where to go? These questions had to be answered on the basis of even scantier information and understanding than that possessed by the internal migrant. In the severest crises these issues were unimportant, as to the Irish peasant in 1846. In general push factors were strongest early in the century and became weaker as it progressed; even so economic depression in the 1880s was one reason for a return of emigration to its highest level since the 1850s. As the century progressed it became easier to assess the opportunities presented by North America and the Antipodes and there were more organised schemes — no guarantee of success — and more official involvement. But such emigration booms as the gold rushes of the years after 1849 contained irrational as well as rational elements.

The greater part of the New World was farmland, at least potentially, and cheap land by Old World standards; it thus exercised a strong appeal to farmers and farm workers. But there was always a place for the skilled craftsman, especially as New World industrial economics developed, and for the young unmarried woman of any occupation or none. The cost of emigration, even to the U.S.A., was a barrier insurmountable to the very poor but not so considerable as to prevent many illiterate, unskilled and near destitute families heading overseas. At the other extreme some of the first Canterbury colonists, university graduates in many cases, watched their flocks by day and read the Latin and Greek classics by night.[6] There is some evidence that the stepwise migration process operated internationally, that the British conurbations as much as or more than the British countryside provided the stream of migrants. Many goldminers of the 1860s had a long migrant history, first to California, thence to Victoria and thence to New Zealand, and this kind of movement was not restricted to such peculiar occupations as the quest for gold.

The likeliest origin of the nineteenth-century emigrant Briton was then the highland zone, urban or rural, and an occupation undergoing crisis or change. On grounds of access, cheapness and size he was more likely to go to the U.S.A. than to the colonies.

But Britain was a land of immigrants as well as of emigrants. The Irish had come to Britain in small numbers as permanent settlers or seasonal workers before the catastrophe of 1846, after which date they became at first a flood, then a steady stream. The main ports of entry, Liverpool and Glasgow, acquired distinctive and persistent Irish enclaves; the former even returned an Irish Nationalist M.P. for its Scotland division between 1885 and 1929. In 1851 13 per cent of the population of Manchester and nine per cent of the population of Bradford was Irish — by 1871 nine per cent and six per cent respectively. The Irish were settling into the role of a minority group concentrated in the worst houses and jobs, practising a religion to which there was still a great deal of hostility, but they were a vital part of the community economically as well as demographically. By the end of the century other immigrant communities had established themselves — refugee Jews in London (in 1901 14 per cent of the population of Stepney was Russian- or Polish-born) and a cosmopolitan dockland community in Cardiff, where in 1901 three per cent of the population had been born outside the United Kingdom. The immigrant and the immigrant community belong to nineteenth- as well as to twentieth-century Britain.

PATTERNS OF SETTLEMENT

More people in new places created new patterns of settlement, of urban settlement in particular; they made new, often frightful, environments and new demands on resources. It was not however merely a matter of weight of numbers and blind economic forces. Deliberate attempts to improve the residential environment emanated from new knowledge and increased wealth, new architectural styles, new social attitudes — did not Prince Albert turn his hand to designing model cottages?[7] — new laws and new institutions. These same forces had unforeseen, and even unwelcome, effects on the geography of settlement; the back-to-back slums of the industrial north used the same materials as the most attractive country cottage, and in the broad sense were created within the same socio-economic environment. To look at the houses the Victorians and their immediate forbears built is at once to register a caveat against over-broad generalisation.

CENTRAL PLACES

Economic growth and a transport revolution generated changes in the system of central places — the hierarchy of city, town, village, hamlet, farm and cottage — which have only begun to be explored. Many old towns ceased to function as central places to some degree, their markets dwindled, their range of shops and services diminished. On the other hand new towns of considerable importance in the national or even the worldwide economy were often central places for only a limited area and in a limited sense, not least because they were so close together.

The spacing of central places early in the nineteenth century varied from one part of the country to another, a consequence of differences of relief, resources, wealth, and historical accident. In East Anglia for example, rich but primarily rural and agricultural, Dickinson has shown that market towns were as little as eight miles apart in the wealthiest areas; he also showed that some of them were declining, as roads improved and rural industry decayed, even before the railways were built. Better communications threatened as many or more central places as they benefited. The railway, or more often its absence, was the *coup de grâce* of many small market towns throughout Britain, although Peake's suggestion[8] of as many as half the total by 1850 is surely an exaggeration. The problem of such towns was not that they became less accessible but that those favoured by the railway — in a few cases created by it, as was Craven Arms — became more accessible. It was the accessible centre which was attractive, both to the local customer and, to a greater extent, to buyer and seller from distant parts, such as the commercial traveller and the cattle dealer. A number of what might be regarded as ephemeral central places were also killed by the railways: the old seasonal livestock fairs, Weyhill and Stenhousemuir for example, dwindled and died as weekly markets in more accessible centres grew and flourished; perhaps some of the rotten boroughs which disappeared in 1832 might almost be regarded as ephemeral central places! By the end of the century the bicycle — and soon the car and bus — appeared as further agents of change, again favouring some larger and more central places over their smaller and peripheral rivals. However it might also be argued that with agricultural depression and rapidly rising living standards late in the century the agricultural market role of many country towns diminished and their importance as shopping and service centres increased, taking away some significance from the railways. Finally, in a number of cases industrial growth, in town or hinterland or both, provided a boost to established central place functions, as happened to many old market towns in South Wales as coalmining developed. The possible implications of the theme are immense and they still await the scrutiny of the geographer.

The new industrial towns were often traditional central places in only a limited sense, for to many of them their local setting was less important than worldwide markets, and their own population was far greater than that of the surrounding area for which they were a service centre. In this latter role retail trade was often well developed however, witness the continuing importance of street or covered markets in many northern industrial towns. Only a few such towns could fulfil traditional central place functions — a market for farmers, a seat for local or regional government. Mining communities and holiday resorts were similarly placed; superimposed upon an older system they served but a limited territory and that primarily for shopping or recreation; their *raison d'être* lay outside the old established system. A few settlements such as Brighton grew so large as to acquire a wider central place role and conversely a large number of specialised settlements shrank, disappeared or changed their character during the century — metalliferous mining communities in the Pennines and many of the lesser ports.

The smaller rural settlements — villages, townships or hamlets — likewise changed. A few grew into market or factory towns or holiday resorts, rather more lost some of their functional centrality, and reputedly their vitality, particularly in the latter half of the century. Early in the century the parish or township, the small rural community, still enjoyed a powerful political central place role. As the basic unit of local government it provided poor relief for those who had a 'settlement' there, and maintained the lesser roads. This was not an efficient system of local government and during the century these powers and rights passed to larger units, such as the Poor Law Unions of 1834. On the other hand population increase, higher real wages (especially for farm workers from mid-century) and perhaps changing taste and custom provided an increased range of shops in many villages. There were also more village schools and post offices, commonly nineteenth-century creations to serve new needs and a larger population. By the end of the century there are signs of some reversal of this situation, a consequence of rural depopulation and increased mobility. The pendulum was swinging back towards greater dependence on the urban central place and the individual's own resources than on village services.

The Cerne Abbas district (a Dorset Poor Law Union of twenty parishes) provides an example of the complexities of this situation in the latter half of the century. The population fell˙ from almost 8,000 in 1851 to little more than 5,000 in 1901, but the provision of retail services slightly improved from one shop to 34 inhabitants to one to 30; many more schools and post offices appeared. The larger villages providing the widest range of services lost not only proportionately more people but also more services; the smaller villages fared better in this respect, perhaps because the advent of school and post office removed a reason for their inhabitants to visit a larger centre. Cerne Abbas itself, a small town not served by the railway, fared very badly. Of the 57 fewer tradesmen in the area in 1901 than 1851, 46 had disappeared from Cerne Abbas and nine from Sydling St Nicholas, another large village. Political and administrative centrality was however retained, since the workhouse, Petty Sessional Court and even a new Rural District Council remained in Cerne Abbas, a situation which did not survive for very long. Commercial functions were lost more readily than administrative — personal decisions are more speedily taken than political. In sum, the changes which occurred reduced large villages and a small town to lower positions in the hierarchy, probably in part because of the remoteness from the railway, rather than making for an overall deterioration in service provision.

The changing commercial central place system contained a large element of logic and order. This was not the case in matters of politics and administration above the decreasingly important parish level. Rather there developed 'a curiously confusing reticulation of mutually intrusive and intersecting jurisdictions' — 'a chaos as regards authorities, a chaos as regards rates, and a worse chaos than all as regards areas'.[10] Until late in the century an *ad hoc* tradition remained stronger than either that of rationalisation or consolidation. Thus within the area of

West Derby (Poor Law) Union (Lancashire) in 1881 lay all or part of ten local boards, one borough, one board of guardians, three burial boards, one school board and one highway board. In 1882 G. J. Goschen M.P. noted, as he later recalled, that he received 87 separate rate demands on a property worth £1,100, the smallest eight for a total of two shillings and fourpence. Reorganisation late in the century (1894) defied the hierarchical logic of central place theory and practice by regarding urban areas as enclaves and separating their local government from that of the countryside. Only in one important instance, the relief of the poor, was a more rational system adopted. This was one of the major concerns of nineteenth-century local government, the one the ordinary citizen was most likely to experience and which, to judge from grandparental reminiscence, was most feared. The Unions of parishes created for this purpose in 1834 were deliberately set up as a central place system - 'the most convenient limit of unions which we have found has been that of a circle, taking a market town as centre and comprehending those surrounding parishes whose inhabitants are accustomed to resort to the same market'[11] − for convenience of management. As such systems focused on the workhouse in the central place[12] the Unions cut across traditional boundaries of hundreds and even counties. Later the unions became the basis of rural districts but, as has been noted, they were decapitated in the process. The fact that they crossed county lines also influenced later changes in county boundaries; nevertheless they remain the great exception to a tradition of local government poorly correlated with central place systems.

NEW FORMS OF SETTLEMENT

The transition from a rural agricultural society to an urban industrial economy not only reorganised the central place system but also created new kinds of settlement. In fact most were not really new. The isolated farmsteads of enclosure and reclamation, mining and fishing villages, decaying market towns and holiday resorts, were certainly more numerous than ever before and with the coming of the railway their forms and details changed. But it is easy to trace their ancestry and recognise their forbears. Three much more novel, if not

completely new, forms of settlement are the factory community, the suburb, and the conurbation. The first was produced by
rapid economic and demographic growth in the absence of
cheap and efficient means of transport; the second by the same
forces in a setting of relative affluence, a shorter working day,
and the horse-bus, tram, or railway. The two converge to
produce the third, albeit to a varying degree. London was
pre-eminently the product of suburban growth, the northern
conurbations of the coalescence of mill communities, suburbs,
and even pit villages. By the end of the century even country
towns, except the most moribund, were experiencing suburban
growth. 'Newtown' is a commonplace of Britain's nineteenth-
century urban growth from Milborne Port to Manchester.

As yet the mill, mine or factory community lacks a generic
name to match suburb or conurbation. It is not quite
exclusively a nineteenth-century phenomenon; its burgeoning
begins late in the eighteenth century and its origins even earlier,
but only during the nineteenth century did it become widespread. A combination of circumstances created such places.
Much early ·nineteenth-century industrial growth took place
beside fast-flowing streams or, and to an increasing extent, on
the coalfields; there were only canals and carthorses to move
coal to consumers, and no means, other than walking, of
moving worker to workplace and home again on a daily basis.
Industrial Britain owes much of its character to this precocious
industrialisation, prior to the building of the railways. Many of
the areas affected were thinly peopled because they were
agriculturally unattractive. Their labour force had to be
imported, at least initially, and housed as close to their
workplace and as cheaply as possible. Thus terraces and blocks
were built alongside factories and mines in a hitherto rural
setting. They were a new kind of community, imposed upon
but not integrated into the rural scene, narrow in their
occupational structure, limited in the range of services they
provided. At worst they were unplanned, ungoverned, undrained and unorganised, monotonous and compact streets of
overcrowded and jerry-built houses (plate 4). They were, like
the factories they served, expected to provide a profit. Yet in a
minority of cases they were model environments, New Lanark
or Saltaire for example. In both instances they outlived the
circumstances of their creation: the worst became slums,

already being demolished by the second half of the century, and the surviving best are as much monuments worthy of preservation as Stonehenge or Salisbury Cathedral.

The suburb, and its close cousin the satellite or dormitory community, are an inherently more varied phenomenon than the factory town, and a very much older one. They share with these industrial settlements a nineteenth-century transformation, but one embracing a much wider range of social classes. The wealthy Evangelicals of the Clapham Sect[13] commuted from a fashionable suburb whereas the continuous line of houses along the Manchester-Oldham road by 1848 represents a less attractive form. Conversely London had a hollow core, a dead heart, by 1800, and such major cities as Glasgow and Birmingham by mid-century. As villages became accessible by horse-bus, tram or even railway, their populations were increased by those who were thus able to leave the city while continuing to work there; such villages often moved down the social scale, as Islington did for example. At the same time new houses were built along or close to the roads linking the urban core to these suburban nuclei, old and new, and then beyond them there was ribbon development as it is commonly called. Much the same might happen along a railway, particularly if its policy was to encourage commuter traffic, an example of which was the Great Eastern in north-east London. The final stage, before redevelopment, was the infilling of the interstices of open space between ribbon and nuclear development. Unforeseen access problems and the use of such space for activities as environmentally destructive as brickmaking might make this a protracted process; surprisingly large areas of undeveloped, even derelict, land thus survive in many suburbs.

The process and product of suburban growth can be related to several factors, the existing template of settlement and communications, changing means (and costs) of transport and the attitude of those providing it, the attitudes and abilities of landowners, local authorities, financial institutions and builders, none of them homogenous groups. The suburb also reflected changes in taste and fashion and in its own social standing – as the century progresses there is an increasing resemblance between working class suburb and factory community in outward appearance. By and large the historical geography of the suburb remains unexplored, Dyos's work on Camberwell being an obvious exception. The time is ripe for such a shift in emphasis, as appears to be beginning, in the study of the urban past.

The conurbation emerges as the combination and climax of urban growth, the fusion of parts into a whole. Geddes coined the word only in 1915 to describe 'these city-regions, these town aggregates'[14] (and as much in terms of becoming as of being) still in a formative stage in most cases. Ought the term to be used only of a continuously built-up area, or more loosely? Should it be conceived in terms of space, function, or population? Britain's conurbations were in fact quite small in 1900 — Manchester for example was but tenuously linked to Eccles, Chorlton and Didsbury. But the nineteenth century had witnessed striking population increase and the West Yorkshire conurbation was, in this sense, already half its present size by 1851; central Clydeside had a million and a half people by 1901. London might by any criteria be regarded as a conurbation by 1801 and other cities passed into this category during the century, creating and swallowing suburbs, embracing a diversity of economic and social activities, establishing an internal central place heirarchy for such matters as shopping. Their system of local government rarely kept up with their growth, their spatial spread in particular. London soon outgrew such recognitions of its special position as the Metropolitan Police of 1829 and the London County Council of 1888. However the inadequacies of local government did not prevent ambitious schemes of central redevelopment, sometimes deliberately associated with the clearance of overcrowded and insanitary districts. Edinburgh provided a magnificent model, emulated by Newcastle upon Tyne and in some degree by London, but too rarely matched in the suburbs and too often destroyed in the 1960s and 1970s.

A NEW FABRIC OF SETTLEMENT

New factories, new churches, and above all new houses had to be built to meet the economic, spiritual, and domestic needs of a growing population. The now inner, often decaying, suburbs of Bristol and Tyneside for example, reflect this need and the way it was met; new cottages, new farm buildings in the countryside were less numerous, but they too reflect the socio-economic circumstances in which they were created. For most of the century the concept of private property and its rights was better developed — and defended — than that of public interest and so the need for housing was generally interpreted in terms of commercial enterprise and private profit. Housing was expected to pay, generally to pay well; even philanthropic housing trusts more often than not operated as dividend- or interest-paying institutions. Housing also had to be paid for and low incomes were probably the most important among many constraints upon quality, but even the middle class who could afford to pay endured defective drains and shoddy masonry (plate 5).

Nineteenth-century builders, developers and speculators operated in a legislative framework minimal by the standards of the 1970s but certainly not non-existent. There occurred a transition from minimum and ineffective control through localised and permissive laws until considerable quality control (but rarely locational control, the quintessence of modern planning) was achieved in the last quarter of the century. Environmental quality was seen as an apt area for legislation earliest in the century with respect to workplace, the more conspicuously dangerous in particular; then, after a period of activity on a voluntary basis, with respect to the setting of the residence or workplace in matters such as water supply, drainage and refuse collection (not of open space provision however) likely to offend or infect the middle class passer-by; and last of all with respect to the structure of the house itself. 'An Englishman's home is his castle'! A mass of often unworkable legislation was created. Urban Improvement Commissioners, concerned with the watch (a rudimentary police) paving and lighting, had existed since the eighteenth century and provided a tradition to build upon. Much nineteenth-century legislation was early and enlightened: Manchester controlled street and court width from 1830, prohibited cellar dwellings from 1853, insisted on water closets from 1881 and damp courses from 1890. But permissive legislation depended upon the inherently changeable attitude of the local authority, thus Manchester also appointed no Medical Officer of Health until 1868 and then limited his activities, a generation after more progressive towns had acted.[15] Even the greatest acts of

environmental legislation were largely permissive, the Public
Health Act of 1848, Torrens's and Cross's Housing Acts of 1868
and 1875 respectively, the Public Health Act of 1875. Back-to-
back housing was forbidden to the speculative builder only in
1925. Implementation depended on the energy and policy of
the local authority, the aim being to set standards for the future
rather than to remedy the mistakes of the past. Nevertheless
housing was marked down as an appropriate area for government intervention and basic principles, such as the duty of the
owner to keep the house in good repair, were established. This
latter problem was as acute a hundred years ago as it is now for
overcrowded, jerry-built nineteenth-century houses were very
prone to the dilapidation and disrepair of even the limited
amenities provided.

Pre-eminent among nineteenth-century building materials was
brick, particularly after the extension of the canal and railway
networks had made it cheaply available almost everywhere.
Cheapness was an important matter not only in terms of the
working man's ability to pay to be housed but also of the
economy's ability to support the huge cost of housing a larger
population, even in an indifferent fashion. Thus cheap bricks
ousted not only stone but a rich variety of more costly local
bricks, in Middlesex for example. Similarly, if less generally,
Welsh slate became the commonest roofing material. Stone and
other expensive or exotic materials were kept for the most part
for prestige buildings, in remote areas, or near to the source of
supply. By 1900 brick was triumphant even in some of the most
substantially stone-built towns such as Sherborne, where for
much of the century it had been no more than a rare intruder.
The industrialisation of brick making followed upon rather than
created this wider market; machinery for brick manufacture was
perfected only in mid-century, the great brickworks like Fletton
only in the last decades. Timber had for the most part to be
imported and thus, for example, the fortunes of the timber
trade at Poole, primarily with Baltic ports, relate closely to the
growth of Bournemouth and its suburbs. The technology and
organisation of the building industry, house building in particular, lagged even further behind. The new factories of the 1890s
might be striking and sophisticated technological monuments,
but the house builder still used large quantities of cheap and
casual labour to place brick upon brick, even if those bricks

might now comprise a damp course and enclose a water closet.

Brick could create a Bryanston or a Bedford Park, but for the most part it was used for small and simple houses meeting, sometimes ingeniously, existing legal requirements. A handful of basic designs covered thousands of acres with some adjustment to the special problems of hilly sites and some minor variation of fashion or ornament. Among widespread early nineteenth-century forms the 'not through' (plate 6) and the 'back-to-back' (figure 9) with common yard, pump, and earth closets were commonplace, as were irregular courtyard arrangements around such amenities. Vestiges of eighteenth-century classicism (plate 7) may appear in their fronts, the veneer of which often hid an appalling situation of disrepair, dirt, darkness and decay. The 'tunnel backs' built later in the century

Figure 9. 'Back-to-back' housing as built in Nottingham between c. 1784 and 1830. Domestic industry was the norm in this city at this date (see Chapter 5), hence the workroom; compare also plate 4. It should also be remembered that it was not uncommon for more than one family to occupy a house. (Redrawn from Chapman, S.D., (ed.), *The History of Working-class Housing : a symposium*, Newton Abbot, 1971, figure 4.1.)

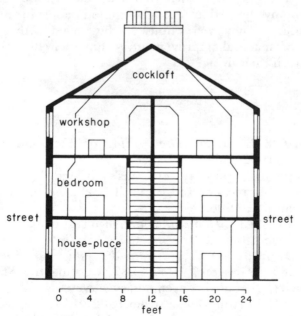

solved the problem of an increasing degree of legislative control; they survive as a common setting for the arrival by train at any major railway station. The form solved the problem not as one devised by the law, nor as a pleasant urban environment, but as the builder's successful attempt to maximise density and minimise cost within the terms of new legislation. The monotony of such order and fashion is however an improvement on the monotony of chaos and squalor, and by the era of the 'tunnel back'[16] a good water supply and a regular refuse collection were adding an element of safety and decency to the urban scene. Local forms — the flat house of Tyneside, the Scottish bungalow or tenement — were created and persisted. By 1900 a few communities designed for working class families were setting standards not always matched in new housing a lifetime later, Bournville and Port Sunlight for example.

Nineteenth-century problems and failures in the area of building in general and housing in particular are now less often derided than even a generation ago.[17] Not only is Victoriana again fashionable but a wealthy society unable adequately to house its citizens is less inclined to scoff at its poorer forbears who, according to their own standards and without crippling their economy, housed an extra 27 million people in the course of a century. They were housed, they lived with a strong prospect of material improvement within their lifetime. How did they earn their living?

NOTES

1 Clark, G.S.R. Kitson, *The Making of Victorian England*, London, 1962. p.64.
2 This unsatisfactory system was initiated by the 1844 Factory Act and lingered on until 1922, but numbers were very few after 1900.
3 Cairncross, A.K., *Home and foreign investment 1870-1913*, Cambridge, 1953, p.79.
4 MacDonald, D.F., *Scotland's shifting population 1770-1850*. Glasgow, 1937, p.87, quoting the *Statistical Accounts*, a detailed contemporary survey.
5 Vicar of Halberton, Devon, from 1862 to 1872, and earlier a curate and incumbent in Lancashire. There seems little

doubt that the contrast between conditions in the two areas roused him to action. He became a prominent member of a minority of 'radical' clergy, reviled by many landowners, farmers and fellow clergy.

6 The best known example, Samuel Butler, used a New Zealand setting for his Utopian novel *Erewhon*. He wrote of his experiences as a colonist in *A First Year In Canterbury Settlement*, 1863.

7 For the Great Exhibition of 1851, where it was awarded the Gold Medal in Class VII.

8. Peake, H.J.E., 'Geographical aspects of administative areas', *Geography*, Vol. 15, 1930, pp. 531-46.

9 For a description see the opening chapter of Thomas Hardy, *The Mayor of Casterbridge*.

10 Lipman, V.D., *Local Government Areas: 1834-1945*, Oxford, 1949, pp. 78 and 81, the latter quoting Goschen.

11 Quoted by Lipman, p. 44.

12 Since many workhouses survive as geriatric hospitals so, in a curious way, has their central place role. Our treatment of the elderly retains some nineteenth-century characteristics!

13 The best known was William Wilberforce, leader of the movement for the abolition of slavery.

14 Geddes, P., *Cities in Evolution*, London, 1915, p. 34.

15 Charles Kingsley's novels *Yeast*, *Alton Locke*, and *Two Years Ago* all relate to mid-century sanitary problems.

16 So called because they were built in terraces, access to the rear of the houses being by tunnels passing through the terrace.

17 A delightful satirical but by no means unsympathetic account of the forms of later nineteenth century urban growth is to be found in the later chapters of Osbert Lancaster's *Draynflete Revealed*.

FURTHER READING

1 POPULATION

Cairncross, A.K., 'Internal migration in Victorian England', *Manchester School*, vol. 17, 1949, pp. 67-87.

Carrier, N.H., and Jeffery, J.R., 'External migration: a study of the available statistics', *Studies on Medical and Population*

Subjects, vol. 6, London (General Register Office), 1953.

Darby, H.C., 'The movement of population to and from Cambridgeshire between 1851 and 1861', *Geographical Journal*, vol. 101, 1943, pp. 118-25.

Deane, P. and Cole, W.A., *British Economic Growth 1688-1959: Trends and Structures*, Cambridge 1967, ch. 3, 'Industrialisation and population change in the eighteenth and early nineteenth centuries'.

Law, C.M., 'The growth of urban population in England and Wales 1801-1911', *Institute of British Geographers: Transactions*, vol. 41, 1967, pp. 125-44.

Lawton, R., 'The population of Liverpool in the mid-nineteenth century', *Transactions of the Historical Society of Lancashire and Cheshire*, vol. 107, 1955, pp. 89-120.

Lawton, R., 'Population movements in the West Midlands 1841-61', *Geography*, vol. 43, pp. 164-77.

Lawton, R., 'Population changes in England and Wales in the later nineteenth century', *Institute of British Geographers: Transactions*, vol. 44, 1968, pp. 55-74.

Lawton, R., 'Rural depopulation in nineteenth century England', in Steel, R.W., and Lawton, R., *Liverpool Essays in Geography*, Liverpool, 1967, pp. 227-55.

MacDonald, D.F., *Scotland's shifting population 1770-1850*, Glasgow, 1937.

McKeown, T., and Record, R.G., 'Reasons for the decline of mortality in England and Wales during the nineteenth century', *Population Studies*, vol. 16, 1962-3, pp. 94-122.

McKeown, T., Brown, R.G., and Record, R.G., 'The modern rise of population in Europe', *Population Studies*, vol. 26, 1972-3, pp. 345-82.

Osborne, R.H., 'The movements of people in Scotland 1851-1951', *Scottish Studies*, vol. 2, 1958, pp. 1-46.

Ravenstein, E.G., 'The laws of migration', *Journal of the Royal Statistical Society*, vol. 48, 1885, pp. 167-235.

Redford, A., *Labour migration in England 1800-1850*, 2nd edition revised by Chaloner, W.H., Manchester, 1964.

Smith, C.T., 'The movement of population in England and Wales in 1851 and 1861', *Geographical Journal*, vol. 117, 1951, pp. 200-10.

Thomas, B., 'The migration of labour into the Glamorganshire coalfield 1861-1911', *Economica*, vol. 10, 1930, pp. 275-94.

Trueman, Sir A.E., 'Population changes in the eastern part of the South Wales coalfield', *Geographical Journal*, vol. 53, 1919, pp. 410-19.

Wallis, B.C., 'Nottinghamshire in the nineteenth century: geographical factors in the growth of the population', *Geographical Journal*, vol. 43, 1914, pp. 34-61.

Welton, T.A., 'On the distribution of the population in England and Wales . . . 1801-91', *Journal of the Royal Statistical Society*, vol. 63, 1900, pp. 527-89.

Wrigley, E.A., *Population and History*, London, 1969.

2   SETTLEMENT

Ashworth, W., *The Genesis of Modern Town Planning*, London, 1954.

Bowley, M., *Innovations in building materials*, London, 1960.

Carter, H., *The Towns of Wales*, Cardiff, 1965.

Carter, H., 'Urban grades in south-west Wales: an historical consideration', *Scottish Geographical Magazine*, vol. 71, 1955, pp. 43-58.

Dickinson, R.E., 'The distribution and functions of the smaller urban settlements of East Anglia', *Geography*, vol. 17, 1932, pp. 19-31.

Dyos, H.J., 'The slums of Victorian London', *Victorian Studies*, vol. 11, 1967-8, pp. 5-40.

Dyos, H.J., 'The speculative builders and developers of Victorian London', *Victorian Studies*, vol. 11 (supplement), 1967-8, pp. 641-90

Dyos, H.J., *Victorian suburb: a study of the growth of Camberwell*, London, 1961.

Frazer, W.M., *History of English public health 1834-1939*, London, 1950.

Gauldie, E., *Cruel Habitations: a history of working-class housing 1780-1918*, London, 1974.

Lipman, V.C., *Local Government Areas 1834-1945*, Oxford, 1949.

Newton, R., *Victorian Exeter*, Leicester, 1968.

Simon, E.D., and Inman, J., *The Rebuilding of Manchester*, London, 1935.

Smailes, A.E., 'The urban grid of England and Wales', *Institute of British Geographers: Transactions and Papers*, vol. 11, 1946, pp. 87-101.

Tarn, J.N., *Five per cent Philanthropy: An Account of Housing in Urban Areas between 1840 and 1914*, Cambridge, 1973.

3 Mines and Metals:
The Geography of Basic Industry

The answer to the rhetorical question posed at the end of the preceding chapter lies in the phrase 'the workshop of the world'. A growing population was sustained and higher living standards were attained by selling raw materials, manufactured goods, and services to the world at large. The bases of this activity were Britain's enormous and accessible reserve of coal, and the technology which exploited it and which matched it to a substantial but less generous reserve of iron ore.

COAL AND STEAM

Among possible themes around which a historical geography of nineteenth-century Britain might be written, coal is pre-eminent. At the end of the century coalmining employed over a million people. Coal was the motive force of Britain and the economically developed world for ships, for railways, for machinery; it was a major export staple, a chemical raw material, a domestic fuel, and not least a locational force. It even begins to appear in the 1970s that present-day dependence on oil and gas may turn out to be no more than an interregnum in the age of coal. Coal was king: 'all the activity and industry of this kingdom is fast concentrating where there are coal pits'[1] wrote Arthur Young as early as 1791. Even by this date precocious industrial development had begun to lay down an industrial geography on the coalfields, half a century before a railway network capable of distributing so bulky a source of power was created.

Britain's coal output increased from about 11 million tons in

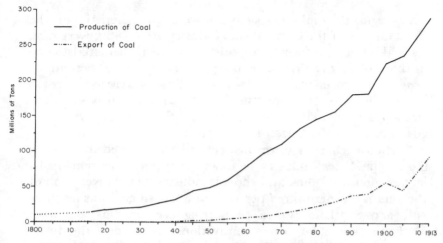

Figure 10. Britain's coal output and exports, 1800-1913. (Drawn from five-yearly date in Deane, P., and Cole, W.A. *British Economic Growth 1688-1959*, Cambridge, 1962, table 54.)

1800 to more than 225 million in 1900 (figure 10), a revolution in itself. An industry made up of small family-owned enterprises in the early nineteenth century, located on the exposed fields, employing no more than a few hundred men to dig a few hundred feet deep, had become in most areas an industry dominated by colliery companies employing several thousand men and sinking shafts as deep as 3,000 feet into 'concealed' coal fields. In the process mining had become safer, largely through legislative action — in the 1850s there were about 4.3 deaths per year for every thousand workers, by the 1900s only 1.4 per thousand.

The early nineteenth-century industry was still largely concerned with traditional domestic and industrial markets, Durham with London, South Wales with its iron-masters for example. Accessibility was of prime importance and until at least mid-century coastal coalfields maintained their long-standing advantage over those of the interior. Thus as late as 1847 the Rhonnda was described as 'the gem of South Wales . . . hardly surpassed throughout the Alpine North'.[2] Railways opened up such inland districts and 'brought a measure of unity to an industry which had hitherto been distinguished by its diversity'.[3] It was only a measure; numerous small workings for local markets survived in such areas as the Forest of Dean, and large regional combines, such as were characteristic of the development of the German coal industry after 1880, were rare. As coal is not a uniform commodity in its own characteristics or in those of its occurrence, mining or marketing, so methods of production, costs, wages and social conditions were as diverse in 1900 as in 1800. They were made more conspicuously so by the size and importance of the industry and the extent to which the government involved itself in its affairs.

Technical changes were unspectacular compared to those in the iron and steel industry or inland transport; coal remained a labour intensive, 'pick and shovel' industry. At the very end of the century a mere three per cent of Scottish coal was machine cut, and Scotland was a pioneering area in this activity.[4] Mechanisation, like other innovations, proceeded discontinuously and at different dates in different fields. Some technical advances are well known, such as the safety lamp and legislative insistence on at least two shafts from 1862.[5] Most are not; in South Wales for example the spread of the longwall method of working in the 1860s, the use of compressed air from about 1865, and improved ventilation by means of fans in the third quarter of the century. Nationwide such advances sustained productivity increase in the face of the inevitable problems of deeper pits, longer underground hauls, and the exhaustion of the thickest and most accessible seams, so that an average output of 220 tons per man per year in 1851 reached 326 tons by the early eighties. Thereafter productivity slowly fell back, not that mining became a technological laggard by comparison with overseas producers — as yet scarcely competitors — the commonplace criticism of late Victorian industry. The problems were organisational and historical, related to such issues as limited finance and bad working conditions. 'The weakness of the early twentieth century coal industry was not that it was under-capitalised . . . but that its assets were too thinly and unevenly spread.'[6] Some degree of weakness and vulnerability is inherent in an old-established extractive industry; some was related to the attitudes of masters and men. Whatever the dimensions of these problems they were, until the 1920s, more often than not concealed by buoyant demand.

The demand for coal in the early nineteenth century contained two components, the domestic and the industrial. Householders needed coal for heating and for cooking; industrialists used coal to raise steam, to boil and evaporate liquids (brine for example) and as a chemical raw material, notably in the manufacture of iron. In every case the coastal, canal-side, or coalfield consumer was in a favoured position — elsewhere coal was because of its bulk a costly raw material, often a luxury. The areas served by the English coalfields appear on a map prepared for the Royal Commission of 1830 (figure 11); the pre-eminence of the north-east coast with its dominance of the London market is evident. There were other coastal fields, among them Fifeshire and Cumberland, and inland fields serving local markets.

Figure 11. Britain's coalfields and their markets in 1830. (Redrawn from Clapham, J.B., *An Economic History of Modern Britain*, Volume 1 ('The early railway age'), Cambridge, 1926, facing p.236, in turn based on *Report of the Select Committee on the Coal Trade*, 1830.)

Coal and iron were associated not only technologically but also geologically, since black-band iron ores occur in the coal measures. By the early nineteenth century this association had a long enough history in Coalbrookdale to drive the iron industry eastward into an area requiring deeper collieries. Shropshire may be regarded as the heartland of this coal-iron relationship, but it was also strong elsewhere. The Ayrshire and Clackmannanshire coalfield served the Devon ironworks (near Clackmannan burgh), the iron industry placed Lanark first among Scottish coalfields, and ironmasters opened up the northern part of the South Wales coalfields in the early nineteenth century. West coast coalfields, Ayrshire for example, could also look to coalless Ireland as a market. The market was, however, changing; industrial demand was more and more for steam, for by the 1830s cotton was essentially a steam industry. In the iron trade Nielsen's hot-blast process of 1828 reduced coal requirements by about two-thirds; in fact as iron production was growing and the process was not adopted instantaneously there was no absolute diminution in the industry's demand for coal, but the tight locational bond of coal to iron had for the first time been loosened.

The great nineteenth-century turning point for the coal industry is however the 1840s. The great expansion of the railway network provided a new and enormous market for steam coal while it facilitated both mining in and the supply of coal to interior Britain. The continuing growth of the industrial economy, driven by steam, likewise extended the market and such enterprises as Bute Dock (Cardiff, 1839) opened up overseas trade. Between 1830 and 1860 output increased almost fourfold to reach 80 million tons, and by the latter date Britain's share of world production was three-fifths. This was the very foundation of Britain's mid-century growth and pre-eminence, so much so as to lead the older Jevons, pessimistic as to the extent of coal reserves, to a gloomy forecast: 'we have to make the choice between brief greatness and longer continued mediocrity'.[7] The north-east coast, the old established producer of high grade steam coal, gradually lost pre-eminence to South Wales, at first to the more accessible Aberdare valleys, later to the Rhonnda. Former ironmasters became primarily mineowners in these areas, their well-established pits having an initial advantage over new, remote, high-wage ventures. By the 1860s the steamship had become an important coal consumer although this market, like overseas exports, reached its apogee only late in the century. The steamer was not, unlike the train, an almost instantaneous success. Mid-century was also the heyday of the black-band iron industry, coal-field based and the *raison d'être* of many collieries in the secondary fields, such as in Scotland. These were the depressed areas of 1920s in the making, where iron works and mines were established which could not carry on seventy years later when coal and iron resources were almost exhausted and prices low. Already by mid-century deeper pits and migration to the concealed field were becoming widely necessary, a development begun in Shropshire fifty years or so earlier, extended to the north east in the 1820s and to the East Midlands in the 1850s. In this expansion the London market played a large part, witness the extensive coal yards to the north of London's northern railway termini. Some secondary fields developed almost wholly for this market at this date, the Leicestershire-South Derbyshire coalfield for example.

The second turning point occurs some time in the 1870s. Productivity per man reached its peak about 1880, thereafter to fall as cheap labour was used as an alternative to machinery. The labour force in fact grew faster than the population, but a continuous influx of new labour into the mines necessarily lowered output per man per hour and thus raised coal prices (mining was by no means an unskilled industry). To some extent this trend was countered by the lessened seasonality of the coal trade as household markets became proportionately less important. The late nineteenth-century coal industry was then a business of mass labour, of limited companies (replacing the older partnerships), and of the pre-eminence of steam coal for shipping and export. This latter situation particularly favoured South Wales. Coal had become a producer good, subject at times to insatiable demand but also vulnerable to trade recession and even to foreign competition. Thus growth was more erratic and less rapid than in mid-century, doubling between 1870 and 1900 where it had trebled in the preceding thirty years. Industrial strife was also important in this context.

By 1900 exports, almost 50 million tons a year, accounted for one quarter of total output (figures 12 and 13). They were made up largely of steam coal from two fields: South Wales sent

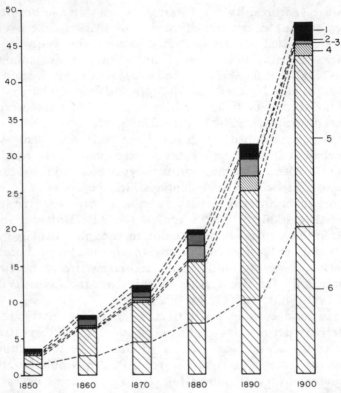

Figure 12. Britain's export trade in coal 1850-1900, in millions of
tons, by destination: 1, South America and Pacific ports of U.S.A.,
(Colombia and Venezuela excepted); 2, North and Central America,
Colombia and Venezuela; 3, East Africa, Asia and Australasia; 4,
West and South Africa; 5, France and the Mediterranean; 6, Baltic
ports, Germany and the Low Countries. (Drawn from Thomas, D.A.,
'The growth and direction of our foreign trade in coal during the last
half century', *Journal of the Royal Statistical Society*, Vol. 66,
1903, appendix C, p.508.)

two-fifths of its output overseas through an elaborate system of
railways and their docks created during the century and the
north-east coast exported one-third of its production via older
established channels. Lower freights facilitated export — the
rate to Buenos Aires was 35s 6d per ton in 1863, 16s in 1900,
the Argentine railways being an important market. More
efficient steamers and a general deflation combined to provide
the world with cheap coal, and by 1900 85 per cent of this

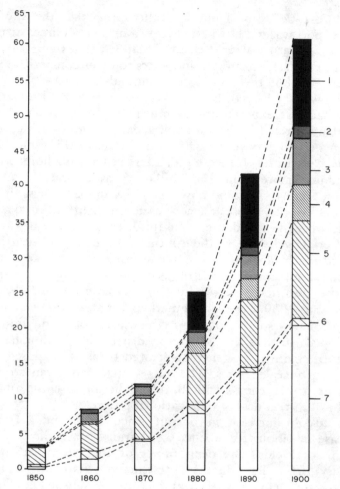

Figure 13. Britain's export trade in coal 1850-1900, in millions of tons, by origin: 1, bunkers in foreign trade (no data for 1850-70); 2, West Scotland; 3, East Scotland; 4, Humber and East Coast ports south of Tees; 5, Durham, Northumberland, and Teesside; 6, North-west England; 7, Bristol Channel. (Drawn from same source as figure 12, p.509.)

international trade was British. Europe, the Mediterranean and South America were markets almost completely dominated by Britain, but in more distant areas, the Pacific for example, only passenger liner operators could stand the cost of shipping best Welsh steam coal in the face of local competition. 'The coal that saved Calliope'[8] came from the Buller rather than the Rhonnda. Coal export was not however merely a matter of direct earnings, since an outward coal cargo ensured that British vessels need rarely travel in ballast, enabling shipowners to offer competitive rates. As early as 1865 this was an important advantage.

Coal was the basis of late nineteenth-century British maritime supremacy, as export cargo as much as motive power. A more mundane parallel is the fact that coal royalties enabled many landowners to survive the agricultural crisis of this same period, in the West Riding for example. There remained a home market consuming more than 150 million tons a year — railways, houses, factories, gas and now electricity undertakings, and iron and steel works. These last now used one-eighth of total output where once they had used one-third. In general coal was used more effectively late in the century; the domestic hearth still pushed much of its heat — to say nothing of its smoke — up the chimney, but possibly as little as one-tenth of the coal required to raise one horse power in 1800 was needed for the same purpose in 1900. Flourishing markets for an extractive industry called for new sources of supply; new areas of production were developed, such as the Ashington district in Northumberland, while the industry in general migrated from old exposed fields to new concealed ones. The pits which had given so much impetus to Manchester and Bradford began to close, and coal itself lost a great deal of its locational power.

A 20-fold increase in output since 1800 and a five-fold increase in labour force since 1841 transformed the landscape of the coalfields. The deep mines of the latter part of the century were less directly destructive than their shallow predecessors, closely spaced and prone to subsidence. On the other hand they required miles of rail and tramway, created huge waste-tips, and since they required a larger labour force they created larger communities. New miners, locally born or immigrant, required new houses, usually cheek by jowl with the pit. The miners' row became as distinctive a part of the landscape of mining as the colliery winding gear. A number of circumstances combined to favour a settlement pattern at best drab and monotonous, at worst dreadful, although the rural setting of many such communities provided a redeeming feature. Much coalmining took place in a harsh physical environment, in Wales for example, where difficult sites for house building favoured high densities; rapid growth of population where the industry grew rapidly led to overcrowding. Housing the miner was expected to be profitable – and thus cheap – an attitude favoured by the inherent risk that a new mining venture would fail and be abandoned. Thus temporary wooden barracks were sometimes built and acquired a particularly bad reputation. Some idea of the appalling conditions in which the miner might be expected to live is provided by an Ayrshire County Council Housing Committee resolution of June 1914 – 'privies should have doors and seats'.[9] The mining village was moreover often isolated, commonly made up solely of workers at one pit, and thus economically and socially vulnerable. These were veritable new towns – Tonypandy and Cowdenbeath – but without the carefully planned housing and social provision of their mid-twentieth-century counterparts.

The colliery owner might support churches and schools, but the chapels and clubs of Durham, the West Riding and South Wales owe much more to the miner. Regional social differences related however not only to living and working conditions, the latter enshrined in official wage differentials, but to cultural antecedents. The Welsh valleys lost their language but retained their music and their religious non-conformity; collections among the mining communities sustained the infant Aberystwyth University College. The cultural antecedents of the leek clubs of Durham and Northumberland are obscure, but they serve to emphasise the existence of distinct coalfield cultural communities. The younger Jevons, writing in 1915, claimed that in general the older coalfields provided the highest quality of life, in part because the skill of the miner and the division of labour there reached the highest level, in Scotland for example. Newer coalfields, such as the East Midlands, provided a coarser and cruder life style. In any event by 1900 the miner was beginning to be able to live at a distance from his work; as well as miners' rows there were extensive services of workmens' trains, some in the Welsh valleys. The collier had become a commuter.

But let D.H. Lawrence have the last word on the colliery community and landscape:

The string of coal-mines of B.W. & Co. had been opened some sixty years before I was born, and Eastwood had come into being as a consequence. It must have been a tiny village at the beginning of the nineteenth century, a small place of cottages and fragmentary rows of little four-roomed miners' dwellings, the homes of the colliers of the eighteenth century, who worked in the bits of mines, foot-hill mines with an opening in the hillside into which the miners walked, or windlass mines, where the men were wound up one at a time, in a bucket, by a donkey. The windlass mines were still working when my father was a boy — and the shafts of some were still there, when I was a boy.

But somewhere about 1820 the company must have sunk the first big shaft — not very deep — and installed the first machinery of the real industrial colliery . . . My grandfather settled in an old cottage down in a quarrybed, by the brook at Old Brinsley, near the pit. A mile away, up at Eastwood, the company built the first miners' dwellings — it must be nearly a hundred years ago. Now Eastwood occupies a lovely position on a hilltop, with the steep slope towards Derbyshire and the long slope towards Nottingham. They put up a new church, which stands fine and commanding, even if it has no real form, looking across the awful Erewash Valley at the church of Heanor, similarly commanding, away on a hill beyond. What opportunities, what opportunities! These mining villages might have been like the lovely hill-towns of Italy, shapely and fascinating. And what happened?

Most of the little rows of dwellings of the old-style miners were pulled down, and dull little shops began to rise along the Nottingham Road, while on the down-slope of the north side the company erected what is still known as the New Buildings, or the Square. These New Buildings consist of two great hollow squares of dwellings planked down on the rough slope of the hill, little four-room houses with the 'front' looking outward into the grim, blank street, and the 'back', with a tiny square brick yard, a low wall, and a w.c. and ash-pit, looking into the desert of the square, hard, uneven, jolting black earth tilting rather steeply down, with these little back yards all round, and openings at the corners. The squares were quite big, and absolutely desert save for the posts for clothes lines, and people passing, children playing on the hard earth. And they were shut in like a barracks enclosure, very strange.

Even fifty years ago the squares were unpopular. It was

'common' to live in the Square. It was a little less common to
live in the Breach, which consisted of six blocks of rather
more pretentious dwellings erected by the company in the
valley below, two rows of three blocks, with an alley
between. And it was most 'common', most degraded of all to
live in Dakins Row, two rows of the old dwellings, very old,
black four-roomed little places, that stood on the hill again,
not far from the Square.

So the place started. Down the steep street between the
squares, Scargill Street, the Wesleyans' chapel was put up,
and I was born in the little corner shop just above. Across the
other side of the Square the miners themselves built the big,
barn-like Primitive Methodist chapel. Along the hill-top ran
the Nottingham Road, with its scrappy, ugly mid-Victorian
shops. The little market-place, with a superb outlook, ended
the village on the Derbyshire side, and was just left bare, with
the Sun Inn on one side, the chemist across, with the gilt
pestle-and-mortar, and a shop at the other corner, the corner
of Alfreton Road and Nottingham Road.

In this queer jumble of the old England and the new, I
came into consciousness. As I remember, little local speculators already began to straggle dwellings in rows, always in
rows, across the fields; nasty red-brick, flat-faced dwellings
with dark slate roofs. The bay-window period only began
when I was a child. But most of the country was untouched.

There must be three or four hundred company houses in
the squares and the streets that surround the squares, like a
great barracks wall. There must be sixty or eighty company
houses in the Breach. The old Dakins Row will have thirty or
forty little holes. Then counting the old cottages and rows
left with their old gardens down the lanes and along the
twitchells, and even in the midst of Nottingham Road itself,
there were houses enough for the population, there was no
need for much building. And not much building went on
when I was small.

We lived in the Breach, in a corner house. A field-path
came down under a great hawthorn hedge. On the other side
was the brook, with the old sheep-bridge going over into the
meadows. The hawthorn hedge by the brook had grown tall
as tall trees, and we used to bathe from there in the
dipping-hole, where the sheep were dipped, just near the fall

from the old mill-dam, where the water rushed. The mill only ceased grinding the local corn when I was a child. And my father, who always worked in Brinsley pit, and who always got up at five o'clock, if not at four, would set off in the dawn across the fields at Coney Grey, and hunt for mushrooms in the long grass, or perhaps pick up a skulking rabbit, which he would bring home at evening inside the lining of his pit-coat.

So that the life was a curious cross between industrialism and the old agricultural England of Shakespeare and Milton and Fielding and George Eliot. The dialect was broad Derbyshire, and always 'thee' and 'thou'. The people lived almost entirely by instinct, men of my father's age could not really read. And the pit did not mechanise men. On the contrary. Under the butty system, the miners worked underground as a sort of intimate community, they knew each other practically naked, and with curious close intimacy, and the darkness and the underground remoteness of the pit 'stall', and the continual presence of danger, made the physical, instinctive, and intuitional contact between men very highly developed, a contact almost as close as touch, very real and very powerful. This physical awareness and intimate togetherness was at its strongest down pit. When the men came up into the light, they blinked. They had, in a measure, to change their flow. Nevertheless, they brought with them above ground the curious dark intimacy of the mine, the naked sort of contact, and if I think of my childhood, it is always as if there was a lustrous sort of inner darkness, like the gloss of coal, in which we moved and had our real being. My father loved the pit. He was hurt badly, more than once, but he would never stay away. He loved the contact, the intimacy, as men in the war loved the intense male comradeship of the dark days. They did not know what they had lost till they lost it. And I think it is the same with the colliers of today.[10]

Coal was to nineteenth century Britain what oil, gas and electricity are to the twentieth — and more besides. Approaching its peak — but past its prime — in 1900 the industry was steam- and export-oriented. As the industry moved more and more on to the concealed fields the popular view was that Kent was the coalfield of the future and the view that its future might be at best difficult and uncertain was scarcely ventured. Many obscure fields survived, meeting local needs by simple methods, the vestiges of 1800 alongside giants of 1900.

IRON AND STEEL

Coal was the motive power of the nineteenth century; iron and later steel were the essential capital goods in such forms as rails and girders, steam engines, screws and eventually ships. To make these goods, coal and limestone were required as well as iron ore and for much of the century the presence of iron ores in the coal measures was an additional force drawing iron-making to the coalfields. Only in the last quarter of the century did imported and non-coalfield ores exert a strong locational influence. It is moreover in this period that the apparent fortunes of the two industries diverge: the export boom in the coal trade was accompanied by general stagnation, occasional sharp depression, and loss of overseas markets in the iron and steel industry. In general iron-making was subject to sharper fluctuations than the coal trade — Scottish pig iron for example fetched 116s per ton in 1873, 46s six years later. If opening an iron works was almost as speculative a venture as sinking a coalmine, the former could more easily be put back into production than an abandoned mine. By comparison with the coal trade some innovations, Nielsen's hot blast for example, were applied relatively quickly. From mid-century however the geography of the industry is more of opportunities rejected than seized, of changes resisted than welcomed (particularly in steel making) as well as of the gradual impact of the depletion of coal and associated iron reserves.

The iron industry expanded quite as remarkably as coal-mining. At the start of the century about a quarter of a million tons of iron were made each year, at its end about ten million (figure 14). An eightfold increase in output between 1830 and 1870 rather outstrips the contemporaneous upsurge in coal production. Moreover locational changes were more marked in the iron and steel industry, thus South Wales and the West Midlands made two-thirds of Britain's pig iron in 1800, whereas between them the north east, the north west, and Scotland

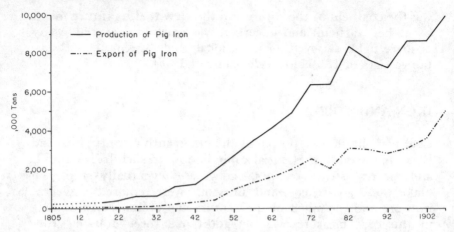

Figure 14. Britain's production and export of pig-iron 1805-1907. (Drawn from five-yearly data in Deane, P., and Cole, W.A., *British Economic Growth 1688-1959*, Cambridge, 1962, table 56.)

produced three-quarters of the iron and steel made in 1900 (figures 15 and 16).

The iron industry of the early nineteenth century occupied some of the best known sites of the Industrial Revelution — Coalbrookdale, Cyfartha, Carron, for example. These were centres of both coal and ore production, and at this period smelting required twice as much coal as ore. During the Napoleonic war the demand for ordnance and the general economic buoyancy boosted the industry's contribution to gross national product to about six per cent; after the war it fell back to about three per cent, but at its peak in 1871 it exceeded 11 per cent. Early in the century many products of the mid-century boom scarcely existed: rails were a trivial concern, the demand was for steam engines, machinery, tools and hardware. Steel was as yet an expensive speciality, required mainly by cutlers and made in Sheffield by 'small scale concerns in the backyards and orchards of the houses of the town'.[11] In South Wales and the West Midlands however iron was big business, albeit already in decline in the more remote Shropshire. A typical early nineteenth-century iron enterprise might be made up of two or three blast furnaces, several coal and iron pits, a refinery, forge, puddling furnace, hammer and rolling mill; a degree of integration and the significance of late eighteenth-century inventions are apparent. By the middle of the 1840s Dowlais

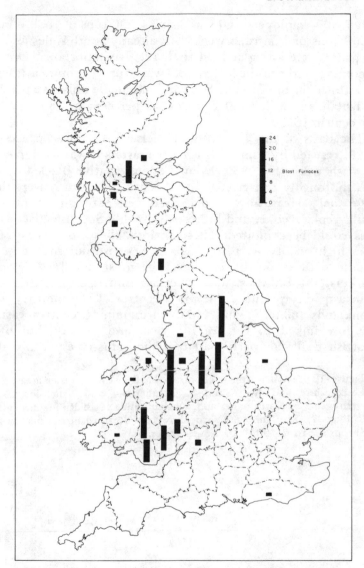

Figure 15. Britain's iron industry in 1796 (Redrawn from Roepke, H.G., *Movements of the British iron and steel industry 1720-1951, Illinois Studies in the Social Sciences,* 36, Urbana, 1956, p.25).

had 7,300 employees and was using 1,200 tons of coal to make 1,600 tons of iron each week, but already South Wales and the Midlands were losing at least their relative importance. Ore was becoming scarce in the latter, coal was to prove a more attractive investment in the former. Scotland had made only five per cent of Britain's iron in 1830; it made 16 per cent in 1839, and 29 per cent in 1852.

The basis of this success was Nielsen's hot blast process of 1828; resisted by some English ironmasters it was used in every Scottish works by 1835. Even the conservative Black Country was thoroughly converted by mid-century. Not only were there huge fuel savings, already discussed, but Scottish 'splint' coal could replace coke, and hitherto unusable Scottish black-band ores could be exploited. These savings, these low costs rather than high quality were the basis of Scottish dominance in the middle decades of the century. The most rapidly developing markets, the railways, wanted cheap iron rails in bulk rather than a quality product. The main centres of the industry were Monklands (plate 8) and Coatbridge, mining centres east of Glasgow linked to the sea by canal and railway, but other Scottish coalfields participated in the industry especially after

Figure 16. Britain's iron production 1796-1913: 1, other areas; 2, Lincolnshire and Northants; 3, Cumberland and Lancashire; 4, Derbyshire; 5, Northumberland, Durham and North Riding; 6, West Riding; 7, Scotland; 8, Shropshire; 9, Staffordshire (including Shropshire from 1905); 10, South Wales.

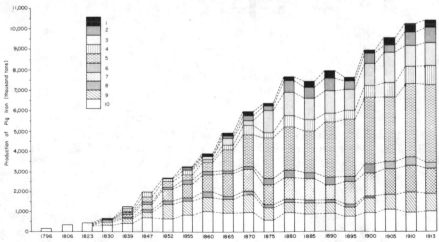

1845. Demand was universal, overseas as well as in Britain, and rails were to the iron trade what steam coal was to the coal trade; to an increasing extent heavier and tougher rails were required. By the 1850s iron rails exported to the U.S.A. were more valuable than cottons or woollens, but inevitably there was also an excess capacity and occasional acute depression. Moreover from 1850 new areas were entering the industry, notably the north-east coast on the basis of Cleveland ironstone and Durham coal. Middlesborough lit its first furnace in 1851, Teesside had 122 by 1871, when the region as a whole made one-quarter of Britain's iron and steel. This shift was largely a response to increased raw material problems in established areas, not felt in Scotland however until the last quarter of the century, and to a constantly improving technology which used less coke. The north-east coast had cheap, albeit low quality ores, and was close to the Durham coalfield; its coastal location was favourable to exports (and a growing shipbuilding industry). It could afford to be wasteful: 'commercial success in spite of wasteful methods [was] . . . a measure of the strength of her raw material resources'.[12]

The major element in the changing geography of the industry in the later nineteenth century is not however the location of new or old indigenous raw materials. It is the creation of a new product — steel — by a new technology and the problems of its adoption and implementation. The Bessemer Converter of 1856 and the Siemens Open-Hearth Furnace of 1868 made steel nearly as cheap as iron and in the long run a better bargain as it was more durable. The cutler's costly raw material became the 'ubiquitous source of strength for the architect, the engineer, the shipbuilder and armaments manufacturer'.[13] Unfortunately the quality of the new material, Bessemer steel in particular, was unreliable until late in the century, and expensive non-phosphoric ores were essential until the Gilchrist-Thomas 'basic' process was developed in 1878.[14] This 'basic' steel also took some time to establish a sound reputation.

The Bessemer process was particularly associated with the ousting of the iron rail by more durable steel in the 1870s — here quality mattered less than price. The supply of ore (non-phosphoric haematite) came from Cumberland, and by 1890 one-fifth of Britain's iron and steel industry was located there on the one British ore field suitable for the new steel processes. Cumberland ore travelled by rail to Cleveland, where local ore was phosphoric, and similar ores imported from Spain served the South Wales industry. Not only was South Wales close to Spain, compared say with Scotland, but steam coal was an attractive return cargo, so the industry, dependent on imported ore, began to move to the coast. Open hearth steel was more important in shipbuilding (and thus in such areas as Scotland and the North east) on account of its higher and more consistent quality. Lloyds first accepted steel ships in 1877[15] and within a decade steel was the almost universal building material. However open hearth steel was not produced in larger quantities than Bessemer steel until 1894, the process having been constantly improved while Britain's Bessemer industry was allowed to become semi-moribund: 'the mid eighties were seminal years for the open hearth steel industry, they were climacteric for the Bessemer industry'.[16] Herein lay one of the problems of the industry in the export market and in its reputation. The Admiralty gave 'basic' (Gilchrist-Thomas) steel parity with 'acid' (open hearth) in 1887 but prejudice against the former remained, and the process accounted for only one-fifth of output in 1900. The argument that the basic process inherently offered more to European producers, Britain's competitors, contains some truth, but the limited growth of the 'basic' industry again bears witness to stagnation and inertia. Thus British steel, wedded to the more costly and less satisfactory Bessemer technology, lost ground as an export save in such new and specialised areas as Sheffield's alloy steels. The industry also failed to make full use of the Jurassic phosphoric ores of the East Midlands. The industry set up there in 1853, to some extent under the auspices of coal and iron companies based in old-established areas, was still of only secondary importance in 1900 and much of the ore that was produced travelled north to be smelted. A degree of geographical inertia accompanied technical stagnation.

It is easy to exaggerate the decadence of the industry in the last years of the century, particularly as an exporter. Britain still accounted for 61 per cent of world steel exports in 1900 compared to 75 per cent in 1870; but between 1875 and 1896 Britain passed from making 47 per cent of the world's pig iron and 40 per cent of its steel, to 29 per cent and 22 per cent. Even more striking changes came in the next decade when

British output grew by one-third, that of Germany doubled, that of the U.S.A. increased fourfold. This was to some extent inevitable: 'the fundamental steelmaking inventions had been made in this country and we benefited from the close juxtaposition of ore and coal and their proximity to the coast. Apart from these there were, by 1880, very few favourable factors'.[17] Overseas producers had their advantages to exploit, their tariff walls to erect. But there is evidence to suggest that recession, relative as it was, went further than can be explained in terms of inherent overseas advantage, of 'some degree of failure . . . in the appreciation of or welcome given to novel principles or in the mode of their application'.[18]

What of the social geography of the iron and steel industry in nineteenth-century Britain? As the geographical patterns of the coal and iron industries slowly diverged, towns of various sizes devoted primarily to iron and steel were created — among them Middlesbrough, Askam and Millom. But such towns were fewer than the single-minded coalmining communities; more often the iron and steel business was carried on alongside others which were favoured by its presence, such as a variety of engineering trades. In environmental terms iron and steel was every bit as unpleasant as coal; on the one hand new communities were created very quickly, with all the problems of low quality and unplanned housing, and on the other the manufacturing process was demanding of space and productive of noise, smoke, dust, and waste. Thus Wolverhampton Corporation threatened to sue the firm of Lysaght for pollution in 1892 and 1895, for which reason the firm moved to Uskmouth in 1896. It was also a damaging consumer of resources — the Whitby ironstone mines for example were marked by 'refuse . . . brought out and deposited on the surface accumulating immense heaps of spoil, damaging and disfiguring the land upon which it was deposited'.[19] In Northamptonshire however it was only when the steam navvy replaced the pick and shovel, enabling deep deposits to be worked, from about 1895 that ironstone mining became seriously destructive of farm land.

At its peak in 1871 the industry, most broadly defined, employed 40 per cent of the adult male labour force, used 25 per cent of static steam power, and accounted for 11 per cent of gross national product. Mid-Victorian supremacy is epitomised in iron and steel; so, regrettably, is mid-Victorian com-

72 *Mines and Metals*

placency. Thus the industry manifested problems which have
since become commonplace, and which worried some contemporaries, earlier than its peers: an indifferent export performance
in a competitive situation, an excess of obsolete plant, an
optimistic – at worst thoughtless – preference for the
traditional and accepted over the innovational and radical.
South Wales epitomises the geographical experience, continuity
on old inland sites generating socio-economic problems only
partly solved by a continuing transfer of the industry to coastal
sites suitable for ore import.

NOTES

1 Young, Arthur, *Tours in England and Wales*, 1791, p. 275.
2 Lewis, E.D., *The Rhonnda Valleys*, London, 1959, p. 15;
quoting Cliffe, C.F., *The Book of South Wales*, London,
1847.
3 Taylor, A.J., 'Combination in the mid-nineteenth century
coal industry', *Transactions of the Royal Historical Society*
(fifth series), vol. 3, 1953, p.23.
4 Machine cutting developed first on the older fields and
thinner seams, not as Jevons suggests (*The British Coal
Trade*, London, 1915, p. 211) in the Midlands. See
Duckham's introduction to the 1969 edition, p.x.
5 The result of a famous accident at Hartley Colliery in
Northumberland when the beam of the engine broke and
blocked the one shaft, preventing access to trapped miners.
6 Taylor, A.J., 'Labour productivity and technological innovation in the British coal industry 1850-1914', *Economic
History Review* (second series), vol. 14, 1961, p. 65.
7 Jevons, W.S., *The Coal Question*, London, 1865 (1st
edition), p. 349. (The closing sentence of the book, Jevons'
italics.).
8 The phrase was used in advertising coal from this New
Zealand field. H.M.S. *Calliope* alone among seven naval
vessels escaped from Apia, Samoa, during a hurricane in
1889. Her escape owed something to the quality of the coal;
at the height of the storm her engines, usually capable of
maintaining 15 knots, were able to sustain no more than
half a knot into the teeth of the gale.

9 Campbell, R.H., 'The iron industry in Ayrshire', *Ayrshire Collections*, vol. 7, 1966, p. 100.

10 Lawrence, D.H., 'Nottingham and the mining country', in *Selected Essays*, London (Penguin), 1950 et seq., pp. 114-17. I am grateful to Dr G.C. Wynn for drawing my attention to this passage.

11 Birch, A., *The Economic History of the British Iron and Steel Industry 1784-1879*, London, 1967. p. 309.

12 Burn, D.L., *The Economic History of Steel Making 1867-1939: a Study in Competition*, Cambridge, 1940. p. 6.

13 Birch, A., op.cit., p. 315.

14 This lined the furnace with chemically 'basic' materials, generally limestones, to neutralise the phosphoric acids. The resultant basic slag turned out to be a valuable artificial fertiliser, rich in phosphorus.

15 Birch, A., op.cit., p. 362.

16 Sinclair, W.A., 'The growth of the British steel industry in the late nineteenth century', *Scottish Journal of Political Economy*, vol. 6, 1959, p. 44.

17 Burnham, T.H., and Hoskins, G.O., *Iron and Steel in Great Britain 1870-1930*, London, 1953, p. 266.

18 Burn, D.L., op.cit., p. 64.

19 Hoskison, T.M., 'Northumberland blast furnace plant in the nineteenth century', *Transactions of the Newcomen Society*, vol. 25, 1945-7, pp. 77-8.

FURTHER READING

1 COAL

Birch, T.W., 'The development and decline of Coalbrookdale coalfield', *Geography*, vol. 19, 1934, pp 114-26.

Crowe, P.R., 'The Scottish Coalfields', *Scottish Geographical Magazine*, vol. 45, 1929, pp 321-36.

Galloway, R., *A History of Coal Mining in Great Britain,* 1882 (reprinted with an introduction by B.F. Duckham, Newton Abbot, 1969).

Green H., 'The Nottinghamshire and Derbyshire coalfield before 1850', *Journal of the Derbyshire Archaeological and Natural History Society,* vol. 56, 1935, pp.44-60.

Holmes, W.D., 'The Leicestershire and South Derbyshire coalfield', *East Midland Geographer,* vol. 10, 1958, pp.16-26.

Jevons, H.S., *The British Coal Trade,* London, 1915 (reprinted Newton Abbot, 1969).

Jevons, W.S., *The Coal Question . . . the probable exhaustion of our coal mines,* London (1st edition), 1865.

Jones, P.N., 'Colliery settlement in the South Wales coalfield', *Hull University Occasional Papers in Geography,* vol. 14, 1969.

Lawrence, D.H., 'Nottingham and the mining country', *in Selected Essays,* London (Penguin), 1950 et seq.

Lebon, J.H.G., 'Development of the Ayshire coalfield', *Scottish Geographical Magazine,* vol. 49, 1933, pp.138-53.

Lewis, E.D., *The Rhonnda Valleys,* London, 1959.

Morris, J.H., and Williams, L.J., *The South Wales Coal Industry 1841-75,* Cardiff, 1958.

Taylor, A.J., 'The Wigan Coalfield in 1851', *Transactions of the Historical Society of Lancashire and Cheshire,* vol. 106, 1954, pp.117-26.

Taylor, A.J., 'Labour productivity and technical innovation in the British coal industry 1850-1914', *Economic History Review,* (2nd series), vol. 14, 1961, pp.48-70.

Taylor, A.J., 'Combination in the mid-nineteenth century coal industry', *Transactions of the Royal Historical Society* (fifth series), vol. 3, 1953, pp.23-40.

Thomas, D.A., 'The growth and direction of our foreign trade in coal', *Journal of the Royal Statistical Society,* vol. 66, 1903, pp.439-522.

2   IRON AND STEEL

Beaver, S.H., 'The development of the Northamptonshire iron industry 1851-1930', in Stamp, L.D., and Wooldridge, S.W., *London Essays in Geography,* London, 1951, pp.33-58.

Birch, A., *The Economic History of the British Iron and Steel Industry 1784-1879,* London, 1967.

Burn, D.L., *The Economic History of Steelmaking,* Cambridge, 1940.

Burnham, T.H., and Hoskins, G.O., *Iron and Steel in Great Britain 1870-1930,* London, 1943.

Campbell, R.H., 'The iron industry in Ayshire', *Ayrshire Collections,* vol. 7, 1966, pp.90-102.

Carr, J.C., and Taplin, W., *A History of the British Steel*

Industry, London, 1962.

Flinn, M.W., and Birch, A., 'The English Steel Industry before 1856', *Yorkshire Bulletin,* vol. 6, 1954, pp.163-77.

Gale, W.K.V., *The Black Country Iron Industry,* Newton Abbot, 1966.

Harris, A., 'Askam iron: the development of Askam-in-Furness, 1850-1920', *Transactions of the Cumberland and Westmorland Antiquarian and Archaeological Society,* vol. 65, 1965, pp.381-407.

Harris, A., 'Millom: a Victorian new town', *Transactions of the Cumberland and Westmorland Antiquarian and Archaeological Society,* vol. 66, 1966, pp.449-67.

Lord, W.M., 'The development of the Bessemer process in Lancashire 1856-1900', *Transactions of the Newcomen Society,* vol. 25, 1945-7, pp.163-80.

Roepke, H.G., 'Movements of the British Iron and Steel Industry 1720 to 1951', *Illinois Studies in the Social Sciences,* vol. 36, 1956.

Scrivenor, H., *History of the Iron Trade,* London, 1841 et seq., (reprinted London, 1967).

Sinclair, W.A., 'The growth of the British steel industry in the late nineteenth century', *Scottish Journal of Political Economy,* vol. 6, 1959, pp.33-47.

Warren, K., *The British Iron and Steel Sheet Industry since 1840,* London, 1970.

Warren, K., 'Locational problems of the Scottish iron and steel industry since 1760', *Scottish Geographical Magazine,* vol. 81, 1965, pp.18-36 and 87-103.

Warren, K., 'The Sheffield rail trade 1861-1930: an episode in the locational history of the British steel industry', *Institute of British Geographers: Transactions,* vol. 34, 1964, pp.131-57.

Wilkins, C., *The History of Merthyr Tydfil,* Merthyr Tydfil, 1867.

4 Cotton and Wool: The New Staple and the Old

COTTON

Cotton was the most important of the great consumer-oriented industries of the nineteenth century; it is also often regarded as occupying a very central position in the Industrial Revolution on account of the rapidity of its growth and the novelty and distinctiveness of its economic organisation (plates 9 and 10). Its historical geography is both simpler and more complex than that of the coal and iron trades. Localisation was carried to extremes — at the end of the nineteenth century the main secondary centre of the industry, around Glasgow, employed little more than one-twentieth the number of hands of the Lancashire industry. Why this should be so is not entirely clear. It was in part the result of a mixture of geographical advantage and chance circumstance operating in the last decades of the eighteenth century and the first of the nineteenth. Furthermore there was extreme specialisation both in the extent to which communities depended on the fortunes of their mills, and in the development of a high degree of local specialisation within the industry. As with coal however growth was no simple and speedy adoption of new technologies but rather their gradual evolution in an often quite conservative and labour intensive business looking for a large share of its profits in overseas markets.

A concentration of the industry around Manchester was evident by the end of the eighteenth century. Here spinners were already showing a preference for coalfield sites for their factories although water power had done much to mould the industry's geography and weaving was still a dispersed domestic trade in the absence of looms suitable for factories. As yet North America supplied only about one-quarter of imported cotton, but by the 1830s it was supplying four-fifths, a dependence which continued, not always to Lanceshire's advantage, through the rest of the century. By 1802 cotton made up between four per cent and five per cent of Britain's gross national product, by 1812 (having overtaken wool) between seven per cent and eight per cent. Exports were basic to the industry: 'the tentacles of the Manchester trade reach out to all corners of the world, and whatever form of manufactured cotton is sought. . . someone can be found in Manchester ready to accept a commission'.[1] Moreover the cotton trade brought foreigners to Manchester, perhaps most notably Friedrich Engels.[2] Only rarely was less than half the output exported, usually by the end of the century four-fifths. Cotton cloth went to China, India and the tropics,[3] and also, early in the century, to Europe and the U.S.A. As these latter developed their own manufacture their importance as export markets diminished, but Europe remained a market for yarn. On this basis the British industry grew from a consumption of 60 million pounds of cotton in 1800 to use over 1,300 million pounds by the 1880s (figure 17). It employed half a million people and controlled almost three-quarters of the world's trade in cotton goods at the end of the century.

Such growth justifies Armitage's use of the word 'procession' to characterise the industry,[4] a procession occasionally and ephemerally interrupted by such crises as the scarcity of raw materials during the American Civil War. But as a procession moves on so did the industry reorganise its geography — Lancastrian pre-eminence was enhanced, regional specialisation became more marked, the industry as a whole adjusted its location remarkably closely to that of the coalfields. And yet the pre-eminence of Lancashire remains something of a mystery: evidently it is related to the rapidity of the early growth of the industry, to the proximity of coal and water power, to the port of Liverpool, perhaps to entrepreneurial traditions and to the Napoleonic War. Why did the industry not thrive in some similar west coast coalfield, Cumberland or Bristol for example, in certain respects seemingly more favourable than the margins of the Pennines for the export processing of imported raw materials? It remains the case, as Deane wrote in 1965, that 'it is not entirely clear why it should have been so concentrated in Lancashire'.[5]

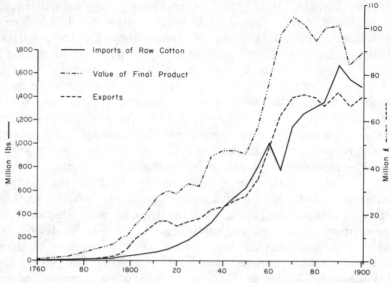

Figure 17. Imports of raw cotton, exports of cotton products, and their value 1760-1901. (Drawn from Deane, P., and Cole, W.A., *British Economic Growth 1688-1959*, Cambridge, 1962, tables 42-3.)

The question of functional specialisation — weaving in the north, spinning in the south — has likewise been no more than partly solved, and until recently has often been overshadowed by the parallel, and dramatic, issue of the plight of the handloom weaver when machinery was adopted in this part of the industry. This too was a geographical phenomenon: 'a good many problems of the weavers stemmed from the fact that the early distribution of factories in general did not always correspond to the still earlier distribution of the hand-loom weavers'.[6] Work was not where the weavers were. A third related issue is the very early development of local specialisation, Bolton's concern with fine spinning and Rochdale's with coarse for example. Nevertheless the basic problem is that of the emergence by mid-century of a weaving north and a spinning south separated by upland Rossendale.

Domestic cotton spinning and weaving had often been carried on under the same roof and although domestic weaving survived until mid-century its migration to factories from the 1820s was often to concerns already active in spinning. A Lancashire witness before a House of Commons Select Committee in 1833 observed that at that date all new spinning mills had weaving sheds attached. These 'combined firms' were the norm for the industry at this period, reaching their zenith in mid-century. Early investment in power looms was in fact often financed from the profits of spinning and thus occurred in the established spinning towns, such as Bolton and Bury. The geographical separation of weaving and spinning began only in the 1840s; new weaving enterprises were set up in such northern towns as Blackburn and Burnley. In part this was a result of the economics of increased specialisation in a growing industry, but it also reflected a divergence in the commercial needs and attitudes of each branch of the industry. The weaver's business was the more risky in the size and variety of stocks which had to be held and successful management seems primarily to have been a matter of matching order book and output. This required constant attention to detail and kept firms relatively small. Association with a spinning mill ceased to be advantageous. What attracted weavers to the north from the 1840s was cheaper labour, in the absence of factory spinning, coal, and improved rail access. The spinner's business was more certain and straightforward allowing considerable scale economies and thus the early development of the large joint-stock company. There was no reason for such firms to go north, to leave the established spinning district and its reservoir of skills and contacts. Thus while the combined firm remained common, by 1884 62 per cent of looms were in the north, 78 per cent of spindles in the south (figure 18).

The close geographical correspondence of coalfields and cotton manifests the industry's increasing dependence on steam, and the desirability of a local supply of coal in the period before the railways were built. Not only was the period prior to about 1840 one of rapid growth in the trade but also of easily accessible local coal and very inefficient — and thus coal-demanding — steam engines. Dependence on coal rather than running water meant a spatially contracting industry, particularly from the steepest and remotest valleys; it was also a further factor removing the size constraint and making possible larger units of production, bigger mill towns. The concentration of weaving into such towns as Burnley is the extreme case of this geographical trend, the dispersed domestic industry re-

Figure 18. Looms and spindles in Lancashire, 1901 (Drawn from data in *Encyclopaedia Brittanica*, 1910 edition, Vol. 7, p.288).

placed by the steam-powered factory centred on coal. By 1900 a third geographical element had appeared, the decline of Manchester as a manufacturing centre and its concentration on an administrative and commercial role, perhaps a result of the position attained by the limited liability company in the industry by this date. The situation was not however without its anomalies: why did Preston, not on the coalfield, attract cotton? is the substitution of cheap labour and food for cheap coal in one of the county's chief market towns a convincing explanation? what part did the mid-century development of a dense railway network in the county play? The industry's failure to develop on the coalfield at St Helens represents the converse situation — a function of pollution created by the chemical manufactures?

By 1840 'cotton manufacture had already taken up a geography which differed only in detail from the present day'.[8] This is perhaps an exaggeration, particularly with respect to the

northern cotton towns, but certainly youth had passed almost
prematurely into middle-aged prosperity; the great investment
phase of 1830-45 had laid down the industry's geography on
the coalfields just before the railways began to create a
close-knit and efficient communications network. The pattern
was to be transformed only by worldwide economic and
political changes after 1918.

COMPARISONS

Cotton, coal and iron are commonly regarded as the heartland
of the nineteenth-century economy, thus some comparison is
apt before the great traditional staple — wool — is examined.
Had the years of maximum contribution to gross national
income of the three industries coincided — which they did not
— they would have contributed about one quarter of that
income. Their role was pivotal in this sense, and in a second
sense in the dependence of almost every branch of industry on
coal and iron. It is, however, unreasonable to estimate the
health or character of nineteenth-century Britain on the basis of
these industries alone, witness Wilson's examination of the
'depression' of the last quarter of the century, an experience
primarily of the iron and steel industry and of agriculture. In
fact of coal, iron and cotton, all three export-oriented industries, only one was in some sense depressed by 1900. Other
parallels present themselves; in each there was a gradual
movement away from a propensity to innovate towards
technological conservatism. These great labour-saving industries
are by the end of the century the great capital-saving industries.
Locational conservatism develops even earlier, favoured by the
extent of their growth before the railways were built; these
served to maintain a geographical *status quo* rather than to
allow the development of new sites, even in the iron and steel
industry where there was considerable technical progress and
stimulus to movement after the railways came. Why no second
or third 'Lancashire'? Why the limited development of the iron
trade on the Jurassic ore-fields? Geographical lethargy belongs
with entrepreneurial shortcomings — of which it is one facet —
and technical conservatism in explaining eventually effective
overseas competition. Coal necessarily escapes this criticism to

some degree, although its reluctance to mechanise should be recalled, and it certainly shared the acute problems of cotton and iron after 1918. The three industries created a substantial portion of the new settlement geography of nineteenth-century Britain, a geography of single-industry communities, of mile upon mile of brick or stone terraces climbing out of the smoky valleys up the hillsides or spreading shapelessly across the plains.

Houses, derelict land, perhaps even a frame of mind, are their legacies to the last quarter of the twentieth century. The industries themselves, cotton and coal in particular, are ghosts by comparison with nineteenth century gigantism. They have experienced almost unceasing problems since 1918. But it is these industries which led Britain's socio-economic trans-formation and created some of its most characteristic land-scapes during the nineteenth century, making Britain as much a New Society as America was a New World. What role then did the older and more conservative industries, wool for example, and new mass-production consumer-oriented industries play in that New Society?

WOOL

The nineteenth-century transformation of Britain's wool manu-facture[10] presents some parallels with cotton; there was a high degree of concentration into one coalfield and intensely localised specialisation within that area. But in most respects the woollen industry was quite a different phenomenon. Traditionally the pre-eminent British manufacturing industry it was relatively in decline during this period and its contribution to the national income shrank from over four per cent in the 1820s to only one and half per cent in 1900. Never more than half of total output, more often only one-quarter or one-third, was exported; a sevenfold expansion of raw material consump-tion, a threefold increase in the value of the end-product is modest by Lancashire standards (figure 19). From about 1850 the industry generally employed somewhere between 250,000 and 300,000 workers, half the number at work in the cotton industry. Ironically the wool industries have survived the stresses and strains of the twentieth century rather better than their youthfully more vigorous trans-Pennine neighbour.

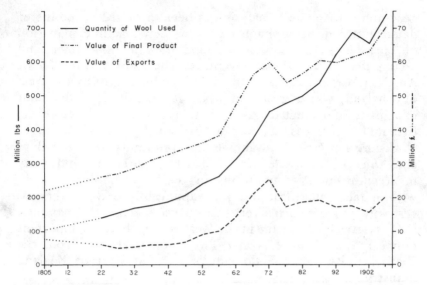

Figure 19. Wool use, export of wool products, and their value 1805-1908 (Drawn from Deane, P., and Cole, W.A., *British Economic Growth 1688-1959*, Cambridge, 1962, table 47).

The pre-eminence of the West Riding in the wool industry dates from the nineteenth century when its ancient and established rivals, Norfolk and the West of England, almost completely gave up the business. Yorkshire never achieved as complete a dominance of wool as did Lancashire of cotton; nevertheless by 1850 the West Riding contained 87 per cent of all worsted spindles and 95 per cent of worsted looms, and Yorkshire and Lancashire (where there were important outliers of the industry) possessed 87 per cent of all woollen spindles and 95 per cent of woollen looms. Only in the Tweed valley, and on a much smaller scale, was there dynamism and momentum in wool comparable to that of the West Riding.

How did this happen? Yorkshire's medieval woollen industry and the rather later worsted industry both grew rapidly during the eighteenth century; the output of broadcloth increased more than sixfold between 1726 and 1790. 'There is not I believe any reason to seek novel causes explanatory of the first rise of Yorkshire. It is the ordinary case of a pushing, hardworking locality, with certain slight advantages, attacking the lower grades of an expanding industry.'[11] The proverbially active and aggressive Yorkshireman is a factor in historical geography. Clapham's analysis has been criticised on points of detail, but majority opinion shares his view that an explanation of Yorkshire's success is to be found more in temperament and tactics than in locational advantage. The conservatism of East Anglia in particular, shared to a considerable degree by the West of England, was a great liability: 'geography alone does not explain the fact that it was more than a generation before the first mill engine was set going in Norwich'[12] (in 1838). Possibly Yorkshire's principal advantage was proximity to Lancashire and. thus to a whole series of late eighteenth- and early nineteenth-century innovations in textile technology which, with suitable modifications, were applicable to wool; there is certainly ample evidence for their diffusion across the Pennines. Coal, relatively abundant in the West Riding, became important only at a later stage — and Tweedside is remote from the coalfields. Part of the domain of the old West of England industry is not.

The two principal elements in the triumph of the West Riding remain matters of entrepeneurial choice: a concentration on the cheaper and coarser end of the market, and thus in the nineteenth century a larger and more readily expanded one, and the early introduction of machinery in the face of technical problems and an unwilling labour force.[13] On the whole it was more difficult to use steam or water driven machinery in the wool industry than in the cotton trade; this was particularly true of woollens where the power loom ousted the hand loom only in mid-century, and where as late as 1856 only half the labour force worked in factories. The West of England and East Anglia stuck to quality and mechanised tardily; as a worsted producer dependent on yarn produced in the West Riding the latter was particularly vulnerable. Moreover cotton was a competitor of some worsteds in the first part of the century. Neither area possessed the dynamism, the fashion sense, or the good fortune of the Tweed mills. Fashion and quality were in fact an integral and permanent problem for so diverse and many sided an industry as wool manufacture: 'there is nothing in the woollen or worsted trade comparable to the demand for plain cotton goods from India and the tropics'.[14] Worsteds in turn faced competition from cottons and from fashion-conscious — even fashion-forming — French weavers. Woollen manufacturers saw their fashionable broadcloths fall into disfavour and there were also prohibitive tariffs, notably in the U.S.A., after mid-century. But as there were problems so there were solutions, a greater emphasis on home markets, the export of worsted yarn rather than fabric, the creation of new materials. In some of these latter the West Riding was never seriously challenged — shoddy was a creation of the first half of the nineteenth century around Batley and Dewsbury for example.

What was the geographical character of this newly pre-eminent industry? In the broadest sense it was contracting. Beverley and York had been medieval woollen towns but were so no longer; Lancashire woollen industry succumbed to cotton competition albeit with important exceptions such as Rochdale flannels and Rossendale felts. Within the West Riding some remote areas decayed — Penistone for example, in a locality oriented primarily towards Sheffield. With the successive concentration of the seemingly innumerable processes of the wool trade into factories the traditional dispersion of the industry diminished but it did not disappear; the process had begun with medieval fulling mills and ended in the second half of the nineteenth century with the factory weaving of woollen cloth. Two circumstances account for the continuance of dispersion and its effects on the location of factories. There were strong, centuries old, commercial links between the industry's commercial centres, like Halifax and Huddersfield, and numerous weaving-cum-farming hamlets. Moreover power weaving was a late arrival, in the woollen trade especially, coming after the development of the railway. Such operations as carding and spinning entered factories and migrated to the valleys early in the century, creating such new and character-istically named settlements as Brighouse and Meltham Mills; water power attracted them there but they soon turned over to steam and were well served by river, canal, and railway. Weaving, domestic and factory, kept to the hills, and by the time the power loom triumphed steam was the motive force and coal was widely, albeit not abundantly, available in the Millstone Grit and Lower Coal Measures of these areas.

Sigsworth, the historian of the worsted trade, aptly summar-ises this process:

'First woollen scribbling (one part of the carding process) and then spinning had been drawn down from the uplands into the valleys by the attractive force of water power to drive the new machines which were being introduced in the late eighteenth century. No similar innovation had been made in weaving where the handloom remained supreme until well into the nineteenth century, and weaving remained on the uplands. With the introduction first of the steam engine and then of the steam-driven power loom ease of access to adequate coal supplies began to influence the location of wool textile mills. Their continued existence on the upland or the successful conversion of an existing domestically organised upland weaving concern into a factory organisation depended on the ease with which coal could be obtained. Where coal was not easily accessible, weaving also migrated to the valleys where engines to drive power-looms could be supplied with coal brought by the canals and roads, and later the railways, which followed the valley floors: "if there was coal to be had near at hand the clothier who was employing many hand-loom weavers built a mill near his warehouse and introduced power-looms. It was the natural course, for his weavers were all round about on the uplands . . . But manufacturing i.e. weaving could only survive on the hills and in the old hill-top towns if coal could be obtained locally or could be brought economically."[15] (figure 20)

Thus arose the geographical amalgam of congested but accessible valleys and seemingly improbable hill-top textile communities such as Queensbury; by mid-century this geography had superimposed itself upon the old pattern of market towns and hamlets. The limits were set firstly by accessibility, notably for coal although wool did not follow the coal industry eastwards, secondly by competition from more dynamic industries, notably cotton, perhaps coal, and thirdly by historical accident, as Charlesworth was able to demonstrate on the industry's southeastern margin.

Within this geographical complex there existed and developed a high degree of geographical specialisation. Woollen and worsted manufacture are very different technologies using different raw materials. Worsted manufacture took more easily and speedily to cotton-derived technology than did woollens; thus geographical correlation with coal appears early in the

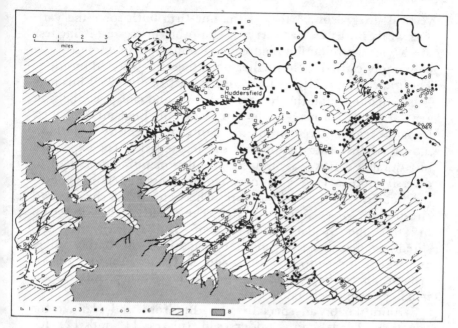

Figure 20. Wool mills, warehouses and coal mines in the Huddersfield district c. 1850: 1, disused mills; 2, mills in use; 3, disused warehouses; 4, warehouses in use; 5, disused mines; 6, mines working; 7, land between 600' and 1250'; 8, land over 1250'. (Redrawn from Crump, W.B., and Ghorbal, G., *History of the Huddersfield Woollen Industry*, Huddersfield, 1935, p.117.)

century, since steam-driven machinery was first used for this branch of the wool trade. Yarn of known quality could be purchased from spinners by weaving firms to produce a range of worsted fabrics. Traditionally Halifax had been Yorkshire's main worsted town but from late in the eighteenth century Bradford ousted its rival, mechanising more willingly and possessed of a better supply of coal. Between 1810 and 1830 Bradford's share of the drawback (rebate) paid to worsted manufacturers from the soap tax increased from 36 per cent of the total to 45 per cent, and by 1850 the city had almost half the county's worsted spindles and more than half the worsted power looms. It was the fastest growing of Yorkshire's large towns, its population increasing from 13,000 in 1801 to 103,000 in 1851. Woollen manufacture was — and is — a more complex process than worsted, and notably one in which the importance and variability of yarn quality is such as to favour vertical integration,[16] that is the one firm both spins the yarn and weaves it as well as carrying out other processes. Being less of a mass-production industry woollen manufacture was commonly carried on in smaller units than the worsted business. The trade comprised both the oldest part of the wool business — broadcloth — and the newest — shoddy and cheap woollens in general. The former, as in the West of England which it imitated, encountered problems during the century — fashion moved against broadcloth and the mass-market for expensive but durable cloths was limited. Woollen manufacturers had to diversify into a variety of new cloths known as 'fancy goods' (particularly on the coal measures where steam was cheap), into cheap cloth, or even into worsted. The shoddy trade was set up in 1813 and by 1858 Batley alone had at least fifty rag-shredding machines; the industry had filled the Batley valley and was spreading to Dewsbury and the Calder. Another area of growth, from the second quarter of the century, was carpet-making around Halifax.

Within the broad specialisation, Bradford and Halifax for worsteds, Leeds and Huddersfield (plates 11 and 12) for woollens, a high degree of local specialisation occurred, favou-red in the latter instance by process complexity and product diversity. Within the heavy district for example Gomersal produced army and navy cloths, Earlsheaton blankets. As the period of most dynamic growth was mid-century, the early railway age, the final stages of movement into factories, so locational patterns and specialisations are of that period. The remarkably persistent geography of woollen and worsted Yorkshire is largely that set up in the middle decades of the last century.

Elsewhere, with one notable exception, the wool business was in decay. Tweedside was that exception. A remote low-quality industry whose production was valued at £26,000 in 1830 was transformed to a £200,000 a year industry by the late 1860s. A locale distant from coal, from markets, even from its main source of raw material, had succeeded by moving into the difficult 'quality' end of the industry. The basis of success was 'fundamental discoveries in the design of woollen cloth',[17] excellent market intelligence, and exploitation of the Victorian mania for Scott and the Scots. The Welsh industry, a possible and potential emulator of the Tweed, failed to follow its northern rivals to success, despite mechanisation and concentration into factories. Evidently Scottish flair for organisation and marketing were missing. The most successful Welsh mills were those of south-west Wales, often nineteenth-century railwayside creations, supplying flannels and blankets to the coalfield. Elsewhere many Welsh mills were extremely isolated, technically primitive, and dependent on local raw materials and markets.

Yorkshire's traditional rivals shared its early nineteenth-century war-based prosperity. Thereafter decline was almost continuous, and in the Norfolk case complete soon after mid-century. If decay was inevitable, disappearance was not: 'if Norfolk had taken full advantage of her opportunities she might conceivably have tided over that period in the early and mid-nineteenth century' — crucial for decaying as for developing industries — 'in which location was all important, diminished but not extinguished'.[18] Part of the West of England industry concentrated around Trowbridge and the Stroud Valley did survive, despite its failure to move out of broadcloths into a wider market. Worsted manufacture was the subject of some experiment, in mid-century of adoption, in the old serge-making region further west, but without much success. However an attenuated industry survived to enjoy some prosperity again in the twentieth century.

The geography of wool like that of cotton derives from past situations, from the changing transport and textile technology of the broad period 1775-1875, from the differing methods and organisations of the two branches of the industry, and from social, commercial, even ecclesiastical[19] circumstances which can be traced back into the Middle Ages. Cotton geography crystallises that of a relatively short period, the geography of wool a much longer time span, but in each case there is a notable correlation with accessible coal, a manifestation of the importance of the early nineteenth-century epoch of immobile steam. 'The historic textile towns . . . all lie on the Lower Coal Measures or within a mile or two either side of them, except Manchester and Wakefield. All but these two have within easy reach of them an area of Millstone Grit country where most of the weaving was done. They were the market towns, each for its own territory — the parish[20] (plate 13). The geography of the industry is thus as much of past patterns of buying and selling as of weaving and spinning.

NOTES

1 Copeland, M.T., *The Cotton Manufacturing Industry of the United States,* Cambridge, Mass., 1912, p.371. The statement neatly epitomises Manchester's role in the cotton industry almost from the start.
2 Engels worked in Manchester as agent for his father's Barmen cotton business in the early 1840s and *The Condition of the Working Class in England* (1844) is based on this experience.
3 The missionary with Bible in one hand, bale of cotton cloth in the other, is a stock — and almost comic — figure of school textbooks: his commercial importance for the cotton trade awaits investigation.
4 Armitage, G., 'The Lancashire cotton trade from the great inventions to the great disasters', *Memoirs and Proceedings of the Manchester Literary and Philosophical Society,* vol. 92, 1950-51, p.24.
5 Deane, P., *The First Industrial Revolution,* Cambridge, 1965, p.91.
6 Bythell, D., 'The handloom weavers in the English cotton industry during the Industrial Revolution: some problems', *Economic History Review* (2nd series), vol. 17, 1964-5, pp.345-6.
7 Discussed by Chapman, S.J., *The Lancashire Cotton Industry,* Manchester, 1904, p.163. The part played by 'accidental causes' is also admitted.
8 Rodgers, H.B., 'The Lancashire cotton industry in 1840', *Institute of British Geographers: Transactions,* vol. 28. 1960, p.136.
9 Wilson, C.H., 'Economy and Society in late Victorian Britain', *Economic History Review* (2nd series), vol. 18, 1965, pp.83-98.
10 A strict usage of the terms wool, woollen and worsted is adopted in this section. 'Wool' applies to the industry as a whole, 'woollen' to the production of cloth from carded fibres with some degree of felting, 'worsted' to the production of a fabric known variously as cloth or stuff from combed fibres with a minimum of felting.
11 Clapham, J.H., 'The transference of the worsted industry from Norfolk to the West Riding', *Economic Journal,* vol.

20, 1910, p.201.
12 Clapham, J.H., *Economic Journal*, vol.20, 1910, p.203.
13 One subject of Charlotte Brontë's novel *Shirley* (*1849*).
14 Clapham, J.H., *The Woollen and Worsted Industries*, London, 1907, p.167.
15 Sigsworth, E.M., *Black Dyke Mills: A History*, Liverpool, 1958, pp.168-9.
16 There was no organised yarn market, as for worsteds, and since the quality of cloth largely reflected that of the yarn the weaver preferred to manufacture his own.
17 Stillie, T.A., 'The evolution of pattern design in the Scottish wool textile industry in the nineteenth century', *Textile History*, vol.1, 1970, p.310.
18 Clapham, J.H., *Economic Journal*, vol. 20, 1910, p.203.
19 Market centres such as Halifax and Huddersfield owed something to their role as centres — parish churches — for very large parishes comprising many wool-working villages and hamlets.
20 Crump, W.B., 'The wool textile industry of the Pennines in its physical setting', *Journal of the Textile Institute*, vol. 26, 1935, P.390.

FURTHER READING

1 COTTON

Baines, E., *History, Directory and Gazatteer* [sic] *of the County Palatine of Lancaster*, Liverpool, 1824-5 (reprinted Newton Abbot, 1968).
Blaug, M., 'Productivity of capital in the Lancashire cotton industry during the nineteenth century', *Economic History Review* (2nd series), vol.13, 1961, pp.358-81.
Bythell, D., 'The handloom weavers in the English cotton industry during the Industrial Revolution: some problems', *Economic History Review* (2nd series), vol.17, 1964, pp.339-53.
Chapman, S.J., *The Lancashire Cotton Industry: a study in economic development*, Manchester, 1904. (See also his article 'Cotton manufacture' in the 11th edition of *Encyclopaedia Brittanica*..)
Daniels G.W., *The Early English Cotton Industry*, Manchester,

1920.

Daniels, G.W., 'The cotton trade during the revolutionary and Napoleonic wars', *Transactions of the Manchester Statistical Society,* vol. 31, 1915-16, pp.53-84.

Edwards, M.M., *The Growth of the British Cotton trade 1780-1815,* Manchester, 1967.

Ellison, T., *The Cotton Trade of Great Britain,* London, 1886.

Jewkes, J., 'The localisation of the cotton industry', *Economic History,* vol. 2, 1930, pp.91-106.

Ogden, H.W., 'The geographical basis of the Lancashire cotton industry', *Journal of the Manchester Geographical Society,* vol. 43, 1927, pp.8-30.

Rogers, H.B., 'The Lancashire Cotton Industry in 1840', *Institute of British Geographers: Transactions,* vol. 28, 1960, pp.135-53.

Sandberg, L.G., *Lancashire in decline: a study in entrepreneurship, technology and international trade,* Columbus, Ohio, 1974.

Smelser, N.J., *Social Change in the Industrial Revolution, an application of theory to the Lancashire cotton industry 1770-1840,* London, 1959.

Shapiro, S., *Capital and the Cotton Industry in the Industrial Revolution,* Ithaca (N.Y.), 1967.

Taylor, A.J., 'Concentration and specialisation in the Lancashire cotton industry', *Economic History Review* (2nd series), vol. 1, 1949. pp.114-22.

Schulze-Galvenitz, G. von., *The Cotton Trade in England and on the Continent,* London and Manchester, 1895.

2   WOOL

Charlesworth, E., 'A local example of the factors influencing industrial location', *Geographical Journal,* vol. 91, 1938, pp.340-51.

Clapham, J.H., 'The transference of the worsted industry from Norfolk to the West Riding', *Economic Journal,* vol. 20, 1910, pp.195-210.

Clapham, J.H., *The Woollen and Worsted Industries,* London, 1907.

Crump, W.B., 'The wool textile industry of the Pennines in its physical setting', *Journal of the Textile Institute*, vol. 26, 1935, P.367-74 and P.383-94.

Crump W.B., and Ghorbal, G., *History of the Huddersfield Woollen Industry*, Huddersfield (Tolson Memorial Museum Publication, Handbook 9), 1935.

Edwards, J.K., 'The decline of the Norwich textile industry', *Yorkshire Bulletin*, vol. 16, 1964, pp.31-41.

Glover, F.J., 'The rise of the heavy woollen trade in the West Riding of Yorkshire in the nineteenth century', *Business History*, vol. 4, 1962, pp.1-21.

Heaton, H., 'Benjamin Gott and the industrial revolution in Yorkshire', *Economic History Review*, vol. 3, 1931, pp.45-66.

Jenkins, J.G., *The Welsh Woollen Industry*, Cardiff, 1969.

Jubb, S., *History of the Shoddy Trade*, London, 1860.

Lipson, E., *A Short History of Wool*, London, 1953.

Moir, E., 'Marling and Evans, King's Stanley and Ebley Mills, Gloucestershire', *Textile History*, vol. 2, 1971, pp.28-56.

Pankhurst, K.V., 'Investment in the West Riding wool textile industry in the nineteenth century', *Yorkshire Bulletin*, vol. 7, 1955, pp.93-116.

Ponting, K.G., *A History of the West of England Cloth Industry*, London, 1957.

Ponting, K.G., *The Woollen Industry of South-West England*, Bath, 1971.

Ponting, K.G. (ed.), *Baines's (1858) Account of the Woollen Manufacture of England*, Newton Abbot, 1970.

Sigsworth, E.M., *Black Dyke Mills: A History*, Liverpool, 1958. (Chapters 1 to 3 are a general history of the nineteenth century worsted industry.).

Sigsworth, E.M., 'Bradford and its worsted industry under Victoria 1837-1901', *Journal of the Bradford Textile Society*, vol. 59, 1952-3, pp.63-70.

Stillie, T.A., 'The evolution of pattern design in the Scottish wool-textile industry in the nineteenth century', *Textile History*, vol. 1. 1970, pp.309-31.

5 Manufacturers and Mass - Producers: The Geography of Necessities and Luxuries

Coal, iron, cotton and wool select themselves as major themes in the historical geography of nineteenth-century industrial Britain. Iron — or by the end of the century steel — provided the hull of the ship of state, coal was the driving force, cotton and wool exemplify new cargoes and old. Consideration of these realms is essential — a comprehensive survey of the other industries of the 'workshop of the world' is impossible. This chapter is then a choice and a selection, as much personal as rational: chemicals and paper represent existing industries which were transformed and which serviced a wide range of other industries and occupations, while brewing and milling were old and dispersed mass-consumption industries affected not only by steam but by government; the hosiery and the boot and shoe trades experienced the move from cottage to factory and in the latter case the rise of new methods of retailing.

CHEMICALS

The chemical industry was neither a huge producer, nor a great exporter, nor a large employer. In 1841 it employed less than one-twentieth of the labour force of the textile industries, and in 1901 still only one-fifth. In 1892 the Leblanc alkali trade in Widnes and Runcorn, one of the main nuclei of chemical manufacture, employed 1,100 specifically 'chemical' workers, aided by 5,000 general labourers. The interest and importance of the industry lies not its size but in that its growth was a prerequisite for more spectacular events elsewhere, in textiles and agriculture for example, and that its locational patterns were of such extreme variety and changeability. Entrepreneurial decision, raw material supplies, technological change, process linkage, and public pressure all played a part. Moreover the industry experienced both great success, in heavy inorganic chemicals, and catastrophic failure — after early pioneering — in some areas of organic chemistry.

Even in the relatively undeveloped chemical industry of the late eighteenth century the key role of sulphuric acid was evident, and Liebig's dictum that 'we may fairly judge of the commercial prosperity of a country by the amount of sulphuric acid it consumes'[1] retains much of its validity in the diversified chemical economy of the 1970s. The most direct, albeit not the most important, use of sulphuric acid at this period was as a bleach, a role it retained in a less direct form in the generation of sulphur dioxide for wool and silk, after bleaching powder came into use for cotton and linen early in the nineteenth century. The eighteenth-century alternatives, sour milk and sunlight, might well have placed severe constraints, locational as well as economic, upon the growth of the textile industries had there been no cheap sulphuric acid. Moreover the acid was also used to make chlorine and thus bleaching powder. The predominant use of sulphuric acid in the first half of the nineteenth century however was in the Leblanc process for soda (sodium carbonate) manufacture, the alkali industry as it was usually called. Devised in the 1790s it was a boom industry of the 1820s — soda was needed by soap makers, by glass makers, and to some extent for making bleaches. From the 1840s artificial fertiliser manufacturers were another important market for sulphuric acid.

Demand for sulphuric acid was thus widespread, but strongest in textile areas. The product was difficult, dangerous, and disagreeable to transport before the railways were built, but its manufacture by the lead-chamber process was simple and profitable, although imperfectly understood[2] and costly to establish. Only the raw materials presented problems. Sulphur was imported from Sicily until the 1840s when, for both political and economic reasons, pyrites from the coalfields and Spain was preferred. It is thus not surprising that even before the alkali boom the industry was dispersed. In 1830 there were 30 producers in Britain, of whom seven were in London, seven in central Scotland, four in Birmingham, three in Lancashire and three in Yorkshire. The surge in demand for alkali fostered the industry's growth, often as a subsidiary part of a Leblanc enterprise, but there were other linkages. As the industry turned to pyrites as a raw material, so copper smelting became associated with sulphuric acid manufacture, notably in South Wales and on Tyneside. And it was in part the copper industry of Tyneside which fostered the development of electrical engineering in that area late in the nineteenth century. A further cheaper and widely available source of sulphur became available and widespread in the 1870s, 'spent oxide' from gasworks. Thus an industry producing 10,000 tons per annum in the 1820s was producing 1,000,000 (a quarter of world output) by 1900; an essential chemical which had cost £30 to £35 a ton in the 1790s sold for 25s (£1.25) in 1885. By the end of the nineteenth century the catalytic contact process was replacing the lead chamber, and by its scale economies served to foster the localisation of a still very dispersed industry.

Sulphuric acid was only a beginning, an industry to meet the needs of other chemical manufacturers rather than the public at large. The main user was as has been mentioned the Leblanc soda maker who, in the early nineteenth century, was responding to a situation in which a surge of demand for his product outran the traditional vegetable (mainly kelp and barilla) source of supply. However the conservatism of users in the face of.a synthetic product was one reason why Leblanc's.idea of the 1790s took 30 years to become the basis of large-scale industry; the war and possibly the salt taxes (repealed in 1822) were also delaying circumstances. Not surprisingly those involved in trades killed by the new process (the barilla importers and the kelp interests in Scotland) also tried to delay its impact. In fact Britain's first small Leblanc industry appeared on Tyneside some time between 1802 and 1806; the process appeared at St Rollox, Clydeside (plate 13), a primarily entrepreneurial location,[4] only in 1818. Muspratt's Liverpool works of 1823 which later moved to St Helens was the first large-scale enterprise. By the 1830s the purer soda of Muspratt's Leblanc process was cheap enough and abundant enough to allow local soap producers to switch to palm oil, thus producing better soap and fostering Liverpool's tropical connections.

These three areas were to remain the heartland of the British inorganic chemical industry until late in the century. However

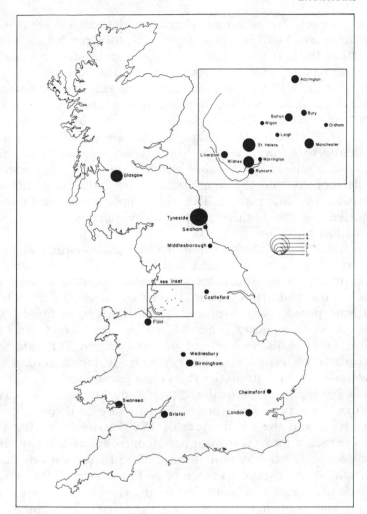

Figure 21. Alkali works registered under the Alkali Acts of 1863. (Drawn from data in Campbell, W.A., *The Chemical Industry*, London, 1971, table 12.)

the salt-coal axis of north Cheshire-south Lancashire linked by river, canal and railway was particularly important. In the two estuaries, Clyde and Tyne, chemicals were eventually over-shadowed by more conspicuous industries, notably shipbuild-ing, and St Rollox, although Europe's largest individual chem-ical works in the 1840s, suffered from remoteness from the major markets for bleaching powder and soda. Of 83 British Leblanc works listed in 1864 (figure 21), 36 were in Lancashire and 20 in the northeast. There were linkages inside the industry — colliers taking coal from the Tyne to the Mersey returned with Cheshire salt. Connections with local markets were strong in Lancashire and Cheshire, soap and bleach for cotton, soda for glass; elsewhere there were less immediately obvious connections. On Tyneside for example the soap industry owed something to coalmining, not however on account of demand among the miners but because the coal industry supported a candle industry and the soap industry used the softer tallows unsuitable for illumination. The wider implications must not be forgotten — cheap soap played an important part in the population explosion.

Until 1867 the Leblanc manufacturers, diversified as their interests often were into acid and bleach, reckoned to make their profits from soda. Exports were increasing (fivefold between the mid-fifties and mid-seventies) and 70 per cent of bleaching powder was exported to the U.S.A. in the 1870s, although as in so many other industries they were to run up against tariff walls by the end of the century. Tyneside was particularly associated with the export trade, and thus hard hit. However from the late sixties the Leblanc trade and its location changed rapidly. Hydrochloric acid, traditionally a waste product — a very noxious one — began to be used for chlorine generation, and the Alkali Acts of 1863, strictly limiting the acid's emission into the atmosphere, controlled technology and raised costs. The Solvay (Ammonia-Soda) process was establishing itself as the cheapest source of soda by the 1870s, forcing Leblanc producers to depend first on the chlorine and bleaching powder side of their trade and then, the price of now abundant chlorine proving so unremunerative, on copper recovery from the pyrites of their sulphuric acid plants for their profits. The Solvay process used brine rather than salt and less coal than the Leblanc system — Widnes alone had used a million tons of coal annually when its Leblanc industry was at its peak — and so the tendency was to move to the sources of brine and to larger works. The Tyne yielded to the Tees, the Weaver and Sankey to Northwich and Fleetwood. The United Alkali Company of 1890, a merger of Leblanc firms, had to rationalise in order to protect its interests, its very *raison d'être;* thus it quickly closed

20 out of 24 Tyneside works at the same time as it opened up the Fleetwood (Lancashire) salt field.

Alkali was not only the most important it was also the dirtiest and most damaging of the nineteenth-century chemical industries. The Leblanc process generated large quantities of hydrogen chloride gas which, being of no value at that period, was discharged into the atmosphere. The 1863 legislation insisted that no more than five per cent of the acid be allowed to escape, but the dilute acid discharged into rivers was almost equally unpleasant. The hallmarks of the industry were tall chimneys[5] to disperse the gas (plate 13), devastated vegetation, complaints, and law suits:

'the gas from these manufactures is of such a deleterious nature as to blight everything within its influence, and is alike harmful to health and property. The herbage of the fields in their vicinity is scorched, the gardens neither yield fruit nor vegetables; many flourishing trees have lately become rotten naked sticks. Cattle and poultry droop and pine away. It tarnishes the furniture in our houses, and when we are exposed to it, which is of frequent occurrence, we are afflicted with coughs and pains in the head'. (1839)[6]

The pollution problem drove Muspratt from both Liverpool and Newton-le-willows in 1849 and made Widnes in 1888 'the dirtiest, ugliest, most depressing town in England'.[7] The Alkali Acts could not reverse damage already done; moreover the industry produced and dumped a second, less dangerous but also less tractable by-product, the 'alkali waste' of calcium sulphide, calcium hydroxide, and coal. The waste tended to smoulder and in wet weather it gave off evil-smelling hydrogen sulphide. Chance's process for sulphur recovery from the 'alkali waste' tips came only in the 1860s after 40 years of accumulation and devastation.

The fertiliser industry, the creation of Leibig's method of superphosphate production in 1840, was basic to Britain's mid-century agricultural prosperity. The process used quite widely available materials — 'bones, bone ash, bone dust, and other phosphoric substances, mixing a quality of sulphuric acid just sufficient to set free such phosphoric acid as will hold in solution the undecomposed phosphate of lime'[8] — to serve a widespread market and was thus itself dispersed. Since bones were often imported coastal towns had some advantage; prizes for top quality superphosphate were awarded in 1881 to works as far apart as Plymouth and Inverness. It was an area of diversification for sulphuric acid makers — the Carnoustie fertiliser works of 1846 for example were an offshoot of St Rollox. Superphosphate manufacture was almost as unpleasant and un-neighbourly a business as the Leblanc trade and came under the control of the Alkali Acts in 1881; unfortunately the trade's characteristic — and even more offensive — associates, horse slaughtering, glue making, the knacker's business in general, did not. The ammoniacal by-products of coal-gas manufacture were another material for the fertiliser trade, and from the 1880s the iron and steel industry made its by-product contribution, basic slag.[9]

Organic chemicals however were one of the conspicuous failures of the nineteenth-century economy. An inability to exploit Perkin's discoveries, an inadequate base in chemical research and teaching, a high degree of dependence on German dyestuffs; this was the kind of commercial failure so frequently discussed in late Victorian Britain. Locationally these industries were footloose, employing such widely available materials as coal tar to make valuable end-products. Perkins set up his works at Harrow because he was a Londoner and the end-product of his process was able to withstand the cost of bringing benzene from Glasgow. The limited availability of technical education, save perhaps in agriculture, was one reason for the limited development of so technically sophisticated an industry; among others were ineffective patent laws, tariff problems, and difficulties with the Excise over the industrial use of alcohol. Dyes were the great failure — surprisingly so when textiles were such a thriving business — other areas less so. The explosives industry was one of the organic chemical industries which did well. The first British factory for organic explosives, built at Ardeer, Ayrshire, in 1871 (plate 14) occupied a classic site and location for so dangerous a trade, remote but with rail and water access to not too distant markets, the dunes facilitating the excavation of bunkers and the creation of embankments.

A note on the principal chemical reactions:

Lead Chamber Sulphuric Acid — in practice a simple process, but one of which the chemistry remains imperfectly understood. Sulphur and saltpetre (in proportions 7: 1) are burnt on trays in a lead-lined chamber, the floor of which is covered with water. Sulphur dioxide is produced, oxidised to sulphur trioxide which combines with water to produce sulphuric acid. Nitrogenous impurities are a problem, as also the time required for the process and the problem of making concentrated acid.

Leblanc Process — salt when heated with. sulphuric acid produces hydrogen chloride (gas) and sodium sulphate. This sulphate is heated with limestone and coal to produce sodium carbonate (soda), calcium sulphide and carbon dioxide. The soda is dissolved out leaving the alkali waste which itself slowly produces hydrogen sulphide in the presence of water.

Solvay Process — a cold concentrated brine solution is saturated with ammonia and carbon dioxide producing ammonium bicarbonate. This reacts with salt to form ammonium chloride (from which ammonia is recoverable) and sodium carbonate, which excess carbon dioxide converts to the bicarbonate. This is insoluble in brine and is precipitated; heating decomposes it to the carbonate. Solvay's contribution was to make a profitable large-scale process out of a well known laboratory reaction.

Bleaching Powder — chlorine is passed over a layer of slaked lime (calcium hydroxide) in a lead or concrete chamber. The end-product, a mixture of calcium hypochlorite and basic calcium chloride, is an easily handled generator of chlorine, useful not only as a bleach but as a disinfectant.

PAPER MAKING

Paper making, like the chemical industry, was a small affair by comparison with textiles or mining, and yet its end product was used in almost every industry and played an integral part in the nineteenth century 'knowledge explosion'. In mid-century, on Coleman's estimate of a labour force of 43,000 people, the industry, broadly defined, employed about one-tenth the labour force of the coal industry, one-fifteenth that of textiles. Its role and status approximated to that of the chemical industry but as a technology it resembled textile manufacture, transforming natural products and wastes into a fabric rather than carrying out newly devised syntheses. As such it was as old established a trade as textiles.

The paper industry of 1800 was a handicraft industry, on the verge of the initial implementation of Fourdrinier's paper-making machine but with its widespread adoption still 30 years away. The basic raw material — rags — was widely available, albeit most readily in the cities and the textile and clothing districts.[10] The raw material supply situation was a perennial problem but was about to be eased by the use of bleaching powder and china clay to clean and add bulk to raw materials. The industry comprised many and widely scattered units, mostly small, rented from landlords and worked within a family or partnership organisation assisted by a small amount of hired labour.[11] The process of rag-pulping was mechanised and large quantities of water were used, hence stream-side locations were normal, often in mills which had begun — as they were to end — their working life in another trade. The working life of mills was often shortened by flood or fire, both particularly damaging and frequent in the paper industry. The growth areas of the early nineteenth-century industry were on the one hand its traditional centres, the Medway and the Chilterns, both of which had the advantage of being handy to London, and a similar market orientation south of Edinburgh; on the other hand the new industrial areas, notably Lancashire, at once a source of raw materials and a market. Other raw materials were also locationally significant, the 'old rope' of the maritime north-east coast, for example, a surprisingly common coastal cargo during the nineteenth century. The industry avoided remote areas, mid-Wales for example, since raw materials and end-product were bulky, and East Anglia, where the rivers were muddy and good sites for water mills relatively few (figure 22).

Mechanisation began in Hertfordshire and Huntingdonshire, but it favoured those areas well placed for coal, as well as a general increase in the scale of enterprise. Thus even before esparto grass in the 1850s and timber in the 1880s became important raw materials, remote inland sites were giving way to estuaries, the eastern margin of the Pennines to Yarm and Jarrow for example. By 1860 mechanisation had reduced hand-made paper to four per cent of an output which had

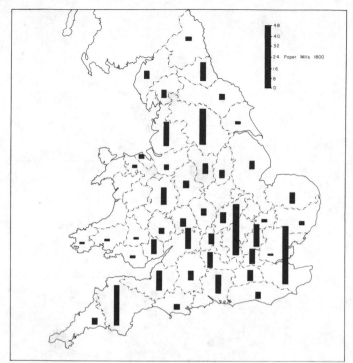

Figure 22. The paper mills of England and Wales, 1800. (Redrawn from Shorter, A.H., *Paper making in the British Isles*, Newton Abbot, 1971, figure 4).

increased sevenfold since 1800; moreover prices had halved. Some makers were vertically integrated, from stationery to rag collecting in a few cases, others horizontally, producing a wide variety of paper types. Cheap brown paper manufacture was more important on the coalfields and in the industrial areas where it was most in demand; quality white paper was more important around London and Edinburgh whose printers and publishers were its markets, and for the remote mills able to survive only by producing quality goods.

Markets, materials and tradition by no means exhaust a list of locational factors. Dickinson established esparto-based paper manufacture in Sunderland to avoid further water pollution in Hertfordshire. The abandonment of suitable buildings by other industries also provided a location for some paper makers. Lewis noted that in the water power period such circumstances

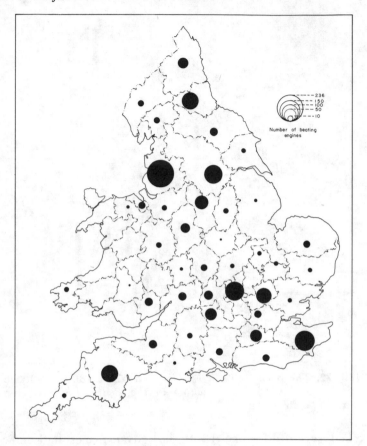

Figure 23. Paper mills (beating engines) in England and Wales 1911.
(Redrawn from same source as figure 22, figure 14.)

favoured dispersion and facilitated the process of 'swarming' around an original mill, since water power limited mill size. Steam reversed this circumstance and favoured larger units. At a more local level he was able to show that in the Maidstone area mills using water from the Hythe aquifer were advantaged over others with a more ferruginous supply, but that narrow valley sites made expansion difficult and these mills thus tended to remain small and to specialise in high grade papers.

The rapid turnover to imported timber as the basic raw material in the last two decades of the century was seen as the final and complete solution to the raw material problem.

Market and material supply ceased to coincide geographically; the use of heavy inorganic chemicals (sulphates and sulphites) became a further locational factor favouring movement to the coast, already a well-established tendency. Areas such as the Medway and the north east were thus well placed for the timber-based industry, but it was able to remain powerful in Lancashire (figure 23). If the general tendency was for remote rural mills to disappear, the railway — and later the lorry — allowed prolonged survival in some such situations, Richmond (North Riding) and Witchampton (Dorset) for example. The pre-eminence of Kent and Lancashire was strengthened but the scattered and rural component and character survived.

BREWING

At the end of the eighteenth century the British spent more money on beer than on any other one item. Brewing could be at the one end of the scale a one-man or domestic business; at the other it could already be — as it generally was in London — big business. There were indeed considerable economies of scale, especially with the coming of steam power, but for these to be effected there had to be retail outlets, a matter of both availability and accessibility. Beer was a perishable and bulky product, and for ordinary beer in a horse and cart age the radius of distribution extended only from three to five miles from the brewery. In these circumstances urbanisation favoured the industrialisation of brewing. Its separation from retail selling has probably begun in London as early as the seventeenth century and by 1815 the 11 leading London brewers were producing 2,000,000 barrels a year, one-fifth of the nation's output. The best London beer, porter[12], enjoyed a wider market; it cost no more to ship a barrel of the very best than of the very worst beer, and it was by sea or canal that such beer travelled.[13] Generally the further one travelled from London, the coastal towns, and the best beers, the more frequently was the beer brewed very locally or even by the publican who sold it. In the highland zone not only was land transport more difficult and costly — to the domestic brewer's advantage — but another of his needs, fuel, was cheaper; moreover porter was still an innovation, and not to everyone's taste. London porter might, ironically, be sold in Dublin, but more generally local tastes, conservatism, and not least local pride favoured the local brewer, especially for everyday beer. Some centres outside London also enjoyed a more than local reputation. Burton upon Trent provides an example;[14] some of its finest beers could compete outside the vicinity of the town, but poor communications and the prevalent taste for porter impeded its growth: 'for centuries a great industrial potential there had lain imprisoned in a narrow overland marketing area by high transport costs until freed by the railway to Derby in 1839'.[15]

The railways allowed quality beer to be sold to a national market and Burton was aided in this respect by a move in public taste away from porter towards the light ales for which its hard water was so suited. Several London brewers migrated to Burton for this reason, Ind Coope in 1858 for example, or to similarly favoured hard water sites, as Courage to Alton. Existing breweries in such locations, as at Tadcaster, were given at least a regional advantage. The railway also generated a phase of public house relocation, away from turnpikes and canals to the 'Station'.[16] Nevertheless the greater part of the brewing business remained local and common beer was made by small brewers or by innkeepers in most areas outside London. In Leeds in 1851, possibly an extreme case, Tetley, the largest brewer, had a mere 32 employees — commercial brewers (as opposed to innkeeper-brewers) made only just over half the beer brewed in Britain. The average Leeds brewery of the mid-nineteenth century employed fewer than ten men. However by the end of the century the number of innkeeper-brewers had fallen to about ten per cent of the mid-century figure, and by 1914 47 large breweries produced 45 per cent of the nation's beer. Tetley was employing 400 men, but the average brewery still only a dozen or so. The stage had not been reached where brewing could cease to be dispersed, because of the limitations of horse and cart distribution, even though many company mergers had taken place. These were concerned more with marketing than with manufacturing, since assured retail outlets were essential for profitable brewing and these were to be found in 'tied' houses. This innovation also diffused outwards from London — half of London's pubs were 'tied' by 1815 — perhaps as part of the process whereby porter lost out to light ale and marketing became more competitive. There was also the question of the complex legal framework — and restrictions — imposed by parliament upon beer selling,[17] and of the capital needed by the retailer and most readily supplied by the brewer. In fact by the end of the century an outright scramble for licensed properties among brewers was adversely affecting profits, but a series and hierarchy of overlapping territories, each focused on a brewery, had been set up.

In 1900 brewing was still a dispersed activity, but more so with respect to plant than to company organisation. Although the family element was strong, even in the large companies, brewing was big business, witness the very scale of operation of the principal companies, their ownership of large numbers of public houses, and their backward integration into malt and hops. The even more radical impact of the motor lorry and van lay in the future.

FLOUR MILLING

The miller, like the brewer, was involved in the production of an everyday necessity, and like him he was to an increasing extent a wholesaler. The industry was geographically dispersed to meet demands for a bulky although not very perishable commodity and technologically conservative. If, as in the London breweries, steam had some impact before 1800, so in the 1830s and 1840s there were still disputes as to manorial rights over mills in Yorkshire.[18] Steam-powered mills became widespread in the first half of the nineteenth century, on the coalfields especially, but for each steam mill there were several water mills and an occasional windmill; the technology of the milling process itself remained medieval. As grain imports became more important and steam pre-eminent coastal locations were increasingly at an advantage and from mid-century millers began to experiment with roller methods, emulating their European (especially Hungarian) counterparts. By 1870 one firm of Liverpool millers had got rid of stones entirely, and it was from this centre and in the succeeding two decades that the large roller mill triumphed, aided by ever improving technology and the near-collapse of British grain farming. Circumstances favoured large coastal mills — Vernon's Birkenhead mill of 1898 (plate 15) had a 1,200 h.p. engine and produced 12,000 28 lb sacks of flour each week — while the old water mills (plate 16) decayed. Where milling was carried on inland the seat of business often shifted to the railway, at Cambridge from Newnham to a new enterprise at the station in 1900. The consumer was an unwitting — possibly willing — victim of progress since roller-milled flour was not only whiter, the popular preference, but often less nutritious. The ubiquitous trade of the early nineteenth century had become a localised, largely coastal, factory industry through the impact of steam, technology and foreign competition.

LEATHER

In 1800 the making of leather goods, and of leather itself, was the country's second largest manufacture. It was an ancient craft, carried on in almost every community, never wholly to lose this character but to be modernised and in many instances relocated, by chance and accident as well as by rational decision.

Tanning, fell-mongery and associated trades were in the early nineteenth century a small-scale, neighbourhood (albeit unneighbourly) activity. Markets and materials were almost universal although availability of the latter may in a few cases have initially favoured certain areas, oak-bark from Rockingham Forest the Northamptonshire leather trade for example. The main concentrations of the industry were near the ports where raw materials came in, at Bermondsey for example, and in areas concerned with leather manufactures like south Somerset. The tanner's trade was not liked by his neighbours,[19] hence the typical location at or beyond the edge of the town. During the century the small tanner tended to disappear, the business to concentrate on London, Leeds — the second largest centre by 1850 — and the ports. Communications mattered more than coal; movement to and from markets and sources of supply mattered more than fuel costs. British industry concentrated on heavy leathers, the lighter leathers were often imported; in general there was much inter-regional movement of the valuable end-product. In the 1860s Yeovil glovers bought leather from Northamptonshire whose bootmakers looked north and even overseas for their supply. As an historian of the county wrote in

1906 'the manufacture of leather . . . never attained to the importance which would be expected'.[20] After all the boot and shoe trade was but one market — heavy leather belting connected steam engine to machine and was thus integral to factory industry. Indeed it has been suggested that its importance was one reason for the industry's tendency to move north and for its neglect of light leathers. While technical changes were not a strong locational force — the industry was notoriously conservative, witness its reluctant adoption of the chrome process in 1884 — prolonged occupation of a particular site was not typical. The urban fringe was a moving frontier and this may in part explain why Northampton's 11 'heavy' tanneries of 1847 had all closed or moved elsewhere by 1906.

The principal leather-using industry was the manufacture of boots and shoes. At the beginning of the century this activity was widespread; Clapham estimated that in 1831 100,000 out of 130,000 bootmakers were local shopkeepers. The remainder, serving wider and more specialised markets, tended to be concentrated in a few provincial cities and towns. Some communities like Northampton had an association with the industry reaching back several centuries while in others it was, as a speciality, a comparatively recent arrival, at Stafford and Norwich for example. The industry was almost completely domestic, since cutting and warehousing alone could be centralised into factories. Most shoe-making processes came to be mechanised only in the 1850s and then with hand machines — steam power was an even later starter. More powerful elements in creating a factory system were compulsory education and extension of the Factory Acts to cover workshops in the 1870s, eliminating cheap labour and cheap premises. The unions and the manufacturers were equally keen to move the business into centralised establishments, the former the more readily to guard their members' rights and interests, the latter for the sake of quality control.

Geographical relocation on a nationwide scale began earlier than movement into factories. If the growth of the Northampton industry is the main feature of the first half of the nineteenth century, it was also during this period that Clarks of Street (Somerset) entered the trade (in the 1820s, at first as a sideline to their tannery and sheepskin slipper business) and the Kendal industry dates from 1842. The second half of the

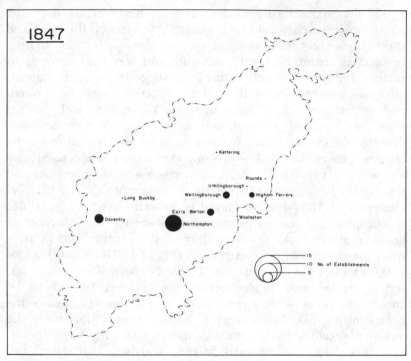

Figure 24. Boot and shoe manufacturing establishments in North-amptonshire, 1847. (Redrawn from Mounfield, P.R. 'The footwear industry of the East Midlands: (III) Northamptonshire 1700-1911', *East Midland Geographer*, Vol. 3 (8), 1965, fig. 2, p.436.)

century, the period of mechanisation and the factory, witnessed the great expansion of the industry in Leicester and rural Northamptonshire (figures 24-27). Leicester had made boots and children's shoes for some time; expansion in the 1850s — as at Kendal — related to the reluctance of Northampton and Stafford to introduce machinery. Leicester possessed a pioneer inventor and innovator, Crick, who invented a boot-riveting machine in 1853 — the first of a series of such inventions — and alone among Leicester bootmakers he was using steam power in the early 1860s. Leicester possessed other advantages — surplus labour in its hosiery and knitwear trade and the presence of an elastic web industry at the time when elastic-sided boots were coming into fashion. By 1891 Leicester had almost twice as many workers in the industry as Northampton and firms from

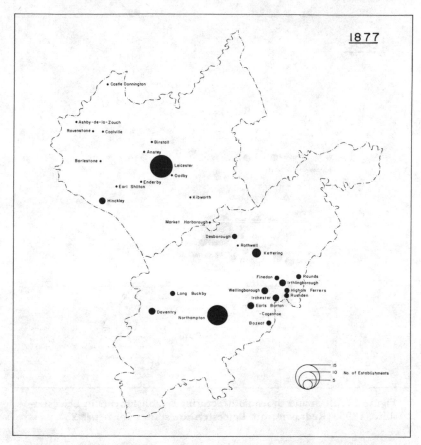

Figure 25. Boot and shoe manufacturing establishments in North-amptonshire and Leicestershire, 1877. (Redrawn from same sources as figure 24, and Mounfield, P.R., 'The footwear industry of the East Midlands: (IV) Leicesershire to 1911', *East Midland Geographer*, Vol. 4 (1), 1966, fig. 2, p.12)

elsewhere were setting up depots and branches in the county. Rural Northamptonshire offered different advantages: the whole outwork tradition of the industry favoured dispersal, and dispersed through the county was a pool of unemployed or underemployed labour, in part from a dying wool trade. This cheap labour was eminently suitable for the new machine boot business and it had provided the base for some development of the industry in the first half of the century. Undoubtedly the railway built through the Ise valley in 1857 facilitated its

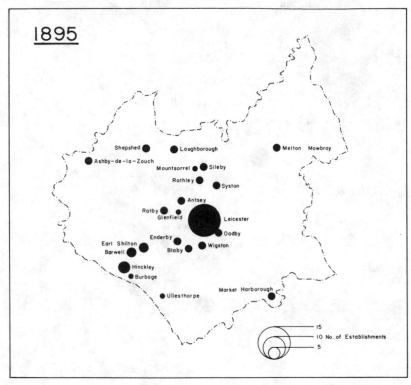

Figure 26. Boot and shoe manufacturing establishments in Leicester-shire, 1895. (Redrawn from Leicestershire source for figure 25).

growth as a centre of the industry, the rapid economic (and demographic) transformation of 11 small centres (two of them old markets) into a boot and shoe manufactory set apart from the local rural economy. Absence of coal may have been a further advantage to the boot and shoe manufacturer as other industries were not attracted to the area to compete for its labour. The middle decades of the century were certainly a boom period — Northamptonshire's boot and shoe manufact-urers (bespoke excepted) numbered 97 in 1847, 220 only 30 years later. But the factory system was still in the future and the industry remained largely domestic — even in northern cities, Leeds for example — and hand- or foot-powered until after 1880. The creation of the modern factory industry relates very largely to the impact of American competition and

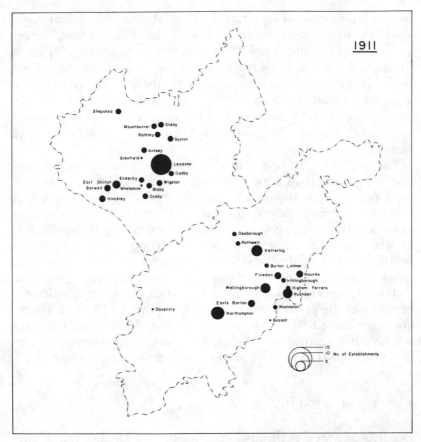

Figure 27. Boot and shoe factories in Northamptonshire and Leicestershire, 1911. (Redrawn from same sources as figures 24 and 25.)

technology by means of the American-owned British United Shoe Machinery Company of 1899.

Spatial differentiation, as complex as in wool or cotton, took two forms. Different processes were carried out in separate plants, presupposing that movement of half-made goods from plant to plant — often in fact a short journey within the one town or village — was economically possible. More significantly, different areas worked for different sections of what the railways had made a single national (and substantial export) market. Stafford made the best women's, Northampton the best

men's, boots and shoes, while Leicestershire and Northamptonshire, the newcomers, made the cheaper grades. In general larger
centres made higher quality goods. Bristol specialised in work
boots, Rossendale in slippers, and, at an even more specialised
level, Raunds had been making army boots since the Napoleonic
War. As a result the bulk of the population were more cheaply
and comfortably[21] shod in 1900 than in 1800; mechanisation
and specialisation had benefited customer, craftsman and
capitalist.

Gloving was an even more tenaciously conservative and
domestic trade than boot and shoe making. London, Worcester
and Yeovil were its ancient centres, the first two concerned
more with fancy gloves, the last with heavier goods. In the
provinces the industry was — and is — very largely domestic, but
as with boot and shoe manufacture cutting was often centralised (plate 17). Unfortunately the industry was one of fashion,
more so and from an earlier date than boots and shoes, liable to
instant changes and fluctuations after such events as Huskisson's
removal of the prohibition of French imports in 1830, or for no
apparent cause at all. Fashion was to the glover what the state
of, say, the Australian economy or North American tariffs, to
cite two important export markets, was to the bootmaker.

KNITWEAR AND HOSIERY

Parallels between the knitwear industry and the boot and shoe
trade in the nineteenth century are at once apparent: Both were
tenaciously domestic, both were carried on — and to some
extent overlapped — in the East Midlands. It seems likely that in
each case localisation reflected broadly similar circumstances,
the availability of labour in a well populated rural area with a
rather moribund domestic textile tradition and no strongly
competing growth industry. However the hosiery and knitwear
trade had a longer history of localisation than boot and shoe
making, it was rather more subject to whims of fashion[22] and
also to the reality of competition from (or at least substitution
by) garments made at home by the housewife and her
daughters, a commonplace even in the 1970s.

The industry's geographical localisation owed something to
William Lee's invention of the stocking frame at Calverton, near

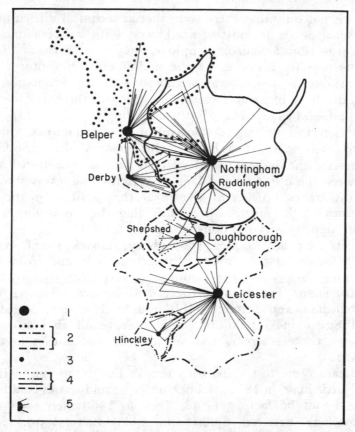

Figure 28. The domestic system in the East Midlands hosiery trade, 1844: 1, principal putting-out centres; 2, spheres of influence of principal centres; 3, secondary putting-out centres; 4, spheres of influence of secondary centres; 5, places for which there is evidence of centre worked for. (Redrawn from Smith, D.M., 'The British hosiery industry at the middle of the nineteenth century', *Institute of British Geographers : Transactions and Papers*, vol. 32, 1963, fig. 4.)

Nottingham, in 1589. By the 1840s 90 per cent of the industry's machines, providing 100,000 jobs, were in Leicestershire, Nottinghamshire or Derbyshire. These were the hand-machines of a domestic industry (plate 18) dispersed within defined areas around central warehouses. Beyond a fixed radius from these depots the quest for cheap labour became uneconomic. The industry remained thus organised until about 1850:

'it was not only that there were special technical difficulties in applying power to knitting machinery. With a superabundance of cheap labour available, employers had no incentive.'[23] Or to quote another historian of the mid-nineteenth century: 'the over-riding impression was of almost complete stagnation . . . not the least important reason for this was the existence of a well-established system of putting out'.[24] (figure 28). This situation had sad social consequences – framework knitters were even more of a byword for poverty than handloom weavers: 'the industry had entered into a transitional stage between the domestic and factory systems, and it was precisely in the trades which had arrived at this position in the first decades of the nineteenth century that the worst abuses and most oppressive conditions could be found'.[25] The industry had its secondary centres, Tewkesbury, Hawick, Dumfries, and its offshoots, most notably Nottingham lace, and from 1816 Tiverton lace when the Luddites forced Heathcoat to leave Nottingham. The main hosiery and knitwear centres were Nottingham and Leicester, followed by Hinckley, Mansfield, and Sutton-in-Ashfield, but it was above all an industry of village workers serving and serviced by warehouses in these towns.

Steam came to the industry first at Loughborough in 1839, to Nottingham in 1851, and not until the mid-sixties could high class goods be factory made. Thus in 1860 there were only somewhere between 3,000 and 4,000 factory workers in Nottingham as against 50,000 domestic; in 1862 only some three per cent of the industry's labour force came under the Factory Acts. In these circumstances the move to factories (plates 18 and 19) reflected not sudden and overwhelming technical change but legislation hostile to domestic manufacture, Frame Rent abolition (1874),[26] the Workshop Acts (1867-76), compulsory education, and the wishes of unions and employers (if not of all work people). Parallels with the boot and shoe industry are evident. The factory came first to the larger towns, the old distributive centres – Nottingham (plate 28) and Leicester which had only 22 per cent of the industry's plant in 1884 had 75 per cent 20 years later – some indication, perhaps an exaggerated one, of the triumph of the urban industry in mid-century. The process was one of some substitution of capital for labour,[27] but also of higher wages, in places

1. A Lancashire colliery, *c.* 1800. The setting is rural but smoky; attention is focused on pumping, weighing, and on moving coal by cart, pack donkey, and even wheelbarrow.

2. The country around Manchester, *c.* 1800. Manchester and to a lesser extent Oldham and Ashton-under-Line are already considerable towns; but despite conspicuous ribbon development along main roads there remains much open country.

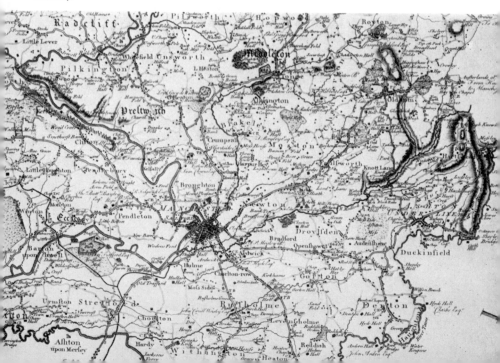

3. The country around Blackpool, *c.* 1800. A rural England of both nuclear villages (e.g. Thistleton) and dispersed hamlets and farms (e.g. east of Kirkham) untouched by industrialisation. Note the incipient Blackpool, the much older Lytham, and the limited extent of coastal settlement.

4. The Red Lion Street area of Narrow Marsh, central Nottingham, prior to demolition in 1919. Note the mixture of industry and housing. Demolition (or decay) has revealed the cross-section of a 'back-to-back' terrace; at right angles to it runs the 'blind back' of a 'not-through' terrace.

THE NEW HOUSE.

PATERFAMILIAS (with his belongings) returned last night from the Sea-side to his new home in the Suburbs. He has slept on his own spring-bed and breakfasted comfortably, and is beginning to forget the misery of the last four weeks. The children are out. The October Sun is shining brightly. A faint fragrance pervades the house, which (he says) reminds him vaguely of days gone by. He strolls into his garden. The young Virginia creeper is turning lovely red ; the kitten has grown into a cat, and a lily has actually burst into blossom from a bulb of his own planting. In the fulness of his heart, he throws himself into a garden chair, takes out his pipe, and begins to warble "*Home! sweet Home!*" when—O horror ! . . . He suddenly descries a series of ominous cracks running up the back of his "*newly-built substantial semi-detached suburban residence*"—and the partner of his joys rushes out to tell him that "that subtle aroma, so poetically suggestive of the past, proceeds from—*THE DRAINS!*"

5. Mr Punch's comment on 19th-century building standards; note the attention paid to both the structure itself and to the drains. Houses in this style survive in large numbers in the inner suburbs of many English towns and cities.

6. The blind back wall of 'not through' houses, Lower Acreman Street, Sherborne. Compare plate 4. These stone-built cottages are probably early nineteenth-century, but note brick chimneys and later addition of the odd window.

7. Choppington Street, Newcastle upon Tyne. Built 1876-7 and photographed
1965; subsequently demolished. Certainly not a mean street with its tiny front
gardens and stone doorways and windows. Note the survival of a cobbled road
surface.

8. The blast furnaces at Summerlea, Monkland, Lanarkshire, in the late 1870s:
the classic Scottish iron and steel industry in its prime, served by canal as well
as railway.

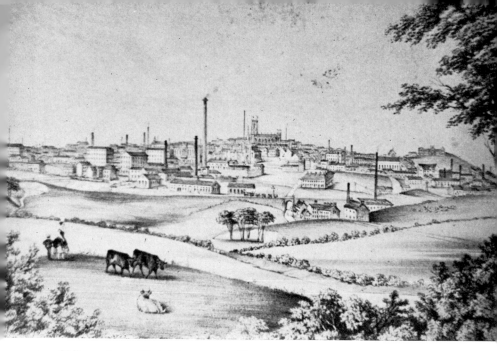

9. Oldham from Glodwick *c.* 1831. Numerous mills and chimneys are in evidence; the new church – a sign of the wealth generated by the cotton industry – is conspicuous on the skyline, but the setting remains rural.

10. Oldham from Glodwick *c.* 1870. A closer and murkier view than plate 9 – a transformation from rural to urban. Several factory chimneys can be identified in both plates; note too the conspicuous presence of mines among mills.

11. (*above*) Huddersfield *c.* 1830. A small town in a rural setting but note the already numerous mill chimneys, bleaching grounds (?) (right middle distance), and mills outside the town (often set in a cluster of houses, e.g. left foreground) and some distance from it.

12. (*below*) Huddersfield in 1900. Note the growth of the town and its
satellites, the numerous churches and schools as well as mills. The railways
have conspicuously occupied the open space prominent in the foreground of
the 1830 view (plate 11) but provision has been made for a park and there is
some evidence of suburban sprawl.

13. St Rollox Chemical Works, Glasgow, *c.* 1878. The very tall chimneys (known locally as 'Tennant's stalks') were typical of the Leblanc process, the rather impermanent looking buildings of most branches of nineteenth-century chemical industry.

14. Ardeer explosive works, Ayrshire, in the early 1870s, shortly after their establishment. Note dispersal among and inside dunes for safety and the conspicuous hill-top lookout. The works eventually became part of ICI.

15. Vernon's new flour mills, Birkenhead Dock. Built in 1899 this mill is a classic example of the large dockside roller mill of the late nineteenth century, dependent on imported supplies and rail distribution.

16. West Mill, Sherborne, *c.* 1900. The opposite end of the spectrum from plate 15. A water-powered mill in a rural area milling local supplies for local needs. As was often the case the mill, now ruinous, is located a short distance from the town.

17. A glove-cutting room in Yeovil c. 1898. As in the boot and shoe trade cutting was early centralised and its practitioners were among the most skilled and most highly paid employees. Note the minimal machinery, the use of hand tools.

18. Framework knitters' cottages, Currant Street, Nottingham; built c. 1800, photographed c. 1919. The well-lit workrooms comprising the upper storeys (and in this case attics) are characteristic of domestic textile manufacture; note also cellars and the effect of the height of the buildings in shutting out sunlight.

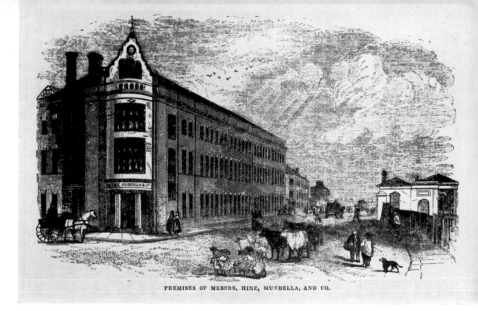

PREMISES OF MESSRS. HINE, MUNDELLA, AND CO.

19. The hosiery factory of Hine, Mundella and Co., Station Street, Nottingham, 1856. The first of the town's hosiery factories, it was opened in 1851. Note sheep and cattle in the street and the paucity of vehicular traffic; the location of the new premises in Station Street is scarcely coincidental.

20. S.S. *Elderslie* berthed at Oamaru, New Zealand. Built by Palmers of Jarrow in 1884 this steamer was the first built specifically for the New Zealand frozen meat trade. Oamaru was the port for the area which pioneered the trade. Thus the picture epitomises British maritime and shipbuilding supremacy and dependence on imported food.

21. Channel Island steamers at Weymouth *c.* 1880. At this date the service was somewhat run-down and the paddle steamers, some 40 years old, do not represent the best contemporary packet steamers. Note numerous sailing vessels astern of steamers.

22. London General Omnibus Company Stables, Hackney 1901: the bus depot of the period, horses requiring space, labour and food.

23. Hayboats on the Thames *c.* 1872. Provisioning London's horses was a very substantial problem and perhaps a limit to city growth.

POST OFFICE REGULATIONS.

On and after the 10th January, a Letter not exceeding HALF AN OUNCE IN WEIGHT, may be sent from any part of the United Kingdom, to any other part, for ONE PENNY, if paid when posted, or for TWO PENCE if paid when delivered.

THE SCALE OF RATES,

If paid when posted, is as follows, for all Letters, whether sent by the General or by any Local Post,

Not exceeding ½ Ounce		**One Penny.**
Exceeding ½ Ounce, but not exceeding 1 Ounce		**Twopence.**
Ditto 1 Ounce .... 2 Ounces		**Fourpence.**
Ditto 2 Ounces.............. 3 Ounces		**Sixpence.**

and so on; an additional Two-pence for every additional Ounce. With but few exceptions, the WEIGHT is limited to Sixteen Ounces.

If not paid when posted, double the above Rates are charged on Inland Letters.

COLONIAL LETTERS.

If sent by Packet Twelve Times, if by Private Ship Eight Times, the above Rates.

FOREIGN LETTERS.

The Packet Rates which vary, will be seen at the Post Office. The Ship Rates are the same as the Ship Rates for Colonial Letters.

As regards Foreign and Colonial Letters, there is no limitation as to weight. All sent outwards, with a few exceptions, which may be learnt at the Post Office, must be paid when posted as heretofore.

Letters intended to go by Private Ship must be marked "*Ship Letter.*"

Some arrangements of minor importance, which are omitted in this Notice, may be seen in that placarded at the Post Office.

No Articles should be transmitted by Post which are liable to *injury* by being stamped, or by being crushed in the Bags.

It is particularly requested that all Letters may be *fully* and *legibly* addressed, and *posted as early* as convenient.

January 7th, 1840.

By Authority :—J. Hartnell. London.

24. The 'penny post' regulation of 1840. Note the geographical emphasis and transformation, 'from any part of the United Kingdom, to any other part', the very high foreign rates, and the perennial appeal for legibility and correct address.

25. An early Victorian milk shop: cows are kept on the premises (hay in the basement) and customers supplied with milk, eggs, cheese and butter.

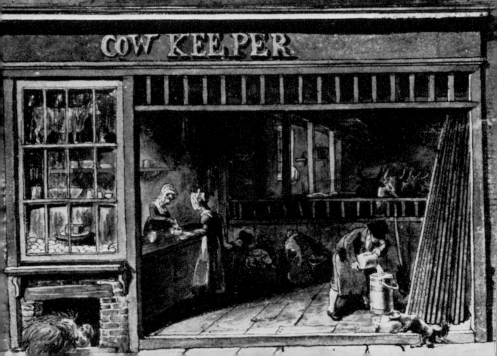

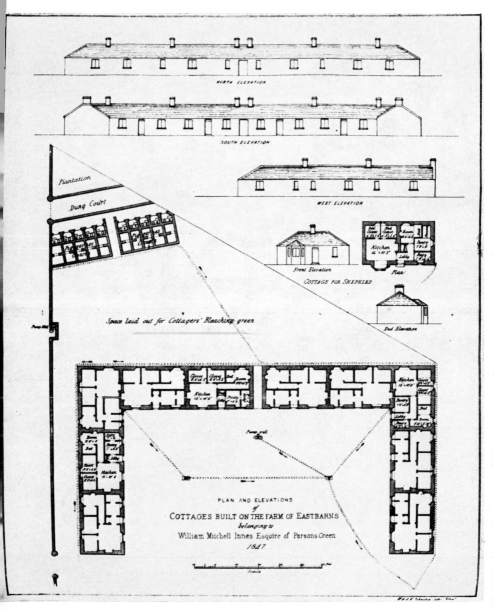

26. Plans for new cottages on an East Lothian farm 1847. Such agricultural 'barracks' can still be seen in this area of traditionally expert farming. The cost of each cottage was about £110; note very small size (about 600 sq. ft.), absence of gardens (but provision of piggery) and the superior, detached shepherd's cottage.

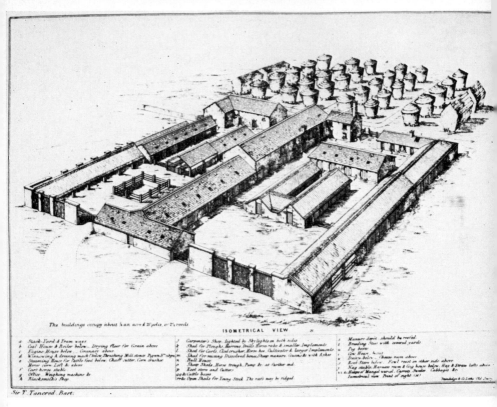

ISOMETRICAL VIEW

27. Prize-winning farm layout of 1850. Note the extensive buildings, the large rickyard, and the engine-house.

28. Smallholder's cottage at Rew, Dorchester, built *c.* 1890 on an 8-acre holding. The pioneer fringe of the depression period was, to some politicians at least, a panacea. This corrugated iron shack suggests another view.

with established transport links to markets and now ready access to coal. However the last decades of the century witnessed a revival of the traditional geography, the spread of factories into rural areas in search of cheap (often non-union) labour, and away from such competitors in the labour market as lace in west Nottinghamshire, the boot and shoe trade in Leicestershire, and Boot, Player and Raleigh in Nottingham. The movement did not take the form of migration to the coalfields since coal was widely available and not very important. Nottingham and Leicester's share of the industry fell from 62 per cent in 1881 to 42 per cent in 1899, but dispersal of the industry was largely contained within its traditional limits. In fact, as Smith has pointed out, there is a remarkable correlation between the size of mid-century domestic manufacture and late nineteenth-century factory industry throughout the northeast Midlands. Regional pre-eminence increased to the extent that this area provided 95 per cent of all hosiery and knitwear employment by the 1890s. Local specialisation existed, but less strongly than in similar industries. Derby made silk hose, Nottinghamshire made cotton hose (having been engaged in cotton manufacture in the first phase of the Industrial Revolution) and lace; Leicestershire made worsted hose and woollen knitwear. Like its peers the industry had to face problems in export markets, notably tariffs and competition; characteristically wool fared better than cotton here. The bureaucrat played his part in sustaining hand-frame industry, according to one writer 'because the War Office had an antiquated specification for military pants'.[28]

SOME CONCLUSIONS

It would be possible to go on to discuss the industrial geography of nineteenth-century Britain at great length. It seems debatable that this would further facilitate generalisation, be it tentative, verbal (and thus unfashionable), confident or numerical. If a first generalisation is to describe nineteenth-century Britain as the age of coal — an almost self-evident statement — what was coal's locational impact? Certainly the iron and steel industry was drawn to the coalfields, in search of ore as well as coal, and cotton and wool were lucky enough to be situated on secondary and easily worked coalfields. The technology of these two textile trades had for the most part reached a fuel-demanding stage in the first half of the century, hence the fact that they thrived on the coalfields and languished elsewhere, although other circumstances were also involved. But it should also be pointed out that the textile trade's propensity to migrate to coal, to follow the miner eastwards in Yorkshire for example, or to venture more widely, was negligible. Other industries found the coalfields equally unattractive having not yet reached the steam power stage — leather and hosiery for example. Even the chemical industry, a considerable coal user, was not tied to the coalfields. Coalmining areas were, after all, in many cases remote, paid high wages to their workers and were equipped by mid-century to move coal to the manufacturer cheaply and reliably. He proved as reluctant to move to coal as did established coalfield industries — notably iron — to leave them.

In such conditions, once the railways could move coal almost everywhere, other factors affected industrial location. Some sought out raw materials or their port of entry — iron and steel in Cleveland, Cumberland and South Wales, paper around London (also a market), flour milling at Liverpool — and settled there. Others kept to a regional pattern set up long ago, perhaps by a forgotten entrepreneur or inventor and his successors. They had reached only a hand tool stage in the first half of the century and by the time they became coal users — footwear and hosiery for example — it was easier for the coal to come to them than for them to move. A pool of cheap rural labour was often to their advantage and played a part in their late nineteenth-century geography, as it had at an earlier date for cotton and wool. Public pressure was by no means insignificant, in the chemical trades for example, and in the guise of specialised markets and tastes it affected the geography of both paper-making and brewing. The importance of inter-industry linkages is evident, as on Tyneside, and their significance within industries increased as the subdivision of processes was extended and specialised common commercial and technical services came into use; hence the propensity for local 'swarming'.

The coal-fired steam locomotive had served to carry coal to the customer rather than customer to coal, save in those instances where the customer ante-dated the means of communication. Timing of technological change — of the application of power and of the direct use of coal — is thus all-important. Broadly speaking if it occurred before mid-century the industry located on the coalfields, if after mid-century there was a high probability, in old-established industries in particular, that the coal would be brought to existing sites or their vicinity. 'Changes in the geographical distribution of industry since 1850 have not been general . . . the major interest of the years 1850-1913 with regard to most industries is of trends in the balance of output as between different regional centres and of changes in the detailed distribution of industries within regions already roughly defined by the middle of the nineteenth century'.[29] The preceding century or so had been quite exceptional in the propensity of industry to move and adjust its locations, but after 1850 there was a return to the more usual inertia and immobility.[30]

NOTES

1 von Liebig, J., *Familiar Letters on Chemistry,* London, 1843, p.30. This book went through four editions in English by 1859, perhaps an indication that science was neither so unpopular nor so neglected in nineteenth-century Britain as has sometimes been suggested.
2 This remains the case, witness any modern textbook of chemistry.
3 Barilla, containing about 25% alkali, was obtained by burning a Mediterranean plant. The trade was closely associated with Alicante and thus very subject to interruption during the several eighteenth-century wars with Spain. Kelp was made by burning sea weed and was one of the staple industries of the Scottish Highlands and Islands. See Clow, A. and N.L., *The Chemical Revolution,* London, 1952, pp.65-90.
4 Charles Tennant, a Scottish linen bleacher — at the time a key local industry — patented bleaching powder in 1798 and set up St Rollox in 1799 for its manufacture. The works soon outgrew the needs or ends of linen, itself a contracting industry.
5 'Tennant's Stalk' at St Rollox (1842) was 420 feet high. In

general the object of tall chimneys was not only dispersal, which up to a point could increase damage, but to make more difficult the tracing of the offender.

6 Proceedings of the Town Council of Newcastle upon Tyne, 9 January 1839, p.19. Quoted by Campbell, W.A., *The Chemical Industry,* London, 1971, p.36.

7 *Daily News,* April, 1888.

8 Quoted from the patent itself by Campbell, W.A., op.cit., pp.75-6.

9 See Chapter 3, note 13. Gilchrist Thomas went so far as to assert that phosphorus would one day be the main product of his process, and threatened to sell out his interest in the North Eastern Steel Company to prevent it making a long-term, low-price contract for disposal of basic slag in 1884.

10 Rags were also used as a fertiliser and became the raw material of the shoddy trade during the first half of the nineteenth century. The concept of recycling is no twentieth-century novelty.

11 Coleman, D.C., *The British Paper Industry 1495-1860,* Oxford, 1958, p.146.

12 Beer is rarely now sold as porter, but porter is much the same as the still popular stout.

13 Even as far as India, hence the term India Pale Ale (I.P.A.).

14 The geographical basis of this advantage was the hardness — especially the gypsum content — and purity of the water supply.

15 Mathias, P., *The Brewing Industry in England 1700-1830,* Cambridge, 1959, p.xxvii.

16 Scarcely a station in Britain has not a hotel, and the course of former railways — or even merely planned lines — is evidenced in public house names, witness the 'Silent Whistle' at Evercreech on the old Somerset and Dorset Line, the 'Railway Dock Hotel' at Weymouth on the proposed, but never executed, line to the new dock.

17 To say nothing of the temperance and abstinence campaigners; the geography of alcohol as a social problem and responses to it in the nineteenth century deserves investigation.

18 In the Middle Ages the lord's mill commonly enjoyed a valuable monopoly and vestiges of this persisted.

19 He himself usually asserts that it is particularly healthy, a confidence shared not only proverbially by the farmer, but — more remarkably — by the nineteenth-century alkali manufacturer!

20 Muscott, B.B., 'Leather', in volume 2 (1906) of the *Victoria History of the County of Northampton,* p.317.

21 Bespoke boots and shoes excepted, all evidence suggests that the average boot of the pre-machine phase was poorly fitting, uncomfortable, and at worst damaging. The distinction of left from right is a late nineteenth-century phenomenon.

22 Perhaps most notable in the nineteenth century is the substitution of trousers for breeches.

23 Patterson, A. Temple, *Radical Leicester,* Leicester, 1954, p.381.

24 Head, P., 'Putting out in the Leicester hosiery industry in the middle of the nineteenth century', *Transactions of the Leicestershire Archaeological and Historical Society,* vol. 37, 1961-2, p.56.

25 Patterson, p.62.

26 Frame rent abolition outlawed the system whereby the knitter hired his machine (frame) from the master hosier, or sometimes from a middleman, to whom also he sold his finished work. Frame renting was a conservative force, favoured by manufacturers, opposed by trades unions; it appears to have been losing both economic and technical advantage even before 1874.

27 Ironically just as such staples as coal and cotton had begun to do the reverse.

28 Clapham, J.H., *An Economic History of Modern Britain: Free Trade and Steel 1850-1886,* Cambridge, 1932, quoting *Royal Commission on Labour,* 1892, Question 13358.

29 Smith, W., *An Historical Introduction to the Economic Geography of Great Britain,* London, 1968, p.161.

30 Rawstron, E.M., 'Some aspects of the location of hosiery and lace manufacture in Great Britain', *East Midland Geographer,* vol. 9, 1958, pp.16-28, ends (pp.26-8) with a useful summary of the locational forces acting on British industry as a whole in the nineteenth century.

FURTHER READING

1 CHEMICALS

Campbell, W.A., *The Chemical Industry*, London, 1971.
Campbell, W.A., *A Century of Chemistry on Tyneside 1868-1968*, Newcastle upon Tyne, 1968.
Clow, A., 'Vitriol and the Industrial Revolution', *Economic History Review*, vol. 15, 1945, pp.44-55.
Clow, A. and N.L., *The Chemical Revolution*, London, 1952.
Haber, L.F., *The Chemical Industry during the Nineteenth Century*, Oxford (2nd edition), 1969.
Hardie, D.W.F., *A History of the Chemical Industry in Widnes*, London, 1950.
Hardie, D.W.F. and Pratt, D., *A History of the Modern British Chemical Industry*, Oxford, 1966.
MacLeod, R.M., 'The Alkali Acts Administration 1863-84', *Victorian Studies*, vol. 9, 1965, pp.85-112.
Taylor, F. Sherwood, *A History of Industrial Chemistry*, London, 1957.
Wallwork, K., 'The mid-Cheshire salt industry', *Geography*, vol. 44, 1959, pp.171-86.

2 PAPER
Coleman, D.C., *The British Paper Industry 1495-1860*, Oxford, 1958.
Lewis, P.W., 'Changing factors of location in the paper-making industry as illustrated by the Maidstone area', *Geography*, vol. 52, 1967, pp.280-93.
Parris, H., 'Adaptation to technical change in the paper-making industry: the paper mill at Richmond, Yorkshire, 1823-46', *Yorkshire Bulletin*, vol. 12, 1960, pp.84-9.
Shorter, A.H., *Paper making in the British Isles: An Historical and Geographical Study*, Newton Abbot, 1971.

3 BREWING
Burnet, J., *Plenty and Want: A Social History of Diet in England from 1815 to the Present Day*, London, 1966 (also for flour-milling).
Mathias, P., *The Brewing Industry in England 1700-1830*, Cambridge, 1959.

Mathias, P., 'Industrial revolution in brewing', *Explorations in Entrepreneurial History*, vol. 5, 1953, pp.208-24.

Monckton, H.A., *A History of English Ale and Beer*, London, 1966.

Sigsworth, E.M., *The brewing trade during the industrial revolution: the case of Yorkshire*, York (Borthwick Papers No. 31), 1967.

Vaizey, J., *The Brewing Industry 1886-1951*, London, 1960.

4   FLOUR MILLING

Bennett, R., and Elton, J., *A History of Corn Milling*, London, 1898-1904.

5   LEATHER, FOOTWEAR, GLOVES

Church, R.A., 'The British leather industry and foreign competition 1870-1914', *Economic History Review* (2nd series), vol. 24, 1971, pp.543-68.

Church, R.A., 'The effect of the American export invasion on the British boot and shoe industry 1885-1914', *Journal of Economic History*, vol. 28, 1968, pp.223-54.

Fox, A., *A History of the National Union of Boot and Shoe Operatives 1874-1957*, Oxford, 1958.

Morley, C.D., 'Population of Northampton and the Ise Valley 1801-1951', *East Midland Geographer*, vol. 11, 1959, pp.20-29 (also hosiery and knitwear).

Mounfield, P.R., 'The footwear industry of the East Midlands', *East Midland Geographer*, vols 3 and 4, 1964-6, pp.293-306, 394-413, 434-53 and 8-23.

Patterson, A. Temple., *Radical Leicester*, Leicester, 1954.

Rimmer, W.G., 'The Leeds leather industry in the nineteenth century', *Thoresby Society Publications*, vol. 46, 1960, pp.119-64.

Weekly, I.G., 'Industry in the small country towns of Lincolnshire, Northamptonshire and Rutland', *East Midland Geographer*, vol. 7, 1957, pp.21-30.

6   HOSIERY AND KNITWEAR

Church, R.A., *Economic and Social Change in a Midland Town: Victorian Nottingham, 1815-1900*, London, 1966.

Head, P., 'Putting out in the Leicester hosiery industry in the middle of the nineteenth century', *Transactions of the*

Leicestershire Archaeological and Historical Society, vol. 37, 1961-2, pp.44-59.

Rawstron, E.M., 'Some aspects of the location of hosiery and lace manufacture in Great Britain', *East Midland Geographer*, vol. 9, 1958, pp.16-28.

Smith, D.M., 'The British hosiery industry at the middle of the nineteenth century: an historical study in economic geography', *Institute of British Geographers : Transactions*, vol. 32, 1963, pp.125-42.

Smith, D.M., 'The location of the British hosiery industry since the late nineteenth century', *East Midland Geographer*, vol. 5, 1970, pp.71-9.

Wells, F.A., *The British Hosiery and Knitwear Industry: Its History and Organisation*, Newton Abbot (revised edition), 1972.

6 Movement and Mobility: The Conquest of Distance

The nineteenth century was a century of easier movement, of the creation of the railway and the steamer and of their colossal impact on the economy and society. This impact is a major theme of most socio-economically oriented studies of nine-teenth-century Britain and the Railway Age has even generated at least one history of the period organised around this topic.[1] More characteristically studies of the period briefly discuss the demise of turnpike and canal and then plunge into a prolonged discussion of the glories of the railway; the steamer, perhaps even the motor car, provides a postcript. This approach, organising the topic of transport in terms of medium, inevitably and rightly gives pride of place to the railway, even in balanced and imaginative studies which have not succumbed to the lure of steam. It is to be doubted however whether this is to put the railway into an apt perspective; railways, like every other means of communication, existed neither in their own right nor to complete a centralised plan — nor even for the delight of later generations — but to facilitate the movement of goods and people either for the profit of promoter and proprietor, or at the behest (and subsidy) of the state or a benefactor-philanthr-opist. The railways of nineteenth-century Britain thus resemble the airlines of the last quarter of the twentieth — they are there, conspicuous and even a matter for intermittent public debate. Evidently they have a considerable impact on economy and society since they are a big business in their own right, but the economy and society had showed themselves capable of advance before they were created, and only a small part of the population is a direct user of their services. Moreover railway and aeroplane depend on other means of transport, the motor vehicle or, in the nineteenth century, the horse, without which they are stranded whales or lame ducks. For most people of the nineteenth century walking was the normal means of movement — the car is becoming a close twentieth-century analogy — and yet the pedestrian rarely enters scholarly discussion of the topic or the period; likewise the horse, although Thompson has begun to redress this omission[2], real and counterfactual. Moreover nineteenth-century Britain was provided with a variety of other means of communication — the telegraph, a much improved postal service, new-style newspapers, and by the end of the century near universal literacy. These new means of spreading ideas and information deserve discussion alongside more visible and conspicuous methods. The framework of this chapter is not, then, how it moved (or was moved), but what moved, and how far, and where? Geographers have often employed this approach, studies of the 'journey to work' for example, and it appears equally appropriate for areas which they have neglected such as information and finance; hopefully it will also prove applicable to coal, corn and commuters. But firstly the distinction between movement inland and overseas must be made.

OVERSEAS

There was only one way of leaving Britain during the nineteenth century — by sea. This might be the 20 or so miles to Calais or the 12,000 to the Antipodes, but in either case there was no alternative to a sea voyage — no airports, no hovercraft, and only the idea of a Channel Tunnel.[3] Nevertheless the nineteenth century witnessed the transformation of every aspect of this maritime traffic; Brittania ruled the waves, commercially as well as militarily, from a position of much loftier and lonelier pre-eminence at the end of the century than at the beginning. By 1914 one-third of the world's merchant shipping — and one half of launchings — were British. Sail had yielded to steam as the steamer had progressed from a primitive and pioneering toy to a peak of near perfection. There is a strong case for regarding the great passenger, or even cargo, liner of the 1890s as the apogee of nineteenth-century technical and organisational attainment. Not only the ships but their management and operations had been transformed, by their owners and operators, by government intervention, by telegraphy.

Britain attained an unquestioned, albeit not unchallenged, maritime supremacy only in the latter half of the century, and as much by accident as by design. It was not only a question of British economic development being dependent upon and the generator of more traffic, for the carrying trade for third parties was a major part of Britain's maritime activity. Nor was it merely the abundance of coal and iron which allowed Britain to take the lead in the technical revolution in ship construction. Britain's principal maritime rival in the early nineteenth century, the U.S.A., suffered greatly from the Civil War, its timing particularly unfortunate from the maritime point of view. The repeal of the protective Navigation Acts in 1849 and 1854 although resisted by British shipowners proved to be to their benefit and demonstrated that most foreign owners were unable to compete in most trades.

Commercial pre-eminence emerged in the two decades 1850-1870; the technical transformation was protracted. If *Charlotte Dundas* (1802) was the first steamer and *Comet* (1812) the first commercial steamer, only about 70 years later did the nominal carrying capacity of British steam exceed that of sail. As late as 1900 it was no problem to obtain a passage to Australia by sail and many of the minor ports of Britain were still concerned largely with sailing vessels. Until the compound steam engine was developed in the 1860s the commercial possibilities of the steam engine were limited by high fuel consumption — which raised costs and limited cargo space — and a limited infrastructure of coaling stations. Steamers were effectively limited to short routes and/or high value traffic, commonly combined in passenger routes. These were the steamer's first area of success so that by 1825 so many were competing for Belfast-Glasgow passengers that the first class fare was 2s (10p), the deck passage free.[4] Customers were ready to pay for the speed and regularity which steam alone, and from early in its history, could provide. On longer routes, the North Atlantic or via the Mediterranean or to India, suitable steamships were slower to develop and a government mail subsidy was essential for viability. On this basis private enterprise, the Pensinular and Oriental (P.&O.) for example, could oust the old East Indiamen and the Admiralty Mail service. The mails also mattered for short routes such as the Channel Islands.[5] By 1860 mail subsidies were costing the government a million pounds a year, a modest price however for so much improved a service. Long haul bulk cargoes remained the realm of sail until the end of the century and some of these trades, newly developed, were ideal for the large sailing vessel. Australian wool for example came from a distant continent by a route remote from bunkering stations and favourable to sail because of the strong westerly winds of the Southern Hemisphere. Even the first cargoes of frozen mutton from New Zealand in 1881 came under sail, a decade and a half after Holt had introduced the first economical long-range cargo steamers in 1865. He operated iron-built, compound-engined, screw-propelled steamers in the rich China trade, where the Suez Canal was to add to steam's advantages; he soon had his successful imitators. As steamers grew bigger so they needed proportionately less power and were cheaper to run; as the steamer became ubiquitous so did the market for British steam coal. Freight rates fell markedly − it had cost £6 to ship a ton of cotton to Shanghai in 1866, £2 in 1913. This was one element in the possibility and actuality of a greater dependence on world trade − 'international trade . . . ceased to be an affair of luxuries and became instead a constant daily procession of indispensable necessities'[6] − and a great increase in tonnage. British ports handled 18.5 million tons of shipping in 1855, 139 million tons in 1912.

The transformation was organisational as well as techno-logical and geographical. The passenger liner, the tramp, and the shipping company are nineteenth-century creations and only the cargo liner (plate 20) can be regarded as a close relative of an early nineteenth-century pattern of operations, the East Indianman or Newfoundland trader for example, working as nearly to a fixed schedule as the elements allowed. Regularity depended on steam, and passenger liners also needed a sure flow of traffic generated on the one hand by new prosperity, on the other by old adversity − emigration. Thus such well known lines as Cunard (1840) and Royal Mail (1840) were set up, though their present form reflects subsequent amalgamations, each specialising in a particular area and set of routes. The tramp[7] arrives later, in the 1880s and 1890s; bulk cargoes had long been carried, but the tramp in its classical form was created by the conjunction of cheap steamers and a worldwide telegraph network. By 1914 they dominated world trade although their eventual rival, the specialist bulk carrier, had already appeared on the scene in the guise of the oil tanker. Moreover oil was starting to displace coal as a fuel. It was the tramp rather than the liner which ousted sail from its last strongholds in overseas and coastwise trade. The role of the telegraph was to give the owner continuous and worldwide commercial control over operations, so increasingly he came to be a London or Liverpool based limited company. After 1875 he was also likely, outside the North Atlantic and tramp trades, to participate in a conference, fixing rates and schedules to his own, and less certainly his customer's, advantage.

Each one of these changes, aided by the railways, acted to concentrate foreign trade more and more onto a few major ports. From an early stage these assisted the process by opening new docks and building more and better warehouses. Liverpool had six docks by 1796 and during the nineteenth century the longest interval between dock openings in the port was only 12 years. London saw a particularly intense period of activity early in the century — it had no docks in 1796, six by 1811. The lesser ports declined relatively and in many cases absolutely. Poole lost its 300-year old Newfoundland and Mediterranean trade for example; Weymouth came to concentrate on old and new Channel Island traffic (plate 21), passengers and potatoes for example, largely to the exclusion of a wider range of continental and coastwise trades. New technology, new telegraphs, new trades transformed a maritime geography of the small, the dispersed, the occasional, into a new geography of the large, the concentrated and the regular.

GOODS

The most general and diverse group of commodities — alum and antimacassars, ale and apples — presents the widest range of alternative, competing, and at times replacing, transport possibilities. As in the 1970s it also presented in the nineteenth century the largest number of special cases, exceptions and anomalies. Thus the Railway Clearing House soon found that any classification brings problems — its own initial (1842) six class (five plus special and exclusions) system had grown to a book of 129 pages by 1879 even though based on the simple

Figure 29. Canals and inland waterways of Britain c. 1820. Note that only in central England and central Scotland was there any kind of continuous system. (Redrawn from Hadfield, C.M., *The Canal Age*, Newton Abbot, 1968, fig. 3.)

idea of value. Pictures, poultry (alive) and silk (manufactured), to name but three 5th (and highest) class items of the 1852 list raise the separate problems of fragility, perishability, and pillageability.

Most early nineteenth-century railway promoters set out to solve the problem of the cost of the carriage of bulky goods.

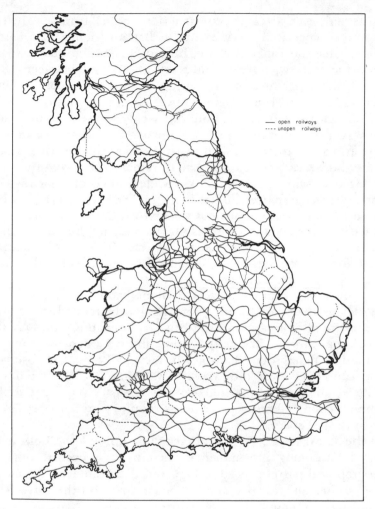

Figure 30. The railways of Britain in 1872. By this date the network was approaching its maximum extent; compare with figure 29. (Redrawn from *Report on Railway Amalgamations*, 1872.)

The railway as we know it grew out of local solutions, coalfield solutions in particular, to this problem, and from efforts to find alternatives to the coaster and canal and their limitations. These flourished in the early nineteenth century; the second canal boom was as late as the 1820s (figure 29) and the Tyne coal trade required as much shipping as the whole overseas trade. But even in the lowland zone many areas were remote from ports and, even after two construction booms, from canals. The railways penetrated every corner of Britain (figure 30), depriving coaster and canal of some, but not all of their business, and reducing waterway freight rates by about half between 1820 and 1866. Their success was neither instantaneous nor absolute, for as late as 1863 eight times as much traffic between Edinburgh/Glasgow and London went by sea as by rail;[8] railway companies had to learn the art and science of railway operation and to create such institutions as the Clearing House. Water-borne carriage, sea or canal, remained optimal for some goods over wide areas and for a wider range of goods within narrower geographical limits. Only in 1867 did more rail than sea coal come to London, and the Oxford Canal was carrying as much traffic in in the 1860s as 40 years earlier, but at one-third of the price to pay one quarter of the dividend. In whatever way goods were carried they generally began and ended their journey by horse and cart, the forgotten transport medium of the nineteenth century. Pickfords alone had 4,000 horses in the 1820s for their fast Birmingham-London boats and, moreover, the coalfield alternative to the canal system, the tramway, also used some horses, just as the whole industry depended on the horse for underground haulage. In fact, as Perkin has observed, one consequence of the railways was that 'more horse drawn vehicles than ever appeared on the roads',[9] requiring skilled labour, country-bred replacements, country-grown oats, and a great deal of space.

The railways did not take over the whole of the bulk trade but in attaining pre-eminence therein they evened out the geographical pattern of advantage and disadvantage inherent in the coaster and canal system. Their impact on the carriage of small consignments of more valuable goods — 'parcels' — was more rapid. The growth of business, of the economy as a whole, in the nineteenth century necessitated such a cheap, speedy and reliable service. The coach, the canal, the carrier's cart could not offer all of these simultaneously, and only in the cities could the pedestrian messenger offer an adequate service — as he still does in some cases. The railways were quick to see and seize the opportunity, and in the absence of competition could maintain rates high enough to pay a good profit. Sometimes they used the experience, personnel, and infrastructure of old-established firms, Pickfords for example, and they also developed their own essential organisation for an effective nationwide service, the Clearing House. This institution acted for the railways in obstructing, and preventing, the establishment of a rival for traffic of this kind, the Post Office Parcel Post, until 1883.

Bulk freight and parcels did not make up the whole goods traffic: a variety of other potentially lucrative, albeit practically inconvenient, business awaited development. From the late 1860s the railways handled the greater part of London's rapidly growing milk demand, likewise — on a smaller scale — in other cities. Perishable fruit and vegetables similarly depended on the railways in many instances — only when an integrated railway and steamer service was provided via Weymouth did the Channel Island tomato trade flourish. Livestock belongs to a similar category, for the railways killed the traditional pattern of movement of lean beasts from Wales and Scotland 'on the hoof' to such markets as Horsham St Faith, and replaced it by a fatstock and dead meat trade serving weekly or daily markets. Towns such as Craven Arms grew up on this basis. The steamer could however still rival the railway for some of the live traffic, from Aberdeenshire to London for example, not because it was speedier or cheaper but because the beasts were delivered in better condition.

The railways grew out of a set of local solutions to a 'goods' problem and though their passenger business soon captured the public and entrepreneurial imagination, by 1852 goods traffic had regained the role of provider of the greater part of the revenue. The railway companies were busily purchasing, neglecting, and less often closing, the canals, reducing them to a local, feeder role; they were cutting back the sphere of influence of the now diminishing number of ports engaged in coastwise trade to a thin fringe within which the railway itself was often a feeder and distributor. The small amount of long-distance road traffic extant in 1800 was taken over and massively developed; the old economic disadvantage of an inland location had largely, but not wholly, disappeared. 'The major contribution of the railways was not so much to lower freight charges . . . as to quicken bulk transport and to extend it to areas beyond the reach of canals'.[10] Flexibility and speed as much as cheapness were the railway's advantages, but it remained dependent on the horse as a distributor and vulnerable to the horseless carriage as a competitor.

PASSENGERS

The travelling public of nineteenth-century Britain was as diverse and varied as its goods, in the purposes for which it travelled, in the length of its purse, in the time at its disposal. The century of the railway was the first in which the common man — proverbially on the Clapham omnibus[11] — might also expect to undertake an occasional long-distance excursion. The Great Exhibition of 1851 was perhaps the first, certainly the best known, but by no means the only such occasion. The journey to work was not a nineteenth-century creation, but nineteenth-century developments provided a range of alternative methods which substantially extended its geographical limits for the greater part of the population. The amalgam of alternatives is however like the iceberg; what is concealed and unseen is more remarkable than what is evident and conspicuous.

For by far the largest group throughout the century the journey to work was a walk. As early as 1836 100,000 pedestrians crossed London Bridge daily. In 1854 four times as many people walked to work in London as used any other method; a survey of trades unionists — skilled and unskilled — in South London in 1896 revealed that only one quarter ever used public transport. In some areas there was no alternative — the farm labourer walked up to four or five miles to work,[12] some country children almost as far to school — and even the workmens' trains and the trams were too costly for some of those they were intended to serve. Society was adjusted and accumstomed to pedestrianism — it may even have preferred it. Jagger's clerk, Wemmick, in *Great Expectations* walked in to work each day from Walworth to Smithfield even though he could probably have afforded to use a bus; Liverpool's suburban expansion in the period 1831-1871 scarcely extends beyond walking distance from the city centre. A large number of the casually and irregularly employed had to live close to where they were likeliest to find work — the docks, the markets — but the overall impression is of a pedestrian society, adjusted to this norm, accepting its advantages, and tolerating the high urban densities it necessitated. No doubt this was one reason why the Sunday excursion was so popular. The decline of pedestrianism is primarily a twentieth-century phenomenon, the impact of the car on the affluent society, but with one major and one minor exception. From the late 1880s the bicycle came into common use, considerably extending the distance which working men could travel to work, and in cities the telephone made it possible to do without large numbers of hitherto commercially indispensable messengers.

The walker was as pre-eminent in the journey to work as the horse in the carriage of goods; for the rest — the minority — there remained several possibilities. A few possessed their own carriage and rather more could run to the habitual or occasional cab. Neither was used exclusively for the journey to work, but this was the role in which they were most susceptible to competition from the horse bus and the tram. These were cheaper, they were increasingly efficient, and by the late nineteenth century they were in competition with the private owner for horses, fodder and labour. The private carriage, as Thompson has pointed out, had become a financial burden of some weight by the last decades of the century. The hansom cab suffered like the messenger from the advent of telegraphy and the telephone. Early in the century river steamers, and to a lesser extent canal fly-boats, enjoyed some short-lived success with commuters as well as long-distance passengers, but the real alternatives to walking to work were the bus, the tram, the railway. On the whole the railways sought out this traffic reluctantly, even those eventually involved on a large scale such as the Great Eastern. Their fares were high, their stations generally on the periphery of the city centre, necessitating a walk, a cab, or a bus, and large numbers of stopping trains on lines used by more and more expresses raised considerable operating problems. The underground 'cut and cover' lines built in London from the 1850s proved over-capitalised and unre-munerative (save to landowners and experts among promoters) like many main lines and were not initially oriented towards suburban traffic but to a role within the city. Here they competed, with no great success, with bus and tram; the great days of the commuter railway came with extensive electrific-ation in the twentieth century.

The omnibus and the tram ruled supreme in the nineteenth century and proved extremely profitable. 'Not the form but the use of the vehicle . . . [was] revolutionary'[13] and even here it has its antecedents in the carrier's cart and short stage journeys in the first decades of the century; by the 1830s the horse bus was established, in the form which was to persist, providing a cheap, convenient, flexible, and profitable service over a radius of about five or six miles. On this basis the London General Omnibus Company often paid a 12½% dividend in the 1880s although by then the tram (horse, electric, or steam) had appeared as a rival. (In London however trams did not serve the central areas.) Between them in London in 1896 horse buses and trams carried almost half as many passengers again as the railways. They were particularly favoured in the last quarter of the century by falling cereal prices, their fuel costs and a large part of their current outlay. On the other hand the horse bus was unwieldy, space consuming (on the road and off it), slow, and created a noise and dirt problem (plates 22 and 23) - no Victorian novel is complete without a crossing sweeper and straw laid in the streets outside an invalid's window.

The limits of the city and its suburbs throughout the nineteenth century were very largely fixed by the horse and the pedestrian; the upper middle class might commute by rail from Brighton, the middle middle class by bus, the lower middle class by tram, the working man on foot! Some suburbs, Edmonton for example, owed almost everything to the railway, but its 'contribution to (urban) growth was shared with other more modest forms of transport to an extent often overlooked'.[14]

It was for long-distance travel, inter-city or from province to metropolis, that the railway met with most success, captured the public imagination, and made its most conspicuous impact on the landscape. Before 1850, when the railways linked almost all major towns and cities and the Railway Clearing House had ironed out practical problems resulting from a multiplicity of companies, it was quite possible to travel long distances by canal or in some cases by sea. But even at the peak of their efficiency around 1830 coaches were slow, costly, and uncomfortable; the prodigious itineraries of Dickens the journalist or Macready the actor were achieved by extreme − perhaps excessive and damaging − effort, no longer needed when the railways were operating. For members of such occupations, for businessmen and bookmakers for example, the express train was a boon; the working man neither needed it nor could afford it. If the excursion return from Leeds to the Great Exhibition was, at 5s (25p), within his means, the normal single fare of 35s

(£1.75) was not; only such special circumstances as the admittedly increasingly common move of job by the skilled man to a fairly distant city were exceptions. Nor did the railways encourage working men to take long journeys any more than to commute; even 'parliamentary' trains[15] were relatively expensive, often inconveniently timed, and sometimes the only daily third class train. Sabbatarians managed to restrict Sunday services and thus the occasional recreational journey. It is scarcely surprising that nineteenth-century expresses were small trains, four or five little coaches full of commercial travellers and boarding school pupils — two activities transformed by the railway — of maiden aunts and governesses.

At a more local level the impact of the railway was less complete. The coach and carrier's cart continued to serve country towns, some cross-country routes poorly served by the railways, and pre-eminently the railway station itself, often a new focus of growth for urban expansion. The coach proper proved very persistent; there was a London-Wendover coach as late as 1892. Likewise the carrier who sometimes turned himself into a bus and lorry owner — as did blacksmith into garage proprietor — early this century. Until the end of the century no aspect of the railway business could be carried on without horses, whether owned by the railway or meeting its needs at another's behest.

It was, as has already been noted, for recreation, for an annual or Sunday excursion, that most people were likely first to use the railway; as leisure, and the money to enjoy it, increased, so did travel. The early steamers were soon in this kind of business, on the Thames and Clyde for example — Margate received 17,000 passengers a year in 1812-13, 105,000 in 1855-6 — where they have retained this role. For the railways, and despite sabbatarian pressures, Sunday was often the busiest day for passengers — the city dweller, the Londoner especially, loved a day in the country and now he could afford and enjoy it. For a smaller section of the population the railway made possible the annual holiday, by the sea for the most part, and was thus the creator or at least the animator of many resorts. But again recreation had a pedestrian aspect; early in the nineteenth century Manchester cotton workers commonly walked to Blackpool — over 40 miles — a traffic which, formalised into 'wakes week', passed to the railways. The countryman as usual walked everywhere, and some recreations were almost universally pedestrian — courting for example. For rural recreation the safety bicycle, ousting and much improving upon the 'ordinary' (penny farthing) in the 1880s was a breakthrough towards mobility and freedom.

It is scarcely surprising that the railway established its public image and reputation in terms of the express rather than the suburban train, of the great rural engineering triumphs — Saltash Bridge, Shap summit — rather than intricate and often inconspicuous urban routes. In these former it had no rivals. Its success with holidays and excursions, its very creations, is more remarkable but it was never quite the sole agency involved. The journey to work, where its part is now taken for granted, was an area of more limited activity, the sphere primarily of pedestrian, horse, and eventually bicycle. These, and their institutional framework, set relatively restricted limits to nineteenth-century urban expansion at the same time as the railways were breaking down at least technical constraints on long-distance movement.

INFORMATION

The movement of information and ideas is less often looked at by geographers than that of goods or people, but information and ideas have to be spread and disseminated through space, and the means available for this were transformed during the nineteenth century. Specialised new technologies played their part — telegraphy, better printing presses — and so did means of distribution — the railway, and the steamer. Their effectiveness depended largely on educational advance, in particular on the elimination of illiteracy. An illiterate society is a society of individuals and groups isolated from one another except when they can meet in person or, uncertainly, through a third party: 'An illiterate maidservant living ten miles from home was cut off from her parents and her brothers and sisters far more effectively than a factory worker in Coventry is separated today from his mother and sister in Glasgow'.[16] In 1800 probably one-third of all males in England and Wales were illiterate, and an even higher proportion of females — by contrast literacy was almost the norm in Scotland. Since there were areas of relatively high literacy in England and Wales, London and the rural north for example, there were also areas of majority illiteracy, much of the rural lowland zone for example, persisting into mid-century. By 1870, the year of Forster's Education Act, four adults in five were literate and by 1900 near universal literacy had been attained, the prerequisite for communicating news, information and ideas by means of the printed word.

The conquest of illiteracy was accompanied by many other favourable circumstances like a shorter working week, higher wages and cheaper travel. Two particular aspects deserve consideration, newspapers and the Post Office, which were ranked by as shrewd a contemporary commentator as Disraeli[17] alongside the more conspicuous railway as key instruments of social change. The expansion of the newspaper industry in the second half of the century owed something to the final abolition of duties and taxes on the Press in 1855, more to the development of a largely literate public. At the same time the telegraph enabled newspapers to become more attractively up to the minute, first with home, later with foreign news. There were nine London dailies in 1830, 22 in 1865; 200 provincial dailies and weeklies in 1846 had passed 750 by 1865, an even faster rate of increase which owed something to the fact that breakfast table delivery of London dailies throughout the country became possible only at the end of the century. The coffee shop gave early nineteenth-century newspapers a wider influence than their small circulation might suggest and contemporary governments might have wished; as they attained mass circulation they turned away from their old role of political ideology and debate towards the supply of more news — local and international — and advertisement, both in bulk. Indeed it might well be argued that from being a menace to the nation's stability they turned to being a menace to its health.[18] Advertisements were not universally pernicious: they played a useful role in putting the reader in touch with the market place, in many cases much more important to him, as well as the metropolis. Nor was the specialist neglected — to cite but two examples, *The Lancet* first appeared in 1823, *The Mining Journal* in 1835.

The expansion and cheapening of postal services broadly parallels that of the Press and slightly precedes the educational revolution. The post Office quickly took to the railway and the steamer, but the creation of the Penny Post in 1840 (plate 24) followed some years of agitation and discussion. It was a dramatic abolition of bureaucracy, taxation, and geography, but as Cobden pointed out in 1841 'all . . . over-rated the immediate advantage of the change to the working class. They are too often unable to write'.[19] Nevertheless where 82 million letters were handled in 1839 there were 2,300 million by 1900. Between 1850 and 1864 delivery services were reorganised so that by the latter date 94 per cent of all letters were delivered, and delivery became a right in 1897.[20] The telegraph service was taken over by the Post Office in 1870, 25 years after it had begun and four years after it crossed the Atlantic; within two years 5,000 post offices were also telegraph offices. Telephone services were acquired more gradually — and not quite completely — between 1892 and 1911. Parcel post, for reasons already discussed, was the area of slowest development, delayed with the exception of some much abused special services, such as book and sample post, until 1883. A regional example serves to summarise progress. Thus in Rutland:

   1848—13 post offices (of which 2 money order) i.e. one office to about 1,600 people.

   1900—33 post offices (of which 12 money order and telegraph, only 13 purely postal) i.e. one to about 600 people.

   The letter had ceased to be an event and had become a commonplace.

MONEY

'The renovation of the economy of Britain during the nineteenth century may be regarded, in one sense, as an act of continuous mobilisation of capital',[21] a movement however of which geographers have taken little notice. This mobilisation was primarily the concern of the banks, but other agencies were involved — insurance companies, even the Post Office. The Post Office Savings Bank (1861) was not only a public service but a source of government borrowing in a formerly almost untapped area.

   In early nineteenth century England and Wales there was on the one hand the Bank of England, on the other numerous private banks. The law limited the number of partners in a bank to six so they were essentially local affairs, the Bank of England excepted, operating in no more than a few towns or part of a county; as yet they were by no means always detached from their mercantile or industrial origins. Banking was a growth industry, the 230 banks of 1797 had become 721 by 1810, but not a reliable one — 240 banks failed in the crisis of 1814-16. Well into the century a 'novelist could always give the story a fresh turn by bringing the local bank crashing down';[22] the City of Glasgow Bank which failed in 1878 (with unlimited liability[23]) was in fact at least a regional concern. Failure often resulted from misfortune and geographical isolation rather than mismanagement or national economic trends, so much so that a commentator in 1822 noted that 'no person in the more northern counties will take a Bank of England note if he can help it',[24] an indication of preference for the known and local over the unknown and distant. Law, local pride and practical managerial considerations all favoured local banks in the first decades of the nineteenth century. As late as 1847 difficulty of communication was the reason why the Doncaster branch of a Wakefield bank was taken over by a Doncaster firm and only exceptional concerns took the plunge into geographical extension as soon as changes in the law (1826-33) allowed banks to become joint stock companies.[25] The National Provincial, as its name implies, was among these.

Country banks were small local businesses but they needed a London bank as their agent to do their City and Bank of England business. The agent's role might be spectacular, to provide gold to a partner who had ridden or coached through the night in order that a run on the bank might be met. More important and persistent was the steady accumulation in the hands of these London banks of the funds of country banks in rural southern and eastern England, where investment opportunities were few, and their use to discount bills for banks[26] in the industrial Midlands and North where local funds fell short of local demands (figure 31). The banks were the mechanism of transfer of capital from the old rural to the new urban and industrial society, an instrument of geographical change. This capital was short-term, used to finance stocks of raw materials and finished goods in transit rather than manufacturing industry in general. Save in a few special cases, canals and railways for

Figure 31. The geographical distribution of note-issuing licences, 1822. Note the concentration in Yorkshire and the agricultural south and west. (Source: Pressnel, L.S., *Country Banking in the Industrial Revolution*, Oxford, 1956, table IX.)

example, where country banks were very active, this latter need had to be met elsewhere until late in the century. Other funds were channelled into foreign investment, creating the City's international role and Britain's continuing, albeit diminished, invisible income. Financial mechanisms and institutions changed during the century; the inter-regional flow of capital described above was crucial to economic growth early in the century but became less important as private banks gave way to joint stock and as industrial areas came to comprise the bulk of the nation's wealth. New financial agencies also possessed a regional elem-ent; the investment trusts of 1868 onwards, a means of organising British overseas investment (in North America in particular), were and are largely Scottish and particularly associated with Dundee.

The increasing importance of joint stock banks, London and provincial, and the decline in private country banking followed legislative changes in 1826-33, 1844 and 1862.[27] However these did not always favour the kinds of changes the bankers sought — fusions of country and metropolitan banks between 1844 and 1861 for example. The changed situation arose from the inadequacy of local banks in a context of rapidly expanding economic activity, and from better communications. As late as 1914 a private country banker hastened to London by train to collect gold during a crisis, but generally the railway and the telegraph made such drama unnecessary, facilitating consultation, forestalling crisis. Nevertheless banks remained relatively localised until late in the century, and inter-bank competition outside the larger towns was restrained and muted. In 1870 the average number of branches per joint stock bank was only nine, and even in 1918 the amalgamation which produced Lloyds Bank was virtually unrepresented in the north outside Tyneside.

Some comparison with the railways may be appropriate at this point. Each was a medium of communication made up of localised parts — much more so in the case of the banks — subject to some government control but not so much so as to prevent frequent calamity, the bank failure, the projected and funded but never executed railway, or even collision. Localised units gave way to regional units earlier in the railway than the banking world. Certain centralised institutions appear in mid-century — the Railway Clearing House, the Country Bankers Clearing House (1858: London banks had long possessed a clearing house) — but amalgamation into 'big four' and 'big five'[28] awaited the twentieth century and was more strongly regional in the case of the railways. The analogy is not exact but the parallels suggest that the great importance attached by geographers to the railways against the apparent insignificance of the banks, is at worst a travesty and at best an imbalance in the geography of nineteenth-century Britain.

Scottish banks were precocious by English standards. By 1800 there were already some banks with nationwide branches like the Royal Bank, the British Linen Bank (indicating its mercantile origins), as well as numerous local banks. Scottish law facilitated branch banking and favoured stability, although limited liability was adopted by banks not chartered in this form only after the 1878 catastrophe. In 1864 the largest Scottish bank with branches had no fewer than 103, the smallest nine — as many as the English average in 1870. A distinctive geography reflected a distinctive legality and an agreement on both sides not to compete across the border.

The Post Office acted as a means of financial communication (as opposed to capital mobilisation already discussed) by providing alternatives to the risky business of sending coin or notes by post. The first such, the money order, begun as a private venture by Post Office staff in 1792, was taken over in 1838 and the poundage reduced in 1840. As a result sales increased threefold. Postal Orders were created in 1883 as a cheap and simple means of transferring small sums which could be purchased (but not paid) at almost any office. How far they were used is uncertain — how, how often, how much (if at all), did rural migrants send money home?[29] — but at least a simple and nationwide service had been set up.

MARKETS AND SHOPS

The distributive apparatus of nineteenth-century Britain served a society where for the most part the seller and his wares were more mobile than the buyer, and where low wages limited the latter to a narrow range of goods and services. The itinerant pedlar or chapman, the weekly or more frequent market for perishables, the annual or occasional fair for durables met the needs of most people to a greater degree than did shops in a central place in the early nineteenth century: perhaps the manufacturer's 'tommy shop' can be considered to belong to the same class, taking goods to people on the canals and in the isolated coal and iron communities, as well as in their more usual and unfavourable light. General and specialised shops served villages and towns, but a wide range of the latter existed only in the towns and to meet middle and upper class needs. These groups had the time to go shopping, the money to pay the price of assembling and preparing a variety of products from a diversity of sources, then the essence of the grocer's trade. A number of shopkeepers such as bakers, tailers and cobblers were still producers (plate 36).

The itinerant salesman and the fair, but not the market, were beginning to lose their hold during the first half of the century. Better roads and faster coaches favoured shopkeepers and particularly the commercial traveller selling by sample. These were numerous by the 1820s and the railways, the telegraph and the penny post greatly facilitated their task and enabled them to offer better service to retailers. The market retained its role however, not only as a matter of custom and convenience, but as the best way of selling perishables. Railways and later refrigerators revolutionised some perishable trades, the supply of fresh milk for example, and enhanced the size and status of some wholesale markets,[30] but popular prejudice against chilled or frozen meat gave way but slowly and the suburban market gardener with his pony and trap enjoyed some indestructible advantages over his competitors. Markets moreover produced a municipal revenue and were popular with purchasers if not shopkeepers — further reasons for their persistence. The producer-retailer or processor-retailer was strongly entrenched in these trades and as late as 1900 the butcher was usually concerned with buying, finishing, slaughtering, and cutting — and thus with the movement of large numbers of animals into the towns — as well as with selling meat.[31]

Despite this persistence of (and some preference for) old methods there was a conspicuous retailing revolution. From 1844 in Rochdale the cooperatives provided comprehensive shops to meet working class needs. They operated in Scotland and the north in particular, and in the process also discovered the advantages of branch operation and of backward integration into production. Each was made possible by better communications and allowed better and cheaper service. Other shops soon took to the branch system, first the specialist newsagents, then — and most famously — the grocery and footwear trades, and by the 1890s the tailors. They too integrated backwards and overseas, for example Lipton's tea estates, or in some instances were a manufacturer's forward integration, as in the case of Freeman Hardy and Willis in footwear. In the process the shop became nothing more than a point of sale, dependent on railway and Post Office to link it to the factory or warehouse. On such a basis Liptons grew from one shop in 1872 to 245 in 1898, a total of 978 multiple store outlets in 1878 to 11,645 in 1900. The cooperatives alone numbered 1,400 societies and 1.7 million members (perhaps 7 million consumers) by 1900. The old-fashioned retailer was threatened, although he is not yet extinct, not only by multiples and cooperatives, which created a market as much as they competed for it, since the city centre department store (and its branches) grew rapidly, usually originating in the drapery trade, from about 1860. As their architecture so often shows their golden age came between 1880 and 1914 and depended on the creation of a substantial urban middle class market — to make their high-turnover, low-mark-up policy practicable — and on means of transport to convey purchaser and purchase — the horse bus, tram and suburban railway. In turn their specialist adaptation to mundane needs and mass markets, the 'penny bazaar', Woolworths, Marks and Spencer, had appeared by the end of the century.

By 1900 mobility had substantially passed from seller to buyer, from part-processed goods or raw materials to finished and marketable products advertised on a national basis. Railways, steamers, the parcel post, higher wages, a shorter working day and week, had enabled shop and store to triumph over pedlar and fair. The market kept much, the producer-retailer some, importance; only the supermarket remained for the twentieth century to make.

MOVEMENT AND ENVIRONMENT

The direct visual and environmental impact of the steamers, railways and canals, of a whole nineteenth-century revolution in movement and mobility, is too easily and too often exaggerated. The railways and steamers provided one base for the huge expansion of the coal and iron trades; the railways in particular captured the public imagination because of their novelty, and the conspicuously monumental character of one part of their capital investment. An ephemeral, and often flamboyantly alien labour force built embankments and excavated tunnels and cuttings on a hitherto unknown scale, dramatised by artists such as Bourne, writers such as Dickens. But even more remarkable is the speed with which abhorrence gave way to approval, and with which the railway, like the canal, merged into the rural landscape, much more so than twentieth-century motorways.

Only in the towns might the railway long remain conspicuously obtrusive (plate 7), in the cases where it had to be elevated, because it required large — and often ostentatious — terminal facilities, and because a high density of traffic made the dirt and noise problem only too evident to too many people. In any event the nineteenth-century city was both dirty and noisy, thanks to horsedrawn traffic on cobbled streets, inadequate drainage and sewerage, the factory whistle as well as its chimney, the hawker. These were not new in the nineteenth century but their scale was greatly increased. Ships and harbours had of course a localised impact, and the roads had always been there; improved surfaces were evident only at close quarters and completely new roads were few, the urban areas excepted. Telegraph, penny post, bank and multiple store had the minimal impact of the occasional new, albeit often assertive, building; only the concentrations of department stores in the West End for example late in the century represent an exception. Outside the towns then new means of movement were soon a no more than modestly obvious addition to the landscape, at most a massive bridge to rival the splendour of a medieval castle;[32] in the towns and cities of the 1870s a perceptive time traveller of the 1770s would probably not lose his way — as he so often would today — but he would certainly marvel at railways and comment on canals, shops, and the ubiquitous and variously employed horse; he would perhaps go on to put these in a wider context of growth and change.

The striking change was not the new media and their appearance but their ready acceptance as an instrument of economic and social change. Their impact had some unlikely components — the popularity of Landseer owes something to the new accessibility of the wilder and savager parts of Britain, Scotland in particular. The Queen could set up a summer residence, the middle class family take a holiday there in the railway age. The impact of a new mobility is not however restricted to exotica. An export economy assumed and depended upon means of assembling and financing imported and local raw materials and shipping manufactures; the conurbation presupposed other means of travelling to work than on foot — the bicycle, the bus, the tram, the train — and a reliable supply of cheap food (perishables included) drawn from a wide area. The repeal of the Corn Laws in 1846 and the decision to allow British farming to decay during the last quarter of the century reflected not only the existence of supplies elsewhere but of means to move them and money to pay for them. On the whole the later Victorians took all this for granted even while searching for better solutions. The social and economic inconvenience of many functionally and financially acceptable means of transport certainly led to a quest for alternatives, such as the railways themselves early in the century, later a steam engine which condensed, electric road traction and the horseless carriage (quiet and pollution free as it then appeared!) but only in a narrow sense, railway rates for example, was the adequacy of existing media challenged when economic and social problems were discussed. After all they did represent a great advance. It seems strange in the 1970s that the horseless carriage (quiet and pollution free as it then appeared!). But only given up save in a few special cases, and even more remarkable that the telephone spread so slowly. What the Victorians posessed seemed adequate to them in terms of comparison with the past, of cost (at least in direct terms), of the needs of the times and of its ability to cope with rapid economic growth. Pressures and possibilities of radical change awaited a new century.

NOTES

1 Perkin, H., *The Age of the Railway*, Newton Abbot, 1971.
2 In a delightful inaugural lecture, *Victorian England: The Horsedrawn Society* , London, 1970.
3 First mooted in 1812: short pilot tunnels were drilled in 1881.
4 Presumably in the hope that they might contribute to profits through their consumption of food and drink?
5 Officially, if not in practice, the Channel Island packets running from Weymouth between 1794 and 1845 were simply a mail service, with passengers no more than a sideline and thus a secondary consideration.
6 Thornton, R.H., *British Shipping*, Cambridge (2nd edition), 1959, p. 64.
7 The *Oxford English Dictionary* states that the word was in colloquial use by *c*. 1880, but gives its first literary

reference as 1886.

8 There was also a phase of incomplete railway growth when some Anglo-Scottish traffic, more particularly passengers, went part way by rail and the rest by sea, e.g. London to Glasgow via Fleetwood and Ardrossan in the early 1840s.

9 Perkin, H., op.cit., p. 112.

10 ibid., p. 103.

11 The phrase was coined by Lord Bowen, a High Court judge. The date is uncertain, the judgement in which it appears being unreported, but must be between 1879 and 1894. I would like to thank Professor R.M. Caldwell for helping me to date this expression.

12 One unfortunate consequence of the existence of 'open' and 'close' villages.

13 Hibbs, J., *History of British Bus Services*, Newton Abbot, 1968, p. 29, quoting C.E. Lee.

14 Kellett, J., *The Impact of Railways on Victorian Cities*, London, 1969, p. 419.

15 In 1844 Parliament required each railway company to operate on each working day a train stopping at all stations, maintaining an average speed of not less than twelve miles per hour, composed of carriages with seats protected from the weather, and at a maximum charge of one penny per mile — the 'parliamentary' train.

16 Laslett, P., *The World we have lost*, London, 1971, pp. 205-6.

17 *Endymion*, ch. 12. The immediate context is rural Berkshire.

18 Advertisements for patent medicines — and quacks — abound, and many are so designed (and placed) in the news columns as to be a considerable nuisance to the present-day researcher. Nationwide promotion and availability of such medicines is of course another facet of the communications revolution.

19 Having given evidence before the Select Committee of 1837-8 which recommended the penny post, his subsequent comment was invited.

20 The Post Office work with which Anthony Trollope the novelist was particularly associated in his professional capacity.

21 Checkland, S.G., *The Rise of Industrial Society in England*

1815-1855 , London, 1964, p. 189.

22 Sayers, R.S., *Lloyd's Bank in the History of English Banking*, Oxford, 1957, p. 204.

23 The shareholders were liable for the bank's deficiency not merely to the extent of their own investment in its capital (limited liability, granted to banks in general — their note issue excepted — in 1862 but not commonly acted upon) but to their last penny, the reality of the case for many unfortunate shareholders in this instance.

24 Joplin, T., *On the General Principles and Present Practice of Banking in England and Scotland*, Newcastle upon Tyne, 1822, p. 545.

25 In 1826 outside a radius of 65 miles from London, in 1833 in London provided they did not issue notes.

26 The operation is explained in Sayers, R.S., *Modern Banking*, Oxford (7th edition), 1967, pp. 46-8.

27 See note 25. In 1844 note issue other than by the Bank of England (and in Scotland) was restricted (ceasing only in 1921); the 1862 legislation allowed ten partners but was otherwise restrictive.

28 Southern, Great Western, London and North-Eastern, London Midland and Scottish Railways; Barclay's, Lloyd's, Midland, Westminster, and National Provincial Banks (these last two now amalgamated, of course). There were several other quite large banks, few other railways.

29 In *Lark Rise to Candleford*, Book 3, Flora Thompson gives a classic account of a country post office in the last years of the nineteenth century. In ch. 35 there is mention of (unofficial) extension of opening hours to enable itinerant Irish labourers to purchase postal orders to send home.

30 Stratford Market in east London for example was very much the creation of the Great Eastern Railway.

31 This is still not uncommon in country towns and villages.

32 Surprisingly often in close proximity, at Newcastle upon Tyne and Conway for example.

FURTHER READING

1 OVERSEAS

Fayle, C.E., *A Short History of the World's Shipping Industry,* London, 1933.

Kirkaldy, A.W., *British Shipping,* Newton Abbot (2nd edition), 1970.

Rowland, K.T., *Steam at Sea,* Newton Abbot, 1970.

Thornton, R.H., *British Shipping,* Cambridge (2nd edition), 1959.

2 INLAND TRANSPORT

Bagwell, P.S., *The Railway Clearing House in the British Economy 1842-1922,* London, 1968.

Barker, T.C., 'Passenger transport in nineteenth century London', *Journal of Transport History,* vol. 6, 1963-4, pp. 166-74.

Barker, T.C., and Robbins, M., *A History of London Transport* (Volume 1: *The Nineteenth Century*), London, 1963.

Channon, G., 'The Aberdeenshire beef trade with London: a study in steamship and railway competition 1850-69', *Transport History,* vol. 2, 1969, pp. 1-24.

Copeland, J. *Roads and their Traffic:* 1750-1850, Newton Abbot, 1968.

Dickinson, C.G., 'Stage coach services in the West Riding of Yorkshire between 1830 and 1840', *Journal of Transport History,* vol. 4, 1959, pp. 1-11.

Dyos, H.J., and Aldcroft, D.H., *British Transport,* Leicester, 1969.

Hadfield, C.M., *British Canals,* Newton Abbot (4th ed.), 1969.

Hibbs, J., *History of British Bus Services,* Newton Abbot, 1968.

Kellett, J., *The Impact of Railways on Victorian Cities,* London, 1969.

Margetson, S.J., *Journey by Stages,* London, 1967.

Perkin, H., *The Age of the Railway,* Newton Abbot, 1971.

Perry, P.J., 'Working class isolation and mobility in rural Dorset 1837-1936: a study of marriage distances', *Institute of British Geographers: Transactions,* vol. 46, 1969, pp. 121-41.

Thompson, F.M.L., *Victorian England: The Horsedrawn Society,* London, 1970 (inaugural lecture).

Turnbull, G.L., 'The railway revolution and carrier's response:

Messrs. Pickford and Co. 1830-50', *Transport History*, vol. 2, 1969, pp. 48-71.

Williamson, G., *Wheels with Wheels*, London, 1966 (bicycles).

3   INFORMATION, MONEY AND MARKETS

Aspinall, A., 'The circulation of newspapers in the early nineteenth century', *Review of English Studies*, vol. 22, 1946, pp. 29-43.

Blackman, J., 'The development of the retail grocery trade in the nineteenth century', *Business History*, vol. 9, 1967, pp. 110-17.

Burnett, J., 'The baking industry in the nineteenth century', *Business History*, vol. 5, 1962, pp. 98-105.

Davis, D., *A History of Shopping* London, 1966.

Jefferys, J.B. *Retail Trading in Britain 1850-1950*, Cambridge, 1954.

Kellett, E.E., 'The Press', in Young, G.M., *Early Victorian England*, London, 1934, vol. 2, pp. 1-98.

Paserunadjian, H., *The Department Store*, London, 1954.

Pressnell, L.S., *Country Banking in the Industrial Revolution*, Oxford, 1956.

Robinson, H., *Britain's Post Office*, London, 1953.

Sayers, R.S., *Lloyd's Bank in the History of English Banking*, Oxford, 1957.

Stone, L., 'Literacy and education in England 1640-1900', *Past and Present*, vol. 42, 1969, pp. 69-139.

Sutton, G.B., 'The marketing of ready made footwear in the nineteenth century', *Business History*, vol. 6, 1964, pp. 93-112.

Sykes, J., *The Amalgamation Movement in English Banking 1825-1924*, London, 1926.

Taylor, A.M., *Gillet's: Bankers at Banbury and Oxford*, Oxford, 1964.

Wadsworth, A.P., 'Newspaper circulation 1800-1954', *Transactions of the Manchester Statistical Society*, 1955, pp. 1-40.

7 The Agricultural Interest: Change and Decay

The landowner, the farmer and the labourer usually make their appearance in one of the earlier chapters of any book dealing with past economies and societies. For much of the past such priority is defensible, serving to emphasise the key role of the land in pre-industrial society, but for the nineteenth century, when the pre-eminence of agriculture is markedly on the wane, this priority is less desirable, for however well qualified, it serves to give the reader an exaggerated sense of the importance of farming. Agriculture was pre-eminent in 1800; landowners dominated parliament, farmers the countryside. Over 2,000,000 farmers and farm labourers were the largest occupational group. Only in mid-century did the greater part of Britain's population cease to live in the countryside, and by 1900 agriculture was small beer by comparison with cotton or coal. The contrast lay not so much in terms of occupied space — 85 per cent of the land was still farmed or grazed, albeit often very badly — or even employment, but in terms of contribution to the economy, and above all to exports, to prosperity, and in public esteem. In a society built upon booming export industries agriculture eventually and inevitably became an industry depressed by competitive imports. There were times when agriculture occupied the centre of the stage — the years culminating in Corn Law repeal in 1846 for example — or enjoyed great prosperity as in the 1850s and 1860s, but for the most part the century witnessed the removal of agriculture from a dominant to a subsidiary socio-economic position, from simple and assured prosperity to a state of adversity which could be countered only by enterprise and ingenuity. In general the agricultural interest retired in good order and periods of rout never lasted more than two or three

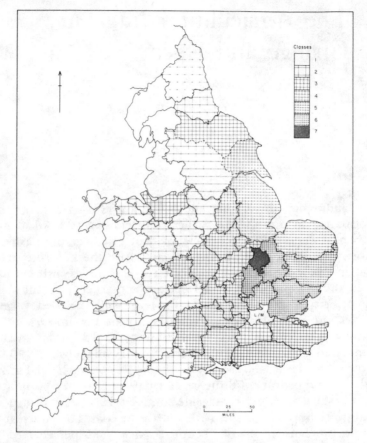

Figure 32. Agricultural failures (assignments and bankruptcies, annual average by counties) 1881-83 as a percentage of the farming population in 1881: 1, less than 0.1%; 2, 0.1% to 0.2%; 3, 0.2% to 0.3%; 4, 0.3% to 0.4%; 5, 0.4% to 0.5%; 6, 0.5% to 0.6%; 7, more than 0.6%; L/M, London and Middlesex. (Source: Perry, P.J., *British Farming in the Great Depression 1870-1914*, Newton Abbot, fig. 1.)

years even in the severe depression of the last quarter of the century (figures 32 and 33). Only in a very few years did agriculture's contribution to the national income diminish. But it was a withdrawal, relative rather than absolute, from prosperity to penury, from prestige to powerlessness.

A sequential typology — Napoleonic prosperity, postwar depression, the splendours of mid-century 'high farming' and the 'great depression' — is commonly used when British farming

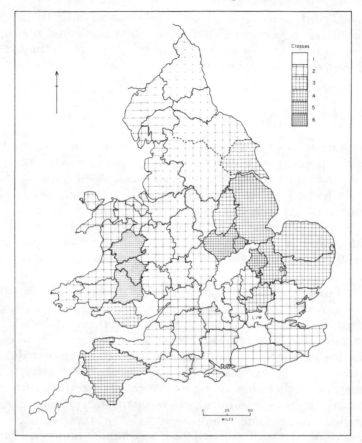

Figure 33. Agricultural failures 1881-83 (a) in relation to agricultural failures 1871-73 (b), (a/b): 1, less than 1.5; 2, 1.5 to 3.0; 3, 3.0 to 4.5; 4, 4.5 to 6.0; 5, 6.0 to 7.5; 6, more than 7.5; L/M, London and Middlesex). Note the general evenness of the incidence of failure compared to figure 32; the high values in some western counties relating to epidemics. (Source: as figure 32, figure 4).

in the nineteenth century is being considered, sometimes with the addition of a third short but severe depression following on Corn Law repeal. The general validity of such an approach can scarcely be questioned, but it requires qualification at almost all points. The prosperity of mid-century for example conceals problems which engendered a shift towards pastoral farming and thus anticipated the depression. A regional approach affords no better solution to these problems, important though regional differences were and local studies are. It is more appropriate to consider firstly the context of change, the forces which were at work and the circumstances in which they acted, and then to examine the changes themselves.

THE CONTEXT OF CHANGE

A rapidly increasing and, for much of the century, increasingly wealthy population provided the most favourable feature of the environment in which the agricultural interest worked. More people had to be fed, and while debate continues as to their standard of living in the first half of the century[1] and certainly while the consumer of 1900 was not the consumer of the 1970s, there is no doubt that the British were much better fed in 1900 than in 1800. Farmers whose products either entered the average man's diet during the century or were transformed from occasional luxuries to everyday necessities were particularly favoured. Thus the dairy farmer, the horticulturalist, even the grazier, prospered more than the traditional arable farmer. Ironically the farmer's preference for engagement in cereal cropping remained very strong, a preference based on habit and social esteem rather than economic returns, a persistent and widespread belief that to be a farmer was to grow corn.[2] By comparison the traditional view, particularly strongly entrenched in wartime conditions early in the century, that Britain must try to feed itself gave way almost imperceptibly to an assumption that a much more populous Britain could and would be fed by the world at large; fears of Napoleonic power gave way to fulmination against high prices, and these to faith in the Pax Brittanica. A larger and richer populace not only ate more food, it occupied more land. By comparison with the present-day situation this competition for space was modest and uncontrolled; but London did spread over the market gardens of Putney and Fulham, Leblanc alkali works devasted Cheshire farms, the new laird's fashionable recreation replaced sheep with grouse or deer. On the whole, population increase favoured the farmer, but not necessarily the British farmer since it took a form which divorced an increasingly large proportion of the population from contact with or understanding of the farming interest and the countryside and its problems. Rural Britain became not the nation's larder but its leisure; the countryman of whatever class was no longer the supplier of essential goods but an anachronism or an irrelevance, be he a reputedly powerful — even wicked — vested interest, an earl or a mere esquire, or a popular subject of derision — toothless and unlettered Hodge.[3]

Nineteenth-century agriculture operated in a legal as well as a demographic framework. Every section of the rural community was subject to legal constraints (and incentives) and to legal intervention; in the century of *laissez faire* these remained somewhat biased in favour of property, maintaining the landlord in a stronger position than his tenant, the farmer than his labourer. This bias was however to be largely broken down if not wholly destroyed by means of agricultural legislation. Some of these laws represented the continuance of an existing situation. In 1800 enclosure by Act of Parliament had been the norm for a century, albeit constantly undergoing modification, and machinery allowing for enclosure without each scheme coming before the legislature was devised only when the process was almost complete.[4] The Napoleonic War witnessed one of the high-water marks of enclosure, both of open fields, in the Midlands in particular, and of wastes and moors, a consequence of high prices and fears for the nation's food supply. Thereafter the nearly but never quite completed operation quickly slackened. Enclosure Acts dealt with property, the Corn Laws with prices — another area of long standing concern.[5] Their repeal marks both the triumph of free trade and the end of a tradition of economic regulation extending back to the Middle Ages. Political and technological circumstance however muted the impact of repeal for nearly 30 years.

In the middle of the century a new legislative pattern emerges, that of selective intervention which, after nearly a century of half-hearted application, transformed British farming from the 1930s. Peel's Public Money Drainage Act of 1846 and its successors encouraged and subsidised the application of a new technology, pipe drains, as well as acting as a modest sop to offended landlowners and farmers. The Agricultural Holdings Acts, of 1883 in particular, ventured to control landlord and tenant relationships, to take away some traditional (landlord) property rights, in the contentious area of the tenant's right to be compensated for the improvements he had made during his tenancy on giving up a farm. The 'whisky money' of 1890,[6] produced by abortive government action in one area, ended up financing agricultural education. In short the conspicuous termination of one kind of legislative support in 1846 is followed by the modest initiation of another kind, more selective and localised, and for a century inadequately protective, but eventually a more satisfactory basis for the prosperity of British farming.

Farming exists not only under the law and to meet the consumers' needs but also in terms of the aspirations of several groups. The largest of these, the public at large, might have summed up their wishes in the phrase 'cheap food', to find them satisfied by the events of 1846 and more generally by an improved agricultural technology. The interests of farmer, landowner and labourer were, in their own view, less satisfactorily met; nor were they wholly economic and rational, each embracing a deal of custom and even ignorance. Nevertheless by 1900 a much greater part of Britain's farming was run as a business than in 1800. The railways, education — both general and technical — hard times, shows and societies, had contributed to a great commercialisation, a realisation that profitable farming now called for the matching — even the measurement — of inputs and outputs. Commercialisation was also one aspect of the rural exodus, of surplus (and often ambitious) labourers, of incompetent or unlucky farmers, of inept or spendthrift landlords. The Victorian belief in progress *per se* was undoubtedly a further element in commercialisation, but progress for progress' sake, so popular in mid-century, could run counter to profitability, a necessary if not total objective for farmer and landlord. Lavish expenditure on drainage, of heavy land in particular, was fashionable and 'progressive' in mid-century, a hallmark of 'high farming'; it often gave a meagre return on capital or none at all. New cottages (plate 26), new branch railway lines in rural areas, had more social than directly economic justification. Some rural fashions were blatantly anti-agricultural, the shooting of the hand-reared pheasant and the hardy Scottish grouse, and even, to a lesser degree, fox-hunting. This was even more the case when management passed out of the hands of resident landowners and their tenants.[7] The personnel of nineteenth-century farming is then an integral part of its context, not merely a statistical background but thousands of individuals, extraordinary or everyday in their behaviour. It is essential to ask, if not always to answer, such questions as what did they want? what could they afford? how well informed were they?

New technologies within agriculture and outside it provided the most conspicuous group of forces for change, and perhaps those most likely to be misunderstood. Not only is there the question of terminology — technology is not synonymous with mechanisation — but of scale of impact. Some of the most evident innovations were among the least important — steam-ploughing — some of the least conspicuous the most significant — ley-farming. Some can be dated with precision, at least as far as their direct impact on farming is concerned, although all have antecedents and all required time for their spatial diffusion: a machine for making cheap drainpipes (1835), the invention of basic slag (1878), the concept of the separation of the maintenance ration and the production ration of the dairy cow (1887) belong in this category.[8] Other innovations spread more slowly, the swede early in the century for example, the use of oil cake as a feed for cattle. The area of least spectacular progress was mechanisation, the substitution of power tools for hand tools in particular. The binder was commonplace by 1900, the farming journals of mid-century advertised clod crushers and chaff cutters, but cheap labour, small fields (often pronouncedly ridged) and above all the absence of a conveniently mobile source of power inhibited progress. The mechanical revolution awaited the internal combustion and diesel engines. New technology cost money, landlord's money or tenant's money, and though at times and in certain parts of the country this was abundantly — even excessively — forthcoming (in mid-century and much of East Anglia for example), elsewhere it was not, in the post Napoleonic depression, in remote Wales and southwest England where labour was abundant.

New technologies directly applicable on the farm were paralleled by developments outside farming. Railways and factory methods, albeit rudimentary, made drainpipes and superphosphate cheaply and widely available; when fat cattle and milk could be sent by train to the city the drover and often the cheesemaker were out of business. But technology had a less happy side where farming was concerned: the steamer and the railway flooded the country with cheap grain, the refrigerator was not yet a household convenience but it quickly brought an end to the protection provided by nature for the British farmer's perishable produce, meat and even milk.[9] New methods might lower prices as well as costs, increase competition as well as production. Prices and costs were what mattered most to the farmer; to the landlord they were filtered through rents and through investment and maintenance programmes, and to the labourer wages and living costs were a sphere of interaction largely beyond his control. But to the farmer, whatever his aims and aspirations, ability to maintain a differential between ever-changing costs and ever-changing returns by means of skilful application of technology was essential if he was to stay in business.

How a farmer stayed in business, and for that matter how the landlord did so and whether the labourer left the land, was a matter of individual decision, of a personal response to the multitude of circumstances outlined above. In this respect farming was very different from most other industries, and particularly from those which were developing most rapidly — coal and iron for example; all farmers, to say nothing of landowners, in all some hundreds of thousands, were policy makers and policy executants. Geography combined with personality to decide how forces for change would be applied. Some were universally applicable, so that an understanding of the separate roles of maintenance and production rations was as meaningful in Kent as in Kirkcudbright. Others were universal in theory but localised in practice — loans for land drainage were widely available but relevant only where drainage was a problem and one which appeared to be potentially soluble; enclosure was complete in many areas before 1800. The largest group of possibilities was geographically the most constrained, thus a new railway opened the urban milk market only to willing farmers within pony and trap distance of a station and the swede, although a response to the environmental shortcomings of the turnip, could not be grown everywhere; new rotations had to match soil and climate as well as costs and prices. Traditionally and actually British farming was environmentally adjusted. Farmers grew wheat, beans, fallow in rotation on the heavy undrained clays because experience showed that no other system worked. It is certainly a perceptive view of nineteenth-century developments which comments that 'the progress of farming technology reduced a farmer's dependence on environmental conditions'; to go on to relate this to 'a declining regional differentiation',[10] as Grigg does, is to venture on to less safe ground, at least outside South Lincolnshire and in the second half of the century. New methods and the circumstances in which they were applied were on the one hand matched to particular tasks or problems and on the other constantly changing; they thus combined as often to enhance as to diminish regional differences. Some periods — mid-century for example — certainly witnessed both an evening-up of standards, the worst coming closer to the best, and widespread imitation of particular techniques, such as oil cake as a cattle feed to produce manure. Other periods saw the reverse, for depression in the last quarter of the century generated both intensive horticulture and 'dog and stick' farming,[11] rendering every advantage of environment, position, and individual skill more rather than less important, thus engendering a higher degree of local and regional variation.

Lastly it is necessary to recall that there were some relatively unchanging elements in the rural scene. Some farms remained more remote than others, some presented more intractable environments, facts which could be modified but not overturned. Rural Britain remained a society and economy of landlord and tenant, the former made up of private individuals and also of corporate bodies such as Cambridge colleges and cathedral chapters. Legislation, public debate, even political agitation did little to change this situation — owner-occupiers remained a small minority. Similarly British agriculture remained an amalgam of large, medium, and small farms but with scarcely a peasant in sight — again this issue from time to time captured public interest and attention, but attempts to establish a peasantry were localised and unsuccessful.[12] The apparent scale of values within farming remained unaltered: arable farming and grazing were fit occupations for a gentleman, a status more and more aspired to by farmers — perhaps under pressure from their wives — during the century, dairying and market gardening were not.

THE CHARACTERISTICS OF CHANGE

Change is of the essence of farming. In most of the world the basis of farming is to exploit a not wholly reliable seasonal cycle as well as a more predictable physical environment both changing sharply over short distances and short periods of time in some cases. There are also frequent and often cumulative adjustments, alterations in practice based on hindsight but which masquerade as foresight; the most hidebound farmer cannot proceed on absolutely identical lines in successive years. Thirdly there are major innovations, the decision to adopt a new crop rotation, to give up pigs, to buy a new implement, merging gradually however into the second 'adjustment' category. Too often only the third of these categories above is considered by scholars, less spectacular considerations are neglected; undoubtedly the overall scale of values is correct, but not to the exclusion of seasons and minor adjustments from all consideration. Moreover the analytical framework which is now widely and aptly employed in considering the process of agricultural innovation — knowledge, decision, action, obstacles, adoption, effects — serves to perpetuate assumptions of this kind.

The farmer exploits the seasonal cycle, he also endures it, and in the nineteenth century did so without the wealth of technology now available as a counter-measure. The weather — the context of farming — was not only intractable and unpredictable but at times an agent of change. Runs of good seasons bred complacency, but more conspicuously adverse seasons, in the late 1870s for example, might both contribute to a crisis by raising costs, reducing yields or decimating sheep flocks, and at the same time serve to mask more fundamental long-term trends.[13] Moreover this particular crisis was both regionally and locally variable. The process of minor adjustment represents an alternative unspectacular process of change which may be at least as important as that of deliberate innovation; highland Britain displays not only the geometry of large-scale enclosure early in the nineteenth century but the small irregular patterns of protracted informal reclamation; the increase in the grassland acreage in late nineteenth-century Britain owed as much or more to a host of little decisions (or indecisions) — not to plough this field, to allow that rotation pasture to run on —

as to deliberate policies to move into grassland farming and lay down permanent pasture.

The most important of all the changes which took place in British agriculture during the nineteenth century had both an innovation and an adjustment component. It was the continuation of the extension of the cultivated acreage, a matter of which the legitimacy in terms of 'agricultural revolution' has been contentiously debated but of which the role in sustaining both eighteenth- and nineteenth-century population increase can scarcely be gainsaid.[14] Early in the century the Napoleonic Wars favoured enclosure of moors, wastes and open fields, and the process continued throughout the century even into the 'great depression'. The margin of cultivation ebbed and flowed but reclamation was never completely halted. In the Fens meres and wastes were drained, Whittlesey and Deeping for example, and the operation of extension merges imperceptibly into that of drainage, so characteristic of heavy land in mid-century, so vigorously debated a hundred years later.[15]

Areal extension embraced not only new land in Britain but also new land overseas, not only outputs but also inputs. Englishmen came to be fed on the wheat of the prairies, the lambs of the Canterbury Plains; the 'high farmer' needed oil cake from the Baltic, guano from Peru. This extension was dependent on discovery, and also upon technology. It contained elements beneficial to the British farmer but others which were to prove his ruin. The resources of the New World bankrupted not a few farmers and landowners (figure 34). In brief an agricultural economy operating on an insular base in 1800, aspiring to occasional export, employing a small range of imports, was in the deep end of a worldwide economy by 1900, an areal extension of greater importance than its own efforts to find more land within its own island limits.

Nineteenth-century farmers were not generally accustomed to think in terms of productivity, and yet this was an area where they were conspicuously successful. Output increased almost continuously, the nation's farmers were still providing the bulk of its food supply in 1900 while employing less labour and less capital. Productivity per unit of labour was a particularly successful area: a large part of the agricultural interest, some 700,000 men, left the land without great social distress, an adverse impact on output, or even a spectacular

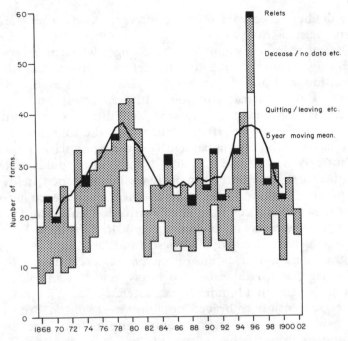

Figure 34. Character of farm sales in Huntingdonshire 1868-1902.
The two peaks in the moving mean correspond to the two periods of
acutest depression. (Source: *Peterborough Advertiser*.)

mechanisation, although the improved hand tool was undoubtedly an important factor. Farming had been grossly over-
manned, its labour force had been inefficient, underpaid and
underfed in southern and eastern England in particular (figure
35). From mid-century this situation, wage differentials excepted, markedly improved. Methods for improving productivity per
acre or per beast developed through the century, but to a
greater degree than improved labour productivity their adoption
depended upon knowledge, willingness to apply them, and
finance for their implementation. There were times when it paid
to farm less well; the technical brilliance of mid-century high
farming did not make money in the 1880s and 1890s. Some
new methods however almost guaranteed a good return, such as
open-field enclosure and application of basic slag to worn out
pastures. Productivity per unit of capital — the farmer's return
on his investment — was less assuredly on the increase during
the century; it was a century of investment, of growing

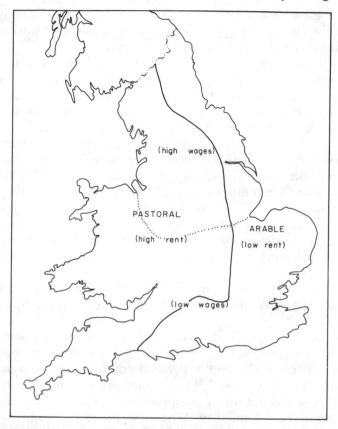

Figure 35. The basic divisions of mid-century British farming as viewed by an expert of the period, James Caird. After 35 unprosperous years the predominantly arable area is at its minimum extent. (Source: Caird, J., *English Agriculture 1850-51*, London, 1852, frontispiece.)

awareness that farming was a business of inputs and outputs, but at times, after 1815 and in the last quarter of the century in particular, a great deal of capital had to be written off. It was often the areas of highest investment — eastern England and the Midlands — which proved most vulnerable, high investment necessitating high prices. Investment tended to be only as profitable as the predictive powers of the investor were reliable. Much mid-century investment, drains and even permanent pasture, paid its way only for a few years, likewise much upland enclosure early in the century, but vegetables, fruit trees and heated glass-houses late in the century paid handsomely. So much depended on management and on timing, and thus on the individual. What were his possible choices?

The landowner was concerned on the one hand with rents and on the other with long-term investment. In each area he was constrained; social considerations[16] made it much easier to lower rents quickly in a crisis than to raise them in a boom, except in parts of the highland zone, and the strict family settlement[17] sometimes inhibited development. Investment was also related to the level of rents, other sources of income and, not least, the personal interest and inclination of the landowner. Enclosure and buildings (plate 27) were traditionally the most important areas of landlord activity, matched by his less tangible and financial exemplary and educative role. By mid-century draining had largely replaced enclosure; late in the century investment was generally but by no means invariably cut back, so too was maintenance, another and often neglected aspect of the landlord's role. The countryside became dilapidated and a few landlords took the ultimate step of selling their estates.

The tenant farmer had a great deal more room for manoeuvre than his landlord, and for that matter the owner-occupier. He was much less in the public eye and could harry and pester his landlord in a way which was unthinkable in the reverse direction. He could move in and out of business, if not easily at least with some flexibility. What was hardest for him was to change everyday practice; attention is rightly and necessarily focused on innovators but they were always a minority, their reluctant and tardy imitators the silent majority. Innate conservatism, limited education, finance and everyday routine inhibited change. So too did geographical considerations; there were always more options open, in good times and bad, to the farmer on a light loam near a big city than to the unfortunate tenant of a heavy clay farm seven miles from the railway. In fact the farmer's most basic decision — corn or horn? — was to some degree made for him by his location. There were few alternatives to pastoral farming in the highland zone although the railways expanded the range of possibilities from stores to fat beasts and dairying, and also made for cheaper fertiliser and easier migration. On the whole farmers in these areas were at the mercy not only of a tough environment but of limited outlets —

the purchasers of store sheep and cattle in English markets, dairy companies, and butchers — although in a few favoured localities, Lancashire and South Wales for example, industrialisation provided booming local markets. In hard times however there was often no alternative to tighter belt and shorter purse other than to give up,[18] perhaps to emigrate.

It was in Midland England and lowland eastern Scotland that horn and corn were most meaningful alternatives. Within the framework of high farming, intensive and integrated arable and livestock husbandry, and underpinned by improvements in drainage — the removal of a major environmental constraint — these two regions oscillated between emphasis upon livestock and grain. If popular preference was for the latter, less demanding of capital and everyday attention, and which long continued to be thought of as the paying side of the business when manifestly it had ceased to be so, price movements in the long run favoured the livestock side. As beef and mutton paid better than wheat and barley, farmers reluctantly kept more stock — a costly investment — fed off more of their corn, and put more land to permanent pasture or feed crops. Primarily arable high farming retreated eastwards. Parts of the Midlands had a long-standing pastoral reputation, Leicestershire for example, but such pastures were not easily made; much of what went under the name in the last quarter of the century was more weed than seed. Temporary grass had a long history — it is no more than another name for the convertible husbandry of the classical agricultural revolution; the nineteenth-century contribution, particularly associated with the Scottish borders, was to devise new systems and to show how to exploit their full potential.[19] There were also opportunities for dairying, in Derbyshire and Staffordshire for example, and for market gardening, as raspberries in Lanarkshire, but the Midlands and central Scotland remained pre-eminently the domain of adjustable mixed farming.

In eastern England this system ran into problems in sustaining grass through often hot, dry summers, on light and infertile soils in particular. Temporary grass was particularly prone to fail; permanent pasture was — wrongly — thought to be impossible. The arable element predominated, the livestock were mere manure machines. It required hard times to demonstrate alternatives, such as supplying London with winter milk from cattle fed on roots in the north Essex clays. Alderman Mechi's high farming was eventually his ruin,[20] but Tiptree fruit and Wisbech strawberries proved rewarding enterprises. In East Anglia, and more widely, traditional views as to profitable farming had given way to new ideas, themselves made practicable by the railways and by rising urban incomes.

The labourer's decision was to stay or to move. Low wages, rural under-employment, poor housing and a tradition of subservience all encouraged the labourer — or more often his children — to move when opportunity presented itself. The railways, universal education and hard times for farming in the last quarter of the century facilitated mobility, even within the 'farming ladder' (plate 28). The process was not of redundancy but of non-replacement, not, with some exceptions, of a direct exodus to mills and mines but, as been noted, of a drift to larger villages and country towns, the first leg of the stepwise migration process. The girls went to domestic service, the men to the railways, the police, the armed forces, or to use rural skills as urban carters and carriers. The lower echelons of the service sector depended on a flow of recruits from the cottages as much as the upper ranks looked to the younger sons from hall and rectory.

Until about the 1860s every circumstance favoured that increasing uniformity of farming practice, at least within lowland Britain, noted by Grigg. The economic base appeared secure, mixed arable-livestock farming paid well, tools such as superphosphate and tile drains were available and could be afforded to counter environmental problems. Already a number of circumstances favouring diversity were at work in the highland zone — railways and industrialisation at the farm gate. It took the hard times which followed 1875 to bring back diversity to the lowland zone: on the one hand the means to conquer the environment could no longer be afforded, on the other difficulties were best overcome by adaptive exploitation of any environmental and locational advantage. Everywhere there were several possible solutions, although many farmers found none of them; overall the answer was a greener and better fed Britain in 1900 than in 1800, a greater diversity of farming practice but not necessarily a higher technical standard than half a century earlier.

NOTES

1 See particularly the writings of R.M. Hartwell and E.J.E. Hobsbawm.

2 See for example Street, A.G., *Farmer's Glory*, London, 1932, where the personal problems of changing from arable farming to dairying in the 1920s are well discussed.

3 The general tendency to regard all landowners as at least potentially wicked, all farm labourers as idiots, is manifest in a variety of ways in the nineteenth century. The rustic of the *Punch* cartoon is almost always a half-wit, and in W.S. Gilbert's words 'All baronets are bad' (*Ruddigore*, Act 1).

4 Notably the General Enclosure Act 1845.

5 Hence too the fact that grain prices alone appeared in the *London Gazette*.

6 So called because it was originally voted as part of a scheme for licensing reform; the scheme fell through but the compensation which was to have been paid was used for educational ends.

7 Damage to crops by game was a constant source of friction between farmers and landlords, even after the Ground Game Act of 1880 strengthened the farmer's position. The few complaints about hunting probably reflect the fact that farmers could take part in this sport whereas shooting was generally reserved for the landowner.

8 That is that the dairy cow requires a basic ration to keep alive, the supply of food over and above this level determining the flow of milk.

9 Fresh milk was occasionally imported from France late in the century. The refrigerated trade in perishable milk products, especially butter from New Zealand, was much more important.

10 Grigg, D.B., *The Agricultural Revolution in South Lincolnshire*, Cambridge, 1966, p. 186.

11 That is extensive grazing for which the only tools needed were a dog and a stick.

12 In both instances agitation was commonplace in the last two decades of the century, and commonly completely oblivious of the realities of agricultural depression.

13 In this case tending to make farmers think that their misfortunes were purely caused by exceptional seasons and

would thus right themselves.

14 See the debate between G.E. Mingay and E. Kerridge in *Agricultural History*, 1969.

15 Summarised by Whetham, E.H., 'Sectoral advance in English agriculture 1850-80: a summary', *Agricultural History Review*, vol. 16, 1968, pp. 46-8.

16 In particular the fact that most English landlords lived on their estates for at least part of the year alongside their tenants, went to church and rode to hounds with them, and commonly hoped to exert a political influence over them.

17 The system whereby to ensure that the estate was handed down more or less intact from generation to generation the owner surrendered his rights as proprietor and became tenant for life. The subject is very complex.

18 Hence the importance of migrant Scots or Welsh farmers from overcrowded districts in England at some periods. See Smith, E.L., *Go East for a Farm*, Oxford, 1932.

19 By 1907 the fourth edition of the classic of the subject, Elliot, R.H., *The Agricultural Changes required by these times*, Kelso, 1898 had been renamed *The Clifton Park System of Farming*.

20 Mechi used the fortune derived from his 'magic razor strop' to reclaim Tiptree Heath from 1841. He wrote many books on farming.

FURTHER READING

1   GENERAL AND REGIONAL

Chambers, J.D., and Mingay, G.E., *The Agricultural Revolution*, London 1966.

Fussell, G.E., *The English Dairy Farmer 1500-1900*, London, 1952.

Fussell, G.E., *The Farmer's Tools 1500-1900*, London, 1952.

Gaskell, P., *Morvern Transformed: A Highland Parish in the Nineteenth Century*, Cambridge, 1968.

Grigg, D.B., *The Agricultural Revolution in South Lincolnshire*, Cambridge, 1966.

Kerr, B., *Bound to the Soil: a social history of Dorset 1750-1918*, London, 1968.

Symon, J.A., *Scottish Farming Past and Present*, Edinburgh,

1959.

Thirsk, J., and Imray, J., *Suffolk Farming in the Nineteenth Century*, Suffolk Record Society, Ipswich, 1958.

Thompson, F.M.L., *English Landed Society in the Nineteenth Century*, London, 1963.

Trow-Smith, R., *A History of British Livestock Husbandry 1700-1900*, London, 1959.

2   EARLY NINETEENTH CENTURY

Adams, L.P., *Agricultural Depression and Farm Relief in England 1813-1852*, London, 1932.

Hunt, H.G., 'Agricultural rent in south-east England 1788-1825', *Agricultural History Review*, vol. 7, 1959, pp. 98-108.

John, A.H., 'Farming in war time 1793-1815', in Jones, E.L., and Mingay, G.E., *Land, Labour and Population in the Industrial Revolution*, London, 1967.

Martin, J.M., 'The parliamentary enclosure movement and rural society in Warwickshire', *Agricultural History Review*, vol. 15, 1967, pp. 19-39.

Tate. W.E., *The English Village Community and the Enclosure Movement*, London, 1967.

3   HIGH FARMING IN MID-CENTURY

Caird, J.B., *English Agriculture in 1850-51,* London, 1852 and subsequent reprints.

Collins, E.T.J., and Jones, E.L., 'Sectoral advance in English agriculture 1850-80', *Agricultural History Review*, vol. 15, 1967, pp. 65-81. (In reply to Sturgess, R.W., cited below).

Darby, H.C., 'The Draining of the English Clay-lands', *Geographische Zeitschrift*, vol. 52, 1964, pp. 190-201.

Hunt, E.H., 'Labour productivity in British agriculture 1850-1914', *Economic History Review*, 2nd series, vol. 29, 1967, pp. 280-92.

Jones, E.L., 'The changing basis of English agricultural prosperity, 1853-1873', *Agricultural History Review*, vol. 10, 1962, pp. 102-19.

Phillips, A.D.M., 'Underdraining and the English claylands 1850-80: a review', *Agricultural History Review*, vol. 17, 1969, pp. 44-55.

Sturgess, R.W., 'The Agricultural Revolution on the English

Clays', *Agricultural History Review*, vol. 14, 1966, pp. 104-121. Also 'A rejoinder', *Agricultural History Review*, vol. 15, 1967, pp. 82-7 (Replying to Collins, E.J.T., and Jones, E.L.).

Whetham, E.H., 'Sectoral advance in English agriculture 1850-80: a summary', *Agricultural History Review*, vol. 16, 1968, pp. 46-8.

4   LATE NINETEENTH-CENTURY 'DEPRESSION'

Haggard, H.R., *Rural England*, London, 1906.

Hall, A.D., *A Pilgrimage of British Farming*, London, 1913.

Perry, P.J., *British Farming in the Great Depression 1875-1914*, Newton Abbot, 1974.

8 Britain in 1900:
The Limits of Prosperity

The reputation which the first decade of the twentieth century still enjoys as a golden age owes something to the subsequent holocaust, but it is also derived from a real renewal of prosperity after 20 years of intermittent depression. Times had begun to improve before 1900, itself a very good year, and between 1896 and 1913 exports doubled in value and imports increased by more than half. But perhaps rather ominously the export boom was led by the old staples, coal and steel, rather than by new lines, and it is arguable that enthusiastic overseas investment and involvement served primarily to deprive British industry of the capital and manpower it needed for modernisation. The geographer concerned with this period is then writing of a boom compounded and complicated by a subsequent tragedy. He is able however to call to his aid a mass of evidence collected and analysed by the many social investigators of a period when 'the attention of the general public has been more directed, probably, to economic and industrial problems, to varying social conditions than ever before'.[1] Evidence of a quickened interest in the state of the nation, these investigations themselves reveal an important aspect of the 'geosophy'[2] of the period, an awareness that in the richest nation and society in the world there existed great social problems of which the geographical characteristics were of basic significance, be they a slum courtyard or an impoverished village. These objective surveys are parallelled by more partisan endeavours, at worst polemic, describing the ills and evils of the nation as a political consequence and for a political purpose; the writings of Masterman and his associates are probably the most significant examples of this genre. Of equal importance but much less widely known or read is Mackinder's *Britain and the British Seas* (1902), the first and incomparably the best modern geography of Britain, an enormous intellectual advance over even the English volume of the *Géographie Universelle* of 1886,[3] and soon to be imitated and influential in a number of county geographies. Victorian self-assurance gave way during no more than a generation to Edwardian self-scrutiny, 'the uneasy feeling . . . that the nineteenth century, which has done such wonderful things, and from which things so much more wonderful were hoped, has been on the whole a failure'.[4] Such an introspective mood sets the scene and provides the framework for this concluding chapter of an historical geography which of necessity anticipates much of the geography of 1900 in its central chapters. What were the geographical problems to be faced and found in early twentieth-century Britain? What were the geographical elements in the transformation of Britain which few would deny had taken place since 1800?

By 1900 Britain was already having to adjust to a status in world affairs — a new political geography — less lofty and certainly less lonely than in mid-century. The internantional prestige and self-confidence of Britain was as yet scarcely touched, even by the misadventures of the Boer War, but economic power and authority had waned considerably, at least on a comparative scale, since the 1870s. Not only were there other producers of the wide range of goods, and at least some of the services, which Britain had supplied to much of the world during the nineteenth century, notably Germany and the U.S.A., but they were often more competitive. As has been mentioned already there is no reason to believe that Britain's mid-century worldwide commercial dominance could have persisted, but successful foreign competition served not only to demonstrate this fact but to generate both political rivalries and realignments. Foreign successes were also taken to reflect upon Britain's social structures in general, educational shortcomings in particular, and upon the experience of half a century of free trade in a world of foreign competitors, foreign tariffs, and a large empire. The geographical re-evaluation implicit in the term 'little Englander' was as yet exceptional, but commercial and political imperialism and protectionism, another new geography were commonplace. Britain's place in the geography of world trade, and thus of world power, was altogether a matter for revision by the end of the century.

Within Britain the principal focus of attention and concern was the cities. Since mid-century Britain had been more an urban than a rural society and for considerably longer had been the most urbanised nation in the world. One great nineteenth-century achievement was to house this rapidly growing urban population, but when the achievement has been admitted there remains the undoubted existence of appalling problems, rural as well as urban, in this area. They presented themselves to educated Edwardians almost as forcefully as they pressed upon their unfortunate proletarian victims. These problems 'were less those of economic depression than of a prosperity unevenly shared'.[5] Charles Booth discovered and publicised the fact that in the richest country in the world a third of the population endured chronic poverty. In 1891 three-fifths of the population of Glasgow, at the apogee of its economic power and prestige, lived in overcrowded conditions[6] and even in London, away from the Scottish tradition of tenement housing and with a less cyclical economic base, the figure was one in five. The Boer War publicised the consequences of this situation when in 1899 three recruits in every five at Manchester proved to be physically unfit even under drastically reduced wartime standards'.[7]

Poverty, physique, and housing were evidently related, albeit regionally variable, problems. They do not exhaust such a list. Every city had a pool of chronically unemployed or irregularly employed men, unskilled workers in trades where the level of demand for their services fluctuated by the day or the hour – the docks, the building industry, shipping. Very often the circumstances of their occasional opportunity of employment necessitated that they live close to the possibility of work, which led to overcrowding. Unemployment was recognised as one of the root causes of poverty and thus of poor physique. Despite some amelioration infant mortality remained high, as high as 200 per 1,000 in the Potteries where many women were engaged in arduous industrial work. The unsatisfactory economic, social and domestic environment in which most of the working class still lived in 1900 may have been necessary for mid-Victorian economic expansion, but that this need not continue to be so – need never have been so? – and that it was an affront to the conscience of a rich and Christian society was beginning to be recognised by 1900.

It is then scarcely surprising that contemporary social critics and commentators were disenchanted with the urban scene. London was particularly singled out — 'some voiceless prophet mutely pointing to the strange wounds and scars upon its face . . . the price paid for its greatness'.[8] Lawrence went so far as to introduce the concept of 'towniness' into his 'model' of housing problems[9] indicating a distaste not merely for the material aspects of urban life but for the very phenomenon. Even in Masterman, the radical and the social reformer, there are shades of Arnold or Ruskin: 'civilize the poor . . . expand their tiny rubbish yards into green gardens, introduce bow windows before and behind; remove from them the actual experience of privation, convert all England into a suburban city — will the completed product be pronounced to be "very good"?'[10] A consequence of such, if less sceptical, attitudes was the countrification of the city: 'England would one day be a huge garden city . . . we find whole village-like new communities created in this great era of domestic and rustic architecture.'[11] But not for the poor.

Ironically the idealisation and idolisation of the countryside, the preaching if rarely the practising of 'back to the land' as a solution for a mass of social and economic problems, coincided with agricultural crisis. The countryside which was worshipped did not exist and had never existed. The reality of 1900 was a slowly waning 20-year old agricultural depression — 1900 itself was a very unprosperous year — rural depopulation and emigration, and a rural labour force as ever the worst paid such group in Britain.[12] Reputedly, if not one suspects everywhere in reality, a deadweight of apathy, decay and inertia had settled like some pestilence over each and every village and hamlet. The illusion that all was well did not even begin to exist save for the privileged few in rural Britain at the end of the nineteenth century.

There were areas of national life which stood up to scrutiny rather better than the economy, the towns and the countryside. Britain had become almost wholly literate in the last quarter of the nineteenth century, a process in which very ancient regional differences disappeared, and an educational system had been set up which achieved this end and which was a contentious issue only on the limited sectarian front. A penny post, a national

Press — potent counterweights to regional isolation if not to regional identity — had been created; there was a superb railway system, worldwide dominance in shipping and, in many areas, at least an adequate system of suburban transport. 'From a collection of regions, separated rather than united by such means of transport as existed, England was becoming unified in a way never possible before.'[13] There were even some commentators who took an optimistic view of economic prospects: it was an American who wrote in 1911 'it is very doubtful whether its [Lancashire cotton] presence and influence in the world markets can be seriously affected, at least for many years to come'.[14]

If there had been a change of heart and mind from mid-century complacency it was evidently set in a context of even more complete geographical upheaval during the course of the century. Comparison with the past gave even Masterman grounds for optimism — 'who could be pessimistic who had traced the history of a hundred years, and compared the England of 1811 with the England of today?'[15] — and it provides the geographer of the 1970s with an appropriate framework with which to conclude a study of nineteenth-century Britain. What were the chief alterations in the geography of Britain between 1800 and 1900?

Britain had ceased to be predominantly rural and had become overwhelmingly urban and industrial. Of course in simple spatial terms Britain remained rural, and, as has been noted, urbanisation was less than wholeheartedly accepted. (A visual comparison of even the depressed countryside of the 1890s with either the manufacturing or residential quarter of a British town at the same date makes it easy to understand why.) By 1900 a mere nine per cent of the populace was in farming and thus the sacrifice of agricultural prosperity to urban well-being, whether or not it was necessary, proved politically palatable. The sacrifice itself depended upon a set of new geographical circumstances, the availability of food from overseas and the Pax Brittanica.

Urbanisation and industrialisation thus epitomise nineteenth-century Britain and the component parts of these developments have made up much of the preceding chapters of this book. Early in the century textiles, the old woollen trade and the new cotton trade, situated for the most part on the margins of the

Pennines, were dominant. Neither diminished in absolute importance during the century and cotton was spectacularly a growth industry, but by 1900 coal and steel occupied pride of place on the industrial scene. An industrial geographer of the period could not neglect Yorkshire and Lancashire but he might be expected first to give his attention to the Clyde, the Tyne and South Wales. Mackinder picked out Middlesborough, Barrow (and Belfast) as the growth centres of his time,[16] steel and shipbuilding towns close to indigenous ores and a little removed from the coalfields.

Coal was commercial king but locationally it was a spent force. One of the more surprising – and more forgotten – aspects of nineteenth-century Britain is how short was the period during which coal was a powerful force for industrial concentration, the brevity of the era between the triumph of the stationary steam engine and the establishment of a widespread railway network. In Mackinder's prescient summary, 'two generations ago men took the raw materials to be manufactured upon the coalfield; one generation ago they began to carry coal to the deposits of the raw material . . . it now appears likely that they will distil power from the coal at the pit mouth'.[17] Only cotton and wool were in that short era securely and rather exclusively tied to coalfield locations – as it happened to second-rank and early depleted coalfields. Iron and chemicals went through a phrase of coalfield fixation, aided in the former case by the black band ores, but new technologies, inside and outside the industries themselves, took them elsewhere in the second half of the century. Footloose industry is in fact a child of the Victorian railways as much as of twentieth-century dynamos and internal combustion engines. In some cases the absence of coal – and coalfield wage levels – appears to have been a boon to manufacturers seeking to implement new methods. By 1900 Britain's premier geographer could not only refer to coal exports as 'decentralisation . . . on an international scale'[18] but point to the re-emergence of old provincial towns and cities, Norwich and Northampton for example, in specialised industrial roles.

London had been recognised as a distinctive urban phenomenon at and even before the start of the nineteenth century, a prosperous and peerless commercial giant. Its peculiar dominance and worldwide role increased rather than diminished during the century even though other conurbations came into existence. It is however to these conurbations and to the manufacturing towns rather than to London that the student of the Victorian city and town *per se* turns for his examples, to Bradford or Birmingham, and then perhaps to Middlesborough or Millom.[19] Although the greatest of these cities had become veritable conurbations by 1900 they remained compact by comparison with their subsequent extension; nineteenth-century suburbanisation was pre-eminently a London phenomenon the creation not of the industrial but of the commercial and business activities'.[20] Whatever its spatial scale the development of residential segregation within cities was very much a nineteenth-century phenomenon, the departure of the upper, middle and even skilled artisan classes towards the periphery. What had occurred on a very limited social and geographical scale early in the century — the Clapham Evangelicals were very rich and by the end of the century Clapham was a largely working class inner suburb — became by 1900 the commonplace of the commercial community. Lady Bell could take it for granted even of a new iron and steel town.[21]

Suburbanisation is one facet, one consequence, of a new mobility. The nineteenth century was the century of the horse and pedestrian, but late in the century the train, the bus, the tram and the bicycle became the everyday means of movement of a large proportion, albeit not necessarily a majority, of the population. More people became more mobile, and often with surprising suddenness. The increase in numbers was however losing its momentum just as widespread personal mobility arrived. A different kind of mobility was manifest in the continuous redistribution of the population onto the coalfields, old and new, and into a discontinuous industrial axis extending from Thames to Mersey or even Clyde. Over much of rural Britain these population changes were small, in terms of density, and inconspicuous compared with either localised urban growth or even occasionally spectacular rural depopulation, but it is this localisation which is the most distinctive and significant feature of the population geography of nineteenth-century Britain.

Of how many Britains then is it legitimate to speak at the turn of the century? Social commentators leave their readers in no doubt as to the continuance of Disraeli's 'two nations' — rich and poor — and the phrase has remained in the political vocabulary. Mackinder chose to echo the *Géographie Universelle* in contrasting metropolitan and industrial Britain,[22] the coal-less and continental oriented south and east with the coal-rich cities and towns of the north and west. This is to emphasise the continuity of the very ancient lowland-highland dichotomy and a geographer of the 1970s might go on to interpret British entry to the European Common Market as a reassertion of metropolitan vitality after two centuries of more peripheral industrial vigour. To Mackinder however the nineteenth century was a period of developing balance between the two parts. Masterman, social critic and foe of that imperial outlook espoused by Mackinder, saw three Englands — and thus surprisingly little change since 1900 — 'there is rural England . . . there is urban England . . . never far from green fields . . . there is London: a population, a nation in itself'.[23] The distant perspective of the 1970s suggests four categories: London, the conurbations and smaller communities created by the century's staple industries for the most part in the north and west, the old provincial towns and cities beginning to experience revival by the last decades of the century, and finally the unprosperous — and forgotten — countryside. But late nineteenth-century Britain, however introspective, was not an essentially inward-looking society. Free trader and imperialist alike recognised that 40 million people living on a small island must needs carry on business with the world at large. This was the realm in which nineteenth-century Britain, the Victorian in particular, was pre-eminently successful; it was from this source that the wealth which enabled the transformation of landscape, economy and society — however unfortunate some aspects of that transformation appear to us — was drawn.

'It would be bold to hazard a prediction as regards England's position as a great power in the immediate future. Her interests are more complex, and through her numerous colonies she is brought into direct contact with a greater variety of nations than can be said of any other state in the world, ancient or modern. Not an event or commercial crisis can take place in any part of the world without England being affected by it. No other state organism is equally sensitive to outside impressions and the fate of Great Britain depends more or less upon the destinies of all those nations with which it entertains commercial relations'.[24]

Reclus' summary of 1886 requires modification on points of detail in 1975, but in general terms it remains as true for Britain entering the last quarter of the twentieth as for the last quarter of the nineteenth century.

NOTES

1 Bell, Lady Florence *At the works*, pp. 10-11. She considered her task as 'to put a piece of prosperity under the microscope' (p. 14), a useful corrective to the gloomy outlook usually ascribed to such writers. The best known of the genre is Charles Booth, *Life and Labour of the People in London*, London, 1891-1903.

2 'The geographical ideas, both true and false, of all manner of people . . . it necessarily has to do in large degree with subjective conceptions.' J.K. Wright. 'Terrae Incognitae: the place of the imagination in geography', *Annals of the Association of American Geographers*, vol. 38, 1947, pp. 1-15.

3 This is a curious, alternating mixture of modern systematic geography and guide-book topography reminiscent of the early nineteenth century.

4 Masterman, C.F.G., *The Heart of the Empire*, p. xx (of author's preface), quoting Mackail, J.W., *William Morris*, a lecture to the City of London, I.L.P., 1901.

5 Taylor, A.J., in Nowell-Smith, S. (ed.), *Edwardian England 1901-1914*, p. 107.

6 As defined by the Registrar General.

7 Discussed in the editorial introduction (Gilbert, B.B.,) to the 1973 reprint of *The Heart of the Empire* pp. xxiv-xxv. The matter became something of a national scandal.

8 Masterman, C.F.G. (ed.), *op.cit.*, p. 112 (in a chapter by Bray, R.A.).

9 Masterman, C.F.G. (ed.), *op.cit.*, p. 55. (in a chapter by Lawrence, F.W.).

10 Masterman, C.F.G., *The Condition of England*, p. 77.

11 Betjeman, J., in Nowell-Smith, S., op.cit., p. 365.

12 A realistic and reasonably objective survey is Haggard, H. Rider, *Rural England*, 1902.
13 Reader, W.J., *Life in Victorian England*, 1964, p. 162.
14 Quoted by Barker, T.C., in Cox, C.B., and Dyson, A.E. (eds), *The Twentieth Century Mind*, p. 61.
15 Masterman, C.F.G., *The Condition of England*, preface to 1911 edition.
16 Mackinder, H.J., *Britain and the British Seas*, 1902, pp. 328-9.
17 ibid., p. 339.
18 ibid p. 329.
19 Briggs, Asa, *Victorian Cities*, 1963, chooses to consider Manchester, Birmingham, Leeds, Middlesborough, Melbourne and London.
20 Masterman, C.F.G., *The Condition of England*, p. 69.
21 Bell, Lady Florence, *At the works*, p. 30.
22 Mackinder, op.cit., titles of chapters 14 and 15: Réclus, E., *The British Isles (Géographie Universelle)*, 1887, p. 486.
23 Masterman, C.F.G., *The Condition of England*, p. 99.
24 Reclus, op. cit., p. 486.

FURTHER READING

Cox, C.B., and Dyson, A.E. (eds), *The Twentieth Century Mind*, London, 1972 (especially Barker, T.C., 'History: economic and social', pp. 51-89).
Mackinder, H.J., *Britain and the British Seas*, London, 1902.
Masterman, C.F.G., *The Condition of England*, London, 1909.
Masterman, C.F.G. (ed.), *The Heart of the Empire*, London, 1901
Nowell-Smith, S. (ed.), *Edwardian England 1901-1914*, London, 1964. (especially Taylor, A.J., 'The economy', pp. 103-38).
Réclus, E. (trans. and ed. Ravenstein, E.G.), *The British Isles* (being volume 4 of *Géographie Universelle*), London, 1887.

Index

Antoine de Saint-Exupéry

Wind, Sand and Stars

Translated from the French
by Lewis Galantière

Penguin Books

Penguin Books Ltd, Harmondsworth, Middlesex, England
Penguin Books Australia Ltd, Ringwood, Victoria, Australia

Terre des hommes first published in 1939
This translation first published by Heinemann 1939
Published in Penguin Books 1966
Reprinted 1969, 1971

Made and Printed in Great Britain by
Hazell Watson & Viney Ltd, Aylesbury, Bucks
Set in Linotype Pilgrim

Contents

1 The Craft

In 1926 I was enrolled as student airline pilot by the Latécoère Company, the predecessors of Aéropostale (now Air France) in the operation of the line between Toulouse, in south-western France, and Dakar, in French West Africa. I was learning the craft, undergoing an apprenticeship served by all young pilots before they were allowed to carry the mails. We took ships up on trial spins, made meek little hops between Toulouse and Perpignan, and had dreary lessons in meteorology in a freezing hangar. We lived in fear of the mountains of Spain, over which we had yet to fly, and in awe of our elders.

These veterans were to be seen in the field restaurant – gruff, not particularly approachable, and inclined somewhat to condescension when giving us the benefit of their experience. When one of them landed, rain-soaked and behind schedule, from Alicante or Casablanca, and one of us asked humble questions about his flight, the very curtness of his replies on these tempestuous days was matter enough out of which to build a fabulous world filled with snares and pitfalls, with cliffs suddenly looming out of fog and whirling air-currents of a strength to uproot cedars. Black dragons guarded the mouths of the valleys and clusters of lightning crowned the crests – for our elders were always at some pains to feed our reverence. But from time to time one or another of them, eternally to be revered, would fail to come back.

I remember, once, a homecoming of Bury, he who was later to die in a spur of the Pyrenees. He came into the restaurant, sat down at the common table, and went stolidly at his food, shoulders still bowed by the fatigue of his recent trial. It was at the end of one of those foul days when from end to end of the line the skies are filled with dirty weather, when the mountains seem to a pilot to be wallowing in slime like exploded cannon on the decks of an antique man-o'-war.

9

I stared at Bury, swallowed my saliva, and ventured after a bit to ask if he had had a hard flight. Bury, bent over his plate in frowning absorption, could not hear me. In those days we flew open ships and thrust our heads out round the windshield, in bad weather, to take our bearings: the wind that whistled in our ears was a long time clearing out of our heads. Finally Bury looked up, seemed to understand me, to think back to what I was referring to, and suddenly he gave a bright laugh. This brief burst of laughter, from a man who laughed little, startled me. For a moment his weary being was bright with it. But he spoke no word, lowered his head, and went on chewing in silence. And in that dismal restaurant, surrounded by the simple government clerks who sat there repairing the wear and tear of their humble daily tasks, my broad-shouldered messmate seemed to me strangely noble; beneath his rough hide I could discern the angel who had vanquished the dragon.

The night came when it was my turn to be called to the field manager's room.

He said: 'You leave tomorrow.'

I stood motionless, waiting for him to dismiss me. After a moment of silence he added:

'I take it you know the regulations?'

In those days the motor was not what it is today. It would drop out, for example, without warning and with a great rattle like the crash of crockery. And one would simply throw in one's hand: there was no hope of refuge on the rocky crust of Spain. 'Here,' we used to say, 'when your motor goes, your ship goes, too.'

An aeroplane, of course, can be replaced. Still, the important thing was to avoid a collision with the range; and blind flying through a sea of clouds in the mountain zones was subject to the severest penalties. A pilot in trouble who buried himself in the white cotton-wool of the clouds might all unseeing run straight into a peak. This was why, that night, the deliberate voice repeated insistently its warning:

'Navigating by the compass in a sea of clouds over Spain is all very well, it is very dashing, but —'

And I was struck by the graphic image:

'But you want to remember that below the sea of clouds lies eternity.'

And suddenly that tranquil cloud-world, that world so harmless and simple that one sees below on rising out of the clouds, took on in my eyes a new quality. That peaceful world became a pitfall. I imagined the immense white pitfall spread beneath me. Below it reigned not what one might think – not the agitation of men, not the living tumult and bustle of cities, but a silence even more absolute than in the clouds, a peace even more final. This viscous whiteness became in my mind the frontier between the real and the unreal, between the known and the unknowable. Already I was beginning to realize that a spectacle has no meaning except it be seen through the glass of a culture, a civilization, a craft. Mountaineers too know the sea of clouds, yet it does not seem to them the fabulous curtain it is to me.

When I left that room I was filled with a childish pride. Now it was my turn to take on at dawn the responsibility of a cargo of passengers and the African mails. But at the same time I felt very meek. I felt myself ill-prepared for this responsibility. Spain was poor in emergency fields; we had no radio; and I was troubled lest when I got into difficulty I should not know where to hunt a landing-place. Staring at the aridity of my maps, I could see no help in them; and so, with a heart full of shyness and pride, I fled to spend this night of vigil with my friend Guillaumet. Guillaumet had been over the route before me. He knew all the dodges by which one got hold of the keys to Spain. I should have to be initiated by Guillaumet.

When I walked in he looked up and smiled.

'I know all about it,' he said. 'How do you feel?'

He went to a cupboard and came back with glasses and a bottle of port, still smiling.

'We'll drink to it. Don't worry. It's easier than you think.'

Guillaumet exuded confidence the way a lamp gives off light. He was himself later on to break the record for postal crossings in the Andes and the South Atlantic. On this night, sitting in his shirtsleeves, his arms folded in the lamplight, smiling the most heartening of smiles, he said to me simply:

'You'll be bothered from time to time by storms, fog, snow. When you are, think of those who went through it before you, and say to yourself, "What they could do, I can do." '

I spread out my maps and asked him hesitantly if he would mind going over the hop with me. And there, bent over in the lamplight, shoulder to shoulder with the veteran, I felt a sort of schoolboy peace.

But what a strange lesson in geography I was given! Guillaumet did not teach Spain to me, he made the country my friend. He did not talk about provinces, or peoples, or livestock. Instead of telling me about Guadix, he spoke of three orange-trees on the edge of the town: 'Beware of those trees. Better mark them on the map.' And those three orange-trees seemed to me thenceforth higher than the Sierra Nevada.

He did not talk about Lorca, but about a humble farm near Lorca, a living farm with its farmer and the farmer's wife. And this tiny, this remote couple, living a thousand miles from where we sat, took on a universal importance. Settled on the slope of a mountain, they watched like lighthouse-keepers beneath the stars, ever on the look-out to succour men.

The details that we drew up from oblivion, from their inconceivable remoteness, no geographer had been concerned to explore. Because it washed the banks of great cities, the Ebro River was of interest to map-makers. But what had they to do with that brook running secretly through the water-weeds to the west of Motril, that brook nourishing a mere score or two of flowers?

'Careful of that brook: it breaks up the whole field. Mark it on your map.' Ah, I was to remember that serpent in the grass near Motril! It looked like nothing at all, and its faint murmur sang to no more than a few frogs; but it slept with one eye open. Stretching its length along the grasses in the paradise of that emergency landing-field, it lay in wait for me a thousand miles from where I sat. Given the chance, it would transform me into a flaming candelabra. And those thirty valorous sheep ready to charge me on the slope of a hill! Now that I knew about them I could brace myself to meet them.

'You think the meadow empty, and suddenly bang! there

are thirty sheep in your wheels.' An astounded smile was all I could summon in the face of so cruel a threat.

Little by little, under the lamp, the Spain of my map became a sort of fairyland. The crosses I marked to indicate safety zones and traps were so many buoys and beacons. I charted the farmer, the thirty sheep, the brook. And, exactly where she stood, I set a buoy to mark the shepherdess forgotten by the geographers.

When I left Guillaumet on that freezing winter night, I felt the need of a brisk walk. I turned up my coat collar, and as I strode among the indifferent passers-by I was escorting a fervour as tender as if I had just fallen in love. To be brushing past these strangers with that marvellous secret in my heart filled me with pride. I seemed to myself a sentinel standing guard over a sleeping camp. These passers-by knew nothing about me, yet it was to me that, in their mail pouches, they were about to confide the weightiest cares of their hearts and their trade. Into my hands were they about to entrust their hopes. And I, muffled up in my cloak, walked among them like a shepherd, though they were unaware of my solicitude.

Nor were they receiving any of those messages now being dispatched to me by the night. For this snow-storm that was gathering, and that was to burden my first flight, concerned my frail flesh, not theirs. What could they know of those stars that one by one were going out? I alone was in the confidence of the stars. To me alone news was being sent of the enemy's position before the hour of battle. My footfall rang in a universe that was not theirs.

These messages of such grave concern were reaching me as I walked between rows of lighted shop-windows, and those windows on that night seemed a display of all that was good on earth, of a paradise of sweet things. In the sight of all this happiness, I tasted the proud intoxication of renunciation. I was a warrior in danger. What meaning could they have for me, these flashing crystals meant for men's festivities, these lamps whose glow was to shelter men's meditations, these cosy furs out of which were to emerge pathetically beautiful solicitous faces? I was still wrapped in the aura of friendship, dazed a little like a child on Christmas Eve, expectant of surprise and palpitatingly prepared for happiness; and yet already I was soaked in spray; a mail pilot, I was already nibbling the bitter pulp of night flight.

It was three in the morning when they woke me. I thrust the shutters open with a dry snap, saw that rain was falling on the town, and got soberly into my harness. A half-hour later I was out on the pavement shining with rain, sitting on my little valise and waiting for the bus that was to pick me up. So many other flyers before me, on their day of ordination, had undergone this humble wait with beating heart.

Finally I saw the old-fashioned vehicle come round the corner and heard its tinny rattle. Like those who had gone before me, I squeezed in between a sleepy custom guard and a few glum government clerks. The bus smelled musty, smelled of the dust of government offices into which the life of a man sinks as into a quicksand. It stopped every five hundred yards to take on another scrivener, another guard, another inspector. Those in the bus who had already gone back to sleep responded with a vague grunt to the greeting of the newcomer, while he crowded in as well as he was able and instantly fell asleep himself. We jolted mournfully over the uneven pavements of Toulouse, I in the midst of these men who in the rain and the breaking day were about to take up again their dreary diurnal tasks, their red tape, their monotonous lives.

Morning after morning, greeted by the growl of the custom guard shaken out of sleep by his arrival, by the gruff irritability of clerk or inspector, one mail pilot or another got into this bus and was for the moment indistinguishable from these bureaucrats. But as the street lamps moved by, as the field drew nearer and nearer, the old omnibus rattling along lost little by little its reality and became a grey chrysalis from which one emerged transfigured.

Morning after morning a flyer sat here and felt of a sudden, somewhere inside the vulnerable man subjected to his neighbour's surliness, the stirring of the pilot of the Spanish and African mails, the birth of him who, three hours later, was to confront in the lightnings the dragon of the mountains; and who, four hours afterwards, having vanquished it, would be free to decide between a détour over the sea and a direct assault upon the Alcoy range, would be free to deal with storm, with mountain, with ocean.

And thus every morning each pilot before me, in his time, had been lost in the anonymity of daybreak beneath the dismal winter sky of Toulouse, and each one, transfigured by this old omnibus, had felt the birth within him of the sovereign who, five hours later, leaving behind him the rains and snows of the North, repudiating winter, had throttled down his motor and begun to drift earthward in the summer air beneath the shining sun of Alicante.

The old omnibus has vanished, but its austerity, its discomfort, still live in my memory. It was a proper symbol of the apprenticeship we had to serve before we might possess the stern joys of our craft. Everything about it was intensely serious. I remember three years later, though hardly ten words were spoken, learning in that bus of the death of Lécrivain, one of those hundred pilots who on a day or a night of fog have retired for eternity.

It was four in the morning, and the same silence was abroad when we heard the field manager, invisible in the darkness, address the inspector:

'Lécrivain didn't land at Casablanca last night.'

'Ah!' said the inspector. 'Ah?'

Torn from his dream he made an effort to wake up, to display his zeal, and added:

'Is that so? Couldn't he get through? Did he come back?'

And in the dead darkness of the omnibus the answer came: 'No.'

We waited to hear the rest, but no word sounded. And as the seconds fell it became more and more evident that that 'no' would be followed by no further word, was eternal and without appeal, that Lécrivain not only had not landed at Casablanca but would never again land anywhere.

And so, at daybreak on the morning of my first flight with the mails, I went through the sacred rites of the craft, and I

15

felt the self-confidence oozing out of me as I stared through the windows at the macadam shining and reflecting back the street lights. Over the pools of water I could see great palms of wind running. And I thought: 'My first flight with the mails! Really, this is not my lucky day.'

I raised my eyes and looked at the inspector. 'Would you call this bad weather?' I asked.

He threw a weary glance out of the window. 'Doesn't prove anything,' he growled finally.

And I wondered how one could tell bad weather. The night before, with a single smile Guillaumet had wiped out all the evil omens with which the veterans overwhelmed us, but they came back into my memory. 'I feel sorry for the man who doesn't know the whole line pebble by pebble, if he runs into a snow-storm. Oh, yes, I pity the fellow.' Our elders, who had their prestige to think of, had all bobbed their heads solemnly and looked at us with embarrassing sympathy, as if they were pitying a flock of condemned sheep.

For how many of us had this old omnibus served as refuge in its day? Sixty? Eighty? All driven on a rainy morning by the same taciturn chauffeur. I looked about me. Luminous points glowed in the darkness. Cigarettes punctuated the meditations. Humble meditations of worn old clerks. How many of us had they escorted on a journey from which there was no coming back?

I heard them talking to one another in murmurs and whispers. They talked about illness, money, shabby domestic cares. Their talk painted the walls of the dismal prison in which these men had locked themselves up. And suddenly I had a vision of the face of destiny.

Old bureaucrat, my comrade, it is not you who are to blame. No one ever helped you to escape. You, like a termite, built your peace by blocking up with cement every chink and cranny through which the light might pierce. You rolled yourself up into a ball in your genteel security, in routine, in the stifling conventions of provincial life, raising a modest rampart against the winds and the tides and the stars. You have chosen not to be perturbed by great problems, having trouble enough to forget your own fate as man. You are not the dweller upon an errant planet and do not ask yourself questions to which there are no answers. You are a petty bourgeois of Toulouse. Nobody grasped you by the shoulder while there was still time. Now the clay of which you were shaped has dried and hardened, and naught in you will ever awaken the sleeping musician, the poet, the astronomer that possibly inhabited you in the beginning.

The squall has ceased to be a cause of my complaint. The magic of the craft has opened for me a world in which I shall confront, within two hours, the black dragons and the crowned crests of a coma of blue lightnings, and when night has fallen I, delivered, shall read my course in the stars.

Thus I went through my professional baptism and I began to fly the mails. For the most part the flights were without incident. Like sea-divers, we sank peacefully into the depths of our element.

Flying, in general, seemed to us easy. When the skies are filled with black vapours, when fog and sand and sea are confounded in a brew in which they become indistinguishable, when gleaming flashes wheel treacherously in these skyey swamps, the pilot purges himself of the phantoms at a single stroke. He lights his lamps. He brings sanity into his house as into a lonely cottage on a fearsome heath. And the crew travel a sort of submarine route in a lighted chamber.

Pilot, mechanic, and radio operator are shut up in what might be a laboratory. They are obedient to the play of dial-hands, not to the unrolling of the landscape. Out of doors the mountains are immersed in tenebrous darkness; but they are no longer mountains, they are invisible powers whose approach must be computed.

The operator sits in the light of his lamp, dutifully setting down figures; the mechanic ticks off points on his chart; the pilot swerves in response to the drift of the mountains as quickly as he sees that the summits he intends to pass on the left have deployed straight ahead of him in a silence and secrecy as of military preparations. And below on the ground the watchful radio men in their shacks take down submissively in their notebooks the diction of their comrade in the air: '12.40 a.m. En route 230. All well.'

So the crew fly on with no thought that they are in motion. Like night over the sea, they are very far from the earth, from towns, from trees. The motors fill the lighted chamber with a quiver that changes its substance. The clock ticks on. The dials, the radio lamps, the various hands and needles go through their invisible alchemy. From second to second these mysterious stirrings, a few muffled words, a concentrated tenseness, contribute to the end result. And when the hour is at hand the pilot may glue his forehead to the window with perfect assurance. Out of oblivion the gold has been smelted : there it gleams in the lights of the airport.

And yet we have all known flights when of a sudden, each for himself, it has seemed to us that we have crossed the border of the world of reality; when, only a couple of hours from port, we have felt ourselves more distant from it than we should feel if we were in India; when there has come a premonition of an incursion into a forbidden world whence it was going to be infinitely difficult to return.

Thus, when Mermoz first crossed the South Atlantic in a hydroplane, as day was dying he ran foul of the Black Hole region, off Africa. Straight ahead of him were the tails of tornadoes rising minute by minute gradually higher, rising as a wall is built; and then the night came down upon these preliminaries and swallowed them up; and when, an hour later, he slipped under the clouds, he came out into a fantastic kingdom.

Great black waterspouts had reared themselves seemingly in the immobility of temple pillars. Swollen at their tops, they were supporting the squat and lowering arch of the tempest, but through the rifts in the arch there fell slabs of light and the full moon sent her radiant beams between the pillars down upon the frozen tiles of the sea. Through these uninhabited ruins Mermoz made his way, gliding slantwise from one channel of light to the next, circling round those giant pillars, in which there must have rumbled the upsurge of the sea, flying for four hours through these corridors of moonlight towards the exit from the temple. And this spectacle was so overwhelming that only after he had got through the Black Hole did Mermoz awaken to the fact that he had not been afraid.

I remember, for my part, another of those hours in which a pilot finds suddenly that he has slipped beyond the confines of this world. All that night the radio messages sent from the ports in the Sahara concerning our position had been inaccurate, and my radio operator, Néri, and I had been drawn out of our course. Suddenly, seeing the gleam of water at the bottom of a crevasse of fog, I tacked sharply in the direction of the coast; but it was by then impossible for us to say how long we had been flying towards the high seas. Nor were we certain of making the coast, for our fuel was probably low. And even so, once we had reached it we would still have to make port – after the moon had set.

We had no means of angular orientation, were already deafened, and were bit by bit growing blind. The moon like a pallid ember began to go out in the banks of fog. Overhead the sky was filling with clouds, and we flew thenceforth between cloud and fog in a world voided of all substance and all light. The ports that signalled us had given up trying to tell us where we were. 'No bearings, no bearings,' was all their message, for our voice reached them from everywhere and nowhere. With sinking hearts Néri and I leaned out, he on his side and I on mine, to see if anything, anything at all, was distinguishable in this void. Already our tired eyes were seeing things – errant signs, delusive flashes, phantoms.

And suddenly, when already we were in despair, low on the horizon a brilliant point was unveiled on our port bow. A wave of joy went through me. Néri leaned forward, and I could hear him singing. It could not but be the beacon of an airport, for after dark the whole Sahara goes black and forms a great dead expanse. That light twinkled for a space – and then went out! We had been steering for a star which was visible for a few minutes only, just before setting on the horizon between the layer of fog and the clouds.

Then other stars took up the game, and with a sort of dogged hope we set our course for each of them in turn. Each time that a light lingered a while, we performed the same crucial experiment. Néri would send his message to the airport at Cisneros: 'Beacon in view. Put out your light and flash three times.' And Cisneros would put out its beacon and flash three times while the hard light at which we gazed would not, incorruptible star, so much as wink. And despite our dwindling fuel we continued to nibble at the golden bait which each time seemed more surely the true light of a beacon, was each time a promise of a landing and of life – and we had each time to change our star.

And with that we knew ourselves to be lost in interplanetary space among a thousand inaccessible planets, we who sought only the one veritable planet, our own, that planet on which alone we should find our familiar countryside, the houses of our friends, our treasures.

On which alone we should find ... Let me draw the picture that took shape before my eyes. It will seem to you childish; but even in the midst of danger a man retains his human concerns. I was thirsty and I was hungry. If we did find Cisneros we should re-fuel and carry on to Casablanca, and there we should come down in the cool of daybreak, free to idle the hours away. Néri and I would go into town. We would go to a little pub already open despite the early hour. Safe and sound, Néri and I would sit down at table and laugh at the night of danger as we ate our warm rolls and drank our bowls of coffee and hot milk. We would receive this matutinal gift at the hands of life. Even as an old peasant woman recognizes her God in a painted image, in a childish medal, in a chaplet, so life would speak to us in its humblest language in order that we understand. The joy of living, I say, was summed up for me in the remembered sensation of that first burning and aromatic swallow, that mixture of milk and coffee and bread by which men hold communion with tranquil pastures, exotic plantations, and golden harvests, communion with the earth. Amidst all these stars there was but one that could make itself significant for us by composing this aromatic bowl that was its daily gift at dawn. And from that earth of men, that earth docile to the reaping of grain and the harvesting of the grape, bearing its rivers asleep in their fields, its villages clinging to their hillsides, our ship was separated by astronomical distances.

All the treasures of the world were summed up in a grain of dust now blown far out of our path by the very destiny itself of dust and of the orbs of night.

And Néri still prayed to the stars.

Suddenly he was pounding my shoulder. On the bit of paper he held forth impatiently to me I read: 'All well. Magnificent news.' I waited with beating heart while he scribbled the half-dozen words that were to save us. At last he put this grace of heaven into my hands.

It was dated from Casablanca, which we had left the night before. Delayed in transmission, it had suddenly found us more than a thousand miles away, suspended between cloud and fog, lost at sea. It was sent by the government representative at the airport. And it said: 'Monsieur de Saint-Exupéry, I am obliged to recommend that you be disciplined at Paris for having flown too close to the hangars on leaving Casablanca.'

It was true that I had done this. It was also true that this man was performing his duty with irritability. I should have been humiliated if this reproach had been addressed to me in an airport. But it reached me where it had no right to reach me. Among these too rare stars, on this bed of fog, in this menacing savour of the sea, it burst like a detonation. Here we were with our fate in our hands, the fate of the mails and of the ship; we had trouble enough to try to keep alive; and this man was purging his petty rancour against us.

But Néri and I were far from nettled. What we felt was a vast and sudden jubilation. Here it was we who were masters, and this man was letting us know it. The impudent little corporal! not to have looked at our stripes and seen that we had been promoted captain! To intrude into our musings when we were solemnly taking our constitutional between Sagittarius and the Great Bear! When the only thing we could be concerned with, the only thing of our order of magnitude, was this appointment we were missing with the moon!

The immediate duty, the only duty of the planet whence this man's message came, was to furnish us accurate figures for our computations among the stars. And its figures had been false. This being so, the planet had only to hold its tongue. Néri scribbled: 'Instead of wasting their time with this nonsense they would do better to haul us back to Cisneros, if they can.' By 'they' he meant all the peoples of the globe, with their parliaments, their senates, their navies, their armies, their emperors. We re-read the message from that man mad enough to imagine that he had business with us, and tacked in the direction of Mercury.

It was by the purest chance that we were saved. I had given up all thought of making Cisneros and had set my course at right angles to the coast-line in the hope that thus we might avoid coming down at sea when our fuel ran out. Meanwhile, however, I was in the belly of a dense fog, so that even with land below it was not going to be easy to set the ship down. The situation was so clear that already I was shrugging my shoulders ruefully when Néri passed me a second message which, an hour earlier, would have been our salvation. 'Cisneros,' it said, 'has deigned to communicate with us. Cisneros says, "216 doubtful." ' Well, that helped. Cisneros was no longer swallowed up in space, it was actually out there on our left, almost within reach. But how far away? Néri and I talked it over briefly, decided it was too late to try for it (since that might mean missing the coast), and Néri replied: 'Only one hour fuel left continuing on 93.'

But the airports one by one had been waking each other up. Into our dialogue broke the voices of Agadir, Casablanca, Dakar. The radio stations at each of these towns had warned the airports and the ports had flashed the news to our comrades. Bit by bit they were gathering round us as round a sickbed. Vain warmth, but human warmth after all. Helpless concern, but affectionate at any rate.

And suddenly into this conclave burst Toulouse, the headquarters of the Line three thousand miles away, worried along with the rest. Toulouse broke in without a word of greeting, simply to say sharply : 'Your reserve tanks bigger than standard. You have two hours' fuel left. Proceed to Cisneros.'

There is no need of nights like the one just described to make the airline pilot find new meanings in old appearances. The scene that strikes the passenger as commonplace is from the very moment of taking off animated with a powerful magic for the crew. It is the duty of the ship's captain to make port, cost what it may. The sight of massing clouds is no mere spectacle to him: it is a matter of concern to his physical being, and to his mind it means a set of problems. Before he is off the ground he has taken its measure, and between him and it a bond is formed which is a veritable language.

There is a peak ahead, still distant. The pilot will not reach it before another hour of flight in the night. What is to be the significance of that peak? On a night of full moon it will be a useful landmark. In fainter moonglow it will be a bit of wreckage strewn in shadow, dangerous but marked clearly enough by the lights of villages. But if the pilot flies blind, has bad luck in correcting his drift, is dubious about his position, that peak begins to stir with a strange life and its threat fills the breadth of the night sky in the same way as a single mine, drifting at the will of the current, can render the whole of the ocean a danger.

The face of the sea is as variable as that of the earth. To passengers, the storm is invisible. Seen from a great height, the waves have no relief and the pockets of fog have no movement. The surface of the sea appears to be covered with great white motionless palm-trees, palms marked with ribs and seams stiff in a sort of frost. The sea is like a splintered mirror. But the hydroplane pilot knows there is no landing here.

The hours during which a man flies over this mirror are hours in which there is no assurance of the possession of anything in the world. These palms beneath the plane are so many poisoned flowers. And even when the flight is an easy one, made under a shining sun, the pilot navigating at some point on the line is not gazing upon a scene. These colours of earth and sky, these traces of wind over the face of the sea, these clouds golden in the afterglow, are not objects of the pilot's admiration but of his cogitation. He looks to them to tell him the direction of the wind or the progress of the storm, and the quality of the night to come.

Even as the peasant strolling about his domain is able to foresee in a thousand signs the coming of the spring, the threat of frost, a promise of rain, so all that happens in the sky signals to the pilot the oncoming snow, the expectancy of fog, or the

23

peace of a blessed night. The machine which at first blush seems a means of isolating man from the great problems of nature, actually plunges him more deeply into them. As for the peasant so for the pilot, dawn and twilight become events of consequence. His essential problems are set him by the mountain, the sea, the wind. Alone before the vast tribunal of the tempestuous sky, the pilot defends his mails and debates on terms of equality with those three elemental divinities.

The mail pouches for which he is responsible are stowed away in the after-hold. They constitute the dogma of the religion of his craft, the torch which, in this aerial race, is passed from runner to runner. What matter though they hold but the scribblings of tradesmen and nondescript lovers. The interests which dictated them may very well not be worth the embrace of man and storm; but I know what they become once they have been entrusted to the crew, taken over, as the phrase is. The crew care not a rap for banker or tradesman. If, some day, the crew are hooked by a cliff it will not have been in the interest of tradespeople that they will have died, but in obedience to orders which ennoble the sacks of mail once they are on board ship.

What concerns us is not even the orders – it is the men they cast in their mould.

2 The Men

Mermoz is one airline pilot, and Guillaumet another, of whom
I shall write briefly in order that you may see clearly what I
mean when I say that in the mould of this new profession a
new breed of men has been cast.

I

A handful of pilots, of whom Mermoz was one, surveyed the
Casablanca–Dakar line across the territory inhabited by the
refractory tribes of the Sahara. Motors in those days being what
they were, Mermoz was taken prisoner one day by the Moors,
The tribesmen were unable to make up their minds to kill him,
kept him a captive a fortnight, and he was eventually ransomed.
Whereupon he continued to fly over the same territory.

When the South American line was opened up Mermoz, ever
the pioneer, was given the job of surveying the division between
Buenos Aires and Santiago de Chile. He who had flung a bridge
over the Sahara was now to do the same over the Andes. They
had given him a plane whose absolute ceiling was sixteen
thousand feet and had asked him to fly it over a mountain
range that rose more than twenty thousand feet into the air.
His job was to search for gaps in the Cordilleras. He who had
studied the face of the sands was now to learn the contours of
the peaks, those crags whose scarfs of snow flutter restlessly in
the winds, whose surfaces are bleached white in the storms,
whose blustering gusts sweep through the narrow walls of their
rocky corridors and force the pilot to a sort of hand-to-hand
combat. Mermoz enrolled in this war in complete ignorance of
his adversary, with no notion at all of the chances of coming
forth alive from battle with this enemy. His job was to 'try
out' for the rest of us. And, 'trying out' one day, he found
himself prisoner of the Andes.

Mermoz and his mechanic had been forced down at an altitude of twelve thousand feet on a table-land at whose edges the mountain dropped sheer on all sides. For two mortal days they hunted a way off this plateau. But they were trapped. Everywhere the same sheer drop. And so they played their last card.

Themselves still in it, they sent the plane rolling and bouncing down an incline over the rocky ground until it reached the precipice, went off into air, and dropped. In falling, the plane picked up enough speed to respond to the controls. Mermoz was able to tilt its nose in the direction of a peak, sweep over the peak, and, while the water spurted through all the pipes burst by the night frost, the ship already disabled after only seven minutes of flight, he saw beneath him like a promised land the Chilean plain.

And the next day he was at it again.

When the Andes had been thoroughly explored and the technique of the crossings perfected, Mermoz turned over this section of the line to his friend Guillaumet and set out to explore the night. The lighting of our airports had not yet been worked out. Hovering in the pitch-black night, Mermoz would land by the faint glimmer of three petrol flares lined up at one end of the field. This trick, too, he taught us, and then, having tamed the night, he tried the ocean. He was the first, in 1931, to carry the mails in four days from Toulouse to Buenos Aires. On his way home he had engine trouble over a stormy sea in mid-Atlantic. A passing steamer picked him up with his mails and his crew.

Pioneering thus, Mermoz had cleared the desert, the mountains, the night, and the sea. He had been forced down more than once in desert, in mountain, in night, and in sea. And each time that he got safely home, it was but to start out again. Finally, after a dozen years of service, having taken off from Dakar bound for Natal, he radioed briefly that he was cutting off his rear right-hand engine. Then silence.

There was nothing particularly disturbing in this news. Nevertheless, when ten minutes had gone by without report there began for every radio station on the South Atlantic line, from Paris to Buenos Aires, a period of anxious vigil. It would be ridiculous to worry over someone ten minutes late in our day-to-day existence, but in the air-mail service ten minutes can be pregnant with meaning. At the heart of this dead slice of time an unknown event is locked up. Insignificant, it may be; a mishap, possibly: whatever it is, the event has taken place. Fate has pronounced a decision from which there is no appeal. An iron hand has guided a crew to a sea-landing that may have been safe and may have been disastrous. And long hours must go by before the decision of the gods is made known to those who wait.

We waited. We hoped. Like all men at some time in their lives we lived through that inordinate expectancy which like a fatal malady grows from minute to minute harder to bear. Even before the hour sounded, in our hearts many among us were already sitting up with the dead. All of us had the same vision before our eyes. It was a vision of a cockpit still inhabited by living men; but the pilot's hands were telling him very little now, and the world in which he groped and fumbled was a world he did not recognize. Behind him, in the glimmer of the cabin light, a shapeless uneasiness floated. The crew moved to and fro, discussed their plight, feigned sleep. A restless slumber it was, like the stirring of drowned men. The only element of sanity, of intelligibility, was the whirring of the three engines with its reassuring evidence that time still existed for them.

We were haunted for hours by this vision of a plane in distress. But the hands of the clock were going round and little by little it began to grow late. Slowly the truth was borne in upon us that our comrades would never return, that they were sleeping in that South Atlantic whose skies they had so often ploughed. Mermoz had done his job and slipped away to rest, like a gleaner who, having carefully bound his sheaf, lies down in the field to sleep.

When a pilot dies in the harness his death seems something that inheres in the craft itself, and in the beginning the hurt it brings is perhaps less than the pain sprung of a different death. Assuredly he has vanished, has undergone his ultimate mutation; but his presence is still not missed as deeply as we might

27

miss bread. For in this craft we take it for granted that we shall meet together only rarely.

Airline pilots are widely dispersed over the face of the world. They land alone at scattered and remote airports, isolated from each other rather in the manner of sentinels between whom no words can be spoken. It needs the accident of journeyings to bring together here or there the dispersed members of this great professional family.

Round the table in the evening, at Casablanca, at Dakar, at Buenos Aires, we take up conversations interrupted by years of silence, we resume friendships to the accompaniment of buried memories. And then we are off again.

Thus is the earth at once a desert and a paradise, rich in secret hidden gardens, gardens inaccessible, but to which the craft leads us ever back, one day or another. Life may scatter us and keep us apart; it may prevent us from thinking very often of one another; but we know that our comrades are somewhere 'out there' – where, one can hardly say – silent, forgotten, but deeply faithful. And when our path crosses theirs, they greet us with such manifest joy, shake us so gaily by the shoulders! Indeed we are accustomed to waiting.

Bit by bit, nevertheless, it comes over us that we shall never again hear the laughter of our friend, that this one garden is for ever locked against us. And at that moment begins our true mourning, which, though it may not be rending, is yet a little bitter. For nothing, in truth, can replace that companion. Old friends cannot be created out of hand. Nothing can match the treasure of common memories, of trials endured together, of quarrels and reconciliations and generous emotions. It is idle, having planted an acorn in the morning, to expect that afternoon to sit in the shade of the oak.

So life goes on. For years we plant the seed, we feel ourselves rich; and then come other years when time does its work and our plantation is made sparse and thin. One by one, our comrades slip away, deprive us of their shade.

This, then, is the moral taught us by Mermoz and his kind. We understand better, because of him, that what constitutes the dignity of a craft is that it creates a fellowship, that it binds men together and fashions for them a common language. For there is but one veritable problem – the problem of human relations.

We forget that there is no hope of joy except in human relations. If I summon up those memories that have left with me an enduring savour, if I draw up the balance sheet of the hours in my life that have truly counted, surely I find only those that no wealth could have procured me. True riches cannot be bought. One cannot buy the friendship of a Mermoz, of a companion to whom one is bound for ever by ordeals suffered in common. There is no buying the night flight with its hundred thousand stars, its serenity, its few hours of sovereignty. It is not money that can procure for us that new vision of the world won through hardship – those trees, flowers, women, those treasures made fresh by the dew and colour of life which the dawn restores to us, this concert of little things that sustain us and constitute our compensation.

Nor that night we lived through in the land of the unconquered tribes of the Sahara, which now floats into my memory.

Three crews of Aéropostale men had come down at the fall of day on the Rio de Oro coast in a part of the Sahara whose denizens acknowledge no European rule. Riguelle had landed first, with a broken connecting rod. Bourgat had come along to pick up Riguelle's crew, but a minor accident had nailed him to earth. Finally, as night was beginning to fall, I arrived. We decided to salvage Bourgat's ship, but we should have to spend the night and do the job of repair by daylight.

Exactly on this spot two of our comrades, Gourp and Erable, had been murdered by the tribesmen a year earlier. We knew that a raiding party of three hundred rifles was at this very moment encamped somewhere nearby, round Cape Bojador. Our three landings had been visible from a great distance and the Moors must have seen us. We began a vigil which might turn out to be our last.

Altogether, there were about ten of us, pilots and mechanics, when we made ready for the night. We unloaded five or six wooden cases of merchandise out of the hold, emptied them, and set them about in a circle. At the deep end of each case, as in a sentry-box, we set a lighted candle, its flame poorly sheltered from the wind. So in the heart of the desert, on the naked rind of the planet, in an isolation like that of the beginnings of the world, we built a village of men.

Sitting in the flickering light of the candles on this kerchief of sand, on this village square, we waited in the night. We were waiting for the rescuing dawn – or for the Moors. Something, I know not what, lent this night a savour of Christmas. We told stories, we joked, we sang songs. In the air there was that slight fever that reigns over a gaily prepared feast. And yet we were infinitely poor. Wind, sand, and stars. The austerity of Trappists. But on this badly lighted cloth, a handful of men who possessed nothing in the world but their memories were sharing invisible riches.

We had met at last. Men travel side by side for years, each locked up in his own silence or exchanging those words which carry no freight – till danger comes. Then they stand shoulder to shoulder. They discover that they belong to the same family. They wax and bloom in the recognition of fellow-beings. They look at one another and smile. They are like the prisoner set free who marvels at the immensity of the sea.

Happiness! It is useless to seek it elsewhere than in this warmth of human relations. Our sordid interests imprison us within their walls. Only a comrade can grasp us by the hand and haul us free.

And these human relations must be created. One must go through an apprenticeship to learn the job. Games and risk are a help here. When we exchange manly handshakes, compete in races, join together to save one of us who is in trouble, cry aloud for help in the hour of danger – only then do we learn that we are not alone on earth.

Each man must look to himself to teach him the meaning of life. It is not something discovered: it is something moulded. These prison walls that this age of trade has built up round us, we can break down. We can still run free, call to our comrades, and marvel to hear once more, in response to our call, the pathetic chant of the human voice.

Guillaumet, old friend, of you too I shall say a few words. Be sure that I shall not make you squirm with any clumsy vaunting of your courage and your professional valour. In telling the story of the most marvellous of your adventures, I am after something quite different.

There exists a quality which is nameless. It may be gravity, but the word does not satisfy me, for the quality I have in mind can be accompanied by the most cheerful gaiety. It is the quality of the carpenter face to face with his block of wood. He handles it, he takes its measure. Far from treating it frivolously, he summons all his professional virtues to do it honour.

I once read, Guillaumet, a tale in which your adventure was celebrated. I have an old score to settle with the infidel who wrote it. You were described as abounding in the witty sallies of the street arab, as if courage consisted in demeaning oneself to schoolboy banter in the midst of danger and the hour of death. The man did not know you, Guillaumet. You never felt the need of cheapening your adversaries before confronting them. When you saw a foul storm you said to yourself: 'Here is a foul storm.' You accepted it, and you took its measure.

These pages, Guillaumet, written out of my memory, are addressed in homage to you.

It was winter and you had been gone a week over the Andes. I had come up from farthest Patagonia to join Deley at Mendoza. For five days the two of us, each in his plane, had ransacked the mountains unavailingly. Two ships! It seemed to us that a hundred squadrons navigating for a hundred years would not have been enough to explore that endless, cloud-piercing range. We had lost all hope. The very smugglers themselves, bandits who would commit a crime for a five-peso note, refused to form a rescue party out of fear of those counterforts. 'We should surely die,' they said; 'the Andes never give up a man in winter.'

And when Deley and I landed at Santiago, the Chilean officers also advised us to give you up. 'It is midwinter,' they said; 'even if your comrade survived the landing, he cannot have survived the night. Night in those passes changes a man into ice.'

And when, a second time, I slipped between the towering walls and giant pillars of the Andes, it seemed to me I was no longer seeking, but was now sitting up with, your body in the silence of a cathedral of snow.

You had been gone a week, I say, and I was lunching between flights in a restaurant in Mendoza when a man stuck his head in the door and called out:

'They've found Guillaumet!'

All the strangers in the restaurant embraced.

Ten minutes later I was off the ground, carrying two mechanics, Lefebvre and Abri. Forty minutes later I had landed alongside a road, having recognized from the air, I know not by what sign, the car in which you were being brought down from San Rafael. I remember that we cried like fools; we put our arms about a living Guillaumet, resuscitated, the author of his own miracle. And it was at that moment that you pronounced your first intelligible sentence, a speech admirable in its human pride:

'I swear that what I went through, no animal would have gone through.'

Later, you told us the story. A storm that brought fifteen feet of snow in forty-eight hours down on the Chilean slope had bottled up all space and sent every other mail pilot back to his starting point. You, however, had taken off in the hope of finding a rift in the sky. You found this rift, this trap, a little to the south, and now, at twenty thousand feet, the ceiling of clouds being a couple of thousand feet below you and pierced by only the highest peaks, you set your course for Argentina.

Down-currents sometimes fill pilots with a strange uneasiness. The engines run on, but the ship seems to be sinking. You jockey to hold your altitude: the ship loses speed and goes mushy. And still you sink. So you give it up, afraid that you may have jockeyed too much; and you let yourself drift to right or left, striving to put at your back a favourable peak, that is, a peak off which the winds rebound as off a springboard.

And yet you go on sinking. The whole sky seems to be coming down on you. You begin to feel like the victim of some cosmic accident. You cannot land anywhere, and you try in vain to turn round and fly back into those zones where the air, as dense and solid as a pillar, had held you up. That pillar has melted away. Everything here is rotten and you slither about in a sort of universal decomposition while the cloud-bank rises apathetically, reaches your level, and swallows you up.

'It almost had me in a corner once,' you explained, 'but I still wasn't sure I was caught. When you get up above the clouds you run into those down-currents that seem to be perfectly stationary for the simple reason that in that very high altitude they never stop flowing. Everything is queer in the upper range.'

And what clouds!

'As soon as I felt I was caught I dropped the controls and grabbed my seat for fear of being flung out of the ship. The jolts were so terrible that my leather harness cut my shoulders and was ready to snap. And what with the frosting on the panes, my artificial horizon was invisible and the wind rolled me over and over like a hat in a road from eighteen thousand feet down to ten.

'At ten thousand I caught a glimpse of a dark horizontal blot that helped me right the ship. It was a lake, and I recognized it as what they call Laguna Diamante. I remembered that it lay at the bottom of a funnel, and that one flank of the funnel, a volcano called Maipu, ran up to about twenty thousand feet.

'There I was, safe out of the clouds; but I was still blinded by the thick swirling snow and I had to hang on to my lake if I wasn't to crash into one of the sides of the funnel. So down I went, and I flew round and round the lake, about a hundred and fifty feet above it, until I ran out of fuel. After two hours of this, I set the ship down on the snow — and over on her nose she went.

'When I dragged myself clear of her I stood up. The wind knocked me down. I stood up again. Over I went a second time. So I crawled under the cockpit and dug me out a shelter in the snow. I pulled a lot of mail sacks round me, and there

I lay for two days and two nights. Then the storm blew over and I started to walk my way out. I walked for five days and four nights.'

But what was there left of you, Guillaumet? We had found you again, true; but burnt to a crisp, shrivelled, and shrunken into an old woman. That same afternoon I flew you back to Mendoza, and there the cool white sheets flowed like a balm down the length of your body.

They were not enough, though. Your own foundered body was an encumbrance: you turned and twisted in your sleep, unable to find lodgement for it. I stared at your face: it was splotched and swollen, like an over-ripe fruit that has been repeatedly dropped on the ground.

You were dreadful to see, and you were in misery, for you had lost the beautiful tools of your work: your hands were numb and useless, and when you sat up on the edge of your bed to draw a free breath, your frozen feet hung down like two dead weights. You had not even finished your long walk back, you were still panting; and when you turned and stirred on the pillow in search of peace, a procession of images that you could not escape, a procession waiting impatiently in the wings moved instantly into action under your skull. Across the stage of your skull it moved, and for the twentieth time you fought once more the battle against these enemies that rose up out of their ashes.

I filled you with herb-teas.

'Drink, old fellow.'

'You know ... what amazed me ...'

Boxer victorious, but punch-drunk and scarred with blows, you were re-living your strange adventure. You could divest yourself of it only in scraps. And as you told your dark tale I could see you trudging without ice-axe, without ropes, without provisions, scaling cols fifteen thousand feet in the air, crawling on the faces of vertical walls, your hands and feet and knees bleeding in a temperature twenty degrees below zero.

Voided bit by bit of your blood, your strength, your reason, you went forward with the obstinacy of an ant, retracing your steps to go round an obstacle, picking yourself up after each fall to earth, climbing slopes that led to abysses, ceaselessly in motion and never asleep, for had you slept, from that bed of snow you would never have risen. When your foot slipped and you went down, you were up again in an instant, else had you been turned into stone. The cold was petrifying you by the minute, and the price you paid for taking a moment too much of rest, when you fell, was the agony of revivifying dead muscles in your struggle to rise to your feet.

You resisted temptation. 'Amid snow,' you told me, 'a man loses his instinct of self-preservation. After two or three or four days of tramping, all you think about is sleep. I would long for it; but then I would say to myself : "If my wife still believes I am alive, she must believe that I am on my feet. The boys all think that I am on my feet. They have faith in me. And I am a skunk if I don't go on." '

So you tramped on; and each day you cut out a bit more of the opening of your shoes so that your swelling and freezing feet might have room in them.

You confided to me this strange thing :

'As early as the second day, you know, the hardest job I had was to force myself not to think. The pain was too much, and I was really up against it too hard. I had to forget that, or I shouldn't have had the heart to go on walking. But I didn't seem able to control my mind. It kept working like a turbine. Still, I could more or less choose what I was to think about. I tried to stick to some film I'd seen, or book I'd read. But the film and the book would go through my mind like lightning. And I'd be back where I was, in the snow. It never failed. So I would think about other things . . .'

There was one time, however, when, having slipped, and finding yourself stretched flat on your face in the snow, you threw in your hand. You were like a boxer emptied of all passions by a single blow, lying and listening to the seconds drop one by one into a distant universe, until the tenth second fell and there was no appeal.

'I've done my best and I can't make it. Why go on ?' All that you had to do in the world to find peace was to shut your eyes. So little was needed to blot out that world of crags and ice and snow. Let drop those miraculous eyelids and there was an end of blows, of stumbling falls, of torn muscles and burning ice, of that burden of life you were dragging along like a worn-out ox, a weight heavier than any wain or cart.

Already you were beginning to taste the relief of this snow that had now become an insidious poison, this morphia that was filling you with beatitude. Life crept out of your extremities and fled to collect round your heart while something gentle and precious snuggled in close at the centre of your being. Little by little your consciousness deserted the distant regions of your body, and your body, that beast now gorged with suffering, lay ready to participate in the indifference of marble.

Your very scruples subsided. Our cries ceased to reach you, or, more accurately, changed for you into dream-cries. You were happy now, able to respond by long confident dream-strides that carried you effortlessly towards the enchantment of the plains below. How smoothly you glided into this suddenly merciful world! Guillaumet, you miser! You had made up your mind to deny us your return, to take your pleasures selfishly without us among your white angels in the snows. And then remorse floated up from the depths of your consciousness. The dream was spoilt by the irruption of bothersome details. 'I thought of my wife. She would be penniless if she couldn't collect the insurance. Yes, but the company . . .'

When a man vanishes, his legal death is postponed for four years. This awful detail was enough to blot out the other visions. You were lying face downward on a bed of snow that covered a steep mountain slope. With the coming of summer your body would be washed with this slush down into one of the thousand crevasses of the Andes. You knew that. But you also knew that some fifty yards away a rock was jutting up out of the snow. 'I thought, if I get up I may be able to reach it. And if I can prop myself up against the rock, they'll find me there next summer.'

Once you were on your feet again, you tramped two nights and three days. But you did not then imagine that you would go on much longer :

'I could tell by different signs that the end was coming. For instance, I had to stop every two or three hours to cut my shoes open a bit more and massage my swollen feet. Or maybe my heart would be going too fast. But I was beginning to lose my memory. I had been going on a long time when suddenly I realized that every time I stopped I forgot something. The first time it was a glove. And it was cold! I had put it down in front of me and had forgotten to pick it up. The next time it was my watch. Then my knife. Then my compass. Each time I stopped I stripped myself of something vitally important. I was becoming my own enemy! And I can't tell you how it hurt me when I found that out.

'What saves a man is to take a step. Then another step. It is always the same step, but you have to take it.'

'I swear that what I went through, no animal would have gone through.' This sentence, the noblest ever spoken, this sentence that defines man's place in the universe, that honours him, that re-establishes the true hierarchy, floated back into my thoughts. Finally you fell asleep. Your consciousness was abolished; but forth from this dismantled, burnt, and shattered body it was to be born again like a flower put forth gradually by the species which itself is born of the luminous pulp of the stars. The body, we may say, then, is but an honest tool, the body is but a servant. And it was in these words, Guillaumet, that you expressed your pride in the honest tool:

'With nothing to eat, after three days on my feet . . . well . . . my heart wasn't going any too well. I was crawling along the side of a sheer wall, hanging over space, digging and kicking out pockets in the ice so that I could hold on, when all of a sudden my heart conked. It hesitated. Started up again. Beat crazily. I said to myself, "If it hesitates a moment too long, I drop." I stayed still and listened to myself. Never, never in my life have I listened as carefully to a motor as I listened to my heart, me hanging there. I said to it: "Come on, old boy. Go to work. Try beating a little." That's good stuff my heart is made of. I hesitated, but it went on. You don't know how proud I was of that heart.'

As I said, in that room in Mendoza where I sat with you, you fell finally into an exhausted sleep. And I thought: If we were to talk to him about his courage, Guillaumet would shrug his

37

shoulders. But it would be just as false to extol his modesty. His place is far beyond that mediocre virtue.

If he shrugs his shoulders, it is because he is no fool. He knows that once men are caught up in an event they cease to be afraid. Only the unknown frightens men. But once a man has faced the unknown, that terror becomes the known.

Especially if it is scrutinized with Guillaumet's lucid gravity. Guillaumet's courage is in the main the product of his honesty. But even this is not his fundamental quality. His moral greatness consists in his sense of responsibility. He knew that he was responsible for himself, for the mails, for the fulfilment of the hopes of his comrades. He was holding in his hands their sorrow and their joy. He was responsible for that new element which the living were constructing and in which he was a participant. Responsible, in as much as his work contributed to it, for the fate of those men.

Guillaumet was one among those bold and generous men who had taken upon themselves the task of spreading their foliage over bold and generous horizons. To be a man is, precisely, to be responsible. It is to feel shame at the sight of what seems to be unmerited misery. It is to take pride in a victory won by one's comrades. It is to feel, when setting one's stone, that one is contributing to the building of the world.

There is a tendency to class such men with toreadors and gamblers. People extol their contempt for death. But I would not give a fig for anybody's contempt for death. If its roots are not sunk deep in an acceptance of responsibility, this contempt for death is the sign either of an impoverished soul or of youthful extravagance.

I once knew a young suicide. I cannot remember what disappointment in love it was which induced him to send a bullet carefully into his heart. I have no notion what literary temptation he had succumbed to when he drew on a pair of white gloves before the shot. But I remember having felt, on learning of this sorry show, an impression not of nobility but of lack of dignity. So! Behind that attractive face, beneath that skull which should have been a treasure chest, there had been nothing, nothing at all. Unless it was the vision of some silly little girl indistinguishable from the rest.

And when I heard of this meagre destiny, I remembered the death of a man. He was a gardener, and he was speaking on his deathbed: 'You know, I used to sweat sometimes when I was digging. My rheumatism would pull at my leg, and I would damn myself for a slave. And now, do you know, I'd like to spade and spade. It's beautiful work. A man is free when he is using a spade. And besides, who is going to prune my trees when I am gone?'

That man was leaving behind him a fallow field, a fallow planet. He was bound by ties of love to all cultivable land and to all the trees of the earth. There was a generous man, a prodigal man, a nobleman! There was a man who, battling against death in the name of his Creation, could, like Guillaumet, be called a man of courage!

3 The Tool

And now, having spoken of the men born of the pilot's craft, I shall say something about the tool with which they work – the aeroplane. Have you looked at a modern aeroplane? Have you followed from year to year the evolution of its lines? Have you ever thought, not only about the aeroplane but about whatever man builds, that all of man's industrial efforts, all his computations and calculations, all the nights spent over working draughts and blue-prints, invariably culminate in the production of a thing whose sole and guiding principle is the ultimate principle of simplicity?

It is as if there were a natural law which ordained that to achieve this end, to refine the curve of a piece of furniture, or a ship's keel, or the fuselage of an aeroplane, until gradually it partakes of the elementary purity of the curve of a human breast or shoulder, there must be the experimentation of several generations of craftsmen. In anything at all, perfection is finally attained not when there is no longer anything to add but when there is no longer anything to take away, when a body has been stripped down to its nakedness.

It results from this that perfection of invention touches hands with absence of invention, as if that line which the human eye will follow with effortless delight were a line that had not been invented but simply discovered, had in the beginning been hidden by nature and in the end been found by the engineer. There is an ancient myth about the image asleep in the block of marble until it is carefully disengaged by the sculptor. The sculptor must himself feel that he is not so much inventing or shaping the curve of breast or shoulder as delivering the image from its prison.

In this spirit do engineers, physicists concerned with thermodynamics, and the swarm of preoccupied draughtsmen tackle their work. In appearance, but only in appearance, they seem to be polishing surfaces and refining away angles, easing this joint or stabilizing that wing, rendering these parts invisible, so that in the end there is no longer a wing hooked to a framework but a form flawless in its perfection, completely disengaged from its matrix, a sort of spontaneous whole, its parts mysteriously fused together and resembling in their unity a poem.

Meanwhile, startling as it is that all visible evidence of invention should have been refined out of this instrument and that there should be delivered to us an object as natural as a pebble polished by the waves, it is equally wonderful that he who uses this instrument should be able to forget that it is a machine.

There was a time when a flyer sat at the centre of a complicated works. Flight sets us factory problems. The indicators that oscillated on the instrument panel warned us of a thousand dangers. But in the machine of today we forget that motors are whirring: the motor, finally, has come to fulfil its function, which is to whirr as a heart beats – and we give no thought to the beating of our heart. Thus, precisely because it is perfect the machine dissembles its own existence instead of forcing itself upon our notice.

And thus, also, the realities of nature resume their pride of place. It is not with metal that the pilot is in contact. Contrary to the vulgar illusion, it is thanks to the metal, and by virtue of it, that the pilot rediscovers nature. As I have already said, the machine does not isolate man from the great problems of nature but plunges him more deeply into them.

Numerous, nevertheless, are the moralists who have attacked the machine as the source of all the ills we bear, who, creating a fictitious dichotomy, have denounced the mechanical civilization as the enemy of the spiritual civilization.

If what they think were really so, then indeed we should have to despair of man, for it would be futile to struggle against this new advancing chaos. The machine is certainly as irresistible in its advance as those virgin forests that encroach upon equatorial domains. A congeries of motives prevents us from blowing up our spinning mills and reviving the distaff. Gandhi had a try at this sort of revolution: he was as simple-minded as a child trying to empty the sea on to the sand with the aid of a tea-cup.

It is hard for me to understand the language of these pseudo-dreamers. What is it makes them think that the ploughshare torn from the bowels of the earth by perforating machines, forged, tempered, and sharpened in the roar of modern industry, is nearer to man than any other tool of steel? By what sign do they recognize the inhumanity of the machine?

Have they ever really asked themselves this question? The central struggle of men has ever been to understand one another, to join together for the common weal. And it is this very thing that the machine helps them to do! It begins by annihilating time and space.

To me, in France, a friend speaks from America. The energy that brings me his voice is born of dammed-up waters a thousand miles from where he sits. The energy I burn up in listening to him is dispensed in the same instant by a lake formed in the River Yser which, four thousand miles from him and five hundred from me, melts like snow in the action of the turbines. Transport of the mails, transport of the human voice, transport of flickering pictures – in this century as in others our highest accomplishments still have the single aim of bringing men together. Do our dreamers hold that the invention of writing, of printing, of the sailing ship, degraded the human spirit?

It seems to me that those who complain of man's progress confuse ends with means. True, that man who struggles in the unique hope of material gain will harvest nothing worth while. But how can anyone conceive that the machine is an end? It is a tool. As much a tool as is the plough. The microscope is a tool. What disservice do we do the life of the spirit when we analyse the universe through a tool created by the science of optics, or seek to bring together those who love one another and are parted in space?

'Agreed!' my dreamers will say, 'but explain to us why it is that a decline in human values has accompanied the rise of the machine.' Oh, I miss the village with its crafts and its folksongs as much as they do! The town fed by Hollywood seems to me, too, impoverished despite its electric street lamps. I quite agree that men lose their creative instincts when they are fed thus without raising a hand. And I can see that it is tempting to accuse industry of this evil.

But we lack perspective for the judgement of transformations that go so deep. What are the hundred years of the history of the machine compared with the two hundred thousand years of the history of man? It was only yesterday that we began to pitch our camp in this country of laboratories and power stations, that we took possession of this new, this still unfinished house we live in. Everything round us is new and different – our concerns, our working habits, our relations with one another.

Our very psychology has been shaken to its foundations, to its most secret recesses. Our notions of separation, absence, distance, return, are reflections of a new set of realities, though the words themselves remain unchanged. To grasp the meaning of the world of today we use a language created to express the world of yesterday. The life of the past seems to us nearer our true natures, but only for the reason that it is nearer our language.

Every step on the road of progress takes us farther from habits which, as the life of man goes, we had only recently begun to acquire. We are in truth emigrants who have not yet founded our homeland. We Europeans have become again young peoples, without tradition or language of our own. We shall have to age somewhat before we are able to write the folksongs of a new epoch.

Young barbarians still marvelling at our new toys – that is what we are. Why else should we race our planes, give prizes to those who fly highest, or fastest? We take no heed to ask ourselves why we race: the race itself is more important than the object.

And this holds true of other things than flying. For the colonial soldier who founds an empire, the meaning of life is conquest. He despises the colonist. But was not the very aim of his conquest the settling up of this same colonist?

In the enthusiasm of our rapid mechanical conquests we have overlooked some things. We have perhaps driven men into the service of the machine, instead of building machinery for the service of man. But could anything be more natural? So

43

long as we were engaged in conquest, our spirit was the spirit of conquerors. The time has now come when we must be colonists, must make this house habitable which is still without character.

Little by little the machine will become part of humanity. Read the history of the railways in France, and doubtless elsewhere too : they had all the trouble in the world to tame the people of our villages. The locomotive was an iron monster. Time had to pass before men forgot what it was made of. Mysteriously, life began to run through it, and now it is wrinkled and old. What is it today for the villager except a humble friend who calls every evening at six?

The sailing vessel itself was once a machine born of the calculations of engineers, yet it does not disturb our philosophers. The sloop took its place in the speech of men. There is a poetry of sailing as old as the world. There have always been seamen in recorded time. The man who assumes that there is an essential difference between the sloop and the aeroplane lacks historic perspective.

Every machine will gradually take on this patina and lose its identity in its function.

Air and water, and not machinery, are the concern of the hydroplane pilot about to take off. The motors are running free and the plane is already ploughing the surface of the sea. Under the dizzying whirl of the scythe-like propellers, clusters of silvery water bloom and drown the flotation gear. The element smacks the sides of the hull with a sound like a gong, and the pilot can sense this tumult in the quivering of his body. He feels the ship charging itself with power as from second to second it picks up speed. He feels the development, in these fifteen tons of matter, of a maturity that is about to make flight possible. He closes his hands over the controls, and little by little in his bare palms he receives the gift of this power. The metal organs of the controls, progressively as this gift is made him, become the messengers of the power in his hands. And when his power is ripe, in a gesture gentler than the culling of a flower, the pilot severs the ship from the water and establishes it in the air.

4 The Elements

When Joseph Conrad described a typhoon he said very little about towering waves, or darkness, or the whistling of the wind in the shrouds. He knew better. Instead, he took his reader down into the hold of the vessel, packed with emigrant coolies, where the rolling and the pitching of the ship had ripped up and scattered their bags and bundles, burst open their boxes, and flung their humble belongings into a crazy heap. Family treasures painfully collected in a lifetime of poverty, pitiful mementoes so alike that nobody but their owners could have told them apart, had lost their identity and lapsed into chaos, into anonymity, into an amorphous magma. It was this human drama that Conrad described when he painted a typhoon.

Every airline pilot has flown through tornadoes, has returned out of them to the fold – to the little restaurant in Toulouse where we sat in peace under the watchful eye of the waitress – and there, recognizing his powerlessness to convey what he has been through, has given up the idea of describing hell. His descriptions, his gestures, his big words would have made the rest of us smile as if we were listening to a little boy bragging. And necessarily so. The cyclone of which I am about to speak was, physically, much the most brutal and overwhelming experience I ever underwent; and yet beyond a certain point I do not know how to convey its violence except by piling one adjective on another, so that in the end I should convey no impression at all – unless perhaps that of an embarrassing taste for exaggeration.

It took me some time to grasp the fundamental reason for this powerlessness, which is simply that I should be trying to describe a catastrophe that never took place. The reason why writers fail when they attempt to evoke horror is that horror is something invented after the fact, when one is re-creating the experience over again in the memory. Horror does not manifest itself in the world of reality. And so, in beginning my story of a revolt of the elements which I myself lived through, I have no feeling that I shall write something which you will find dramatic.

I had taken off from the field at Trelew and was flying down to Comodoro-Rivadavia, in the Patagonian Argentine. Here the crust of the earth is as dented as an old boiler. The high-pressure regions over the Pacific send the winds past a gap in the Andes into a corridor fifty miles wide through which they rush to the Atlantic in a strangled and accelerated buffeting that scrapes the surface of everything in their path. The sole vegetation visible in this threadbare landscape is a series of oil derricks looking like the after-effects of a forest fire. Towering over the round hills on which the winds have left a residue of stony gravel, there rises a chain of prow-shaped, saw-toothed, razor-edged mountains stripped by the elements down to the bare rock.

For three months of the year the speed of these winds at ground level is up to a hundred miles an hour. We who flew the route knew that once we had crossed the marshes of Trelew and had reached the threshold of the zone they swept, we should recognize the winds from afar by a grey-blue tint in the atmosphere at the sight of which we would tighten our belts and shoulder-straps in preparation for what was coming. From then on we had an hour of stiff fighting and of stumbling again and again into invisible ditches of air. This was manual labour, and our muscles felt it pretty much as if we had been carrying a longshoreman's load. But it lasted only an hour. Our machines stood up under it. We had no fear of wings suddenly dropping off. Visibility was generally good, and not a problem. This section of the line was a stint, yes; it was certainly not a drama.

But on this particular day I did not like the colour of the sky.

The sky was blue. Pure blue. Too pure. A hard blue sky that shone over the scraped and barren world while the fleshless vertebrae of the mountain chain flashed in the sunlight. Not a cloud. The blue sky glittered like a new-honed knife. I felt in advance the vague distaste that accompanies the prospect of physical exertion. The purity of the sky upset me. Give me a good black storm in which the enemy is plainly visible. I can measure its extent and prepare myself for its attack. I can get my hands on my adversary. But when you are flying very high in clear weather the shock of a blue storm is as disturbing as if something collapsed that had been holding up your ship in the air. It is the only time when a pilot feels that there is a gulf beneath his ship.

Another thing bothered me. I could see on a level with the mountain peaks not a haze, not a mist, not a sandy fog, but a sort of ash-coloured streamer in the sky. I did not like the look of that scarf of filings scraped off the surface of the earth and borne out to sea by the wind. I tightened my leather harness as far as it would go and I steered the ship with one hand while with the other I hung on to one of the struts that ran alongside my seat. I was still flying in remarkably calm air.

Very soon came a slight tremor. As every pilot knows, there are secret little quiverings that foretell your real storm. No rolling, no pitching. No swing to speak of. The flight continues horizontal and rectilinear. But you have felt a warning drum on the wings of your plane, little intermittent rappings scarcely audible and infinitely brief, little cracklings from time to time as if there were traces of gunpowder in the air.

And then everything round me blew up.

Concerning the next couple of minutes I have nothing to say. All that I can find in my memory are a few rudimentary notions, fragments of thoughts, direct observations. I cannot compose them into a dramatic recital because there was no drama. The best I can do is to line them up in a kind of chronological order.

In the first place, I was standing still. Having veered right in order to correct a sudden drift, I saw the landscape freeze abruptly where it was and remain jiggling on the same spot. I was making no headway. My wings had ceased to nibble into the outline of the earth. I could see the earth buckle, pivot – but it stayed put. The plane was skidding as if on a toothless cogwheel.

Meanwhile I had the absurd feeling that I had exposed myself completely to the enemy. All those peaks, those crests,

47

those teeth that were cutting into the wind and unleashing its gusts in my direction, seemed to me so many guns pointed straight at my defenceless person. I was slow to think, but the thought did come to me that I ought to give up altitude and make for one of the neighbouring valleys where I might take shelter against a mountainside. As a matter of fact, whether I liked it or not I was being helplessly sucked down towards the earth.

Trapped this way in the first breaking waves of a cyclone about which I learned, twenty minutes later, that at sea-level it was blowing at the fantastic rate of one hundred and fifty miles an hour, I certainly had no impression of tragedy. Now, as I write, if I shut my eyes, if I forget the plane and the flight and try to express the plain truth about what was happening to me, I find that I felt weighed down, I felt like a porter carrying a slippery load, grabbing one object in a jerky movement that sent another slithering down, so that, overcome by exasperation, the porter is tempted to let the whole load drop. There is a kind of law of the shortest distance to the image, a psychological law by which the event to which one is subjected is visualized in a symbol that represents its swiftest summing up: I was a man who, carrying a pile of plates, had slipped on a waxed ffoor and let his scaffolding of porcelain crash.

I found myself imprisoned in a valley. My discomfort was not less, it was greater. I grant you that backwash has never killed anybody, that the expression 'flattened out on the ground by backwash' belongs to journalism and not to the language of flyers. How could air possibly pierce the ground? But here I was in a valley at the wheel of a ship that was three-quarters out of my control. Ahead of me a rocky prow swung to left and right, rose suddenly high in the air for a second like a wave over my head, and then plunged down below my horizon.

Horizon? There was no longer a horizon. I was in the wings of a theatre cluttered up with bits of scenery. Vertical, oblique, horizontal, all of plane geometry was awhirl. A hundred transversal valleys were muddled in a jumble of perspectives. Whenever I seemed about to take my bearings a new eruption would swing me round in a circle or send me tumbling wing over wing and I would have to try all over again to get clear of all this rubbish. Two ideas came into my mind. One was a discovery: for the first time I understood the cause of certain accidents in the mountains when no fog was present to explain them. For a single second, in a waltzing landscape like this, the flyer had been unable to distinguish between vertical mountainsides and horizontal planes. The other idea was a fixation: The sea is flat: I shall not hook anything out at sea.

I banked – or should I use that word to indicate a vague and stubborn jockeying through the east-west valleys? Still nothing pathetic to report. I was wrestling with disorder, was wearing myself out in a battle with disorder, struggling to keep in the air a gigantic house of cards that kept collapsing despite all I could do. Scarcely the faintest twinge of fear went through me when one of the walls of my prison rose suddenly like a tidal wave over my head. My heart hardly skipped a beat when I was tripped up by one of the whirling eddies of air that the sharp ridge darted into my ship. If I felt anything unmistakably in the haze of confused feelings and notions that came over me each time one of these powder magazines blew up, it was a feeling of respect. I respected that sharp-toothed ridge. I respected that peak. I respected that dome. I respected that transversal valley opening out into my valley and about to toss me God knew how violently as soon as its torrent of wind flowed into the one on which I was being borne along.

What I was struggling against, I discovered, was not the wind but the ridge itself, the crest, the rocky peak. Despite my distance from it, it was the wall of rock I was fighting with. By some trick of invisible prolongation, by the play of a secret set of muscles, this was what was pummelling me. It was against this that I was butting my head. Before me on the right I recognized the peak of Salamanca, a perfect cone which, I knew, dominated the sea. It cheered me to think I was about to escape out to sea. But first I should have to wrestle with the wind off that peak, try to avoid its down-crushing blow. The peak of Salamanca was a giant. I was filled with respect for the peak of Salamanca.

There had been granted me one second of respite. Two seconds. Something was collecting itself into a knot, coiling itself up, growing taut. I sat amazed. I opened astonished eyes. My whole plane seemed to be shivering, spreading outward, swelling up. Horizontal and stationary it was, yet lifted before I knew it fifteen hundred feet straight into the air in a kind of apotheosis. I who for forty minutes had not been able to climb higher than two hundred feet off the ground was suddenly able to look down on the enemy. The plane quivered as if in boiling water. I could see the wide waters of the ocean. The valley opened out into this ocean, this salvation. – And at that very moment, without any warning whatever, half a mile from Salamanca, I was suddenly struck straight in the midriff by the gale off that peak and sent hurtling out to sea.

There I was, throttle wide open, facing the coast. At right angles to the coast and facing it. A lot had happened in a single minute. In the first place, I had not flown out to sea. I had been spat out to sea by a monstrous cough, vomited out of my valley as from the mouth of a howitzer. When, what seemed to me instantly, I banked in order to put myself where I wanted to be in respect of the coast-line, I saw that the coast-line was a mere blur, a characterless strip of blue; and I was five miles out to sea. The mountain range stood up like a crenellated fortress against the pure sky while the cyclone crushed me down to the surface of the waters. How hard that wind was blowing I found out as soon as I tried to climb, as soon as I became conscious of my disastrous mistake: throttle wide open, engines running at maximum, which was one hundred and fifty miles an hour, my plane hanging sixty feet over the water, I was unable to budge. When a wind like this one attacks a tropical forest it swirls through the branches like a flame, twists them into corkscrews, and uproots giant trees as if they were radishes. Here, bounding off the mountain range, it was levelling out the sea.

Hanging on with all the power in my engines, face to the coast, face to that wind where each gap in the teeth of the range sent forth a stream of air like a long reptile, I felt as if I were clinging to the tip of a monstrous whip that was cracking over the sea.

In this latitude the South American continent is narrow and the Andes are not far from the Atlantic. I was struggling not merely against the crushing winds that blew off the east-coast range, but more likely also against a whole sky blown down upon me off the peaks of the Andean chain. For the first time in four years of airline flying I began to worry about the strength of my wings. Also, I was fearful of bumping the sea – not because of the down-currents which, at sea-level, would necessarily provide me with a horizontal air mattress, but because of the helplessly acrobatic positions in which this wind was buffeting me. Each time that I was tossed I became afraid that I might be unable to straighten out. Besides, there was a chance that I should find myself out of fuel and simply drown. I kept expecting the petrol plungers to stop priming, and indeed the plane was so violently shaken up that in the half-filled tanks as well as in the feed pipes the petrol was having trouble coming through and the engines, instead of their steady roar, were giving forth a sort of dot-and-dash series of uncertain explosions.

I hung on, meanwhile, to the controls of my heavy transport plane, my attention monopolized by the physical struggle and my mind occupied by the very simplest thoughts. I was feeling practically nothing as I stared down at the imprint made by the wind on the sea. I saw a series of great white puddles, each perhaps eight hundred yards in extent. They were running towards me at a speed of one hundred and fifty miles an hour where the down-surging wind-spouts broke against the surface of the sea in a succession of horizontal explosions. The sea was white and it was green – white with the whiteness of crushed sugar and green in puddles the colour of emeralds. In this tumult one wave was indistinguishable from another. Torrents of air were pouring down upon the sea. The winds were sweeping past in giant gusts as when, before the autumn harvests, they blow a great flowing change of colour over a wheatfield. Now and again the water went incongruously transparent between the white pools, and I could see a green and black sea-bottom. And then the great glass of the sea would be shattered anew into a thousand glittering fragments.

It seemed hopeless. In twenty minutes of struggle I had not moved forward a hundred yards. What was more, with flying as hard as it was out here five miles from the coast, I wondered how I could possibly buck the winds along the shore, assuming I was able to fight my way in. I was a perfect target for the enemy there on shore. Fear, however, was out of the question. I was incapable of thinking. I was emptied of everything except the vision of a very simple act. I must straighten out. Straighten out. Straighten out.

There were moments of respite, nevertheless. I dare say those moments themselves were equal to the worst storms I had hitherto met, but by comparison with the cyclone they were moments of relaxation. The urgency of fighting off the wind was not quite so great. And I could tell when these intervals were coming. It was not I who moved towards those zones of relative calm, those almost green oases clearly painted on the sea, but they that flowed towards me. I could read clearly in the waters the advertisement of a habitable province. And with each interval of repose the power to feel and to think was restored to me. Then, in those moments, I began to feel I was doomed. Then was the time that little by little I began to tremble for myself. So much so that each time I saw the unfurling of a new wave of the white offensive I was seized by a brief spasm of panic which lasted until the exact instant when, on the edge of that bubbling cauldron, I bumped into the invisible wall of wind. That restored me to numbness again.

Up! I wanted to be higher up. The next time I saw one of those green zones of calm it seemed to me deeper than before and I began to be hopeful of getting out. If I could climb high enough, I thought, I would find other currents in which I could make some headway. I took advantage of the truce to essay a swift climb. It was hard. The enemy had not weakened. Three hundred feet. Six hundred feet. If I could get up to three thousand feet I was safe, I said to myself. But there on the horizon I saw again that white pack unleashed in my direction. I gave it up. I did not want them at my throat again; I did not want to be caught off balance. Too late, though. The first blow sent me rolling over and over and the sky became a slippery dome on which I could not find a footing.

One has a pair of hands and they obey. How are one's orders transmitted to one's hands?

I had made a discovery which horrified me: my hands were numb. My hands were dead. They sent me no message. Probably they had been numb a long time and I had not noticed it. The pity was that I had noticed it, had raised the question. That was serious.

Lashed by the wind, the wings of the plane had been dragging and jerking at the cables by which they were controlled from the stick, and the stick in my hands had not ceased jerking a single second. I had been gripping the stick with all my might for forty minutes, fearful lest the strain snap the cables. So desperate had been my grip that now I could not feel my hands.

What a discovery! My hands were not my own. I looked at them and decided to lift a finger: it obeyed me. I looked away and issued the same order: now I could not feel whether the finger had obeyed or not. No message had reached me. I thought: 'Suppose my hands were to open: how would I know it?' I swung my head round and looked again: my hands were still locked round the wheel. Nevertheless, I was afraid. How can a man tell the difference between the sight of a hand opening and the decision to open that hand, when there is no longer an exchange of sensations between the hand and the brain? How can one tell the difference between an image and an act of the will? Better stop thinking of the picture of open hands. Hands live a life of their own. Better not offer them this monstrous temptation. And I began to chant a silly litany which went on uninterruptedly until this flight was over. A single thought. A single image. A single phrase tirelessly chanted over and over again: 'I shut my hands. I shut my hands. I shut my hands.' All of me was condensed into that phrase and for me the white sea, the whirling eddies, the saw-toothed range ceased to exist. There was only 'I shut my hands.' There was no danger, no cyclone, no land unattained. Somewhere there was a pair of rubber hands which, once they let go the wheel, could not possibly come alive in time to recover from the tumbling drop into the sea.

I had no thoughts. I had no feelings, except the feeling of being emptied out. My strength was draining out of me and so was my impulse to go on fighting. The engines continued their dot-and-dash explosions, their little crashing noises that were like the intermittent cracklings of a splitting canvas. Whenever they were silent longer than a second I felt as if a heart had stopped beating. There! that's the end. No, they've started up again.

The thermometer on the wing, I happened to see, stood at twenty below zero, but I was bathed in sweat from head to foot. My face was running with perspiration. What a dance! Later I was to discover that my storage batteries had been jerked out of their steel flanges and hurtled up through the roof of the plane. I did not know then, either, that the strips on my wings had come unglued and that certain of my steel cables had been filed down to the last thread. And I continued to feel strength and will oozing out of me. Any minute now I should be overcome by the indifference born of utter weariness and by the mortal yearning to take my rest.

What can I say about this? Nothing. My shoulders ached. Very painfully. As if I had been carrying too many sacks too heavy for me. I leaned forward. Through a green transparency I saw sea-bottom so close that I could make out all the details. Then the wind's hand brushed the picture away.

In an hour and twenty minutes I had succeeded in climbing to nine hundred feet. A little to the south – that is, on my left – I could see a long trail on the surface of the sea, a sort of blue stream. I decided to let myself drift as far down as that stream. Here where I was, facing west, I was as good as motionless, unable either to advance or retreat. If I could reach that blue pathway, which must be lying in the shelter of something not the cyclone, I might be able to move in slowly to the coast. So I let myself drift to the left. I had the feeling, meanwhile, that the wind's violence had perhaps slackened.

It took me an hour to cover the five miles to shore. There in the shelter of a long cliff I was able to finish my journey south. Thereafter I succeeded in keeping enough altitude to fly inland to the field that was my destination. I was able to stay up at nine hundred feet. It was very stormy, but nothing like the cyclone I had come out of. That was over.

On the ground I saw a platoon of soldiers. They had been sent down to watch for me. I landed nearby and we were a whole hour getting the plane into the hangar. I climbed out of the cockpit and walked off. There was nothing to say. I was very sleepy. I kept moving my fingers, but they stayed numb. I could not collect my thoughts enough to decide whether or not I had been afraid. Had I been afraid? I couldn't say. I had witnessed a strange sight. What strange sight? I couldn't say. The sky was blue and the sea was white. I felt I ought to tell someone about it, since I was back from so far away! But I had no grip on what I had been through. 'Imagine a white sea ... very white ... whiter still.' You cannot convey things to people by piling up adjectives, by stammering.

You cannot convey anything because there is nothing to convey. My shoulders were aching. My insides felt as if they had been crushed in by a terrible weight. You cannot make drama out of that, or out of the cone-shaped peak of Salamanca. That peak was charged like a powder magazine; but if I said so people would laugh. I would myself. I respected the peak of Salamanca. That is my story. And it is not a story.

There is nothing dramatic in the world, nothing pathetic, except in human relations. The day after I landed I might get emotional, might dress up my adventure by imagining that I who was alive and walking on earth was living through the hell of a cyclone. But that would be cheating, for the man who fought tooth and nail against that cyclone had nothing in common with the fortunate man alive the next day. He was far too busy.

I came away with very little booty indeed, with no more than this meagre discovery, this contribution: How can one tell an act of the will from a simple image when there is no transmission of sensation?

I could perhaps succeed in upsetting you if I told you some story of a child unjustly punished. As it is, I have involved you in a cyclone, probably without upsetting you in the least. This is no novel experience for any of us. Every week men sit comfortably at the cinema and look on the bombardment of some Shanghai or other, some Guernica, and marvel without a trace of horror at the long fringes of ash and soot that twist their slow way into the sky from those man-made volcanoes. Yet we all know that together with the grain in the granaries, with the heritage of generations of men, with the treasures of families, it is the burning flesh of children and their elders that, dissipated in smoke, is slowly fertilizing those black cumuli.

The physical drama itself cannot touch us until some one points out its spiritual sense.

5 The Plane and the Planet

The aeroplane has unveiled for us the true face of the earth. For centuries, highways had been deceiving us. We were like that queen who determined to move among her subjects so that she might learn for herself whether or not they rejoiced in her reign. Her courtiers took advantage of her innocence to garland the road she travelled and set dancers in her path. Led forward on their halter, she saw nothing of her kingdom and could not know that over the countryside the famished were cursing her.

Even so have we been making our way along the winding roads. Roads avoid the barren lands, the rocks, the sands. They shape themselves to man's needs and run from stream to stream. They lead the farmer from his barns to his wheatfields, receive at the thresholds of stables the sleepy cattle and pour them forth at dawn into meadows of alfalfa. They join village to village, for between villages marriages are made.

And even when a road hazards its way over the desert, you will see it make a thousand détours to take its pleasure at the oases. Thus, led astray by the divagations of roads, as by other indulgent fictions, having in the course of our travels skirted so many well-watered lands, so many orchards, so many meadows, we have from the beginning of time embellished the picture of our prison. We have elected to believe that our planet was merciful and fruitful.

But a cruel light has blazed, and our sight has been sharpened. The plane has taught us to travel as the crow flies. Scarcely have we taken off when we abandon these winding highways that slope down to watering troughs and stables or run away to towns dreaming in the shade of their trees. Freed henceforth from this happy servitude, delivered from the need of fountains, we set our course for distant destinations. And then, only, from the height of our rectilinear trajectories, do we discover the essential foundation, the fundament of rock and sand and salt in which here and there and from time to time life like a little moss in the crevices of ruins has risked its precarious existence.

We to whom humble journeyings were once permitted have now been transformed into physicists, biologists, students of the civilizations that beautify the depths of valleys and now and again, by some miracle, bloom like gardens where the climate allows. We are able to judge man in cosmic terms, scrutinize him through our portholes as through instruments of the laboratory. I remember a few of these scenes.

I

The pilot flying towards the Straits of Magellan sees below him, a little to the south of the Gallegos River, an ancient lava flow, an erupted waste of a thickness of sixty feet that crushes down the plain on which it has congealed. Farther south he meets a second flow, then a third; and thereafter every hump on the globe, every mound a few hundred feet high, carries a crater in its flank. No Vesuvius rises up to reign in the clouds; merely, flat on the plain, a succession of gaping howitzer mouths.

This day, as I fly, the lava world is calm. There is something surprising in the tranquillity of this deserted landscape where once a thousand volcanoes boomed to each other in their great subterranean organs and spat forth their fire. I fly over a world mute and abandoned, strewn with black glaciers.

South of these glaciers there are yet older volcanoes veiled with the passing of time in a golden sward. Here and there a tree rises out of a crevice like a plant out of a cracked pot. In the soft and yellow light the plain appears as luxuriant as a garden; the short grass seems to civilize it, and round its giant throats there is scarcely a swelling to be seen. A hare scampers off; a bird wheels in the air; life has taken possession of a new planet where the decent loam of our earth has at last spread over the surface of the star.

Finally, crossing the line into Chile, a little north of Punta Arenas, you come to the last of the craters, and here the mouths have been stopped with earth. A silky turf lies snug over the curves of the volcanoes, and all is suavity in the scene. Each fissure in the crust is sutured up by this tender flax. The earth is smooth, the slopes are gentle; one forgets the travail that gave them birth. This turf effaces from the flanks of the hillocks the sombre sign of their origin.

We have reached the most southerly habitation of the world, a town born of the chance presence of a little mud between the timeless lava and the austral ice. So near the black scoria, how thrilling it is to feel the miraculous nature of man! What a strange encounter! Who knows how, or why, man visits these gardens ready to hand, habitable for so short a time – a geologic age – for a single day blessed among days?

I landed in the peace of evening. Punta Arenas! I leaned against a fountain and looked at the girls in the square. Standing there within a couple of feet of their grace, I felt more poignantly than ever the human mystery.

In a world in which life so perfectly responds to life, where flowers mingle with flowers in the wind's eye, where the swan is the familiar of all swans, man alone builds his isolation. What a space between men their spiritual natures create! A girl's reverie isolates her from me, and how shall I enter into it? What can one know of a girl who passes, walking with slow steps homeward, eyes lowered, smiling to herself, filled with adorable inventions and with fables? Out of the thoughts, the voice, the silences of a lover, she can form an empire, and thereafter she sees in all the world but him a people of barbarians. More surely than if she were on another planet, I feel her to be locked up in her language, in her secret, in her habits, in the singing echoes of her memory. Born yesterday of the volcanoes, of greenswards, of brine of the sea, she walks here already half divine.

Punta Arenas! I lean against a fountain. Old women come up to draw water: of their drama I shall know nothing but these gestures of farm servants. A child, his head against a wall, weeps in silence: there will remain of him in my memory only a beautiful child for ever inconsolable. I am a stranger. I know nothing. I do not enter into their empires. Man in the presence of man is as solitary as in the face of a wide winter sky in which there sweeps, never to be tamed, a flight of trumpeting geese.

How shallow is the stage on which this vast drama of human hates and joys and friendships is played! Whence do men draw this passion for eternity, flung by chance as they are upon a scarcely cooled bed of lava, threatened from the beginning by the deserts that are to be, and under the constant menace of the snows? Their civilizations are but fragile gildings: a volcano can blot them out, a new sea, a sand-storm.

This town seemed to be built upon a true humus, a soil one might imagine to be as rich as the wheatlands of the Beauce. These men live heedless of the fact that, here as elsewhere, life is a luxury; and that nowhere on the globe is the soil really rich beneath the feet of men.

Yet, ten miles from Punta Arenas there is a lake that ought to be reminding them of this. Surrounded by stunted trees and squat huts, as modest as a pool in a farm-yard, this lake is subject to the preternatural pull of the tides. Night and day, among the peaceful realities of swaying reeds and playing children, it performs its slow respiration, obedient to unearthly laws. Beneath the glassy surface, beneath the motionless ice, beneath the keel of the single dilapidated bark on the waters, the energy of the moon is at work. Ocean eddies stir in the depths of this black mass. Strange digestions take their peristaltic course there and down as far as the Straits of Magellan, under the thin layer of grasses and flowers. This lake that is a hundred yards wide, that laps the threshold of a town which seems to be built on man's own earth and where men believe themselves secure, beats with the pulse of the sea.

2

But by the grace of the aeroplane I have known a more extraordinary experience than this, and have been made to ponder with even more bewilderment the fact that this earth that is our home is yet in truth a wandering star.

A minor accident had forced me down in the Rio de Oro region, in Spanish Africa. Landing on one of those table-lands of the Sahara which fall away steeply at the sides, I found myself on the flat top of the frustum of a cone, an isolated vestige of a plateau that had crumbled round the edges. In this part of the Sahara such truncated cones are visible from the air every hundred miles or so, their smooth surfaces always at about the same altitude above the desert and their geologic substance always identical. The surface sand is composed of minute and distinct shells; but progressively as you dig along a vertical section, the shells become more fragmentary, tend to cohere, and at the base of the cone form a pure calcareous deposit.

Without question, I was the first human being ever to wander over this ... this iceberg: its sides were remarkably steep, no Arab could have climbed them, and no European had as yet ventured into this wild region.

I was thrilled by the virginity of a soil which no step of man or beast had sullied. I lingered there, startled by this silence that never had been broken. The first star began to shine, and I said to myself that this pure surface had lain here thousands of years in sight only of the stars.

But suddenly my musings on this white sheet and these shining stars were endowed with a singular significance. I had kicked against a hard, black stone, the size of a man's fist, a sort of moulded rock of lava incredibly present on the surface of a bed of shells a thousand feet deep. A sheet spread beneath an apple-tree can receive only apples; a sheet spread beneath the stars can receive only star-dust. Never had a stone fallen from the skies made known its origin so unmistakably.

And very naturally, raising my eyes, I said to myself that from the height of this celestial apple-tree there must have dropped other fruits, and that I should find them exactly where they fell, since never from the beginning of time had anything been present to displace them.

Excited by my adventure, I picked up one and then a second and then a third of these stones, finding them at about the rate of one stone to the acre. And here is where my adventure became magical, for in a striking foreshortening of time that embraced thousands of years, I had become the witness of this miserly rain from the stars. The marvel of marvels was that there on the rounded back of the planet, between this magnetic sheet and those stars, a human consciousness was present in which as in a mirror that rain could be reflected.

3

Once, in this same mineral Sahara, I was taught that a dream might partake of the miraculous. Again I had been forced down, and until day dawned I was helpless. Hillocks of sand offered up their luminous slopes to the moon, and blocks of shadow rose to share the sands with the light. Over the deserted work-yard of darkness and moonray there reigned a peace as of work suspended and a silence like a trap in which I fell asleep.

When I opened my eyes I saw nothing but the pool of nocturnal sky, for I was lying on my back with outstretched arms, face to face with that hatchery of stars. Only half awake, still unaware that those depths were sky, having no roof between those depths and me, no branches to screen them, no root to cling to, I was seized with vertigo and felt myself as if flung forth and plunging downward like a diver.

But I did not fall. From nape to heel I discovered myself bound to earth. I felt a sort of appeasement in surrendering to it my weight. Gravitation had become as sovereign as love. The earth, I felt, was supporting my back, sustaining me, lifting me up, transporting me through the immense void of night. I was glued to our planet by a pressure like that with which one is glued to the side of a car on a curve. I leaned with joy against this admirable breast-work, this solidity, this security, feeling against my body this curving bridge of my ship.

So convinced was I that I was in motion that I should have heard without astonishment, rising from below, a creaking of something material adjusting itself to the effort, that groaning of old sailing vessels as they heel, that long sharp cry drawn from pinnaces complaining of their handling. But silence continued in the layers of the earth, and this density that I could feel at my shoulders continued harmonious, sustained, unaltered through eternity. I was as much the inhabitant of this homeland as the bodies of dead galley-slaves, weighted with lead, were the inhabitants of the sea.

I lay there pondering my situation, lost in the desert and in danger, naked between sky and sand, withdrawn by too much silence from the poles of my life. I knew that I should wear out days and weeks returning to them if I were not sighted by some plane, or if next day the Moors did not find and murder me. Here I possessed nothing in the world. I was no more than a mortal strayed between sand and stars, conscious of the single blessing of breathing. And yet I discovered myself filled with dreams.

They came to me soundlessly, like the waters of a spring, and in the beginning I could not understand the sweetness that was invading me. There was neither voice nor vision, but the presentiment of a presence, of a warmth very close and already half guessed. Then I began to grasp what was going on, and shutting my eyes I gave myself up to the enchantment of my memory.

Somewhere there was a park dark with firs and linden-trees and an old house that I loved. It mattered little that it was far away, that it could not warm me in my flesh, nor shelter me, reduced here to the role of dream. It was enough that it existed to fill my night with its presence. I was no longer this body flung up on a strand; I oriented myself; I was the child of this house, filled with the memory of its odours, with the cool breath of its vestibules, with the voices that had animated it, even to the very frogs in the pools that came here to be with me. I needed these thousand landmarks to identify myself, to discover of what absences the savour of this desert was composed, to find a meaning in this silence made of a thousand silences, where the very frogs were silent.

No, I was no longer lodged between sand and stars. I was no longer receiving from this scene its chill message. And I had found out at last the origin of the feeling of eternity that came over me in this wilderness. I had been wrong to believe it was part of sky and sand. I saw again the great stately cupboards of our house. Their doors opened to display piles of linen as white as snow. They opened on frozen stores of snow. The old housekeeper trotted like a rat from one cupboard to the next, for ever counting, folding, unfolding, recounting the white linen; exclaiming: 'Oh, good Heavens, how terrible!' at each sign of wear which threatened the eternity of the house; running instantly to burn out her eyes under a lamp so that the woof of these altar-cloths should be repaired, these three-master's sails be mended, in the service of something greater than herself – a god, a ship.

Ah, I owe you a page, Mademoiselle! When I came home from my first journeyings I found you, needle in hand, up to the knees in your white surplices, each year a little more wrinkled, a little more round-shouldered, still preparing for our slumbers those sheets without creases, for our dinners those cloths without seams, those feasts of crystal and of snow.

I would go up to see you in your sewing-room, would sit down beside you and tell you of the dangers I had run in order that I might thrill you, open your eyes to the world, corrupt you. You would say that I hadn't changed a whit. Already as a child I had torn my shirts – 'How terrible!' – and skinned my knees, coming home as day fell to be bandaged.

No, Mademoiselle, no! I have not come back from the other end of the park but from the other end of the world! I have brought back with me the acrid smell of solitude, the tumult of sand-storms, the blazing moonlight of the tropics! 'Of course!' you would say. 'Boys *will* run about, break their bones and think themselves great fellows.'

No, Mademoiselle, no! I have seen a good deal more than the shadows in our park. If you knew how insignificant these shadows are, how little they mean beside the sands, the granite, the virgin forests, the vast swamplands of the earth! Do you realize that there are lands on the globe where, when men meet you, they bring up their rifles to their cheeks? Do you know that there are deserts on earth where men lie down on freezing nights to sleep without roof or bed or snowy sheet? 'What a wild lad!' you would say.

I could no more shake her faith than I could have shaken the faith of a candle-woman in a church. I pitied her humble destiny which had made her blind and deaf.

But that night, in the Sahara, naked between the stars and the sand, I did her justice.

What is going on inside me I cannot tell. In the sky a

64

thousand stars are magnetized, and I lie glued by the swing of the planet to the sand. A different weight brings me back to myself. I feel the weight of my body drawing me towards so many things. My dreams are more real than these dunes, than that moon, than these presences. My civilization is an empire more imperious than this empire. The marvel of a house is not that it shelters or warms a man, nor that its walls belong to him. It is that it leaves its trace on the language. Let it remain a sign. Let it form, deep in the heart, that obscure range from which, as waters from a spring, are born our dreams.

Sahara, my Sahara! You have been bewitched by an old woman at a spinning-wheel!

6 Oasis

I have already said so much about the desert that before speaking of it again I should like to describe an oasis. The oasis that comes into my mind is not, however, remote in the deep Sahara. One of the miracles of the aeroplane is that it plunges a man directly into the heart of mystery. You are a biologist studying, through your porthole, the human ant-hill, scrutinizing objectively those towns seated in their plain at the centre of their highways which go off like the spokes of a wheel and, like arteries, nourish them with the quintessence of the fields. A needle trembles on your manometer, and this green clump below you becomes a universe. You are the prisoner of a greensward in a slumbering park.

Space is not the measure of distance. A garden wall at home may enclose more secrets than the Great Wall of China, and the soul of a little girl is better guarded by silence than the Sahara's oases by the surrounding sands. I dropped down to earth once somewhere in the world. It was near Concordia, in the Argentine, but it might have been anywhere at all, for mystery is everywhere.

A minor mishap had forced me down in a field, and I was far from dreaming that I was about to live through a fairy-tale. The old Ford in which I was driven to town betokened nothing extraordinary, and the same was to be said for the unremarkable couple who took me in.

'We shall be glad to put you up for the night,' they said.

But round a corner of the road, in the moonlight, I saw a clump of trees, and behind those trees a house. What a queer house! Squat, massive, almost a citadel guarding behind its tons of stone I knew not what treasure. From the very threshold this legendary castle promised an asylum as assured, as peaceful, as secret as a monastery.

Then two young girls appeared. They seemed astonished to

see me, examined me gravely as if they had been two judges posted on the confines of a forbidden kingdom, and while the younger of them sulked and tapped the ground with a green switch, they were introduced :

'Our daughters.'

The girls shook hands without a word but with a curious air of defiance, and disappeared. I was amused and I was charmed. It was all as simple and silent and furtive as the first word of a secret.

'The girls are shy,' their father said, and we went into the house.

One thing that I had loved in Paraguay was the ironic grass that showed the tip of its nose between the pavements of the capital, that slipped in on behalf of the invisible but ever-present virgin forest to see if man still held the town, if the hour had not come to send all these stones tumbling.

I liked the particular kind of dilapidation which in Paraguay was the expression of an excess of wealth. But here, in Concordia, I was filled with wonder. Here everything was in a state of decay, but adorably so, like an old oak covered with moss and split in places with age, like a wooden bench on which generations of lovers had come to sit and which had grown sacred. The wainscoting was worn, the hinges rusted, the chairs rickety. And yet, though nothing had ever been repaired, everything had been scoured with zeal. Everything was clean, waxed, gleaming.

The drawing-room had about it something extraordinarily intense, like the face of a wrinkled old lady. The walls were cracked, the ceiling stripped; and most bewildering of all in this bewildering house was the floor : it had simply caved in. Waxed, varnished, and polished though it was, it swayed like a ship's gangway. A strange house, evoking no neglect, no slackness, but rather an extraordinary respect. Each passing year had added something to its charm, to the complexity of its visage and its friendly atmosphere, as well as to the dangers encountered on the journey from the drawing-room to the dining-room.

'Careful !'

There was a hole in the floor; and I was warned that if I

stepped into it I might easily break a leg. This was said as simply as 'Don't stroke the dog, he bites.' Nobody was responsible for the hole, it was the work of time. There was something lordly about this sovereign contempt for apologies.

Nobody said : 'We could have these holes repaired; we are well enough off; but . . .' And neither did they say – which was true enough – 'We have taken this house from the town under a thirty-year lease. They should look after the repairs. But they won't, and we won't, so . . .' They disdained explanation, and this superiority to circumstance enchanted me. The most that was said was :

'The house is a little run down, you see.'

Even this was said with such an air of satisfaction that I suspected my friends of not being saddened by the fact. Do you see a crew of bricklayers, carpenters, cabinet-workers, plasterers intruding their sacrilegious tools into so vivid a past, turning this in a week into a house you would never recognize, in which the family would feel that they were visiting strangers? A house without secrets, without recesses, without mysteries, without traps beneath the feet, or dungeons, a sort of town-hall reception room?

In a house with so many secret passages it was natural that the daughters should vanish before one's eyes. What must the attics be, when the drawing-room already contained all the wealth of an attic? When one could guess already that, the least cupboard opened, there would pour out sheaves of yellowed letters, grandpapa's receipted bills, more keys than there were locks and not one of which of course would fit any lock. Marvellously useless keys that confounded the reason and made it muse upon subterranean chambers, buried chests, treasures.

'Shall we go in to dinner?'

We went in to dinner. Moving from one room to the next I inhaled in passing that incense of an old library which is worth all the perfumes of the world. And particularly I liked the lamps being carried with us. Real lamps, heavy lamps, transported from room to room as in the time of my earliest childhood; stirring into motion as they passed great wondrous shadows on the walls. To pick one up was to displace bouquets of light and great black palms. Then, the lamps finally set down, there was a settling into motionlessness of the beaches of clarity and the vast reserves of surrounding darkness in which the wainscoting went on creaking.

As mysteriously and as silently as they had vanished, the girls reappeared. Gravely they took their places. Doubtless they had fed their dogs, their birds; had opened their windows on the bright night and breathed in the smell of the woods brought by the night wind. Now, unfolding their napkins, they were inspecting me cautiously out of the corners of their eyes, wondering whether or not they were going to make a place for me among their domestic animals. For among others they had an iguana, a mongoose, a fox, a monkey, and bees. All these lived promiscuously together without quarrelling in this new earthly paradise. The girls reigned over all the animals of creation, charming them with their little hands, feeding them, watering them, and telling them tales to which all, from mongoose to bees, gave ear.

I firmly expected that these alert young girls would employ all their critical faculty, all their shrewdness, in a swift, secret, and irrevocable judgement upon the male who sat opposite them.

When I was a child my sisters had a way of giving marks to guests who were honouring our table for the first time. Conversation might languish for a moment, and then in the silence we would hear the sudden impact of 'Sixty!' – a word that could tickle only the family, who knew that one hundred was par. Branded by this low mark, the guest would all unknowing continue to spend himself in little courtesies while we sat screaming inwardly with delight.

Remembering that little game, I was worried. And it upset me a bit more to feel my judges so keen. Judges who knew how to distinguish between candid animals and animals that cheated; who could tell from the tracks of the fox whether he was in a good temper or not; whose instinct for inner movements was so sure and deep.

I liked the sharp eyes of these straightforward little souls, but I should so much have preferred that they play some other game. And yet, in my cowardly fear of their 'sixty' I passed them the salt, poured out their wine; though each time that

69

I raised my eyes I saw in their faces the gentle gravity of judges who were not to be bought.

Flattery itself was useless: they knew no vanity. Although they knew not it, they knew a marvellous pride, and without any help from me they thought more good of themselves than I should have dared utter. It did not even occur to me to draw any prestige from my craft, for it is extremely dangerous to clamber up to the topmost branches of a plane-tree simply to see if the nestlings are doing well or to say good morning to one's friends.

My taciturn young friends continued their inspection so imperturbably, I met so often their fleeting glances, that soon I stopped talking. Silence fell, and in that silence I heard something hiss faintly under the floor, rustle under the table, and then stop. I raised a pair of puzzled eyes. Thereupon, satisfied with her examination but applying her last touchstone, as she bit with savage young teeth into her bread, the younger daughter explained to me with a candour by which she hoped to slaughter the barbarian (if that was what I was):

'It's the snakes.'

And content, she said no more, as if that explanation should have sufficed for anyone in whom there remained a last glimmer of intelligence. Her sister sent a lightning glance to spy out my immediate reflex, and both bent with the gentlest and most ingenuous faces in the world over their plates.

'Ah! Snakes, are they?'

Naturally, the words escaped from me against my will. This that had been gliding between my legs, had been brushing my calves, was snakes!

Fortunately for me I smiled. Effortlessly. They would have known if it had been otherwise. I smiled because my heart was light, because each moment this house was more and more to my liking. And also because I wanted to know more about the snakes. The elder daughter came to my rescue.

'They nest in a hole under the table.'

And her sister added: 'They go back into their nest at about ten o'clock. During the day they hunt.'

Now it was my turn to look at them out of the corner of the eye. What shrewdness! what silent laughter behind those candid faces! And what sovereignty they exercised, these princesses guarded by snakes! Princesses for whom there existed no scorpion, no wasp, no serpent, but only little souls of animals!

As I write, I dream. All this is very far away. What has become of these two fairy princesses? Girls so fine-grained, so upright, have certainly attracted husbands. Have they changed, I wonder? What do they do in their new houses? Do they feel differently now about the jungle growth and the snakes? They had been fused with something universal, and then the day had come when the woman had awaked in the maiden, when there had surged in her a longing to find someone who deserved a 'Ninety-five'. The dream of a ninety-five is a weight on the heart.

And then an imbecile had come along. For the first time those sharp eyes were mistaken and they dressed him in gay colours. If the imbecile recited verse he was thought a poet. Surely he must understand the holes in the floor, must love the mongoose! The trust one put in him, the swaying of the snakes between his legs under the table – surely this must flatter him! And that heart which was a wild garden was given to him who loved only trim lawns. And the imbecile carried away the princess into slavery.

7 Men of the Desert

These, then, were some of the treasures that passed us by when for weeks and months and years we, pilots of the Sahara line, were prisoners of the sands, navigating from one stockade to the next with never an excursion outside the zone of silence. Oases like these did not prosper in the desert; these memories it dismissed as belonging to the domain of legend. No doubt there did gleam in distant places scattered round the world – places to which we should return once our work was done – there did gleam lighted windows. No doubt somewhere there did sit young girls among their white lemurs or their books patiently compounding souls as rich in delight as secret gardens. No doubt there did exist such creatures waxing in beauty. But solitude cultivates a strange mood.

I know that mood. Three years of the desert taught it to me. Something in one's heart takes fright, not at the thought of growing old, not at feeling one's youth used up in this mineral universe, but at the thought that far away the whole world is ageing. The trees have brought forth their fruit; the grain has ripened in the fields; the women have bloomed in their loveliness. But the season is advancing and one must make haste; but the season is advancing and still one cannot leave; but the season is advancing . . . and other men will glean the harvest.

Many a night have I savoured this taste of the irreparable, wandering in a circle round the fort. our prison, under the burden of the trade-winds. Sometimes, worn out by a day of flight, drenched in the humidity of the tropical climate, I have felt my heart beat in me like the wheels of an express train; and suddenly, more immediately than when flying, I have felt myself on a journey. A journey through time. Time was running through my fingers like the fine sand of the dunes; the poundings of my heart were bearing me onward towards an unknown future.

Ah, those fevers at night after a day of work in the silence! We seemed to ourselves to be burning up, like flares set out in the solitude.

And yet we knew joys we could not possibly have known elsewhere. I shall never be able to express clearly whence comes this pleasure men take from aridity, but always and everywhere I have seen men attach themselves more stubbornly to barren lands than to any other. Men will die for a calcined, leafless, stony mountain. The nomads will defend to the death their great store of sand as if it were a treasure of gold dust. And we, my comrades and I, we too have loved the desert to the point of feeling that it was there we had lived the best years of our lives. I shall describe for you our stations (Port Étienne, Villa Cisneros, Cape Juby, were some of their names) and shall narrate for you a few of our days.

I

I succumbed to the desert as soon as I saw it, and I saw it almost as soon as I had won my wings. As early as the year 1926 I was transferred out of Europe to the Dakar–Juby division, where the Sahara meets the Atlantic and where, only recently, the Arabs had murdered two of our pilots, Erable and Gourp. In those days our planes frequently fell apart in mid-air, and because of this the African divisions were always flown by two ships, one without the mails trailing and convoying the other, prepared to take over the sacks in the event the mail plane broke down.

Under orders, I flew an empty ship down to Agadir. From Agadir I was flown to Dakar as a passenger, and it was on that flight that the vast sandy void and the mystery with which my imagination could not but endow it first thrilled me. But the heat was so intense that despite my excitement I dozed off soon after we left Port Étienne. Riguelle, who was flying me down, moved out to sea a couple of miles in order to get away from the sizzling surface of sand. I woke up, saw in the distance the thin white line of the coast, and said to myself fearfully that if anything went wrong we should surely drown. Then I dozed off again.

I was startled out of my sleep by a crash, a sudden silence, and then the voice of Riguelle saying: 'Damn! There goes a connecting rod!' As I half rose out of my seat to send a regretful look at that white coast-line, now more precious than ever, he shouted to me angrily to stay as I was. I knew Riguelle had been wrong to go out to sea; I had been on the point of mentioning it; and now I felt a complete and savage satisfaction in our predicament. 'This', I said to myself, 'will teach him a lesson.'

But this gratifying sense of superiority could obviously not last very long. Riguelle sent the plane earthward in a long diagonal line that brought us within sixty feet of the sand – an altitude at which there was no question of picking out a landing-place. We lost both wheels against one sand-dune, a wing against another, and crashed with a sudden jerk into a third.

'You hurt?' Riguelle called out.

'Not a bit,' I said.

'That's what I call piloting a ship!' he boasted cheerfully.

I, who was busy on all fours extricating myself from what had once been a ship, was in no mood to feed his pride.

'Guillaumet will be along in a minute to pick us up,' he added.

Guillaumet was flying our convoy, and very shortly we saw him come down on a stretch of smooth sand a few hundred yards away. He asked if we were all right, was told no damage had been done, and then proposed briskly that we give him a hand with the sacks. The mail transferred out of the wrecked plane, they explained to me that in this soft sand it would not be possible to lift Guillaumet's plane clear if I was in it. They would hop to the next outpost, drop the mail there, and come back for me.

Now this was my first day in Africa. I was so ignorant that I could not tell a zone of danger from a zone of safety – I mean by that, a zone where the tribes had submitted peacefully to European rule from a zone where the tribes were still in rebellion. The region in which we had landed happened to be considered safe, but I did not know that.

'You've got a gun, of course,' Riguelle said.

I had no gun and said so.

'My dear chap, you'll have to have a gun,' he said, and very kindly he gave me his. 'And you'll want these extra clips of cartridges,' he went on. 'Just bear in mind that you shoot at anything and everything you see.'

They had started to walk across to the other plane when Guillaumet, as if driven by his conscience, came back and handed me his cartridge clips, too. And with this they took off.

I was alone. They knew, though I did not, that I could have sat on one of these dunes for half a year without running the least danger. What they were doing was to implant in the imagination of a recruit a proper feeling of solitude and danger and respect with regard to the desert. What I was really feeling, however, was an immense pride. Sitting on the dune, I laid out beside me my gun and my five cartridge clips. For the first time since I was born it seemed to me that my life was my own and that I was responsible for it. Bear in mind that only two nights before I had been dining in a restaurant in Toulouse.

I walked to the top of a sand-hill and looked round the horizon like a captain on his bridge. This sea of sand bowled me over. Unquestionably it was filled with mystery and with danger. The silence that reigned over it was not the silence of emptiness but of plotting, of imminent enterprise. I sat still and stared into space. The end of the day was near. Something half revealed yet wholly unknown had bewitched me. The love of the Sahara, like love itself, is born of a face perceived and never really seen. Ever after this first sight of your new love, an indefinable bond is established between you and the veneer of gold on the sand in the late sun.

Guillaumet's perfect landing broke the charm of my musings. 'Anything turn up?' he wanted to know.

I had seen my first gazelle. Silently it had come into view. I felt that the sands had shown me the gazelle in confidence, so I said nothing about it.

'You weren't frightened?'

I said no and thought, gazelles are not frightening.

The mails had been dropped at an outpost as isolated as an island in the Pacific. There, waiting for us, stood a colonial army sergeant. With his squad of fifteen black troops he stood guard on the threshold of the immense expanse. Every six months a caravan came up out of the desert and left him supplies.

Again and again he took our hands and looked into our eyes, ready to weep at the sight of us. 'By God, I'm glad to see you! You don't know what it means to me to see you!' Only twice a year he saw a French face, and that was when, at the head of the camel corps, either the captain or the lieutenant came out of the inner desert.

We had to inspect his little fort – 'built it with my own hands' – and swing his doors appreciatively – 'as solid as they make 'em' – and drink a glass of wine with him.

'Another glass. Please! You don't know how glad I am to have some wine to offer you. Why, last time the captain came round I didn't have any for the captain. Think of that! I couldn't clink glasses with the captain and wish him luck! I was ashamed of myself. I asked to be relieved, I did!'

Clink glasses. Call out: 'Here's luck!' to a man, running with sweat, who has just jumped down from the back of a camel. Wait six months for this great moment. Polish up your equipment. Scour the post from cellar to attic. Go up on the roof day after day and scan the horizon for that dust-cloud that serves as the envelope in which will be delivered to your door the Atar Camel Corps. And after all this, to have no wine in the house! To be unable to clink glasses. To see oneself dishonoured.

'I keep waiting for the captain to come back,' the sergeant said.

'Where is he, sergeant?'

And the sergeant, waving his arm in an arc that took in the whole horizon, said: 'Nobody knows. Captain is everywhere at once.'

We spent the night on the roof of the outpost, talking about the stars. There was nothing else in sight. All the stars were present, all accounted for, the way you see them from a plane, but fixed.

When the night is very fine and you are at the wheel of your ship, you half forget yourself and bit by bit the plane begins to tilt on the left. Pretty soon, while you still imagine yourself in plumb, you see the lights of a village under your right wing.

There are no villages in the desert. A fishing-fleet in mid-ocean, then? There are no fishing-fleets in mid-Sahara. What —? Of course! You smile at the way your mind has wandered and you bring the ship back to plumb again. The village slips into place. You have hooked that particular constellation back in the panoply out of which it had fallen. Village? Yes, village of stars.

The sergeant had a word to say about them. 'I know the stars,' he said. 'Steer by that star yonder and you make Tunis.'

'Are you from Tunis?'

'No. My cousin, she is.'

A long silence. But the sergeant could not keep anything back.

'I'm going to Tunis one of these days.'

Not, I said to myself, by making a bee-line for that star and tramping across the desert; that is, not unless in the course of some raid a dried-up well should turn the sergeant over to the poetry of delirium. If that happened, star, cousin, and Tunis would melt into one, and the sergeant would certainly be off on that inspired tramp which the ignorant would think of as torture.

He went on: 'I asked the captain for leave to go to Tunis, seeing my cousin is there and all. He said . . .'

'What did the captain say, sergeant?'

'Said: "World's full of cousins." Said: "Dakar's nearer" and sent me there.'

'Pretty girl, your cousin?'

'In Tunis? You bet! Blonde, she is.'

'No, I mean at Dakar.'

Sergeant, we could have hugged you for the wistful disappointed voice in which you answered: 'She was a nigger.'

2

Port Étienne is situated on the edge of one of the unsubdued regions of the Sahara. It is not a town. There is a stockade, a hangar, and a wooden quarters for the French crews. The desert all round is so unrelieved that despite its feeble military strength Port Étienne is practically invincible. To attack it means crossing such a belt of sand and flaming heat that the razzias (as the bands of armed marauders are called) must arrive exhausted and waterless. And yet, in the memory of man there has always been, somewhere in the North, a razzia marching on Port Étienne. Each time that the army captain who served as commandant of the fort came to drink a cup of tea with us, he would show us its route on the map the way a man might tell the legend of a beautiful princess.

But the razzia never arrived. Like a river, it was each time dried up by the sands, and we called it the phantom razzia. The cartridges and hand-grenades that the government passed out to us nightly would sleep peacefully in their boxes at the foot of our beds. Our surest protection was our poverty, our single enemy silence. Night and day, Lucas, who was chief of the airport, would wind his gramophone; and Ravel's *Bolero*, flung up here so far out of the path of life, would speak to us in a half-lost language, provoking an aimless melancholy which curiously resembled thirst.

One evening we had dined at the fort and the commandant had shown off his garden to us. Someone had sent him from France, three thousand miles away, a few boxes of real soil, and out of this soil grew three green leaves which we caressed as if they had been jewels. The commandant would say of them: 'This is my park.' And when there arose one of those sand-storms that shrivelled everything up, he would move the park down into the cellar.

Our quarters stood about a mile from the fort, and after dinner we walked home in the moonlight. Under the moon the sands were rosy. We were conscious of our destitution, but the sands were rosy. A sentry called out, and the pathos of our world was re-established. The whole of the Sahara lay in fear of our shadows and called for the password, for a razzia was on the march. All the voices of the desert resounded in that sentry's challenge. No longer was the desert an empty prison: a Moorish caravan had magnetized the night.

We might believe ourselves secure; and yet, illness, accident, razzia – how many dangers were afoot! Man inhabits the earth, a target for secret marksmen. The Senegalese sentry was there like a prophet of old to remind us of our destiny. We gave the password, *Français!* and passed before the black angel. Once in quarters, we breathed more freely. With what nobility that threat had endowed us! Oh, distant it still was, and so little urgent, deadened by so much sand; but yet the world was no longer the same. Once again this desert had become a sumptuous thing. A razzia that was somewhere on the march, yet never arrived, was the source of its glory.

It was now eleven at night. Lucas came back from the wireless and told me that the plane from Dakar would be in at midnight. All well on board. By ten minutes past midnight the mails would be transferred to my ship and I should take off for the North. I shaved carefully in a cracked mirror. From time to time, a Turkish towel hanging at my throat, I went to the door and looked at the naked sand. The night was fine but the wind was dropping. I went back again to the mirror. I was thoughtful.

A wind that has been running for months and then drops sometimes fouls the entire sky. I got into my harness, snapped my emergency lamps to my belt along with my altimeter and my pencils. I went over to Néri, who was to be my radio operator on this flight. He was shaving, too. I said: 'Everything all right?' For the moment everything was all right. But I heard something sizzling. It was a dragonfly knocking against the lamp. Why it was I cannot say, but I felt a twinge in my heart.

I went out of doors and looked round. The air was pure. A cliff on the edge of the aerodrome stood in profile against the sky as if it were daylight. Over the desert reigned a vast silence as of a house in order. But here were a green butterfly and two dragonflies knocking against my lamp. And again I felt a dull ache which might as easily have been joy as fear but came up from the depths of me, so vague that it could scarcely be said to be there. Someone was calling to me from a great distance. Was it instinct?

Once again I went out. The wind had died down completely. The air was still cool. But I had received a warning. I guessed, I believed I could guess, what I was expecting. Was I right? Neither the sky nor the sand had made the least sign to me; but two dragonflies and a moth had spoken.

I climbed a dune and sat down face to the east. If I was right, the thing would not be long coming. What were they after here, those dragonflies, hundreds of miles from their oases inland? Wreckage thrown up on the strand bears witness to a storm at sea. Even so did these insects declare to me that a sand-storm was on the way, a storm out of the east that had blown them out of their oases.

Solemnly, for it was fraught with danger, the east wind rose. Already its foam had touched me. I was the extreme edge lapped by the wave. Fifty feet behind me no sail would have flapped. Its flame wrapped me round once, only once, in a caress that seemed dead. But I knew, in the seconds that followed, that the Sahara was catching its breath and would send forth a second sigh. And that before three minutes had passed the air-sock of our hangar would be whipped into action. And that before ten minutes had gone by the sand would fill the air. We should shortly be taking off in this conflagration, in this return of the flames from the desert.

But that was not what excited me. What filled me with a barbaric joy was that I had understood a murmured monosyllable of this secret language, had sniffed the air and known what was coming, like one of those primitive men to whom the future is revealed in such faint rustlings; it was that I had been able to read the anger of the desert in the beating wings of a dragonfly.

3

But we were not always in the air, and our idle hours were spent taming the Moors. They would come out of their forbidden regions (those regions we crossed in our flights and where they would shoot at us the whole length of our crossing), would venture to the stockade in the hope of buying loaves of sugar, cotton cloth, tea, and then would sink back again into their mystery. Whenever they turned up we would try to tame a few of them in order to establish little nuclei of friendship in the desert; thus if we were forced down among them there would be at any rate a few who might be persuaded to sell us into slavery rather than massacre us.

Now and then an influential chief came up, and him, with the approval of the Line, we would load into the plane and carry off to see something of the world. The aim was to soften their pride, for, repositories of the truth, defenders of Allah, the only God, it was more in contempt than in hatred that he and his kind murdered their prisoners.

When they met us in the region of Juby or Cisneros, they never troubled to shout abuse at us. They would merely turn away and spit; and this not by way of personal insult but out of sincere disgust at having crossed the path of a Christian. Their pride was born of the illusion of their power. Allah renders a believer invincible. Many a time a chief has said to me, pointing to his army of three hundred rifles: 'Lucky it is for France that she lies more than a hundred days' march from here.'

And so we would take them up for a little spin. Three of them even visited France in our planes. I happened to be present when they returned. I met them when they landed, went with them to their tents, and waited in infinite curiosity to hear their first words. They were of the same race as those who, having once been flown by me to the Senegal, had burst into tears at the sight of trees. What a revelation Europe must have been for them! And yet their first replies astonished me by their coolness.

'Paris? Very big.'

Everything was 'very big' – in Paris, the Trocadéro, the automobiles.

What with everyone in Paris asking if the Louvre was not 'very big' they had gradually learned that this was the answer that flattered us. And with a sort of vague contempt, as if pacifying a lot of children, they would grant that the Louvre was 'very big'.

These Moors took very little trouble to dissemble the freezing indifference they felt for the Eiffel Tower, the steamships, and the locomotives. They were ready to agree once and for always that we knew how to build things out of iron. We also knew how to fling a bridge from one continent to another. The plain fact was that they did not know enough to admire our technical progress. The wireless astonished them less than the telephone, since the mystery of the telephone resided in the very fact of the wire.

It took a little time for me to understand that my questions were on the wrong track. For what they thought admirable was not the locomotive but the tree. When you think of it, a tree does possess a perfection that a locomotive cannot know. And then I remembered the Moors who had wept at the sight of trees.

Yes, France was in some sense admirable, but it was not because of those stupid things made of iron. They had seen pastures in France in which all the camels of Er-Raguibat could have grazed! There were forests in France! The French had cows, cows filled with milk! And of course my three Moors were amazed by the incredible customs of the people.

'In Paris,' they said, 'you walk through a crowd of a thousand people. You stare at them. And nobody carries a rifle!'

But there were better things in France than this inconceivable friendliness between men. There was the circus, for example.

'Frenchwomen,' they said, 'can jump standing from one galloping horse to another.'

Thereupon they would stop and reflect.

'You take one Moor from each tribe,' they went on. 'You take him to the circus. And nevermore will the tribes of Er-Reguibat make war on the French.'

I remember my chiefs sitting among the crowding tribesmen in the opening of their tents, savouring the pleasure of reciting this new series of Arabian Nights, extolling the music halls in which naked women dance on carpets of flowers.

Here were men who had never seen a tree, a river, a rose; who knew only through the Koran of the existence of gardens where streams run, which is their name for Paradise. In their desert, Paradise and its beautiful captives could be won only by bitter death from an infidel's rifle-shot, after thirty years of a miserable existence. But God had tricked them, since from the Frenchmen to whom he grants these treasures he exacts payment neither by thirst nor by death. And it was upon this that the chiefs now mused. This was why, gazing out at the Sahara surrounding their tents, at that desert with its barren promise of such thin pleasures, they let themselves go in murmured confidences.

'You know . . . the God of the French . . . he is more generous to the French than the God of the Moors is to the Moors.'

Memories that moved them too deeply rose to stop their speech. Some weeks earlier they had been taken up into the French Alps. Here in Africa they were still dreaming of what they saw. Their guide had led them to a tremendous waterfall, a sort of braided column roaring over the rocks. He had said to them :

'Taste this.'

It was sweet water. Water ! How many days were they wont to march in the desert to reach the nearest well; and when they had arrived, how long they had to dig before there bubbled a muddy liquid mixed with camel's urine ! Water ! At Cape Juby, at Cisneros, at Port Étienne, the Moorish children did not beg for coins. With empty tins in their hands they begged for water.

'Give me a little water, give !'

'If you are a good lad . . .'

Water ! A thing worth its weight in gold ! A thing the least drop of which drew from the sand the green sparkle of a blade of grass ! When rain has fallen anywhere, a great exodus animates the Sahara. The tribes ride towards that grass that will have sprung up two hundred miles away. And this water, this miserly water of which not a drop had fallen at Port Étienne in ten years, roared in the Savoie with the power of a cataclysm as if, from some burst cistern, the reserves of the world were pouring forth.

'Come, let us leave,' their guide had said.

But they would not stir.

'Leave us here a little longer.'

They had stood in silence. Mute, solemn, they had stood gazing at the unfolding of a ceremonial mystery That which came roaring out of the belly of the mountain was life itself, was the life-blood of man. The flow of a single second would have resuscitated whole caravans that, mad with thirst, had pressed on into the eternity of salt lakes and mirages. Here God was manifesting himself : it would not do to turn one's back on him. God had opened the locks and was displaying his puissance. The three Moors had stood motionless.

'That is all there is to see,' their guide had said. 'Come.'

'We must wait.'

'Wait for what?'

'The end.'

They were awaiting the moment when God would grow weary of his madness. They knew him to be quick to repent, knew he was miserly.

'But that water has been running for a thousand years!'

And this was why, at Port Étienne, they did not too strongly stress the matter of the waterfall. There were certain miracles about which it was better to be silent. Better, indeed, not to think too much about them, for in that case one would cease to understand anything at all. Unless one was to doubt the existence of God. . . .

'You see . . . the God of the Frenchmen . . .'

But I knew them well, my barbarians. There they sat, perplexed in their faith, disconcerted, and henceforth quite ready to acknowledge French overlordship. They were dreaming of being victualled in barley by the French administration, and assured of their security by our Saharan regiments. There was no question but that they would, by their submission, be materially better off.

But all three were of the blood of el Mammun.

I had known el Mammun when he was our vassal. Loaded with official honours for services rendered, enriched by the French Government and respected by the tribes, he seemed to lack for nothing that belonged to the state of an Arab prince. And yet one night, without a sign of warning, he had massacred all the French officers in his train, had seized camels and rifles, and had fled to rejoin the refractory tribes in the interior.

Treason is the name given to these sudden uprisings, these flights at once heroic and despairing of a chieftain henceforth proscribed in the desert, this brief glory that will go out like a rocket against the low wall of European carbines. This sudden madness is properly a subject for amazement.

And yet the story of el Mammun was that of many other

Arab chiefs. He grew old. Growing old, one begins to ponder. Pondering thus, el Mammun discovered one night that he had betrayed the God of Islam and had sullied his hand by sealing in the hand of the Christians a pact in which he had been stripped of everything.

Indeed what were barley and peace to him? A warrior disgraced and become a shepherd, he remembered a time when he had inhabited a Sahara where each fold in the sands was rich with hidden mysteries; where forward in the night the tip of the encampment was studded with sentries; where the news that spread concerning the movements of the enemy made all hearts beat faster round the night fires. He remembered a taste of the high seas which, once savoured by man, is never forgotten. And because of his pact he was condemned to wander without glory through a region pacified and voided of all prestige. Then, truly and for the first time, the Sahara became a desert.

It is possible that he was fond of the officers he murdered. But love of Allah takes precedence.

'Good night, el Mammun.'

'God guard thee!'

The officers rolled themselves up in their blankets and stretched out upon the sand as on a raft, face to the stars. High overhead all the heavens were wheeling slowly, a whole sky marking the hour. There was the moon, bending towards the sands, and the Frenchmen, lured by her tranquillity into oblivion, fell asleep. A few minutes more, and only the stars gleamed. And then, in order that the corrupted tribes be regenerated into their past splendour, in order that there begin again those flights without which the sands would have no radiance, it was enough that these Christians drowned in their slumber send forth a feeble wail. Still a few seconds more, and from the irreparable will come forth an empire.

And the handsome sleeping lieutenants were massacred.

4

Today at Cape Juby, Kemal and his brother Mouyan have invited me to their tent. I sit drinking tea while Mouyan stares at me in silence. Blue sand-veil drawn across his mouth, he maintains an unsociable reserve. Kemal alone speaks to me and does the honours:

'My tent, my camels, my wives, my slaves are yours.'

Mouyan, his eyes still fixed on me, bends towards his brother, pronounces a few words, and lapses into silence again.

'What does he say?' I ask.

'He says that Bonnafous has stolen a thousand camels from the tribes of Er-Reguibat.'

I have never met this Captain Bonnafous, but I know that he is an officer of the camel corps garrisoned at Atar and I have gathered from the Moors that to them he is a legendary figure. They speak of him with anger, but as of a sort of god. His presence lends price to the sand. Now once again, no one knows how, he has outflanked the southward marching razzias, taken them in the rear, driven off their camels by the hundred, and forced them to turn about and pursue him unless they are to lose those treasures which they had thought secure. And now, having saved Atar by this archangelic irruption and planted his camp upon a high limestone plateau, he stands there like a guerdon to be won, and such is his magnetism that the tribes are obliged to march towards his sword.

With a hard look at me, Mouyan speaks again.

'What now?' I ask.

'He says we are off tomorrow on a razzia against Bonnafous. Three hundred rifles.'

I had guessed something of the sort. These camels led to the wells for three days past; these powwows; this fever running through the camp: it was as if men had been rigging an invisible ship. Already the air was filled with the wind that would take her out of port. Thanks to Bonnafous, each step to the South was to be a noble step rich in honour. It has become impossible to say whether love or hate plays the greater part in this setting forth of the warriors.

There is something magnificent in the possession of an enemy of Bonnafous' mettle. Where he turns up, the nearby tribes fold their tents, collect their camels and fly, trembling to think they might have found themselves face to face with him; while the more distant tribes are seized by a vertigo resembling love.

They tear themselves from the peace of their tents, from the embraces of their women, from the happiness of slumber, for suddenly there is nothing in the world that can match in beauty, after two months of exhausting march, of burning thirst, of halts crouching under the sand-storm, the joy of falling unexpectedly at dawn upon the Atar camel corps and there, God willing, killing Captain Bonnafous.

'Bonnafous is very clever,' Kemal avows.

Now I know their secret. Even as men who desire a woman dream of her indifferent footfall, toss and turn in the night, scorched and wounded by the indifference of that stroll she takes through their dream, so the distant progress of Bonnafous torments these warriors.

This Christian in Moorish dress at the head of his two hundred marauding cameleers, Moors themselves, outflanking the razzias hurled against him, has marched boldly into the country of the refractory tents where the least of his own men, freed from the constraint of the garrison, might with impunity shake off his servitude and sacrifice the captain to his God on the stony table-lands. He has gone into a world where only his prestige restrains his men, where his weakness itself is the cause of their dread. And tonight, through their raucous slumber he strolls to and from with heedless step, and his footfall resounds in the innermost heart of the desert.

Mouyan ponders, still motionless against the back wall of the tent, like a block of blue granite cut in low relief. Only his eyes gleam, and his silver knife has ceased to be a plaything. I have the feeling that since becoming part of a razzia he has entered into a different world. To him the dunes are alive. The wind is charged with odours. He senses as never before his own nobility and crushes me beneath his contempt; for he is to ride against Bonnafous, he is to move at dawn impelled by a hatred that bears all the signs of love.

Once again he leans towards his brother, whispers, and stares at me.

'What is he saying?' I ask once again.

'That he will shoot you if he meets you outside the fort.'

'Why?'

'He says you have aeroplanes and the wireless; you have Bonnafous; but you have not the Truth.'

Motionless in the sculptured folds of his blue cloak, Mouyan has judged me.

'He says you eat greens like the goat and pork like the pigs. Your wives are shameless and show their faces – he has seen them. He says you never pray. He says, what good are your aeroplanes and wireless and Bonnafous, if you do not possess the Truth?'

And I am forced to admire this Moor who is not about to defend his freedom, for in the desert a man is always free; who is not about to defend his visible treasures, for the desert is bare; but who is about to defend a secret kingdom.

In the silence of the sand-waves Bonnafous leads his troop like a corsair of old; by the grace of Bonnafous the oasis of Cape Juby has ceased to be a haunt of idle shepherds and has become something as signal, as portentous, as admirable as a ship on the high seas. Bonnafous is a storm beating against the ship's side, and because of him the tent-cloths are closed at night. How poignant is the southern silence! It is Bonnafous' silence. Mouyan, that old hunter, listens to his footfall in the wind.

When Bonnafous returns to France his enemies, far from rejoicing, will bewail his absence, as if his departure had deprived the desert of one of its magnetic poles and their existence of a part of its prestige. They will say to me:

'Why does Bonnafous leave us?'

'I do not know.'

For years he had accepted their rules as his rules. He had staked his life against theirs. He had slept with his head pillowed on their rocks. Like them he had known Biblical nights of stars and wind in the course of the ceaseless pursuit. And of a sudden he proves to them, by the fact of leaving the desert, that he has not been gambling for a stake he deemed essential. Unconcernedly, he throws in his hand and rises from the table. And those Moors he leaves at their gambling lose confidence in the significance of a game which does not involve this man to the last drop of his blood. Still, they try to believe in him:

'Your Bonnafous will come back.'

'I do not know.'

He will come back, they tell themselves. The games of Europe will never satisfy him – garrison bridge, promotion, women, and the rest. Haunted by his lost honour he will come back to this land where each step makes the heart beat faster like a step towards love or towards death. He had imagined that the Sahara was a mere adventure and that what was essential in life lay in Europe; but he will discover with disgust that it was here in the desert he possessed his veritable treasures – this prestige of the sand, the night, the silence, this homeland of wind and stars.

And if Bonnafous should come back one day, the news will spread in a single night throughout the country of the refractory tribes. The Moors will know that somewhere in the Sahara, at the head of his two hundred marauders, Bonnafous is again on the march. They will lead their dromedaries in silence to the wells. They will prepare their provisions of barley. They will clean and oil their breech-loaders, impelled by a hatred that partakes of love.

5

'Hide me in the Marrakesh plane!'

Night after night, at Cape Juby, this slave would make his prayer to me. After which, satisfied that he had done what he could for his salvation, he would sit down upon crossed legs and brew my tea. Having put himself in the hands of the only doctor (as he believed) who could cure him, having prayed to the only god who might save him, he was at peace for another twenty-four hours.

Squatting over his kettle, he would summon up the simple vision of his past – the black earth of Marrakesh, the pink houses, the rudimentary possessions of which he had been despoiled. He bore me no ill-will for my silence, nor for my delay in restoring him to life. I was not a man like himself but a power to be invoked, something like a favourable wind which one of these days might smile upon his destiny.

I, for my part, did not labour under these delusions concerning my power. What was I but a simple pilot, serving my few months as chief of the airport at Cape Juby and living in a wooden hut built over against the Spanish fort, where my worldly goods consisted of a basin, a jug of brackish water, and a cot too short for me?

'We shall see, Bark.'

All slaves are called Bark, so Bark was his name. But despite four years of captivity he could not resign himself to it and remembered constantly that he had been a king.

'What did you do at Marrakesh, Bark?'

At Marrakesh, where his wife and three children were doubtless still living, he had plied a wonderful trade.

'I was a drover, and my name was Mohammed!'

The very magistrates themselves would send for him.

'Mohammed, I have some steers to sell. Go up into the mountains and bring them down.'

Or:

'I have a thousand sheep in the plain. Lead them up into the higher pastures.'

And Bark, armed with an olive-wood sceptre, governed their exodus. He and no other held sway over the nation of ewes, restrained the liveliest because of the lambkins about to be born, stirred up the laggards, strode forward in a universe of confidence and obedience. Nobody but him could say where lay the promised land towards which he led his flock. He alone could read his way in the stars, for the science he possessed was not shared by the sheep. Only he, in his wisdom, decided when they should take their rest, when they should drink at the springs. And at night while they slept, Bark, physician and prophet and king, standing in wool to the knees and swollen with tenderness for so much feeble ignorance, would pray for his people.

One day he was stopped by some Arabs.

'Come with us to fetch cattle up from the South,' they said.

They had walked him a long time, and when, after three days, they found themselves deep in the mountains, on the borders of rebellion, the Arabs had quietly placed a hand on his shoulder, christened him Bark, and sold him into slavery.

He was not the only slave I knew. I used to go daily to the tents to take tea. Stretched out with naked feet on the thick woollen carpet which is the nomad's luxury and upon which for a time each day he builds his house, I would taste the happiness of the journeying hours. In the desert, as on shipboard, one is sensible of the passage of time. In that parching heat a man feels that the day is a voyage towards the goal of evening, towards the promise of a cool breeze that will bathe the limbs and wash away the sweat. Under the heat of the day beasts and men plod towards the sweet well of night as confidently as towards death. Thus, idleness here is never vain; and each day seems as comforting as the roads that lead to the sea.

I knew the slaves well. They would come in as soon as the chief had taken out the little stove, the kettle, and the glasses from his treasure chest – that chest heavy with absurd objects, with locks lacking keys, vases for non-existent flowers, three-penny mirrors, old weapons, things so disparate that they might have been salvaged from a ship cast up here in the desert.

Then the mute slave would cram the stove with twigs, blow on the embers, fill the kettle with water, and in this service that a child could perform, set into motion a play of muscles able to uproot a tree.

I would wonder what he was thinking of, and would sense that he was at peace with himself. There was no doubt that he was hypnotized by the motions he went through – brewing tea, tending the camels, eating. Under the blistering day he walked towards the night; and under the ice of the naked stars he longed for the return of day. Happy are the lands of the North whose seasons are poets, the summer composing a legend of snow, the winter a tale of sun. Sad the tropics, where in the sweating-room nothing changes very much. But happy also the Sahara, where day and night swing man so evenly from one hope to the other.

Tea served, the black will squat outside the tent, relishing the evening wind. In this sluggish captive hulk, memories have ceased to swarm. Even the moment when he was carried off is faint in his mind – the blows, the shouts, the arms of men that brought him down into his present night. And since that hour he has sunk deeper and deeper into a queer slumber, divested like a blind man of his Senegalese rivers or his white Moroccan towns, like a deaf man of the sound of familiar voices.

This black is not unhappy; he is crippled. Dropped down one day into the cycle of desert life, bound to the nomadic migrations, chained for life to the orbits they describe in the sand, how could he retain any memory of a past, a home, a wife and children, all of them for him as dead as the dead?

Men who have lived for years with a great love, and have lived on in noble solitude when it was taken from them, are likely now and then to be worn out by their exaltation. Such men return humbly to a humdrum life, ready to accept contentment in a more commonplace love. They find it sweet to abdicate, to resign themselves to a kind of servility and to enter into the peace of things. This black is proud of his master's embers.

Like a ship moving into port, we of the desert come up into the night. In this hour, because it is the hour when all the weariness of day is remitted and its heats have ceased, when master and slave enter side by side into the cool of evening, the master is kind to the slave.

'Here, take this,' the chief says to the captive.

He allows him a glass of tea. And the captive, overcome with gratitude for a glass of tea, would kiss his master's knees. This man before me is not weighed down with chains. How little need he has of them! How faithful he is! How submissively he forswears the deposed king within him! Truly, the man is a mere contented slave.

And yet the day will come when he will be set free. When he has grown too old to be worth his food or his cloak he will be inconceivably free. For three days he will offer himself in vain from tent to tent, growing each day weaker; until towards the end of the third day, still uncomplaining, he will lie down on the sand.

I have seen them die naked like this at Cape Juby. The Moors jostle their long death-struggle, though without ill intent; and the children play in the vicinity of the dark wreck, running with each dawn to see if it is still stirring, yet without mocking the old servitor. It is all in the nature of things. It is as if they had said to him : 'You have done a good day's work and have the right to sleep. Go to bed.'

And the old slave, still outstretched, suffers hunger which is but vertigo, and not injustice which alone is torment. Bit by bit he becomes one with the earth, is shrivelled up by the sun and received by the earth. Thirty years of toil, and then this right to slumber and to the earth.

The first one I saw did not moan; but then he had no one to moan against. I felt in him an obscure acquiescence, as of a mountaineer lost and at the end of his strength who sinks to earth and wraps himself up in dreams and snow. What was painful to me was not his suffering (for I did not believe he was suffering); it was that for the first time it came on me that when a man dies, an unknown world passes away.

I could not tell what visions were vanishing in the dying slave, what Senegalese plantations or white Moroccan towns. It was impossible for me to know whether, in this black heap, there was being extinguished merely a world of petty cares in the breast of a slave – the tea to be brewed, the camels watered; or whether, revived by a surge of memories, a man lay dying in the glory of humanity. The hard bone of his skull was in a sense an old treasure chest; and I could not know what coloured stuffs, what images of festivities, what vestiges, obsolete and vain in this desert, had here escaped the shipwreck.

The chest was there, locked and heavy. I could not know what bit of the world was crumbling in this man during the gigantic slumber of his ultimate days, was disintegrating in this consciousness and this flesh which little by little was reverting to night and to root.

'I was a drover, and my name was Mohammed !'

Before I met Bark I had never met a slave who offered the least resistance. That the Moors had violated his freedom, had in a single day stripped him as naked as a new-born infant, was not the point. God sometimes sends cyclones which in a single hour wipe out a man's harvests. But deeper than his belongings, these Moors had threatened him in his very essence.

Many another captive would have resigned himself to the death in him of the poor herdsman who toiled the year round for a crust of bread. Not so Bark. He refused to settle into a life of servitude, to surrender to the weariness of waiting and resign himself to a passive contentment. He rejected the slave-joys that are contingent upon the kindness of the slave-owner. Within his breast Mohammed absent held fast to the house Mohammed had lived in. That house was sad for being empty, but none other should live in it. Bark was like one of those white-haired caretakers who die of their fidelity in the weeds of the paths and the tedium of silence.

He never said: 'I am Mohammed ben Lhaoussin'; he said: 'My name was Mohammed', dreaming of the day when that obliterated figure would again live within him in all its glory and by the power of its resuscitation would drive out the ghost of the slave.

There were times when, in the silence of the night, all his memories swept over him with the poignancy of a song of childhood. Our Arab interpreter said to me: 'In the middle of the night he woke up and talked about Marrakesh; and he wept.' No man in solitude can escape these recurrences. The old Mohammed awoke in him without warning, stretched himself in his limbs, sought his wife against his flank in this desert where no woman had ever approached Bark, and listened to the water purling in the fountains here where no fountain ran.

And Bark, his eyes shut, sitting every night under the same star, in a place where men live in houses of air and follow the wind, told himself that he was living in his white house in Marrakesh. His body charged with tenderness and mysteriously magnetized, as if the pole of these emotions were very near at hand, Bark would come to see me. He was trying to let me know that he was ready, that his over-full heart was quivering on the brim and needed only to find itself back in Marrakesh to be poured out. And all that was wanted was a sign from me. Bark would smile, would whisper to me how it could be done – for of course I should not have thought of this dodge:

'The mails leave tomorrow. You stow me away in the Marra-kesh plane.'

'Poor old Bark!'

We were stationed among the unsubdued tribes, and how could we help him away? God knows what massacre the Moors would have done among us that very day to avenge the insult of this theft. I had, indeed, tried to buy him, with the help of the mechanics at the port – Laubergue, Marchal, and Abgrall. But it was not every day that the Moors met Europeans in quest of a slave, and they took advantage of the occasion.

'Twenty thousand francs.'

'Don't make me laugh!'

'But look at those strong arms. . . .'

Months passed before the Moors came down to a reasonable figure and I, with the help of friends at home to whom I had written, found myself in a position to buy old Bark. There was a week of bargaining which we spent, fifteen Moors and I, sitting in a circle in the sand. A friend of Bark's master who was also my friend, Zin Ould Rhattari, a bandit, was privately on my side.

'Sell him,' he would argue in accordance with my coaching. 'You will lose him one of these days, you know. Bark is a sick man. He is diseased. You can't see yet, but he is sick inside. One of these days he will swell right up. Sell him as soon as you can to the Frenchman.'

I had promised fifty Spanish pesetas to another bandit, Raggi, and Raggi would say:

'With the money you get for Bark you will be able to buy camels and rifles and cartridges. Then you can go off on a razzia against these French. Go down to Atar and bring back three or four young Senegalese. Get rid of the old carcass.'

And so Bark was sold to me. I locked him up for six days in our hut, for if he had wandered out before the arrival of a plane the Moors would surely have kidnapped him. Meanwhile, although I would not allow him out, I set him free with a flourish of ceremony in the presence of three Moorish witnesses. One was a local marabout, another was Ibrahim, the mayor of Cape Juby, and the third was his former owner. These three pirates, who would gladly have cut off Bark's head within fifty feet of the fort for the sole pleasure of doing me in the eye, embraced him warmly and signed the official act of manumission. That done, they said to him:

'You are now our son.'

He was my son, too, by law. Dutifully, Bark embraced all his fathers.

He lived on in our hut in comfortable captivity until we could ship him home. Over and over again, twenty times a day, he would ask to have the simple journey described. We were flying him to Agadir. There he would be given an omnibus ticket to Marrakesh. He was to be sure not to miss the bus. That was all there was to it. But Bark played at being free the way a child plays at being an explorer, going over and over his journey back to life – the bus, the crowds, the towns he would pass through.

One day Laubergue came to talk to me about Bark. He said that Marchal and Abgrall and he rather felt it would be a shame if Bark was flung into the world without a copper. They had made up a purse of a thousand francs: didn't I think that would see Bark through till he found work? I thought of all the old ladies who run charities and insist upon gratitude in exchange for every twenty francs they part with. These aeroplane mechanics were parting with a thousand francs, had no thought of charity, and were even less concerned about gratitude.

Nor were they acting out of pity, like those old ladies who want to believe they are spreading happiness. They were contributing simply to restore to a man his lost dignity as a human being. They knew quite as well as anybody else that once the initial intoxication of his homecoming was past, the first faithful friend to step up and take Bark's hand would be Poverty; and that before three months had gone by he would be tearing up sleepers somewhere on the railway line for a living. He was sure to be less well off there than here in the desert. But in their view he had the right to live his life among his own people.

'Good-bye, old Bark. Be a man!'

The plane quivered, ready to take off. Bark took his last look at the immense desolation of Cape Juby. Round the plane two hundred Moors were finding out what a slave looked like when he stood on the threshold of life. They would make no bones about snatching him back again if a little later the ship happened to be forced down.

We stood about our fifty-year-old, new-born babe, worried a little at having launched him forth on the stream of life.

'Good-bye, Bark!'

'No!'

'What do you mean?'

'No. I am Mohammed ben Lhaoussin.'

The last news we had of him was brought back to us by Abdullah, who at our request had looked after Bark at Agadir. The plane reached Agadir in the morning, but the bus did not leave until evening. This was how Bark spent his day.

He began by wandering through the town and remaining silent so long that his restlessness upset Abdullah.

'Anything the matter?'

'No.'

This freedom had come too suddenly: Bark was finding it hard to orient himself. There was a vague happiness in him, but with this exception there was scarcely any difference between the Bark of yesterday and the Bark of today. Yet he had as much right to the sun, henceforth, as other men; as much right as they to sit in the shade of an Arab café.

He sat down and ordered tea for Abdullah and himself. This was his first lordly gesture, a manifestation of a power that ought to have transfigured him in other men's eyes. But the waiter poured his tea quite without surprise, quite unaware that in this gesture he was doing homage to a free man.

'Let us go somewhere else,' Bark had said; and they had gone off to the Kasbah, the licensed quarter of the town. The little Berber prostitutes came up and greeted them, so kind and tame that here Bark felt he might be coming alive.

These girls were welcoming a man back to life, but they knew nothing of this. They took him by the hand, offered him tea, then love, very nicely; but exactly as they would have offered it to any man. Bark, preoccupied with his message, tried to tell them the story of his resurrection. They smiled most sympathetically. They were glad for him, since he was glad. And to make the wonder more wonderful he added: 'I am Mohammed ben Lhaoussin.'

But that was no surprise to them. All men have names, and

so many return from afar! They could guess, nevertheless, that this man had suffered, and they strove to be as gentle as possible with the poor black devil. He appreciated their gentleness, this first gift that life was making him; but his restlessness was yet not stilled. He had not yet rediscovered his empire.

Back to town went Bark and Abdullah. He idled in front of the Jewish shops, stared at the sea, repeated to himself that he could walk as he pleased in any direction, that he was free. But this freedom had in it a taste of bitterness: what he learned from it with most intensity was that he had no ties with the world.

At that moment a child had come up. Bark stroked the soft cheek. The child smiled. This was not one of the master's children that one had to flatter. It was a sickly child whose cheek Bark was stroking. And the child was smiling at him. The child awoke something in Bark, and Bark felt himself more important on earth because of the sickly child whose smile was his due. He began to sense confusedly that something was stirring within him, was striding forward with swift steps.

'What are you looking for?' Abdullah had asked him.

'Nothing,' was again Bark's answer.

But when, rounding a corner, he came upon a group of children at play, he stopped. This was it. He stared at them in silence. Then he went off to the Jewish shops and came back laden with treasure. Abdullah was nettled:

'Fool! Throwing away your money!'

Bark gave no heed. Solemnly he beckoned to each child in turn, and the little hands rose towards the toys and the bangles and the gold-sewn slippers. Each child, as soon as he had a firm grip on his treasure, fled like a wild thing, and Bark went back to the Jewish shops.

Other children in Agadir, hearing the news, ran after him; and these too were shod by Bark in golden slippers. The tale spread to the outskirts of Agadir, whence still other children scurried into town and clustered round the black god, clinging to his threadbare cloak and clamouring for their due. Bark, that victim of a sombre joy, spent on them his last copper.

Abdullah was sure that he had gone mad, 'mad with joy,' he said afterward. But I incline to believe that Bark was not sharing with others an overflow of happiness. He was free, and therefore he possessed the essential of wealth – the right to the love of Berber girls, to go north or south as he pleased, to earn his bread by his toil. What good was this money when the thing for which he was famished was to be a man in the family of men, bound by ties to other men?

The town prostitutes had been kind to old Bark, but he had been able to get away from them as easily as he had come to them : they had no need of him. The waiter in the café, the passers-by in the streets, the shopkeepers, had respected the free man he was, sharing their sun with him on terms of equality; but none of them had indicated that he needed Bark.

He was free, but too infinitely free; not striding upon the earth but floating above it. He felt the lack in him of that weight of human relations that trammels a man's progress; tears, farewells, reproaches, joys – all those things that a man caresses or rips apart each time he sketches a gesture; those thousand ties that bind him to others and lend density to his being. But already Bark was in ballast of a thousand hopes.

And so the reign of Bark began in the glory of the sun setting over Agadir, in that evening coolness that so long had been for him the single sweetness, the unique stall in which he could take his rest. And as the hour of leaving approached, Bark went forward lapped in this tide of children as once in his sea of ewes, ploughing his first furrow in the world. He would go back next day to the poverty of his family, to responsibility for more lives than perhaps his old arms would be able to sustain; but already, among these children, he felt the pull of his true weight. Like an archangel too airy to live the life of man, but who had cheated, had sewn lead into his girdle, Bark dragged himself forward, pulling against the pull of a thousand children who had such great need of golden slippers.

Such is the desert. A Koran which is but a handbook of the rules of the game transforms its sands into an empire. Deep in the seemingly empty Sahara a secret drama is being played that stirs the passions of men. The true life of the desert is not made up of the marches of tribes in search of pasture, but of the game that goes endlessly on. What a difference in substance between the sands of submission and the sands of unruliness! The dunes, the salines, change their nature according as the code changes by which they are governed.

And is not all the world like this? Gazing at this transfigured desert I remember the games of my childhood – the dark and golden park we peopled with gods; the limitless kingdom we made of this square mile never thoroughly explored, never thoroughly charted. We created a secret civilization where footfalls had a meaning and things a savour known in no other world.

And when we grow to be men and live under other laws, what remains of that park filled with the shadows of childhood, magical, freezing, burning? What do we learn when we return to it and stroll with a sort of despair along the outside of its little wall of grey stone, marvelling that within a space so small we should have founded a kingdom that had seemed to us infinite – what do we learn except that in this infinity we shall never again set foot, and that it is into the game and not the park that we have lost the power to enter?

8 Prisoner of the Sand

After three years of life in the desert, I was transferred out. The fortunes of the air service sent me wandering here and there until one day I decided to attempt a long-distance flight from Paris to Saigon. When, on 29 December 1935, I took off, I had no notion that the sands were preparing for me their ultimate and culminating ordeal.

This is the story of the Paris–Saigon flight.

I paid my final visit to the weather bureau, where I found Monsieur Viaud stooped over his maps like a medieval alchemist over an alembic. Lucas had come with me, and we stared together at the curving lines marking the new-sprung winds. With their tiny flying arrows, they put me in mind of curving tendrils studded with thorns. All the atmospheric depressions of the world were charted on this enormous map, ochre-coloured, like the earth of Asia.

'Here is a storm that we'll not hear from before Monday,' Monsieur Viaud pointed out.

Over Russia and the Scandinavian peninsula the swirling lines took the form of a coiled demon. Out in Iraq, in the neighbourhood of Basra, an imp was whirling.

'That fellow worries me a little,' said Monsieur Viaud.

'Sand-storm, is it?'

I was not being idly curious. Day would not yet be breaking when I reached Basra and I was fearful of flying at night in one of those desert storms that turn the sky into a yellow furnace and wipe out hills, towns, and river-banks, drowning earth and sky in one great conflagration. It would be bad enough to fly in daylight through a chaos in which the very elements themselves were indistinguishable.

'Sand-storm? No, not exactly.'

'So much the better,' I said to myself, and I looked round the room. I liked this laboratory atmosphere. Viaud, I felt, was a man escaped from the world. When he came in here and hung up his hat and coat on the peg, he hung up with them all the confusion in which the rest of mankind lived. Family cares, thoughts of income, concerns of the heart – all that vanished on the threshold of this room as at the door of a hermit's cell, or an astronomer's tower, or a radio operator's shack. Here was one of those men who are able to lock themselves up in the secrecy of their retreat and hold discourse with the universe.

Gently – for he was reflecting – Monsieur Viaud rubbed the palms of his hands together.

'No, not a sand-storm. See here.'

His finger travelled over the map and pointed out why.

At four in the morning Lucas shook me into consciousness. 'Wake up!'

And before I could so much as rub my eyes he was saying: 'Look here, at this report. Look at the moon. You won't see much of her tonight. She's new, not very bright, and she'll set at ten o'clock. And here's something else for you: sunrise in Greenwich Meridian Time and in local time as well. And here: here are your maps, with your course all marked out. And here –'

'– is your bag packed for Saigon,' my wife broke in.

A razor and a change of shirt. He who would travel happily must travel light.

We got into a car and motored out to Le Bourget while Fate spying in ambush put the finishing touches to her plans. Those favourable winds that were to wheel in the heavens, that moon that was to sink at ten o'clock, were so many strategic positions at which Fate was assembling her forces.

It was cold at the airport, and dark. The *Simoon* was wheeled out of her hangar. I walked round my ship, stroking her wings with the back of my hand in a caress that I believe was love. Eight thousand miles I had flown in her, and her engines had not skipped a beat; not a bolt in her had loosened. This was the marvel that was to save our lives the next night by refusing to be ground to powder on meeting the upsurging earth.

Friends had turned up. Every long flight starts in the same

atmosphere, and nobody who has experienced it once would ever have it otherwise: the wind, the drizzle at daybreak, the engines purring quietly as they are warmed up; this instrument of conquest gleaming in her fresh coat of 'dope' – all of it goes straight to the heart.

Already one has a foretaste of the treasures about to be garnered on the way – the green and brown and yellow lands promised by the maps; the rosary of resounding names that make up the pilot's beads; the hours to be picked up one by one on the eastward flight into the sun.

There is a particular flavour about the tiny cabin in which, still only half awake, you stow away your thermos flasks and odd parts and overnight bag; in the fuel tanks heavy with power; and best of all, forward, in the magical instruments set like jewels in their panel and glimmering like a constellation in the dark of night. The mineral glow of the artificial horizon, these stethoscopes designed to take the heart-beat of the heavens, are things a pilot loves. The cabin of a plane is a world unto itself, and to the pilot it is home.

I took off, and though the load of fuel was heavy, I got easily away. I avoided Paris with a jerk and up the Seine, at Melun, I found myself flying very low between showers of rain. I was heading for the valley of the Loire. Nevers lay below me, and then Lyon. Over the Rhône I was shaken up a bit. Mt Ventoux was capped in snow. There lies Marignane and here comes Marseille.

The towns slipped past as in a dream. I was going so far – or thought I was going so far – that these wretched little distances were covered before I was aware of it. The minutes were flying. So much the better. There are times when, after a quarter-hour of flight, you look at your watch and find that five minutes have gone by; other days when the hands turn a quarter of an hour in the wink of an eye. This was a day when time was flying. A good omen. I started out to sea.

Very odd, that little stream of vapour rising from the fuel gauge on my port wing! It might almost be a plume of smoke.

'Prévot!'

My mechanic leaned toward me.

'Look! Isn't that petrol? Seems to me it's leaking pretty fast.'

He had a look and shook his head .

'Better check our consumption,' I said.

I wasn't turning back yet. My course was still set for Tunis. I looked round and could see Prévot at the gauge on the second fuel tank aft. He came forward and said :

'You've used up about fifty gallons.'

Nearly twenty had leaked away in the wind! That was serious. I put back to Marignane, where I drank a cup of coffee while the time lost hurt like an open wound. Flyers in the Air France service wanted to know whether I was bound for Saigon or Madagascar and wished me luck. The tank was patched up and refilled, and I took off once more with a full load, again without mishap despite a bit of rough going over the soggy field.

As soon as I reached the sea I ran into low-hanging clouds that forced me down to sixty feet. The driving rain spattered against the windshield and the sea was churning and foaming. I strained to see ahead and keep from hooking the mast of some ship, while Prévot lit cigarettes for me.

'Coffee!'

He vanished into the stern of the cockpit and came back with the thermos flask. I drank. From time to time I flicked the throttle to keep the engines at exactly 2,100 revolutions and ran my eye over the dials like a captain inspecting his troops. My company stood trim and erect: every needle was where it should be.

I glanced down at the sea and saw it bubbling under the steaming rain like a boiling cauldron. In a hydroplane this bumpy sea would have bothered me; but in this ship of mine, which could not possibly be set down here, I felt differently. It was silly, of course, but the thought gave me a sense of security. The sea was part of a world that I had nothing to do with. Engine trouble here was out of the question : there was not the least danger of such a thing. Why, I was not rigged for the sea !

After an hour and a half of this, the rain died down, and though the clouds still hung low a genial sun began to break through. I was immensely cheered by this promise of good weather. Overhead I could feel a thin layer of cotton wool and

I swerved aside to avoid a downpour. I was past the point where I had to cut through the heart of squalls. Was not that the first rift in the cloud-bank, there ahead of me?

I sensed it before I saw it, for straight ahead on the sea lay a long meadow-coloured swath, a sort of oasis of deep and luminous green reminding me of those barley fields in southern Morocco that would make me catch my breath each time I sighted them on coming up from Senegal across two thousand miles of sand. Here as at such times in Morocco I felt we had reached a place a man could live in, and it bucked me up. I flung a glance backward at Prévot and called out:

'We're over the worst of it. This is fine.'

'Yes,' he said, 'fine.'

This meant that I would not need to do any stunt flying when Sardinia hove unexpectedly into view. The island would not loom up suddenly like a mass of wreckage a hundred feet ahead of me: I should be able to see it rising on the horizon in the distant play of a thousand sparkling points of light.

I moved into this region bathed by the sun. No doubt about it, I was loafing along. Loafing at the rate of one hundred and seventy miles an hour, but loafing nevertheless. I smoked a few leisurely cigarettes. I lingered over my coffee. I kept a cautious fatherly eye on my brood of instruments. These clouds, this sun, this play of light, lent to my flight the relaxation of a Sunday afternoon stroll. The sea was as variegated as a country landscape broken into fields of green and violet and blue. Off in the distance, just where a squall was blowing, I could see the fermenting spray. Once again I recognized that the sea was of all things in the world the least monotonous, was formed of an ever-changing substance. A gust of wind mantles it with light or strips it bare. I turned back to Prévot.

'Look!' I said.

There in the distance lay the shores of Sardinia that we were about to skirt to the southward.

Prévot came forward and sat down beside me. He squinted with wrinkled forehead at the mountains struggling out of their shroud of mist. The clouds had been blown away and the island was coming into view in great slabs of field and woodland. I climbed to forty-five hundred feet and drifted along the coast of this island dotted with villages. After the flower-strewn but uninhabitable sea, this was the place where I could take things easily. For a little time I clung to our great-hearted mother earth. Then, Sardinia behind me, I headed for Tunis.

I picked up the African continent at Bizerta and there I began to drop earthward. I was at home. Here was a place where I could dispense with altitude which, as every pilot knows, is our particular store of wealth. Not that we squander it when it is no longer needed: we swap it for another kind of treasure. When a flyer is within a quarter of an hour of port, he sets his controls for the down swing, throttling his motor a little – just enough to keep it from racing while the needle on his speedometer swings round from one hundred and seventy to two hundred miles an hour.

At that rate of speed the impalpable eddies of evening air drum softly on the wings and the plane seems to be drilling its way into a quivering crystal so delicate that the wake of a passing swallow would jar it to bits. I was already skirting the undulations of the hills and had given away almost the whole of my few hundred feet of altitude when I reached the aerodrome, and there, shaving the roofs of the hangars, I set down my ship on the ground.

While the tanks were being refilled I signed some papers and shook hands with a few friends. And just as I was coming out of the administration building I heard a horrible grunt, one of those muffled impacts that tell their fatal story in a single sound; one of those echoless thuds complete in themselves, without appeal, in which fatality delivers its message. Instantly there came into my mind the memory of an identical sound – an explosion in a garage. Two men had died of that hoarse bark.

I looked now across to the road that ran alongside the aerodrome: there in a puff of dust two high-powered cars had crashed head-on and stood frozen into motionlessness as if imprisoned in ice. Men were running towards the cars while others ran from them to the field office.

'Get a doctor . . . Skull crushed. . . .'

My heart sank. In the peace of the evening light Fate had taken a trick. A beauty, a mind, a life – something had been

106

destroyed. It was as sudden as a raid in the desert. Marauding tribesmen creep up on silent feet in the night. The camp resounds briefly with the clashing tumult of a razzia. A moment later everything has sunk back into the golden silence. The same peace, the same stillness, followed this crash.

Nearby, someone spoke of a fractured skull. I had no mind to be told about that crushed and bloody cranium. Turning my back to the road, I went across to my ship, in my heart a foreboding of danger. I was to recognize that sound when I heard it again very soon. When the *Simoon* scraped the black plateau at a speed of one hundred and seventy miles an hour I should recognize that hoarse grunt, that same snarl of destiny keeping its appointment with us.

Off to Benghazi! We still have two hours of daylight. Before we crossed into Tripolitania I took off my glare glasses. The sands were golden under the slanting rays of the sun. How empty of life is this planet of ours! Once again it struck me that its rivers, its woods, its human habitations were the product of chance, of fortuitous conjunctions of circumstance. What a deal of the earth's surface is given over to rock and sand!

But all this was not my affair. My world was the world of flight. Already I could feel the oncoming night within which I should be enclosed as in the precincts of a temple – enclosed in the temple of night for the accomplishment of secret rites and absorption in inviolable contemplation.

Already this profane world was beginning to fade out: soon it would vanish altogether. This landscape was still laved in golden sunlight, but already something was evaporating out of it. I know nothing, nothing in the world, equal to the wonder of nightfall in the air.

Those who have been enthralled by the witchery of flying will know what I mean – and I do not speak of the men who, among other sports, enjoy taking a turn in a plane. I speak of those who fly professionally and have sacrificed much to their craft. Mermoz said once: 'It's worth it, it's worth the final smash-up.'

No question about it; but the reason is hard to formulate. A novice taking orders could appreciate this ascension towards the essence of things, since his profession too is one of renunciation: he renounces the world; he renounces riches; he renounces the love of woman. And by renunciation he discovers his hidden god.

I, too, in this flight, am renouncing things. I am giving up the broad golden surfaces that would befriend me if my engines were to fail. I am giving up the landmarks by which I might be taking my bearings. I am giving up the profiles of mountains against the sky that would warn me of pitfalls. I am plunging into the night. I am navigating. I have on my side only the stars.

The diurnal death of the world is a slow death. It is only little by little that the divine beacon of daylight recedes from me. Earth and sky begin to merge into each other. The earth rises and seems to spread like a mist. The first stars tremble as if shimmering in green water. Hours must pass before their glimmer hardens into the frozen glitter of diamonds. I shall have a long wait before I witness the soundless frolic of the shooting stars. In the profound darkness of certain nights I have seen the sky streaked with so many trailing sparks that it seemed to me a great gale must be blowing through the outer heavens.

Prévot was testing the lamps in their sockets and the emergency torches. Round the bulbs he was wrapping red paper.

'Another layer.'

He added another wrapping of paper and touched a switch. The dim light within the plane was still too bright. As in a photographer's dark-room, it veiled the pale picture of the external world. It hid that glowing phosphorescence which sometimes, at night, clings to the surface of things. Now night has fallen, but it is not yet true night. A crescent moon persists.

Prévot dove aft and came back with a sandwich. I nibbled a bunch of grapes. I was not hungry. I was neither hungry nor thirsty. I felt no weariness. It seemed to me that I could go on like this at the controls for ten years. I was happy.

The moon had set. It was pitch dark when we came in sight of Benghazi. The town lay at the bottom of an obscurity so dense that it was without a halo. I saw the place only when I was over it. As I was hunting for the aerodrome the red obstruction lights were switched on. They cut out a black rectangle in the earth.

I banked, and at that moment the rays of a floodlight rose into the sky like a jet from a fire-hose. It pivoted and traced a golden lane over the landing-field. I circled again to get a clear view of what might be in my way. The port was equipped with everything to make a night-landing easy. I throttled down my engine and dropped like a diver into black water.

It was eleven o'clock, local time, when I landed and taxied across to the beacon. The most helpful ground crew in the world wove in and out of the blinding ray of a searchlight, alternately visible and invisible. They took my papers and began promptly to fill my tanks. Twenty minutes of my time was all they asked for, and I was touched by their great readiness to help. As I was taking off, one of them said :

'Better circle round and fly over us; otherwise we shan't be sure you got off all right.'

I rolled down the golden lane towards an unimpeded opening. My *Simoon* lifted her overload clear of the ground well before I reached the end of the runway. The searchlight following me made it hard for me to wheel. Soon it let me go : the men on the ground had guessed that it was dazzling me. I turned right about and banked vertically, and at that moment the searchlight caught me between the eyes again; but scarcely had it touched me when it fled and sent elsewhere its long golden flute. I knew that the ground crew were being most thoughtful and I was grateful. And now I was off to the desert.

All along the line, at Paris, at Tunis, and at Benghazi, I had been told that I should have a following wind of up to twenty-five miles an hour. I was counting on a speed of 190 m.p.h. as I set my course on the middle of the stretch between Alexandria and Cairo. On this course I should avoid the danger zones along the coast, and despite any drifting I might do without knowing it, I should pick up either to port or to starboard the lights of one of those two cities. Failing them I should certainly not miss the lights of the Nile valley. With a steady wind I should reach the Nile in three hours and twenty minutes; if the wind fell, three hours and three-quarters. Calculating thus I began to eat up the six hundred and fifty miles of desert ahead of me.

There was no moon. The world was a bubble of pitch that had dilated until it reached the very stars in the heavens. I should not see a single gleam of light, should not profit by the faintest landmark. Carrying no wireless, I should receive no message from the earth until I reached the Nile. It was useless to try to look at anything other than the compass and the artificial horizon. I might blot the world out of my mind and concentrate my attention upon the slow pulsation of the narrow thread of radium paint that ran along the dark background of the dials.

Whenever Prévot stirred I brought the plane smoothly back to plumb. I went up to six thousand feet, where I had been told the winds would be favourable. At long intervals I switched on a lamp to glance at the engine dials, not all of which were phosphorescent; but most of the time I wrapped myself closely round in darkness among my miniature constellations which gave off the same mineral glow as the stars, the same mysterious and unwearied light, and spoke the same language.

Like the astronomers, I too was reading in the book of celestial mechanics. I too seemed to myself studious and uncorrupted. Everything in the world that might have lured me from my studies had gone out. The external world had ceased to exist.

There was Prévot, who, after a vain resistance, had fallen asleep and left me to the greater enjoyment of my solitude. There was the gentle purr of my beautiful little motor, and before me, on the instrument panel, there were all those tranquil stars. I was most decidedly not sleepy. If this state of quiet well-being persisted until tomorrow night, I intended to push on without a stop to Saigon.

Now the flight was beginning to seem to me short. Benghazi, the only troublesome night-landing on the route, had banked its fires and settled down behind the horizon in that dark shuttering in which cities take their slumber.

Meanwhile I was turning things over in my mind. We were without the moon's help and we had no wireless. No slightest tenuous tie was to bind us to earth until the Nile showed its thread of light directly ahead of us. We were truly alone in the universe – a thought that caused me not the least worry. If my motor were to cough, that sound would startle me more than if my heart should skip a beat.

Into my mind came the image of Sabathier, the white-haired engineer with a clear eye. I was thinking that, from one point of view, it would be hard to draw a distinction in the matter of human values between a profession like his and that of the painter, the composer, or the poet. I could see in the mind's eye those watchmaker's hands of his that had brought into being this clockwork I was piloting. Men who have given their lives to labours of love go straight to my heart.

'Couldn't I change this?' I had asked him.

'I shouldn't advise it,' he had answered.

I was remembering our last conversation. He had thought it inadvisable, and of course that had settled it. A physician, that's it! Exactly the way one puts oneself into the hands of one's doctor – when he has that look in his eye. It was by his motor that we hung suspended in air and were able to go on living with the ticking of time in this penetrable pitch. We were crossing the great dark valley of a fairy-tale, the Valley of Ordeal. Like the prince in the tale, we must meet the test without succour. Failure here would not be forgiven. We were in the lap of the inexorable gods.

A ray of light was filtering through a joint in the lamp shaft. I woke up Prévot and told him to put it out. Prévot stirred in the darkness like a bear, snorted, and came forward. He fumbled for a bit with handkerchiefs and black paper, and the ray of light vanished. That light had bothered me because it was not of my world. It swore at the pale and distant gleam of the phosphorescence and was like a night-club spotlight compared to the gleam of a star. Besides, it had dazzled me and had outshone all else that gleamed.

We had been flying for three hours. A brightness that seemed to me a glare spurted on the starboard side. I stared. A streamer of light which I had hitherto not noticed was fluttering from a lamp at the tip of the wing. It was an intermittent glow, now brilliant, now dim. It told me that I had flown into a cloud, and it was on the cloud that the lamp was reflected.

I was nearing the landmarks upon which I had counted; a clear sky would have helped a lot. The wing shone bright under the halo. The light steadied itself, became fixed, and then began to radiate in the form of a bouquet of pink blossoms. Great eddies of air were swinging me to and fro. I was navigating somewhere in the belly of a cumulus whose thickness I could not guess. I rose to seventy-five hundred feet and was still in it. Down again to three thousand, and the bouquet of flowers was still with me, motionless and growing brighter.

Well, there it was and there was nothing to do about it. I would think of something else, and wait to get clear of it. Just the same, I did not like this sinister glitter of a one-eyed grog-shop.

'Let me think,' I said to myself. 'I am bouncing round a bit, but there's nothing abnormal about that. I've been bumped all the way, despite a clear sky and plenty of ceiling. The wind has not died down, and I must be doing better than the 190 m.p.h. I counted on.' This was about as far as I could get. Oh well, when I got through the cloud-bank I would try to take my bearings.

Out of it we flew. The bouquet suddenly vanished, letting me know I was in the clear again. I stared ahead and saw, if one can speak of 'seeing' space, a narrow valley of sky and the wall of the next cumulus. Already the bouquet was coming to life again. I was free of that viscous mess from time to time, but only for a few seconds each time. After three and a half hours of flying it began to get on my nerves. If I had made the time I imagined, we were certainly approaching the Nile. With a little luck I might be able to spot the river through the rifts, but they were getting rare. I dared not come down, for if I was actually slower than I thought, I was still over high-lying country.

Thus far I was entirely without anxiety; my only fear was that I might presently be wasting time. I decided that I would take things easy until I had flown four and a quarter hours: after that, even in a dead calm (which was highly unlikely), I should have crossed the Nile. When I reached the fringes of the cloud-bank the bouquet winked on and off more and more swiftly and then suddenly went out. Decidedly, I did not like these dot-and-dash messages from the demons of the night.

A green star appeared ahead of me, flashing like a lighthouse. Was it a lighthouse? or really a star? I took no pleasure from this supernatural gleam, this star the Magi might have seen, this dangerous decoy.

Prévot, meanwhile, had waked up and turned his electric torch on the engine dials. I waved him off, him and his torch. We had just sailed into the clear between two clouds and I was busy staring below. Prévot went back to sleep. The gap in the clouds was no help: there was nothing below.

Four hours and five minutes in the air. Prévot awoke and sat down beside me.

'I'll bet we're near Cairo,' he said.

'We must be.'

'What's that? A star? or is it a lighthouse?'

I had throttled the engine down a little. This, probably, was what had awakened Prévot. He is sensitive to all the variations of sound in flight.

I began a slow descent, intending to slip under the mass of clouds. Meanwhile I had had a look at my map. One thing was sure – the land below me lay at sea-level, and there was no risk of conking against a hill. Down I went, flying due north so that the lights of the cities would strike square into my windows. I must have overflown them, and should therefore see them on my left.

Now I was flying below the cumulus. But alongside was another cloud hanging lower down on the left. I swerved so as not to be caught in its net, and headed north-north-east. This second cloud-bank certainly went down a long way, for it blocked my view of the horizon. I dared not give up any more altitude. My altimeter registered 1200 feet, but I had no notion of the atmospheric pressure here. Prévot leaned toward me and I shouted to him: 'I'm going out to sea. I'd rather come down on it than risk a crash here.'

As a matter of fact, there was nothing to prove that we had not drifted over the sea already. Below that cloud-bank visibility was exactly nil. I hugged my window, trying to read below me, to discover flares, signs of life. I was a man raking dead ashes, trying in vain to retrieve the flame of life in a hearth.

'A lighthouse!'

Both of us spied it at the same moment, that winking decoy! What madness! Where was that phantom light, that invention of the night? For at the very second when Prévot and I leaned forward to pick it out of the air where it had glittered nine hundred feet below our wings, suddenly, at that very instant . . .

'Oh!'

I am quite sure that this was all I said. I am quite sure that all I felt was a terrific crash that rocked our world to its foundations. We had crashed against the earth at a hundred and seventy miles an hour. I am quite sure that in the split second that followed, all I expected was the great flash of ruddy light of the explosion in which Prévot and I were to be blown up together. Neither he nor I had felt the least emotion of any kind. All I could observe in myself was an extraordinary tense feeling of expectancy, the expectancy of that resplendent star in which we were to vanish within the second.

But there was no ruddy star. Instead there was a sort of earthquake that splintered our cabin, ripped away the windows, blew sheets of metal hurtling through space a hundred yards away, and filled our very entrails with its roar. The ship quivered like a knife-blade thrown from a distance into a block of oak, and its anger mashed us as if we were so much pulp.

One second, two seconds passed, and the plane still quivered while I waited with a grotesque impatience for the forces within it to burst it like a bomb. But the subterranean quakings went on without a climax of eruption while I marvelled uncomprehendingly at its invisible travail. I was baffled by the quaking, the anger, the interminable postponement. Five seconds passed; six seconds. And suddenly we were seized by a spinning motion, a shock that jerked our cigarettes out of the window, pulverized the starboard wing – and then nothing, nothing but a frozen immobility. I shouted to Prévot:

'Jump!'

And in that instant he cried out:

'Fire!'

We dove together through the wrecked window and found ourselves standing side by side, sixty feet from the plane. I said:

'Are you hurt?'

He answered:

'Not a bit.'

But he was rubbing his knee.

'Better run your hands over yourself,' I said; 'move about a bit. Sure no bones are broken?'

He answered:

'I'm all right. It's that emergency pump.'

Emergency pump! I was sure he was going to keel over any minute and split open from head to navel there before my eyes. But he kept repeating with a glassy stare:

'That pump, that emergency pump.'

He's out of his head, I thought. He'll start dancing in a minute.

Finally he stopped staring at the plane – which had not gone up in flames – and stared at me instead. And he said again:

'I'm all right. It's that emergency pump. It got me in the knee.'

Why we were not blown up I do not know. I switched on my electric torch and went back over the furrow in the ground traced by the plane. Two hundred and fifty yards from where we stopped the ship had begun to shed the twisted iron and sheet-metal that spattered the sand the length of her traces. We were to see, when day came, that we had run almost tangentially into a gentle slope at the top of a barren plateau. At the point of impact there was a hole in the sand that looked as if it had been made by a plough. Maintaining an even keel, the plane had run its course with the fury and the tail-lashings of a reptile gliding on its belly at the rate of a hundred and seventy miles an hour. We owed our lives to the fact that this desert was surfaced with round black pebbles which had rolled over and over like ball-bearings beneath us. They must have rained upward to the heavens as we shot through them.

Prévot disconnected the batteries for fear of fire by short-circuit. I leaned against the motor and turned the situation over in my mind. I had been flying high for four hours and a quarter, possibly with a thirty-mile following wind. I had been jolted a good deal. If the wind had changed since the weather people forecast it, I was unable to say into what quarter it had veered. All I could make out was that we had crashed in an empty square two hundred and fifty miles on each side.

Prévot came up and sat down beside me.

'I can't believe that we're alive,' he said.

I said nothing. Even that thought could not cheer me. A germ of an idea was at work in my mind and was already bothering me. Telling Prévot to switch on his torch as a land-mark, I walked straight out, scrutinizing the ground in the light of my own torch as I went.

I went forward slowly, swung round in a wide arc, and changed direction a number of times. I kept my eyes fixed on the ground like a man hunting a lost ring.

Only a little while before I had been straining just as hard to see a gleam of light from the air. Through the darkness I went, bowed over the travelling disc of white light. 'Just as I thought,' I said to myself, and I went slowly back to the plane. I sat down beside the cabin and ruminated. I had been looking for a reason to hope and had failed to find it. I had been look-ing for a sign of life, and no sign of life had appeared.

'Prévot, I couldn't find a single blade of grass.'

Prévot said nothing, and I was not sure he had understood. Well, we could talk about it again when the curtain rose at dawn. Meanwhile I was dead tired and all I could think was: 'Two hundred and fifty miles more or less in the desert.'

Suddenly I jumped to my feet. 'Water!' I said.

Petrol tanks and oil tanks were smashed in. So was our supply of drinking-water. The sand had drunk everything. We found a pint of coffee in a battered thermos flask and half a pint of white wine in another. We filtered both, and poured them into one flask. There were some grapes, too, and a single orange. Meanwhile I was computing: 'All this will last us five hours of tramping in the sun.'

We crawled into the cabin and waited for dawn. I stretched out, and as I settled down to sleep I took stock of our situa-tion. We didn't know where we were; we had less than a quart of liquid between us; if we were not too far off the Benghazi–Cairo lane we should be found in a week, and that would be too late. Yet it was the best we could hope for. If, on the other hand, we had drifted off our course, we shouldn't be found in six months. One thing was sure – we could not count on being picked up by a plane; the men who came out for us would have two thousand miles to cover.

'You know, it's a shame,' Prévot said suddenly.

'What's a shame?'

'That we didn't crash properly and have it over with.'

It seemed pretty early to be throwing in one's hand. Prévot and I pulled ourselves together. There was still a chance, slender as it was, that we might be saved miraculously by a plane. On the other hand, we couldn't stay here and perhaps miss a near-by oasis. We would walk all day and come back to the plane before dark. And before going off we would write our plan in huge letters in the sand.

With this I curled up and settled down to sleep. I was happy to go to sleep. My weariness wrapped me round like a multiple presence. I was not alone in the desert: my drowsiness was peopled with voices and memories and whispered confidences. I was not yet thirsty; I felt strong; and I surrendered myself to sleep as to an aimless journey. Reality lost ground before the advance of dreams.

Ah, but things were different when I awoke!

In times past I have loved the Sahara. I have spent nights alone in the path of marauding tribes and have waked up with untroubled mind in the golden emptiness of the desert where the wind like a sea had raised sandwaves upon its surface. Asleep under the wing of my plane I have looked forward with confidence to being rescued next day. But this was not the Sahara!

Prévot and I walked along the slopes of rolling mounds. The ground was sand covered over with a single layer of shining black pebbles. They gleamed like metal scales and all the domes about us shone like coats of mail. We had dropped down into a mineral world and were hemmed in by iron hills.

When we reached the top of the first crest we saw in the

distance another just like it, black and gleaming. As we walked we scraped the ground with our boots, marking a trail over which to return to the plane. We went forward with the sun in our eyes. It was not logical to go due east like this, for everything – the weather reports, the duration of the flight – had made it plain that we had crossed the Nile. But I had started tentatively towards the west and had felt a vague foreboding I could not explain to myself. So I had put off the west till tomorrow. In the same way, provisionally, I had given up going north, though that led to the sea.

Three days later, when scourged by thirst into abandoning the plane and walking straight on until we dropped in our tracks, it was still eastward that we tramped. More precisely, we walked east-north-east. And this too was in defiance of all reason and even of all hope. Yet after we had been rescued we discovered that if we had gone in any other direction we should have been lost.

Northward, we should never have had the endurance to reach the sea. And absurd as it may appear, it seems to me now, since I had no other motive, that I must have chosen the east simply because it was by going eastward that Guillaumet had been saved in the Andes, after I had hunted for him everywhere. In a confused way the east had become for me the direction of life.

We walked on for five hours and then the landscape changed. A river of sand seemed to be running through a valley, and we followed this river-bed, taking long strides in order to cover as much ground as possible and get back to the plane before night fell, if our march was in vain. Suddenly I stopped.

'Prévot!'

'What's up?'

'Our tracks!'

How long was it since we had forgotten to leave a wake behind us? We had to find it or die.

We went back, bearing to the right. When we had gone back far enough we would make a right angle to the left and eventually intersect our tracks where we had still remembered to mark them.

This we did and were off again. The heat rose and with it

came the mirages. But these were still the commonplace kind – sheets of water that materialized and then vanished as we neared them. We decided to cross the valley of sand and climb the highest dome in order to look round the horizon. This was after six hours of march in which, striding along, we must have covered twenty miles.

When we had struggled up to the top of the black hump we sat down and looked at each other. At our feet lay our valley of sand opening into a desert of sand whose dazzling brightness seared our eyes. As far as the eye could see lay empty space. But in that space the play of light created mirages which, this time, were of a disturbing kind, fortresses and minarets, angular geometric hulks. I could see also a black mass that pretended to be vegetation, overhung by the last of those clouds that dissolve during the day only to return at night. This mass of vegetation was the shadow of a cumulus.

It was no good going on. The experiment was a failure. We would have to go back to our plane, to that red-and-white beacon which, perhaps, would be picked out by a flyer. I was not staking great hopes on a rescue party, but it did seem to me our last chance of salvation. In any case, we had to get back to our few drops of liquid, for our throats were parched. We were imprisoned in this iron circle, captives of the curt dictatorship of thirst.

And yet, how hard it was to turn back when there was a chance that we might be on the road to life! Beyond the mirages the horizon was perhaps rich in veritable treasures, in meadows and runnels of sweet water. I knew I was doing the right thing by returning to the plane, and yet as I swung round and started back I was filled with portents of disaster.

We were resting on the ground beside the plane. Nearly forty miles of wandering this day. The last drop of liquid had been drained. No sign of life had appeared to the east. No plane had soared overhead. How long should we be able to hold out? Already our thirst was terrible.

We had built up a great pyre out of bits of the splintered wing. Our petrol was ready, and we had flung on the heap sheets of metal whose magnesium coating would burn with a hard white flame. We were waiting now for night to come down before we lighted our conflagration. But where were there men to see it?

Night fell and the flames rose. Prayerfully we watched our mute and radiant fanion mount resplendent into the night. As I looked I said to myself that this message was not only a cry for help, it was fraught also with a great deal of love. We were begging water, but we were also begging the communion of human society. Only man can create fire: let another flame light up the night; let man answer man!

I was haunted by a vision of my wife's eyes under the halo of her hat. Of her face I could see only the eyes, questioning me, looking at me yearningly. I am answering, answering with all my strength! What flame could leap higher than this that darts up into the night from my heart?

What I could do, I have done. What we could do, we have done. Nearly forty miles, almost without a drop to drink. Now there was no water left. Was it our fault that we could wait no longer? Suppose we had sat quietly by the plane, taking suck at the mouths of our water-bottles? But from the moment I breathed in the moist bottom of the tin cup, a clock had started up in me. From the second when I had sucked up the last drop, I had begun to slip downhill. Could I help it if time, like a river, was carrying me away? Prévot was weeping. I tapped him on the shoulder and said, to console him:

'If we're done for we're done for, and that's all there is to it.'

He said:

'Do you think it's me I'm bawling about?'

I might have known it. It was evident enough. Nothing is unbearable. Tomorrow, and the day after, I should learn that nothing was really unbearable. I had never really believed in torture. Reading Poe as a kid, I had already said as much to myself. Once, jammed in the cabin of a plane, I thought I was going to drown; and I had not suffered much. Several times it had seemed to me that the final smash-up was coming, and I don't remember that I thought of it as a cosmic event. And I didn't believe this was going to be agonizing either. There will be time tomorrow to find out stranger things about it. Meanwhile, God knows that despite the bonfire I had decidedly given up hope that our cries would be heard by the world.

'Do you think it's me . . .' There you have what is truly unbearable! Every time I saw those yearning eyes it was as if a flame were searing me. They were like a scream for help, like the flares of a sinking ship. I felt that I should not sit idly by: I should jump up and run – anywhere! straight ahead of me!

What a strange reversal of roles! But I have always thought it would be like this. Still, I needed Prévot beside me to be quite sure of it. Prévot was a level-headed fellow. He loved life. And yet Prévot no more than I was wringing his hands at the sight of death the way we are told men do. But there did exist something that he could not bear any more than I could. I was perfectly ready to fall asleep, whether for a night or for eternity. If I did fall asleep, I could not even know whether it was for the one or for the other. And the peace of sleep! But that cry that would be sent up at home, that great wail of desolation – that was what I could not bear. I could not stand idly by and look on that disaster. Each second of silence drove the knife deeper into someone I loved. At the thought, a blind rage surged up in me. Why do these chains bind me and prevent me from rescuing those who are drowning? Why does our conflagration not carry our cry to the ends of the world? Hear me, you out here! Patience. We are coming to save you.

The magnesium had been licked off and the metal was glowing red. There was left only a heap of embers round which we crouched to warm ourselves. Our flaming call had spent itself. Had it set anything in the world in motion? I knew well enough that it hadn't. Here was a prayer that had of necessity gone unheard.

That was that.

I ought to get some sleep.

At daybreak I took a rag and mopped up a little dew on the wings. The mixture of water and paint and oil yielded a spoonful of nauseating liquid which we sipped because it would at least moisten our lips. After this banquet Prévot said:

'Thank God we've got a gun.'

Instantly I became furious and turned on him with an aggressiveness which I regretted directly I felt it. There was nothing I should have loathed more at that moment than a gush of sentimentality. I am so made that I have to believe that everything is simple. Birth is simple. Growing up is simple. And dying of thirst is simple. I watched Prévot out of the corner of my eye, ready to wound his feelings, if that was necessary to shut him up.

But Prévot had spoken without emotion. He had been discussing a matter of hygiene, and might have said in the same tone: 'We ought to wash our hands.' That being so, we were agreed. Indeed already yesterday, my eye falling by chance on the leather holster, the same thought had crossed my mind, and with me too it had been a reasonable reflex, not an emotional one. Pathos resides in social man, not in the individual; what was pathetic was our powerlessness to reassure those for whom we were responsible, not what we might do with the gun.

There was still no sign that we were being sought; or rather they were doubtless hunting for us elsewhere, probably in Arabia. We were to hear no sound of plane until the day after we had abandoned our own. And if ships did pass overhead, what could that mean to us? What could they see in us except two black dots among the thousand shadowy dots in the desert? Absurd to think of being distinguishable from them. None of the reflections that might be attributed to me on the score of this torture would be true. I should not feel in the least tortured. The aerial rescue party would seem to me, each time I sighted one, to be moving through a universe that was not mine. When searchers have to cover two thousand miles of territory, it takes them a good two weeks to spot a plane in the desert from the sky.

They were probably looking for us all along the line from Tripoli to Persia. And still with all this, I clung to the slim chance that they might pick us out. Was that not our only chance of being saved? I changed my tactics, determining to go reconnoitring by myself. Prévot would get another bonfire together and kindle it in the event that visitors showed up. But we were to have no callers that day.

So off I went without knowing whether or not I should have

the stamina to come back. I remembered what I knew about this Libyan desert. When, in the Sahara, humidity is still at forty per cent of saturation, it is only eighteen here in Libya. Life here evaporates like a vapour. Bedouins, explorers, and colonial officers all tell us that a man may go nineteen hours without water. Thereafter his eyes fill with light, and that marks the beginning of the end. The progress made by thirst is swift and terrible. But this north-east wind, this abnormal wind that had blown us out off our course and had marooned us on this plateau, was now prolonging our lives. What was the length of the reprieve it would grant us before our eyes began to fill with light? I went forward with the feeling of a man canoeing in mid-ocean.

I will admit that at daybreak this landscape seemed to me less infernal, and that I began my walk with my hands in my pockets, like a tramp on a high road. The evening before we had set snares at the mouths of certain mysterious burrows in the ground, and the poacher in me was on the alert. I went first to have a look at our traps. They were empty.

Well, this meant that I should not be drinking blood today; and indeed I hadn't expected to. But though I was not disappointed, my curiosity was aroused. What was there in the desert for these animals to live on? These were certainly the holes of fennecs, a long-eared carnivorous sand-fox the size of a rabbit. I spotted the tracks made by one of them, and gave way to the impulse to follow them. They led to a narrow stream of sand where each footprint was plainly outlined and where I marvelled at the pretty palm formed by the three-toes spread fanwise on the sand.

I could imagine my little friend trotting blithely along at dawn and licking the dew off the rocks. Here the tracks were wider apart: my fennec had broken into a run. And now I see that a companion has joined him and they have trotted on side by side. These signs of a morning stroll gave me a strange thrill. They were signs of life, and I loved them for that. I almost forgot that I was thirsty.

Finally I came to the pasture-ground of my foxes. Here, every hundred yards or so, I saw sticking up out of the sand a small dry shrub, its twigs heavy with little golden snails. The fennec came here at dawn to do his marketing. And here I was able to observe another of nature's mysteries.

My fennec did not stop at all the shrubs. There were some weighed down with snails which he disdained. Obviously he avoided them with some wariness. Others he stopped at but did not strip of all they bore. He must have picked out two or three shells and then gone on to another restaurant. What was he up to? Was he nurseryman to the snails, encouraging their reproduction by refraining from exhausting the stock on a given shrub, or a given twig? Or was he amusing himself by delaying repletion, putting off satiety in order to enhance the pleasure he took from his morning stroll?

The tracks led me back to the hole in which he lived. Doubtless my fennec crouched below, listening to me and startled by the crunching of my footsteps. I said to him:

'Fox, my little fox, I'm done for; but somehow that doesn't prevent me from taking an interest in your mood.'

And there I stayed a bit, ruminating and telling myself that a man was able to adapt himself to anything. The notion that he is to die in thirty years has probably never spoiled any man's fun. Thirty years ... or thirty days: it's all a matter of perspective.

Only, you have to be able to put certain visions out of your mind.

I went on, finally, and the time came when, along with my weariness, something in me began to change. If those were not mirages, I was inventing them.

'Hi! Hi, there!'

I shouted and waved my arms, but the man I had seen waving at me turned out to be a black rock. Everything in the desert had grown animate. I stopped to waken a sleeping Bedouin and he turned into the trunk of a black tree. A tree-trunk? Here in the desert? I was amazed and bent over to lift a broken bough. It was solid marble.

Straightening up I looked round and saw more black marble. An antediluvian forest littered the ground with its broken tree-tops. How many thousand years ago, under what hurricane of the time of Genesis, had this cathedral of wood crumbled in this spot? Countless centuries had rolled these fragments of giant pillars at my feet, polished them like steel, petrified and vitrified them and indued them with the colour of jet.

I could distinguish the knots in their branches, the twistings of their once living boughs, could count the rings of life in them. This forest had rustled with birds and been filled with music that now was struck by doom and frozen into salt. And all this was hostile to me. Blacker than the chain-mail of the hummocks, these solemn derelicts rejected me. What had I, a living man, to do with this incorruptible stone? Perishable as I was, I whose body was to crumble into dust, what place had I in this eternity?

Since yesterday I had walked nearly fifty miles. This dizziness that I felt came doubtless from my thirst. Or from the sun. It glittered on these hulks until they shone as if smeared with oil. It blazed down on this universal carapace. Sand and fox had no life here, but only a gigantic anvil upon which the sun beat down. I strode across this anvil and at my temples I could feel the hammer-strokes of the sun.

'Hi! Hi, there!' I called out.

'There is nothing there,' I told myself. 'Take it easy. You are delirious.'

I had to talk to myself aloud, had to bring myself to reason. It was hard for me to reject what I was seeing, hard not to run towards that caravan plodding on the horizon. There! Do you see it?

'Fool! You know very well that you are inventing it.'

'You mean that nothing in the world is real?'

Nothing in the world is real if that cross which I see ten miles off on the top of a hill is not real. Or is it a lighthouse? No, the sea does not lie in that direction. Then it must be a cross.

I had spent the night studying my map – but uselessly, since I did not know my position. Still, I had scrutinized all the signs that marked the marvellous presence of man. And somewhere on the map I had seen a little circle surmounted by just such a cross. I had glanced down at the legend to get an explanation of the symbol and had read: 'Religious institution.'

Close to the cross there had been a black dot. Again I had

run my finger down the legend and had read: 'Permanent well.' My heart had jumped and I had repeated the legend aloud: 'Permanent well, permanent well.' What were all of Ali Baba's treasures compared with a permanent well? A little farther on were two white circles. 'Temporary wells,' the legend said. Not quite so exciting. And round about them was nothing ... unless it was the blankness of despair.

But this must be my 'religious institution'! The monks must certainly have planted a great cross on the hill expressly for men in our plight! All I had to do was to walk across to them. I should be taken in by those Dominicans. ...

'But there are only Coptic monasteries in Libya!' I told myself.

... by those learned Dominicans. They have a great cool kitchen with red tiles, and out in the courtyard a marvellous rusted pump. Beneath the rusted pump; beneath the rusted pump ... you've guessed it! ... beneath the rusted pump is dug the permanent well! Ah, what rejoicing when I ring at their gate, when I get my hands on the rope of the great bell.

'Madman! You are describing a house in Provence; and what's more, the house has no bell!'

... on the rope of the great bell. The porter will raise his arms to Heaven and cry out: 'You are the messenger of the Lord!' and he will call aloud to all the monks. They will pour out of the monastery. They will welcome me with a great feast, as if I were the Prodigal Son. They will lead me to the kitchen and will say to me: 'One moment, my son, one moment. We'll just be off to the permanent well.' And I shall be trembling with happiness.

No, no! I will *not* weep just because there happens to be no cross on the hill.

The treasures of the west turned out to be mere illusion. I have veered due north. At least the north is filled with the sound of the sea.

Over the hilltop. Look there, at the horizon! The most beautiful city in the world!

'You know perfectly well that is a mirage.'

Of course I know it is a mirage! Am I the sort of man who

can be fooled? But what if I *want* to go after that mirage? Suppose I enjoy indulging my hope? Suppose it suits me to love that crenellated town all beflagged with sunlight? What if I choose to walk straight ahead on light feet? – for you must know that I have dropped my weariness behind me, I am happy now ... Prévot and his gun! Don't make me laugh! I prefer my drunkenness. I am drunk. I am dying of thirst.

It took the twilight to sober me. Suddenly I stopped, appalled to think how far I was from our base. In the twilight the mirage was dying. The horizon had stripped itself of its pomp, its palaces, its priestly vestments. It was the old desert horizon again.

'A fine day's work you've done! Night will overtake you. You won't be able to go on before daybreak, and by that time your tracks will have been blown away and you'll be properly nowhere.'

In that case I may as well walk straight on. Why turn back? Why should I bring my ship round when I may find the sea straight ahead of me?

'When did you catch a glimpse of the sea? What makes you think you could walk that far? Meanwhile there's Prévot watching for you beside the *Simoon*. He may have been picked up by a caravan, for all you know.'

Very good. I'll go back. But first I want to call out for help.

'Hi! Hi!'

By God! You can't tell me this planet is not inhabited. Where are its men?

'Hi! Hi!'

I was hoarse. My voice was gone. I knew it was ridiculous to croak like this, but – one more try :

'Hi! Hi!'

And I turned back.

I had been walking two hours when I saw the flames of the bonfire that Prévot, frightened by my long absence, had sent up. They mattered very little to me now.

Another hour of trudging. Five hundred yards away. A hundred yards. Fifty yards.

'Good Lord!'

Amazement stopped me in my tracks. Joy surged up and filled my heart with its violence. In the firelight stood Prévot, talking to two Arabs who were leaning against the motor. He had not noticed me, for he was too full of his own joy. If only I had sat still and waited with him! I should have been saved already. Exultantly I called out:

'Hi! Hi!'

The two Bedouins gave a start and stared at me. Prévot left them standing and came forward to meet me. I opened my arms to him. He caught me by the elbow. Did he think I was keeling over? I said:

'At last, eh?'

'What do you mean?'

'The Arabs!'

'What Arabs?'

'Those Arabs there, with you.'

Prévot looked at me queerly, and when he spoke I felt as if he was very reluctantly confiding a great secret to me:

'There are no Arabs here.'

This time I know I am going to cry.

A man can go nineteen hours without water, and what have we drunk since last night? A few drops of dew at dawn. But the north-east wind is still blowing, still slowing up the process of our evaporation. To it, also, we owe the continued accumulation of high clouds. If only they would drift straight overhead and break into rain! But it never rains in the desert.

'Look here, Prévot. Let's rip up one of the parachutes and spread the sections out on the ground, weighed down with stones. If the wind stays in the same quarter till morning, they'll catch the dew and we can wring them out into one of the tanks.'

We spread six triangular sections of parachute under the stars, and Prévot unhooked a fuel tank. This was as much as we could do for ourselves till dawn. But, miracle of miracles! Prévot had come upon an orange while working over the tank. We share it, and though it was little enough to men who could have used a few gallons of sweet water, still I was overcome with relief.

Stretched out beside the fire I looked at the glowing fruit and said to myself that men did not know what an orange was. 'Here we are, condemned to death,' I said to myself, 'and still the certainty of dying cannot compare with the pleasure I am feeling. The joy I take from this half of an orange which I am holding in my hand is one of the greatest joys I have ever known.'

I lay flat on my back, sucking my orange and counting the shooting stars. Here I was, for one minute infinitely happy. 'Nobody can know anything of the world in which the individual moves and has his being,' I reflected. 'There is no guessing it. Only the man locked up in it can know what it is.'

For the first time I understood the cigarette and glass of rum that are handed to the criminal about to be executed. I used to think that for a man to accept these wretched gifts at the foot of the gallows was beneath human dignity. Now I was learning that he took pleasure from them. People thought him courageous when he smiled as he smoked or drank. I knew now that he smiled because the taste gave him pleasure. People could not see that his perspective had changed, and that for him the last hour of his life was a life in itself.

We collected an enormous quantity of water – perhaps as much as two quarts. Never again would we be thirsty! We were saved; we had a liquid to drink!

I dipped my tin cup into the tank and brought up a beautifully yellow-green liquid the first mouthful of which nauseated me so that despite my thirst I had to catch my breath before swallowing it. I would have swallowed mud, I swear; but this taste of poisonous metal cut keener than thirst.

I glanced at Prévot and saw him going round and round with his eyes fixed to the ground as if looking for something. Suddenly he leaned forward and began to vomit without interrupting his spinning. Half a minute later it was my turn. I was seized by such convulsions that I went down on my knees and dug my fingers into the sand while I puked. Neither of us spoke, and for a quarter of an hour we remained thus shaken, bringing up nothing but a little bile.

After a time it passed and all I felt was a vague, distant nausea. But our last hope had fled. Whether our bad luck was due to a sizing on the parachute or to the magnesium lining of the tank, I never found out. Certain it was that we needed either another set of cloths or another receptacle.

Well, it was broad daylight and time we were on our way. This time we should strike out as fast as we could, leave this cursed plateau, and tramp till we dropped in our tracks. That was what Guillaumet had done in the Andes. I had been thinking of him all the day before and had determined to follow his example. I should do violence to the pilot's unwritten law, which is to stick by the ship; but I was sure no one would be along to look for us here.

Once again we discovered that it was not we who were shipwrecked, not we but those who were waiting for news of us, those who were alarmed by our silence, were already torn with grief by some atrocious and fantastic report. We could not but strive towards them. Guillaumet had done it, had scrambled towards his lost ones. To do so is a universal impulse.

'If I were alone in the world,' Prévot said, 'I'd lie down right here. Damned if I wouldn't.'

East-north-east we tramped. If we had in fact crossed the Nile, each step was leading us deeper and deeper into the desert.

I don't remember anything about that day. I remember only my haste. I was hurrying desperately towards something – towards some finality. I remember also that I walked with my eyes to the ground, for the mirages were more than I could bear. From time to time we would correct our course by the compass, and now and again we would lie down to catch our breath. I remember having flung away my waterproof, which I had held on to as covering for the night. That is as much as I recall about the day. Of what happened when the chill of evening came, I remember more. But during the day I had simply turned to sand and was a being without mind.

When the sun set we decided to make camp. Oh, I knew as well as anybody that we should push on, that this one waterless night would finish us off. But we had brought along the bits of parachute, and if the poison was not in the sizing, we might get a sip of water next morning. Once again we spread our trap for the dew under the stars.

But the sky in the north was cloudless. The wind no longer had the same taste on the lip. It had moved into another quarter. Something was rustling against us, but this time it seemed to be the desert itself. The wild beast was stalking us, had us in its power. I could feel its breath in my face, could feel it lick my face and hands. Suppose I walked on: at the best I could do five or six miles more. Remember that in three days I had covered one hundred miles, practically without water.

And then, just as we stopped, Prévot said:

'I swear to you I see a lake!'

'You're crazy.'

'Have you ever heard of a mirage after sunset?' he challenged.

I didn't seem able to answer him. I had long ago given up believing my own eyes. Perhaps it was not a mirage; but in that case it was a hallucination. How could Prévot go on believing? But he was stubborn about it.

'It's only twenty minutes off. I'll go have a look.'

His mulishness got on my nerves.

'Go ahead!' I shouted. 'Take your little constitutional. Nothing better for a man. But let me tell you, if your lake exists it is salt. And whether it's salt or not, it's a devil of a way off. And besides, there is no damned lake!'

Prévot was already on his way, his eyes glassy. I knew the strength of these irresistible obsessions. I was thinking: 'There are somnambulists who walk straight into locomotives.' And I knew that Prévot would not come back. He would be seized by the vertigo of empty space and would be unable to turn back. And then he would keel over. He somewhere, and I somewhere else. Not that it was important.

Thinking thus, it struck me that this mood of resignation was doing me no good. Once when I was half drowned I had let myself go like this. Meanwhile, flat on my face on the stony ground, I took this occasion to write a letter for posthumous delivery. It gave me a chance, also, to take stock of myself again. I tried to bring up a little saliva: how long was it since I had spit? No saliva. If I kept my mouth closed, a kind of glue sealed my lips together. It dried on the outside of the lips and formed a hard crust. However, I found I was still able to swallow, and I bethought me that I was still not seeing a blinding light in my eyes. Once I was treated to that radiant spectacle I might know that the end was a couple of hours away.

Night fell. The moon had swollen since I last saw it. Prévot was still not back. I stretched out on my back and turned these few data over in my mind. A familiar impression came over me, and I tried to seize it. I was ... I was ... I was at sea. I was on a ship going to South America and was stretched out, exactly like this, on the boat deck. The tip of the mast was swaying to and fro, very slowly, among the stars. That mast was missing tonight, but again I was at sea, bound for a port I was to make without raising a finger. Slave-traders had flung me on this ship.

I thought of Prévot who was still not back. Not once had I heard him complain. That was a good thing. To hear him whine would have been unbearable. Prévot was a man.

What was that? Five hundred yards ahead of me I could see the light of his lamp. He had lost his way. I had no lamp with which to signal back. I stood up and shouted, but he could not hear me.

A second lamp, and then a third! God in Heaven! It was a search party and it was me they were hunting!

'Hi! Hi!' I shouted.

But they had not heard me. The three lamps were still signalling me.

'Tonight I am sane,' I said to myself. 'I am relaxed. I am not out of my head. Those are certainly three lamps and they are about five hundred yards off.' I stared at them and shouted again, and again I gathered that they could not hear me.

Then, for the first and only time, I was really seized with panic. I could still run, I thought. 'Wait! Wait!' I screamed. They seemed to be turning away from me, going off, hunting me elsewhere! And I stood tottering, tottering on the brink of life when there were arms out there ready to catch me! I shouted and screamed again and again.

They had heard me! An answering shout had come. I was

strangling, suffocating, but I ran on, shouting as I ran, until I saw Prévot and keeled over.

When I could speak again I said: 'Whew! When I saw all those lights . . .'

'What lights?'

God in Heaven, it was true! He was alone!

This time I was beyond despair. I was filled with a sort of dumb fury.

'What about your lake?' I rasped.

'As fast as I moved towards it, it moved back. I walked after it for about half an hour. Then it seemed still too far away, so I came back. But I am positive, now, that it is a lake.'

'You're crazy. Absolutely crazy. Why did you do it? Tell me. Why?'

What had he done? Why had he done it? I was ready to weep with indignation, yet I scarcely knew why I was so indignant. Prévot mumbled his excuse:

'I felt I had to find some water. You . . . your lips were awfully pale.'

Well! My anger died within me. I passed my hand over my forehead as if I were walking out of sleep. I was suddenly sad. I said:

'There was no mistake about it. I saw them as clearly as I see you now. Three lights there were. I tell you, Prévot, I saw them!'

Prévot made no comment.

'Well,' he said finally, 'I guess we're in a bad way.'

In this air devoid of moisture the soil is swift to give off its temperature. It was already very cold. I stood up and stamped about. But soon a violent fit of trembling came over me. My dehydrated blood was moving sluggishly and I was pierced by a freezing chill which was not merely the chill of night. My teeth were chattering and my whole body had begun to twitch. My hand shook so that I could not hold an electric torch. I who had never been sensitive to cold was about to die of cold. What a strange effect thirst can have!

Somewhere, tired of carrying it in the sun, I had let my waterproof drop. Now the wind was growing bitter and I was learning that in the desert there is no place of refuge. The desert is as smooth as marble. By day it throws no shadow; by night it hands you over naked to the wind. Not a tree, not a hedge, not a rock behind which I could seek shelter. The wind was charging me like a troop of cavalry across open country. I turned and twisted to escape it: I lay down, stood up, lay down again, and still I was exposed to its freezing lash. I had no strength to run from the assassin and under the sabre-stroke I tumbled to my knees, my head between my hands.

A little later I pieced these bits together and remembered that I had struggled to my feet and had started to walk on, shivering as I went. I had started forward wondering where I was and then I had heard Prévot. His shouting had jolted me into consciousness.

I went back toward him, still trembling from head to foot – quivering with the attack of hiccups that was convulsing my whole body. To myself I said: 'It isn't the cold. It's something else. It's the end.' The simple fact was that I hadn't enough water in me. I had tramped too far yesterday and the day before when I was off by myself, and I was dehydrated.

The thought of dying of the cold hurt me. I preferred the phantoms of my mind, the cross, the trees, the lamps. At least they would have killed me by enchantment. But to be whipped to death like a slave! ...

Confound it! Down on my knees again! We had with us a little store of medicines – a hundred grammes of ninety per cent alcohol, the same of pure ether, and a small bottle of iodine. I tried to swallow a little of the ether: it was like swallowing a knife. Then I tried the alcohol: it contracted my gullet. I dug a pit in the sand, lay down in it, and flung handfuls of sand over me until all but my face was buried in it.

Prévot was able to collect a few twigs, and he lit a fire which soon burnt itself out. He wouldn't bury himself in the sand, but preferred to stamp round and round in a circle. That was foolish.

My throat stayed shut, and though I knew that was a bad sign, I felt better. I felt calm. I felt a peace that was beyond all hope. Once more, despite myself, I was journeying, trussed up on the deck of my slave-ship under the stars. It seemed to me that I was perhaps not in such a bad pass after all.

So long as I lay absolutely motionless, I no longer felt the cold. This allowed me to forget my body buried in the sand. I said to myself that I would not budge an inch, and would therefore never suffer again. As a matter of fact, we really suffer very little. Back of all these torments there is the orchestration of fatigue or of delirium, and we live on in a kind of picture-book, a slightly cruel fairy-tale.

A little while ago the wind had been after me with whip and spur, and I was running in circles like a frightened fox. After that came a time when I couldn't breathe. A great knee was crushing in my chest. A knee. I was writhing in vain to free myself from the weight of the angel who had overthrown me. There had not been a moment when I was alone in this desert. But now I have ceased to believe in my surroundings; I have withdrawn into myself, have shut my eyes, have not so much as batted an eyelid. I have the feeling that this torrent of visions is sweeping me away to a tranquil dream: so rivers cease their turbulence in the embrace of the sea.

Farewell, eyes that I loved! Do not blame me if the human body cannot go three days without water. I should never have believed that man was so truly the prisoner of the springs and freshets. I had no notion that our self-sufficiency was so circumscribed. We take it for granted that a man is able to stride straight out into the world. We believe that man is free. We never see the cord that binds him to wells and fountains, that umbilical cord by which he is tied to the womb of the world. Let man take but one step too many ... and the cord snaps.

Apart from your suffering, I have no regrets. All in all, it has been a good life. If I got free of this I should start right in again. A man cannot live a decent life in cities, and I need to feel myself live. I am not thinking of aviation. The aeroplane is a means, not an end. One doesn't risk one's life for a plane any more than a farmer ploughs for the sake of the plough. But the aeroplane is a means of getting away from towns and their book-keeping and coming to grips with reality.

Flying is a man's job and its worries are a man's worries. A pilot's business is with the wind, with the stars, with night, with sand, with the sea. He strives to outwit the forces of nature. He stares in expectancy for the coming of dawn the way a gardener awaits the coming of spring. He looks forward to port as to a promised land, and truth for him is what lives in the stars.

I have nothing to complain of. For three days I have tramped the desert, have known the pangs of thirst, have followed false scents in the sand, have pinned my faith on the dew. I have struggled to rejoin my kind, whose very existence on earth I had forgotten. These are the cares of men alive in every fibre, and I cannot help thinking them more important than the fretful choosing of a night-club in which to spend the evening. Compare the one life with the other, and all things considered this is luxury! I have no regrets. I have gambled and lost. It was all in the day's work. At least I have had the unforgettable taste of the sea on my lips.

I am not talking about living dangerously. Such words are meaningless to me. The toreador does not stir me to enthusiasm. It is not danger I love. I know what I love. It is life.

The sky seemed to me faintly bright. I drew up one arm through the sand. There was a bit of the torn parachute within reach, and I ran my hand over it. It was bone-dry. Let's see. Dew falls at dawn. Here was dawn risen and no moisture on the cloth. My mind was befuddled and I heard myself say: 'There is a dry heart here, a dry heart that cannot know the relief of tears.'

I scrambled to my feet. 'We're off, Prévot,' I said. 'Our throats are still open. Get along, man!'

The wind that shrivels up a man in nineteen hours was now blowing out of the west. My gullet was not yet shut, but it was hard and painful and I could feel that there was a rasp in it. Soon that cough would begin that I had been told about and was now expecting. My tongue was becoming a nuisance. But most serious of all, I was beginning to see shining spots before my eyes. When those spots changed into flames, I should simply lie down.

The first morning hours were cool and we took advantage of them to get on at a good pace. We knew that once the sun was high there would be no more walking for us. We no longer had the right to sweat. Certainly not to stop and catch our breath. This coolness was merely the coolness of low humidity. The prevailing wind was coming from the desert, and under its soft and treacherous caress the blood was being dried out of us.

Our first day's nourishment had been a few grapes. In the next three days each of us ate half an orange and a bit of cake. If we had had anything left now, we couldn't have eaten it because we had no saliva with which to masticate it. But I had stopped being hungry. Thirsty I was, yes, and it seemed to me that I was suffering less from thirst itself than from the effects of thirst. Gullet hard. Tongue like plaster of Paris. A rasping in the throat. A horrible taste in the mouth.

All these sensations were new to me, and though I believed water could rid me of them, nothing in my memory associated them with water. Thirst had become more and more a disease and less and less a craving. I began to realize that the thought of water and fruit was now less agonizing than it had been. I was forgetting the radiance of the orange, just as I was forgetting the eyes under the hat-brim. Perhaps I was forgetting everything.

We had sat down after all, but it could not be for long. Nevertheless, it was impossible to go five hundred yards without our legs giving way. To stretch out on the sand would be marvellous – but it could not be.

The landscape had begun to change. Rocky places grew rarer and the sand was now firm beneath our feet. A mile ahead stood dunes and on those dunes we could see a scrubby vegetation. At least this sand was preferable to the steely surface over which we had been trudging. This was the golden desert. This might have been the Sahara. It was in a sense my country.

Two hundred yards had now become our limit, but we had determined to carry on until we reached the vegetation. Better than that we could not hope to do. A week later, when we went back over our traces in a car to have a look at the *Simoon*, I measured this last lap and found that it was just short of fifty miles. All told we had done one hundred and twenty-four miles.

The previous day I had tramped without hope. Today the word 'hope' had grown meaningless. Today we were tramping simply because we were tramping. Probably oxen work for the same reason. Yesterday I had dreamed of a paradise of orange-trees. Today I would not give a button for paradise; I did not believe oranges existed. When I thought about myself I found in me nothing but a heart squeezed dry. I was tottering but emotionless. I felt no distress whatever, and in a way I regretted it : misery would have seemed to me as sweet as water. I might then have felt sorry for myself and commiserated with myself as with a friend. But I had not a friend left on earth.

Later, when we were rescued, seeing our burnt-out eyes men thought we must have called aloud and wept and suffered. But cries of despair, misery, sobbing grief are a kind of wealth, and we possessed no wealth. When a young girl is disappointed in love she weeps and knows sorrow. Sorrow is one of the vibrations that prove the fact of living. I felt no sorrow. I was the desert. I could no longer bring up a little saliva; neither could I any longer summon those moving visions towards which I should have loved to stretch forth arms. The sun had dried up the springs of tears in me.

And yet, what was that? A ripple of hope went through me like a faint breeze over a lake. What was this sign that had awakened my instinct before knocking on the door of my consciousness? Nothing had changed, and yet everything was changed. This sheet of sand, those low hummocks and sparse tufts of verdure that had been a landscape, were now become a stage setting. Thus far the stage was empty, but the scene was set. I looked at Prévot. The same astonishing thing had happened to him as to me, but he was as far from guessing its significance as I was.

I swear to you that something is about to happen. I swear that life has sprung in this desert. I swear that this emptiness, this stillness, has suddenly become more stirring than a tumult on a public square.

'Prévot! Footprints! We are saved!'

We had wandered from the trail of the human species; we had cast ourselves forth from the tribe; we had found ourselves alone on earth and forgotten by the universal migration; and here, imprinted in the sand, were the divine and naked feet of man!

'Look, Prévot, here two men stood together and then separated.'

'Here a camel knelt.'

'Here . . .'

But it was not true that we were already saved. It was not enough to squat down and wait. Before long we should be past saving. Once the cough has begun, the progress made by thirst is swift.

Still, I believed in that caravan swaying somewhere in the desert, heavy with its cargo of treasure.

We went on. Suddenly I heard a cock crow. I remembered what Guillaumet had told me: 'Towards the end I heard cocks crowing in the Andes. And I heard the railway train.' The instant the cock crowed I thought of Guillaumet and I said to myself: 'First it was my eyes that played tricks on me. I suppose this is another of the effects of thirst. Probably my ears have merely held out longer than my eyes.' But Prévot grabbed my arm:

'Did you hear that?'

'What?'

'The cock.'

'Why . . . why, yes, I did.'

To myself I said: 'Fool! Get it through your head! This means life!'

I had one last hallucination – three dogs chasing one another. Prévot looked, but could not see them. However, both of us waved our arms at a Bedouin. Both of us shouted with all the breath in our bodies, and laughed for happiness.

But our voices could not carry thirty yards. The Bedouin on his slow-moving camel had come into view from behind a dune and now he was moving slowly out of sight. The man was probably the only Arab in this desert, sent by a demon to materialize and vanish before the eyes of us who could not run.

We saw in profile on the dune another Arab. We shouted, but our shouts were whispers. We waved our arms and it seemed to us that they must fill the sky with monstrous signals. Still the Bedouin stared with averted face away from us.

At last, slowly, slowly he began a right-angle turn in our direction. At the very second when he came face to face with us, I thought, the curtain would come down. At the very second when his eyes met ours, thirst would vanish and by this man would death and the mirages be wiped out. Let this man but make a quarter-turn left and the world is changed. Let him bring his torso round, but sweep the scene with a glance, and like a god he can create life.

The miracle had come to pass. He was walking towards us over the sand like a god over the waves.

The Arab looked at us without a word. He placed his hands upon our shoulders and we obeyed him : we stretched out upon the sand. Race, language, religion were forgotten. There was only this humble nomad with the hands of an archangel on our shoulders.

Face to the sand, we waited. And when the water came, we drank like calves with our faces in the basin, and with a greediness which alarmed the Bedouin so that from time to time he pulled us back. But as soon as his hand fell away from us we plunged our faces anew into the water.

Water, thou hast no taste, no colour, no odour; canst not be defined, art relished while ever mysterious. Not necessary to life, but rather life itself, thou fillest us with a gratification that exceeds the delight of the senses. By thy might, there return into us treasures that we had abandoned. By thy grace, there are released in us all the dried-up runnels of our heart. Of the riches that exist in the world, thou art the rarest and also the most delicate – thou so pure within the bowels of the earth! A man may die of thirst lying beside a magnesian spring. He may die within reach of a salt lake. He may die though he hold in his hand a jug of dew, if it be inhabited by evil salts. For thou, water, art a proud divinity, allowing no alteration, no foreignness in thy being. And the joy that thou spreadest is an infinitely simple joy.

You, Bedouin of Libya who saved our lives, though you will

dwell for ever in my memory, yet I shall never be able to recapture your features. You are Humanity and your face comes into my mind simply as man incarnate. You, our beloved fellow-man, did not know who we might be, and yet you recognized us without fail. And I, in my turn, shall recognize you in the faces of all mankind. You came towards me in an aureole of charity and magnanimity bearing the gift of water. All my friends and all my enemies marched towards me in your person. It did not seem to me that you were rescuing me: rather did it seem that you were forgiving me. And I felt I had no enemy left in all the world.

This is the end of my story. Lifted on to a camel, we went on for three hours. Then, broken with weariness, we asked to be set down at a camp while the cameleers went on ahead for help. Towards six in the evening a car manned by armed Bedouins came to fetch us. A half-hour later we were set down at the house of a Swiss engineer named Raccaud who was operating a soda factory beside saline deposits in the desert. He was unforgettably kind to us. By midnight we were in Cairo.

I awoke between white sheets. Through the curtains came the rays of a sun that was no longer an enemy. I spread butter and honey on my bread. I smiled. I recaptured the savour of my childhood and all its marvels. And I read and re-read the telegram from those dearest to me in all the world whose three words had shattered me :

'So terribly happy !'

9 Barcelona and Madrid (1936)

Once again I had found myself in the presence of a truth and had failed to recognize it. Consider what had happened to me: I had thought myself lost, had touched the very bottom of despair; and then, when the spirit of renunciation had filled me, I had known peace. I know now what I was not conscious of at the time – that in such an hour a man feels that he has finally found himself and has become his own friend. An essential inner need has been satisfied, and against that satisfaction, that self-fulfilment, no external power can prevail. Bonnafous, I imagine, he who spent his life racing before the wind, was acquainted with this serenity of spirit. Guillaumet, too, in his snows. Never shall I forget that, lying buried to the chin in sand, strangled slowly to death by thirst, my heart was infinitely warm beneath the desert stars.

What can men do to make known to themselves this sense of deliverance? Everything about mankind is paradox. He who strives and conquers grows soft. The magnanimous man grown rich becomes mean. The creative artist for whom everything is made easy nods. Every doctrine swears that it can breed men, but none can tell us in advance what sort of men it will breed. Men are not cattle to be fattened for market. In the scales of life an indigent Newton weighs more than a parcel of prosperous nonentities. All of us have had the experience of a sudden joy that came when nothing in the world had forewarned us of its coming – a joy so thrilling that if it was born of misery we remember even the misery with tenderness. All of us, on seeing old friends again, have remembered with happiness the trials we lived through with those friends. Of what can we be certain except this – that we are fertilized by mysterious circumstances? Where is man's truth to be found?

Truth is not that which can be demonstrated by the aid of logic. If orange-trees are hardy and rich in fruit in this bit of soil and not that, then this bit of soil is what is truth for orange-trees. If a particular religion, or culture, or scale of values, if one form of activity rather than another, brings self-fulfilment to a man, releases the prince asleep within him unknown to himself, then that scale of values, that culture, that form of activity, constitute his truth. Logic, you say? Let logic wangle its own explanation of life.

Because it is man and not flying that concerns me most, I shall close this book with the story of man's gropings towards self-fulfilment as I witnessed them in the early months of the civil war in Spain. One year after crashing in the desert I made a tour of the Catalan front in order to learn what happens to man when the scaffolding of his traditions suddenly collapses. To Madrid I went for an answer to another question: How does it happen that men are sometimes willing to die?

I

Flying west from Lyon, I veered left in the direction of the Pyrenees and Spain. Below me floated fleecy white clouds, summer clouds, clouds made for amateur flyers in which great gaps opened like skylights. Through one of these windows I could see Perpignan lying at the bottom of a well of light.

I was flying solo, and as I looked down on Perpignan I was day-dreaming. I had spent six months there once while serving as test pilot at a nearby aerodrome. When the day's work was done I would drive into this town where every day was as peaceful as Sunday. I would sit in a wicker chair within sound of the café band, sip a glass of port, and look idly on at the provincial life of the place, reflecting that it was as innocent as a review of lead soldiers. These pretty girls, these carefree strollers, this pure sky. . . .

But here came the Pyrenees. The last happy town was left behind.

Below me lay Figueras, and Spain. This was where men killed one another. What was most astonishing here was not the sight of conflagration, ruin, and signs of man's distress – it was the absence of all these. Figueras seemed no different from Perpignan. I leaned out and stared hard.

There were no scars on that heap of white gravel, that church gleaming in the sun, which I knew had been burnt. I could not distinguish its irreparable wounds. Gone was the pale smoke that had carried off its gilding, had melted in the blue of the sky its altar screens, its prayer books, its sacerdotal treasures. Not a line of the church was altered. This town, seated at the heart of its fan-shaped roads like a spider at the centre of its silken trap, looked very much like the other.

Like other towns, this one was nourished by the fruits of the plain that rose along the white highways to meet it. All that I could discern was the slow gnawing which, through the centuries, had swallowed up the soil, driven away the forests, divided up the fields, dug out these life-giving irrigation ditches. Here was a face unlikely to change much, for it was already old. A colony of bees, I said to myself, once it was established so solidly within the boundaries of an acre of flowers, would be assured of peace. But peace is not given to a colony of men.

Human drama does not show itself on the surface of life. It is not played out in the visible world, but in the hearts of men. Even in happy Perpignan a victim of cancer walled up behind his hospital window goes round and round in a circle striving helplessly to escape the pain that hovers over him like a relentless kite. One man in misery can disrupt the peace of a city. It is another of the miraculous things about mankind that there is no pain nor passion that does not radiate to the ends of the earth. Let a man in a garret but burn with enough intensity and he will set fire to the world.

Gerona went by, Barcelona loomed into view, and I let myself glide gently down from the perch of my observatory. Even here I observed nothing out of the way, unless it was that the avenues were deserted. Again there were devastated churches which, from above, looked untouched. Faintly visible was something that I guessed to be smoke. Was that one of the signs I was seeking? Was this a scrap of evidence of that nearly soundless anger whose all-destroying wrath was so hard to measure? A whole civilization was contained in that faint golden puff so lightly dispersed by a breath of wind.

I am quite convinced of the sincerity of people who say: 'Terror in Barcelona? Nonsense. That great city in ashes? A

mere twenty houses wrecked. Streets heaped with the dead?
A few hundred killed out of a population of a million. Where
did you see a firing line running with blood and deafening with
the roar of guns?'

I agree that I saw no firing line. I saw groups of tranquil
men and women strolling on the Ramblas. When, on occasion,
I ran against a barricade of militiamen in arms, a smile was
often enough to open the way before me. I did not come at
once upon the firing line. In a civil war the firing line is invisible; it passes through the hearts of men. And yet, on my very
first night in Barcelona I skirted it.

I was sitting on the pavement of a café, sipping my drink
surrounded by light-hearted men and women, when suddenly
four armed men stopped where I sat, stared at a man at the
next table, and without a word pointed their guns at his stomach. Streaming with sweat the man stood up and raised leaden
arms above his head. One of the militiamen ran his hands over
his clothes and his eyes over some papers he found in the man's
pockets, and ordered him to come along.

The man left his half-emptied glass, the last glass of his life,
and started down the road. Surrounded by the squad, his
hands stuck up like the hands of a man going down for the
last time.

'Fascist!' A woman behind me said it with contempt. She
was the only witness who dared betray that anything out of
the ordinary had taken place. Untouched, the man's glass stood
on the table, a mute witness to a mad confidence in chance,
in forgiveness, in life. I sat watching the disappearance in a
ring of rifles of a man who, five minutes before, within two
feet of me, had crossed the invisible firing line.

My guides were anarchists. They led me to the railway station
where troops were being entrained. Far from the platforms
built for tender farewells, we were walking in a desert of signal
towers and switching points, stumbling in the rain through a
labyrinthine yard filled with blackened goods wagons where
tarpaulins the colour of lard were spread over carloads of stif-
fened forms. The world had lost its human quality, had become
a world of iron, and therefore uninhabitable. A ship remains a

living thing only so long as man with his brushes and oils swabs an artificial layer of light over it. Leave them to themselves a couple of weeks and the life dies out of your ship, your factory, your railway; death covers their faces. After six thousand years the stones of a temple still vibrate with the passage of man; but a little rust, a night of rain, and this railway yard is eaten away to its very skeleton.

Here are our men. Cannon and machine-guns are being loaded on board with the straining muscles and the hoarse gaspings that are always drawn from men by these monstrous insects, these fleshless insects, these lumps of carapace and vertebra. What is startling here is the silence. Not a note of song, not a single shout. Only, now and then, when a gun-carriage lands, the hollow thump of a steel plate. Of human voices no sound.

No uniforms, either. These men are going off to be killed in their working garb. Wearing their dark clothes stiff with mud, the column heaving and sweating at their work look like the denizens of a night shelter. They fill me with the same uneasiness I felt when the yellow fever broke out among us at Dakar, ten years ago.

The chief of the detachment had been speaking to me in a whisper. I caught the end of his speech :

'. . . and we move up to Saragossa.'

Why the devil did he have to whisper? The atmosphere of this yard made me think of a hospital. But of course! That was it. A civil war is not a war, it is a disease. These men were not going up to the front in the exultation of certain victory; they were struggling blindly against infection.

And the same thing was going on in the enemy camp. The purpose of this struggle was not to rid the country of an invading foreigner but to eradicate a plague. A new faith is like a plague. It attacks from within. It propagates in the invisible. Walking in the streets, whoever belongs to a Party feels himself surrounded by secretly infected men.

This must have been why these troops were going off in silence with their instruments of asphyxiation. There was not the slightest resemblance between them and regiments that go into battle against foreign armies and are set out on the chess-

146

board of the fields and moved about by strategists. These men had gathered together haphazardly in a city filled with chaos.

There was not much to choose between Barcelona and its enemy, Saragossa : both were composed of the same swarm of communists, anarchists, and fascists. The very men who collected on the same side were perhaps more different from one another than from their enemies. In civil war the enemy is inward; one as good as fights against oneself.

What else can explain the particular horror of this war in which firing squads count for more than soldiers of the line? Death in this war is a sort of quarantine. Purges take place of germ-carriers. The anarchists go from house to house and load the plague-stricken into their tumbrils, while on the other side of the barricade Franco is able to utter that horrible boast: 'There are no more communists among us.'

The conscripts are weeded out by a kind of medical board; the officer in charge is a sort of army doctor. Men present themselves for service with pride shining in their eyes and the belief in their hearts that they have a part to play in society.

'Exempt from service for life !' is the decision.

Fields have been turned into charnel-houses and the dead are burned in lime or petroleum. Respect for the dignity of man has been trampled under foot. Since on both sides the political parties spy upon the stirrings of man's conscience as upon the workings of a disease, why should the urn of his flesh be respected? This body that clothes the spirit, that moves with grace and boldness, that knows love, that is apt for self-sacrifice – no one now so much as thinks of giving it decent burial.

I thought of our respect for the dead. I thought of the white sanatorium where the light of a man's life goes quietly out in the presence of those who love him and who garner as if it were an inestimable treasure his last words, his ultimate smile. How right they are ! Seeing that this same whole is never again to take shape in the world. Never again will be heard exactly that note of laughter, that intonation of voice, that quality of repartee. Each individual is a miracle. No wonder we go on speaking of the dead for twenty years.

Here, in Spain, a man is simply stood up against a wall and

he gives up his entrails to the stones of the courtyard. You have been captured. You are shot. Reason: your ideas were not our ideas.

This entrainment in the rain is the only thing that rings true about their war. These men stand round and stare at me, and I read in their eyes a mournful sobriety. They know the fate that awaits them if they are captured. I begin to shiver with the cold and observe of a sudden that no woman has been allowed to see them off.

The absence of women seems to me right. There is no place here for mothers who bring children into the world in ignorance of the faith that will some day flare up in their sons, in ignorance of the ideologist who, according to his lights, will prop up their sons against a wall when they have come to their twenty years of life.

We went up by motor into the war zone. Barricades became more frequent, and from place to place we had to negotiate with revolutionary committees. Passes were valid only from one village to the next.

'Are you trying to get closer to the front?'

'Exactly.'

The chairman of the local committee consulted a large-scale map.

'You won't be able to get through. The rebels have occupied the road four miles ahead. But you might try swinging left here. This road ought to be free. Though there was talk of rebel cavalry cutting it this morning.'

It was very difficult in those early days of the revolution to know one's way about in the vicinity of the front. There were loyal villages, rebel villages, neutral villages, and they shifted their allegiance between dawn and dark. This tangle of loyal and rebel zones made me think the push must be pretty weak. It certainly bore no resemblance to a line of trenches cutting off friend from enemy as cleanly as a knife. I felt as if I were walking in a bog. Here the earth was solid beneath our feet: there we sank into it. We moved in a maze of uncertainty. Yet what space, what air between movements! These military operations are curiously lacking in density.

Once again we reached a point beyond which we were told we could not advance. Six rifles and a low wall of paving stones blocked the road. Four men and two women lay stretched on the ground behind the wall. I made a mental note that the women did not know how to hold a rifle.

'This is as far as you can go.'

'Why?'

'Rebels.'

We got out of the car and sat down with the militiamen upon the grass. They put down their rifles and cut a few slices of fresh bread.

'Is this your village?' we asked.

'No, we are Catalans, from Barcelona. Communist Party.'

One of the girls stretched herself and sat up on the barricade, her hair blowing in the wind. She was rather thick-set, but young and healthy. Smiling happily she said:

'I am going to stay in this village when the war is over. I didn't know it, but the country beats the city all hollow.'

She cast a loving glance round at the countryside, as if stirred by a revelation. Her life had been the grey slums, days spent in a factory, and the sordid compensation afforded by the cafés. Everything that went on here seemed to her as jolly as a picnic. She jumped down and ran to the village well. Probably she believed she was drinking at the very breast of mother earth.

'Have you done any fighting here?'

'No. The rebels kick up a little dust now and then, but ... We see a lorryload of men from time to time and hope that they will come along this road. But nothing has come by in two weeks.'

They were awaiting their first enemy. In the rebel village opposite sat another half-dozen militiamen awaiting a first enemy. Twelve warriors alone in the world.

Each side was waiting for something to be born in the invisible. The rebels were waiting for the host of hesitant people in Madrid to declare themselves for Franco. Barcelona was waiting for Saragossa to waken out of an inspired dream, declare itself Socialist, and fall. It was the thought more than the soldier that was besieging the town. The thought was the great hope and the great enemy.

It seemed to me that the bombers, the shells, the militiamen under arms, by themselves had no power to conquer. On each side a single man entrenched behind his line of defence was better than a hundred besiegers. But thought might worm its way in.

From time to time there is an attack. From time to time the tree is shaken. Not to uproot it, but merely to see if the fruit is yet ripe. And if it is, a town falls.

2

Back from the front, I found friends in Barcelona who allowed me to join in their mysterious expeditions. We went deep into the mountains and were now in one of those villages which are possessed by a mixture of peace and terror.

'Oh, yes, we shot seventeen of them.'

They had shot seventeen 'fascists'. The parish priest, the priest's housekeeper, the sexton, and fourteen village notables. Everything is relative, you see. When they read in their provincial newspaper the story of the life of Basil Zaharoff, master of the world, they transpose it into their own language. They recognize in him the nurseryman, or the pharmacist. And when they shoot the pharmacist, in a way they are shooting Basil Zaharoff. The only one who does not understand is the pharmacist.

'Now we are all Loyalists together. Everything has calmed down.'

Almost everything. The conscience of the village is tormented by one man whom I have seen at the tavern, smiling, helpful, so anxious to go on living! He comes to the pub in order to show us that, despite his few acres of vineyard, he too is part of the human race, suffers with rheumatism like it, mops his face like it with a blue handkerchief. He comes, and he plays billiards. Can one shoot a man who plays billiards? Besides, he plays badly with his great trembling hands. He is upset; he still does not know whether he is a fascist or not. He puts me in mind of those poor monkeys who dance before the boa-constrictor in the hope of softening it.

There was nothing we could do for the man. For the time

being we had another job in hand. Sitting on a table and swinging my legs at committee headquarters, while my companion, Pépin, pulled a bundle of soiled papers out of his pocket, I had a good look at these terrorists. Their looks belied their name: honourable peasants with frank eyes and sober attentive faces, they were the same everywhere we went; and though we were foreigners possessing no authority, we were everywhere received with the same grave courtesy.

'Yes, here it is,' said Pépin, a document in his hand. 'His name is Laporte. Any of you know him?'

The paper went from hand to hand and the members of the committee shook their heads.

'No. Laporte? Never heard of him.'

I started to explain something to them, but Pépin motioned me to be silent. 'They won't talk,' he said, 'but they know him well enough.'

Pépin spread his references before the chairman, saying casually:

'I am a French socialist. Here is my party card.'

The card was passed round and the chairman raised his eyes to us:

'Laporte. I don't believe. . . .'

'Of course you know him. A French monk. Probably in disguise. You captured him yesterday in the woods. Laporte, his name is. The French consulate wants him.'

I sat swinging my legs. What a strange session! Here we were in a mountain village sixty miles from the French frontier, asking a revolutionary committee that shot even parish priests' housekeepers to surrender to us in good shape a French monk. Whatever happened to us, we would certainly have asked for it. Nevertheless, I felt safe. There was no treachery in these people. And why, as a matter of fact, should they bother to play tricks? We had absolutely no protection; we meant no more to them than Laporte; they could do anything they pleased.

Pépin nudged me. 'I've an idea we have come too late,' he said.

The chairman cleared his throat and made up his mind.

'This morning,' he said, 'we found a dead man on the road just outside the village. He must be there still.'

And he pretended to send off for the dead man's papers.

'They've already shot him,' Pépin said to me. 'Too bad! They would certainly have turned him over to us. They are good kind people.'

I looked straight into the eyes of these curious 'good kind people'. Strange: there was nothing in their eyes to upset me. There seemed nothing to fear in their set jaws and the blank smoothness of their faces. Blank, as if vaguely bored. A rather terrible blankness. I wondered why, despite our unusual mission, we were not suspect to them. What difference had they established in their minds between us and the 'fascist' in the neighbouring tavern who was dancing his dance of death before the unavailing indifference of these judges? A crazy notion came into my head, forced upon my attention by all the power of my instinct: If one of those men yawned I should be afraid. I should feel that all human communication had snapped between us.

After we left, I said to Pépin:

'That is the third village in which we have done this job and I still cannot make up my mind whether the job is dangerous or not.'

Pépin laughed and admitted that although he had saved dozens of men on these missions, he himself did not know the answer.

'Yesterday', he confessed, 'I had a narrow squeak. I snaffled a Carthusian monk away from them just as they were about to shoot the fellow. The smell of blood was in the air, and ... Well, they growled a bit, you know.'

I know the end of that story. Pépin, the socialist and notorious anti-church political worker, having staked his life to get that Carthusian, had hustled him into a motor-car and there, by way of compensation, he sought to insult the priest by the finest bit of blasphemy he could summon:

'You ... you ... you triple damned monk!' he had finally spluttered.

This was Pépin's triumph. But the monk, who had not been listening, flung his arms round Pépin's neck and wept with happiness.

In another village they gave up a man to us. With a great air of mystery, four militiamen dug him up out of a cellar. He was a lively bright-eyed monk whose name I have already forgotten, disguised as a peasant and carrying a long gnarled stick scarred with notches.

'I kept track of the days,' he explained. 'Three weeks in the woods is a long time. Mushrooms are not specially nourishing, and they grabbed me when I came near a village.'

The mayor of the village, to whom we owed this gift, was very proud of him.

'We shot at him a lot and thought we had killed him,' he said. And then, by way of excuse for the bad marksmanship, he added : 'I must say it was at night.'

The monk laughed.

'I wasn't afraid.'

We put him into the car, and before we threw in the clutch everybody had to shake hands all round with these terrible terrorists. The monk's hand was shaken hardest of all and he was repeatedly congratulated on being alive. To all these friendly sentiments he responded with a warmth of unquestionably sincere appreciation.

As for me, I wish I understood mankind.

We went over our lists. At Sitges lived a man who, we had been told, was in danger of being shot. We drove round and found his door wide open. Up a flight of stairs we ran into our skinny young man.

'It seems that these people are likely to shoot you,' we told him. 'Come back to Barcelona with us and you will be shipped home to France in the *Duquesne*.'

The young man took a long time to think this over and then said :

'This is some trick of my sister's.'

'What?'

'She lives in Barcelona. She would never pay for the child's keep and I always had to. . . .'

'Your family troubles are none of our affair. Are you in danger here, yes or no?'

'I don't know. I tell you, my sister . . .'

'Do you want to get away, yes or no?'

'I really don't know. What do you think? In Barcelona, my sister . . .'

The man was carrying on his family quarrel through the revolution. He was going to stay here in order to do his sister in the eye.

'Do as you please,' we said, finally, and we left him where he was.

We stopped the car and got out. A volley of rifle-shot had crackled in the still country air. From the top of the road we looked down upon a clump of trees out of which, a quarter of a mile away, stuck two tall chimneys. A squad of militiamen came up and loaded their guns. We asked what was going on. They looked round, pointed to the chimneys, and decided that the firing must have come from the factory.

The shooting died down almost immediately, and silence fell again. The chimneys went on smoking peacefully. A ripple of wind ran over the grass. Nothing had changed visibly, and we ourselves were unchanged. Nevertheless, in that clump of trees someone had just died.

One of the militiamen said that a girl had been killed at the factory, together with her brothers, but there was still some uncertainty about this. What excruciating simplicity! Our own peace of mind had not been invaded by those muffled sounds in the clump of greenery, by that brief partridge drive. The angelus, as it were, that had rung out in that foliage had left us calm and unrepentant.

Human events display two faces, one of drama and the other of indifference. Everything changes according as the event concerns the individual or the species. In its migrations, in its imperious impulses, the species forgets its dead. This, perhaps, explains the unperturbed faces of these peasants. One feels that they have no special taste for horror; yet they will come back from that clump of trees on the one hand content to have administered their kind of justice, and on the other hand quite indifferent to the fate of the girl who stumbled against the root of the tree of death, who was caught by death's harpoon as she fled, and who now lies in the wood, her mouth filled with blood.

Here I touch the inescapable contradiction I shall never be able to resolve. For man's greatness does not reside merely in the destiny of the species: each individual is an empire. When a mine caves in and closes over the head of a single miner, the life of the community is suspended.

His comrades, their women, their children, gather in anguish at the entrance to the mine, while below them the rescue party scratch with their picks at the bowels of the earth. What are they after? Are they consciously saving one unit of society? Are they freeing a human being as one might free a horse, after computing the work he is still capable of doing? Ten other miners may be killed in the attempted rescue: what inept cost-accounting! Of course it is not a matter of saving one ant out of the colony of ants! They are rescuing a consciousness, an empire whose significance is incommensurable with any-thing else.

Inside the narrow skull of the miner pinned beneath the fallen timber, there lives a world. Parents, friends, a home, the hot soup of evening, songs sung on feast-days, loving-kindness and anger, perhaps even a social consciousness and a great uni-versal love, inhabit that skull. By what are we to measure the value of a man? His ancestor once drew a reindeer on the wall of a cave; and two hundred thousand years later that gesture still radiates. It stirs us, prolongs itself in us. Man's gestures are an eternal spring. Though we die for it, we shall bring up that miner from his shaft. Solitary he may be; universal he surely is.

In Spain there are crowds in movement, but the individual, that universe, calls in vain for help from the bottom of the mine.

3

Machine-gun bullets cracked against the stone above our heads as we skirted the moonlit wall. Low-flying lead thudded into the rubble of an embankment that rose on the other side of the road. Half a mile away a battle was in progress, the line of fire drawn in the shape of a horseshoe ahead of us and on our flanks.

Walking between wall and parapet on the white highway, my guide and I were able to disregard the spatter of missiles in a feeling of perfect security. We could sing, we could laugh, we could strike matches, without drawing upon ourselves the direct fire of the enemy. We went forward like peasants on their way to market. Half a mile away the iron hand of war would have set us inescapably upon the black chessboard of battle; but here, out of the game ignored, the Republican lieutenant and I were as free as air.

Shells filled the night with absurd parabolas during their three seconds of freedom between release and exhaustion. There were the duds that dove without bursting into the ground; there were the travellers in space that whipped straight overhead, elongated in their race to the stars. And the leaden bullets that ricocheted in our faces and tinkled curiously in our ears were like bees, dangerous for the twinkling of an eye, poisonous but ephemeral.

Walking on, we reached a point where the embankment had collapsed.

'We might follow the cross-trench from here,' my guide suggested.

Things had suddenly turned serious. Not that we were in the line of machine-gun fire, or that a roving searchlight was about to spot us. It was not as bad as that. There had simply been a rustling overhead; a sort of celestial gurgle had sounded. It meant no harm to us, but the lieutenant remarked suddenly: 'That is meant for Madrid,' and we went down into the trench.

The trench ran along the crest of a hill a little before reaching the suburb of Carabanchel. In the direction of Madrid a part of the parapet had crumbled and we could see the city in the gap, white, strangely white, under the full moon. Hardly a mile separated us from those tall structures dominated by the tower of the Telephone Building.

Madrid was asleep – or rather Madrid was feigning sleep. Not a light; not a sound. Like clockwork, every two minutes the funereal fracas that we were henceforth to hear roared forth and was dissolved in a dead silence. It seemed to waken no sound and no stirring in the city, but was swallowed up each time like a stone in water.

Suddenly in the place of Madrid I felt that I was staring at a face with closed eyes. The hard face of an obstinate virgin taking blow after blow without a moan. Once again there sounded overhead that gurgling in the stars of a newly uncorked bottle. One second, two seconds, five seconds went by. There was an explosion and I ducked involuntarily. There goes the whole town, I thought.

But Madrid was still there. Nothing had collapsed. Not an eye had blinked. Nothing was changed. The stone face was as pure as ever.

'Meant for Madrid,' the lieutenant repeated mechanically. He taught me to tell these celestial shudders apart, to follow the course of these sharks rushing upon their prey :

'No, that is one of our batteries replying. . . . That's theirs, but firing somewhere else. . . . There's one meant for Madrid.'

Waiting for an explosion is the longest passage of time I know. What things go on in that interminable moment! An enormous pressure rises, rises. Will that boiler ever make up its mind to burst? At last! For some that meant death, but there are others for whom it meant escape from death. Eight hundred thousand souls, less half a score of dead, have won a last-minute reprieve. Between the gurgling and the explosion eight hundred thousand lives were in danger of death.

Each shell in the air threatened them all. I could feel the city out there, tense, compact, a solid. I saw them all in the mind's eye – men, women, children, all that humble population crouching in the sheltering cloak of stone of a motionless virgin. Again I heard the ignoble crash and was gripped and sickened by the downward course of the torpedo. . . . Torpedo? I scarcely knew what I was saying. 'They . . . they are torpedoing Madrid.' And the lieutenant, standing there counting the shells, said :

'Meant for Madrid. Sixteen.'

I crept out of the trench, lay flat on my stomach on the parapet, and stared. A new image has wiped out the old. Madrid with its chimney-pots, its towers, its portholes, now looks like a ship on the high seas. Madrid all white on the black waters of the night. A city outlives its inhabitants.

Madrid, loaded with emigrants, is ferrying them from one shore to the other of life. It has a generation on board. Slowly it navigates through the centuries. Men, women, children fill it from garret to hold. Resigned or quaking with fear, they live only for the moment to come. A vessel loaded with humanity is being torpedoed. The purpose of the enemy is to sink Madrid as if she were a ship.

Stretched out on the parapet I do not care a curse for the rules of war. For justifications or for motives. I listen. I have learned to read the course of these gurglings among the stars. They pass quite close to Sagittarius. I have learned to count slowly up to five. And I listen. But what tree has been sundered by this lightning, what cathedral has been gutted, what poor child has just been stricken, I have no means of knowing.

That same afternoon I had witnessed a bombardment in the town itself. All the force of this thunderclap had to burst on the Gran Vía in order to uproot a human life. One single life. Passers-by had brushed rubbish off their clothes; others had scattered on the run; and when the light smoke had risen and cleared away, the betrothed, escaped by miracle without a scratch, found at his feet his *novia*, whose golden arm a moment before had been in his, changed into a blood-filled sponge, changed into a limp packet of flesh and rags.

He had knelt down, still uncomprehending, had nodded his head slowly, as if saying to himself: 'Something very strange has happened.'

This marvel spattered on the pavement bore no resemblance to what had been his beloved. Misery was excruciatingly slow to engulf him in its tidal wave. For still another second, stunned by the feat of the invisible prestidigitator, he cast a bewildered glance round him in search of the slender form, as if it at least should have survived. Nothing was there but a packet of muck.

Gone was the feeble spark of humanity. And while in the man's throat there was brewing that shriek which I know not what deferred, he had the leisure to reflect that it was not those lips he had loved but their pout, not them but their smile. Not those eyes, but their glance. Not that breast, but its gentle swell. He was free to discover at last the source of the anguish love had been storing up for him, to learn that it was the unattainable he had been pursuing. What he had yearned to embrace was not the flesh but a downy spirit, a spark, the impalpable angel that inhabits the flesh.

I do not care a curse for the rules of war and the law of reprisal. As for the military advantage of such a bombardment, I simply cannot grasp it. I have seen housewives disembowelled, children mutilated; I have seen the old itinerant market crone sponge from her treasures the brains with which they were spattered. I have seen a janitor's wife come out of her cellar and douse the sullied pavement with a bucket of water, and I am still unable to understand what part these humble slaughterhouse accidents play in warfare.

A moral role? But a bombardment turns against the bombarder! Each shell that fell upon Madrid fortified something in the town. It persuaded the hesitant neutral to plump for the defenders. A dead child weighs heavily in the balance when it is one's own. It was clear to me that a bombardment did not disperse – it unified. Horror causes men to clench their fists, and in horror men join together.

The lieutenant and I crawled along the parapet. Face or ship, Madrid stood erect, receiving blows without a moan. But men are like this: slowly but surely, ordeal fortifies their virtues.

Because of the ordeal my companion's heart was high. He was thinking of the hardening of Madrid's will. He stood up with his fists on his hips, breathing heavily. Pity for the women and the children had gone out of him.

'That makes sixty,' he counted grimly.

The blow resounded on the anvil. A giant smith was forging Madrid.

One side or the other would win. Madrid would resist or it would fall. A thousand forces were engaged in this mortal confusion of tongues from which anything might come forth. But one did not need to be a Martian, did not need to see these men dispassionately in a long perspective, in order to perceive that they were struggling against themselves, were their own enemy. Mankind perhaps was being brought to bed of something here in Spain; something perhaps was to be born of this chaos, this disruption. For indeed not all that I saw in Spain was horror, not all of it filled my mouth with a taste of ashes.

4

On the Guadalajara front I sat at night in a dugout with a Republican squad made up of a lieutenant, a sergeant, and three men. They were about to go out on patrol duty. One of them – the night was cold – stood half in shadow with his head not quite through the neck of a sweater he was pulling on, his arms caught in the sleeves and waving slowly and awkwardly in the air like the short arms of a bear. Smothered curses, stubbles of beard, distant muffled explosions – the atmosphere was a strange compound of sleep, waking, and death. I thought of tramps on the road bestirring themselves, raising themselves up off the ground on heavy sticks. Caught in the earth, painted by the earth, their hands grubby with their gardenless gardening, these men were raising themselves painfully out of the mud in order to emerge under the stars. In these blocks of caked clay I could sense the awakening of consciousness, and as I looked at them I said to myself that across the way, at this very moment, the enemy was getting into his harness, was thickening his body with woollen sweaters; earth-crusted, he was breaking out of his mould of hardened mud. Across the way the same clay shaping the same beings was wakening in the same way into consciousness.

The patrol moved forward across fields through crackling stubble, knocking its toes against unseen rocks in the dark. We were making our way down into a narrow valley on the other side of which the enemy was entrenched. Caught in the crossfire of artillery, the peasants had evacuated this valley, and their deserted village lay here drowned in the waters of war. Only their dogs remained, ghostly creatures that hunted their pitiful prey in the day and howled in the night. At four in the morning, when the moon rose white as a picked bone, a whole village bayed at the dead divinity.

'Go down and find out if the enemy is hiding in that village,' the commanding officer had ordered. Very likely on the other side the same order had been given.

We were accompanied by a sort of political agent, a civilian, whose name I have forgotten, though not what he looked like. It seems to me he must have been rheumatic, and I remember that he leaned heavily on a knotted stick as we tramped forward in the night. His face was the face of a conscientious and elderly workman. I would have sworn that he was above politics and parties, above ideological rivalries. 'Pity it is', he would say, 'that as things are we cannot explain our point of view to the other fellow.' He walked weighed down by his doctrine, like an evangelist. Across the way, meanwhile, was the other evangelist, a believer just as enlightened as this one, his boots just as muddy, his duty taking him on exactly the same errand.

'You'll hear them pretty soon,' my commissar said. 'When we get close enough we'll call out to the enemy, ask him questions; and he may answer tonight.'

Although we don't yet know it, we are in search of a gospel to embrace all gospels, we are on the march towards a stormy Sinai.

And we have arrived. Here is a dazed sentry, half asleep in the shadow of a stone wall.

'Yes,' says my commissar, 'sometimes they answer. Sometimes they call out first and ask questions. Of course they don't answer, too, sometimes. Depends on the mood they're in.'

Just like the gods.

A hundred yards behind us lie our trenches. I strike a match, intending to light a cigarette, and two powerful hands duck my head. Everybody has ducked, and I hear the whistle of bullets in the air. Then silence. The shots were fired high and the volley was not repeated – a mere reminder from the enemy of what constitutes decorum here. One does not light a cigarette in the face of the enemy.

We are joined by three or four men, wrapped in blankets, who had been posted behind neighbouring walls.

'Looks as if the lads across the way were awake,' one of them remarks.

'Do you think they'll talk tonight? We'd like to talk to them.'

'One of them, Antonio, he talks sometimes.'

'Call him.'

The man in the blanket straightens up, cups his hands round his mouth, takes a deep breath, and calls out slowly and loudly: 'An . . . to . . . ni . . . o !'

The call swells, unfurls, floats across the valley and echoes back.

'Better duck,' my neighbour advises. 'Sometimes when you call them, they let fly.'

Crouched behind the stone wall, we listen. No sound of a shot. Yet we cannot say we have heard nothing at all, for the whole night is singing like a sea-shell.

'Hi ! Antonio . . . o ! Are you . . .'

The man in the blanket draws another deep breath and goes on :

'Are you asleep ?'

'Asleep ?' says the echo. 'Asleep ?' the valley asks. 'Asleep ?' the whole night wants to know. The sound fills all space. We scramble to our feet and stand erect in perfect confidence. They have not touched their guns.

I stand imagining them on their side of the valley as they listen, hear, receive this human voice, this voice that obviously has not stirred them to anger since no finger has pressed a trigger. True, they do not answer, they are silent; but how attentive must be that silent audience from which, a moment ago, a match had sufficed to draw a volley. Borne on the breeze of a human voice, invisible seeds are fertilizing that black earth across the valley. Those men thirst for our words as we for theirs. But their fingers, meanwhile, are on their triggers. They put me in mind of those wild things we would try in the desert to tame and that would stare at us, eat the food and drink the water we set out for them, and would spring at our throats when we made a move to stroke them.

We squatted well down behind the wall and held up a lighted match above it. Three bullets passed overhead. To the match they said : 'You are forgetting that we are at war.' To us : 'We are listening, nevertheless. We can still love, though we stick to our rules.'

Another giant peasant rested his gun against the wall, stood up, drew a deep breath, and let go:

'Antonio ... o! It's me! Leo!'

The sound moved across the valley like a ship new-launched. Eight hundred yards to the far shore, eight hundred back – sixteen hundred yards. If they answered, there would be five seconds of time between our questions and their replies. Five seconds of silence, in which all war would be suspended, would go by between each question and each answer. Like an embassy on a journey, each time. What this meant was that even if they answered, we should still feel ourselves separated from them. Between them and us the inertia of an invisible world would still be there to be stirred into action. For the considerable space of five seconds we should be like men shipwrecked and fearful lest the rescue party had not heard their cries.

'... ooo!'

A distant voice like a feeble wave has curled up to die on our shore. The phrase, the word, was lost on the way and the result is an undecipherable message. Yet it strikes me like a blow. In this impenetrable darkness a sudden flash of light has gleamed. All of us are shaken by a ridiculous hope. Something has made known to us its existence. We can be sure now that there are men across the way. It is as if in invisibility a crack had opened, as if ... Imagine a house at night, dark and its doors all locked. You, sitting in its darkness, suddenly feel a breath of cold air on your face. A single breath. What a presence!

There it comes again! '... time ... sleep!'

Torn, mutilated as a truly urgent message must be, washed by the waves and soaked in brine, here is our message. The men who fired at our cigarettes have blown up their chests with air in order to send us this motherly bit of advice:

'Quiet! Go to bed! Time to sleep!'

It excites us. You who read this will perhaps think that these men were merely playing a game. In a sense they were. I am sure that, being simple men, if you had caught them at their sport they would have denied that it was serious. But games always cover something deep and intense, else there would be no excitement in them, no pleasure, no power to stir us. Here was a game that made our hearts beat too wildly not to satisfy a real though undefined need within us. It was as if we were marrying our enemy before dying of his blow.

But so slight, so fragile was the pontoon flung between our two shores that a question too awkward, a phrase too clumsy, would certainly upset it. Words lose themselves: only essential words, only the truth of truths would leave this frail bridge whole. And I can see him now, that peasant who stirred Antonio to speech and thus made himself our pilot, our ambassador; I can see him as he stood erect, as he rested his strong hands on the low stone wall and sent forth from his great chest that question of questions:

'Antonio! What are you fighting for?'

Let me say again that he and Antonio would be ashamed to think that you took them seriously. They would insist that it was all in fun. But I was there as he stood waiting, and I know that his whole soul gaped wide to receive the answer. Here is the truncated message, the secret mutilated by five seconds of travel across the valley as an inscription in stone is defaced by the passing of the centuries:

'... Spain!'

And then I heard:

'... You?'

He got his answer. I heard the great reply as it was flung forth into space:

'The bread of our brothers!'

And then the amazing:

'Good night, friend!'

And the response from the other side of the world:

'Good night, friend!'

And silence.

Their words were not the same, but their truths were identical. Why has this high communion never yet prevented men from dying in battle against each other?

5

Back on the Madrid front I sat again at night in a subterranean chamber, at supper with a young captain and a few of his

164

men. The telephone had rung and the captain was being ordered to prepare to attack before daybreak. Twenty houses in this industrial suburb, Carabanchel, constituted the objective. There would be no support: one after the other the houses were to be blown in with hand grenades and occupied.

I felt vaguely squeamish as I took something like a last look at these men who were shortly to dive into the great bowl of air, suck the blue night into their lungs, and then be blown to bits before they could reach the other side of the road. They were taking it easily enough, but the captain came back to table from the telephone shrugging his shoulders. 'The first man out ...' He started to say something, changed his mind, pushed two glasses and a bottle of brandy across the table, and said to the sergeant:

'You lead the file with me. Have a drink and go get some sleep.'

The sergeant drank and went off to sleep. Round the table a dozen of us were sitting up. All the chinks in this room were caulked up; not a trickle of light could escape; the glare within was so dazzling that I blinked. The brandy was sweet, faintly nauseating, and its taste was as mournful as a drizzle at daybreak. I was in a daze, and when I had drunk I shut my eyes and saw behind my lids those ruined and ghostly houses bathed in a greenish radiance as of moonglow under water, that I had stared at a few minutes before through the sentry's loophole. Someone on my right was telling a funny story. He was talking very fast and I understood about one word in three.

A man came in half-drunk, reeling gently in this half-real world. He stood rubbing a stubble of beard and looking us over with vague affectionate eyes. His glance slid across to the bottle, avoided it, came back to it, and turned pleadingly to the captain.

The captain laughed softly, and the man, suddenly hopeful, laughed too. A light gust of laughter ran over the roomful of men. The captain put out his hand and moved the bottle noiselessly out of reach. The man's glance simulated despair, and a childish game began, a sort of mute ballet which, in the fog of cigarette smoke and the weariness of the watch with its anticipation of the coming attack, was utterly dream-like. I sat hypnotized by this atmosphere of the slowly ending vigil, reading the hour in the stubbles of beard while out of doors a sea-like pounding of cannon waxed in intensity.

Soon afterwards these men were to scour themselves clean of their sweat, their brandy, the filth of their vigil, in the regal waters of the night of war. I felt in them something so near to spotless purity! Meanwhile, as long as it would last, they were dancing the ballet of the drunkard and the bottle. They were determined that this game should absorb them utterly. They were making life last as long as it possibly could. But there on a shelf stood a battered alarm clock, set to sound the zero-hour. No one so much as glanced at it but me, and my glance was furtive. They would all hear it well enough, never fear! Its ringing would shatter the stifling air.

The clock would ring out. The men would rise to their feet and stretch themselves. They would be sure to make this gesture which is instinctive in every man about to tackle the problem of survival. They would stretch themselves, I say, and they would buckle on their harness. The captain would pull his revolver out of his holster. The drunk would sober up. And all these men, without undue haste, would file into the passage. They would go as far as that rectangle of pale light which is the sky at the end of the passage, and there they would mutter something simple like 'Look at the moon!' or 'What a night!' And then they would fling themselves into the stars.

Scarcely had the attack been called off by telephone, scarcely had these men, most of whom had been doomed to die in the attack upon that concrete wall, begun to feel themselves safe, begun to realize that they were certain of trampling their sweet planet in their rough clogs one more day, scarcely were their minds at peace, when all in chorus began to lament their fate.

'Do they think we are a lot of women?' 'Is this a war or isn't it?' A fine general staff! they grumbled sarcastically. Can't make up its mind about anything! Wants to see Madrid bombarded and kids smashed to bits. Here they were, ready to rip up those enemy batteries and fling them over the backs of mountains to save innocence imperilled, and the staff tied them hand and foot, condemned them to inaction.

It was clear enough, and the men admitted it, that none of them might have come up again after their dive into the moonlight, and that they ought in reality to be very happy to be alive and able to grouse against G.H.Q. and go on drinking their consoling brandy; and, by the way, since the second telephone message, two curious things had happened: the brandy tasted better and the men were now drinking it cheerfully instead of moodily.

Yet at the same time I saw nothing in their vehemence that made me think it either silly or boastful. I could not but remember that all of them had been ready to die with simplicity.

Day broke. I scrubbed my face in the freezing water of the village pump. Coffee steamed in the bowls under an arbour forty yards from the enemy outpost, half-wrecked by the midnight firing but safe in the truce of dawn. Now freshly washed, the survivors gathered here to commune in life rather than in death, to share their white bread, their cigarettes, their smiles. They came in one by one, the captain, Sergeant R—, the lieutenant, and the rest, planted their elbows solidly on the table, and sat facing this treasure which they had been judicious enough to despise at a moment when it seemed it must be abandoned, but which had now recovered its price. '*Salud, amigo!*' – 'Hail, friend!' – they sang out as they clapped one another on the shoulder.

I loved the freezing wind that caressed us and the shining sun that warmed us beneath the touch of the wind. I loved the mountain air that was filling me with gladness. I rejoiced in the cheer of these men who sat in their shirt-sleeves gathering fresh strength from their repast and making ready, once they had finished and risen to their feet, to knead the stuff of the world.

A ripe pod burst somewhere. From time to time a silly bullet spat against the stone wall. Death was abroad, of course, but wandering aimlessly and without ill intent. This was not death's hour. We in the arbour were celebrating life.

This whole platoon had risen up *de profundis*; and the captain sat breaking the white bread, that densely baked bread of

Spain so rich in wheat, in order that each of his comrades, having stretched forth his hand, might receive a chunk as big as his fist and turn it into life.

These men had in truth risen *de profundis*. They were in very fact beginning a new life. I stared at them, and in particular at Sergeant R—, he who was to have been the first man out and who had gone to sleep in preparation for the attack. I was with them when they woke him up. Now Sergeant R— had been well aware that he was to be the first man to step out into the line of fire of a machine-gun nest and dance in the moonlight that brief ballet at the end of which is death. His awakening had been the awakening of a prisoner in the death cell.

At Carabanchel the trenches wound among little workmen's houses whose furnishings were still in place. In one of these, a few yards from the enemy, Sergeant R— was sleeping fully dressed on an iron cot. When we had lighted a candle and had stuck it into the neck of a bottle, and had drawn forth out of the darkness that funereal bed, the first thing that came into view was a pair of clogs. Enormous clogs, iron-shod and studded with nails, the clogs of a sewer-worker or a railway track-walker. All the poverty of the world was in those clogs. No man ever strode with happy steps through life in clogs like these: he boarded life like a longshoreman for whom life is a ship to be unloaded.

This man was shod in his tools, and his whole body was covered with the tools of his trade – cartridge belt, gun, leather harness. His neck was bent beneath the heavy collar of the draught horse. Deep in caves, in Morocco, you can see millstones worked by blind horses. Here in the ruddy wavering light of the candle we were waking up a blind horse and sending him out to the mill.

'Hi! Sergeant!'

He sent forth a sigh as heavy as a wave and turned slowly and massively over towards us so that we saw a face still asleep and filled with anguish. His eyes were shut, and his mouth, to which clung a bubble of air, was half open like the mouth of a drowned man. We sat down on his bed and watched his laborious awakening. The man was clinging like a crab to submarine depths, grasping in his fists I know not what dark seaweed. He opened and shut his hands, pulled up another deep sigh, and escaped from us suddenly with his face to the wall, obstinate with the stubbornness of an animal refusing to die, turning its back on the slaughter-house.

'Hi! Sergeant!'

Once again he was drawn up from the bottom of the sea, swam towards us, and we saw again his face in the candle-light. This time we had hobbled our sleeper; he would not get away from us again. He blinked with closed eyes, moved his mouth round as if swallowing, ran his hand over his forehead, made one great effort to sink back into his happy dreams and reject our universe of dynamite, weariness, and glacial night, but it was too late. Something from without was too strong for him.

Like the punished schoolboy stirred by the insistent bell out of his dream of a school-less world, Sergeant R— began to clothe himself in the weary flesh he had so recently shed, that flesh which in the chill of awakening was soon to know the old pains in the joints, the weight of the harness, and the stumbling race towards death. Not so much death as the dis-comfort of dying, the filth of the blood in which he would steep his hands when he tried to rise to his feet; the stickiness of that coagulating syrup. Not so much death as the Calvary of a punished child.

One by one he stretched his arms and then his legs, bringing up an elbow, straightening a knee, while his straps, his gun, his cartridge belt, the three grenades hanging from his belt, all hampered the final strokes of this swimmer in the sea of sleep. At last he opened his eyes, sat up on the bed, and stared at us, mumbling:

'Huh! Oh! Are we off?'

And as he spoke, he simply stretched out his hand for his rifle.

'No,' said the captain. 'The attack has been called off.'

Sergeant R—, let me tell you that we made you a present of your life. Just that. As much as if you had stood at the foot of the electric chair. And God knows, the world sheds ink enough on the pathos of pardon at the foot of the electric chair. We brought you your pardon *in extremis*. No question about it. In your mind there was nothing between you and death but a thickness of tissue-paper. Therefore you must forgive me my curiosity. I stared at you, and I shall never forget your face. It was a face touching and ugly, with a humped nose a little too big, high cheek-bones, and the spectacles of an intellectual. How does a man receive the gift of life? I can answer that. A man sits still, pulls a bit of tobacco out of his pocket, nods his head slowly, looks up at the ceiling, and says:

'Suits me.'

Then he nods his head again and adds:

'If they'd sent us a couple of platoons the attack might have made sense. The lads would have pitched in. You'd have seen what they can do.'

Sergeant, Sergeant, what will you do with this gift of life?

Now, Sergeant at peace, you are dipping your bread into your coffee. You are rolling cigarettes. You are like the lad who has been told he will not be punished after all. And yet, like the rest, you are ready to start out again tonight on that brief dash at the end of which the only thing a man can do is kneel down.

Over and over in my head there goes the question I have wanted to ask you ever since last night: 'Sergeant, what is it makes you willing to die?'

But I know that it is impossible to ask such a question. It would offend a modesty in you which you yourself do not know to be there, but which would never forgive me. You could not answer with high-sounding words: they would seem false to you and in truth they would be false. What language could be chaste enough for a modest man like you? But I am determined to know, and I shall try to get round the difficulty. I shall ask you seemingly idle questions, and you will answer.

'Tell me, why did you join up?'

If I understood your answer, Sergeant, you hardly know yourself. You were a book-keeper in Barcelona. You added up your columns of figures every day without worrying much about the struggle against the rebels. But one of your friends joined up, and then a second friend; and you were disturbed to find yourself undergoing a curious transformation: little by little your columns of figures seemed to you futile. Your pleasures, your work, your dreams, all seemed to belong to another age.

But even that was not important, until one day you heard that one of your friends had been killed on the Málaga front. He was not a friend for whom you would ever have felt you had to lay down your life. Yet that bit of news swept over you, over your narrow little life, like a wind from the sea. And that morning another friend had looked at you and said: 'Do we or don't we?' And you had said: 'We do.'

You never really wondered about the imperious call that compelled you to join up. You accepted a truth which you could never translate into words, but whose self-evidence overpowered you: And while I sat listening to your story, an image came into my mind, and I understood.

When the wild ducks or the wild geese migrate in their season, a strange tide rises in the territories over which they sweep. As if magnetized by the great triangular flight, the barnyard fowl leap a foot or two into the air and try to fly. The call of the wild strikes them with the force of a harpoon and a vestige of savagery quickens their blood. All the ducks on the farm are transformed for an instant into migrant birds, and into those hard little heads, till now filled with humble images of pools and worms and barnyards, there swims a sense of continental expanse, of the breadth of seas and the salt taste of the ocean wind. The duck totters to right and left in its wire enclosure, gripped by a sudden passion to perform the impossible and a sudden love whose object is a mystery.

Even so is man overwhelmed by a mysterious presentiment of truth, so that he discovers the vanity of his book-keeping and the emptiness of his domestic felicities. But he can never put a name to this sovereign truth. Men explain these brusque vocations by the need to escape or the lure of danger, as if we knew where the need to escape and the lure of danger themselves came from. They talk about the call of duty, but what is it that makes the call of duty so pressing? What can you tell me, Sergeant, about that uneasiness that seeped in to disturb your peaceful existence?

The call that stirred you must torment all men. Whether we

dub it sacrifice, or poetry, or adventure, it is always the same voice that calls. But domestic security has succeeded in crushing out that part in us that is capable of heeding the call. We scarcely quiver; we beat our wings once or twice and fall back into our barnyard.

We are prudent people. We are afraid to let go of our petty reality in order to grasp at a great shadow. But you, Sergeant, did discover the sordidness of those shopkeepers' bustlings, those petty pleasures, those petty needs. You felt that men did not live like this. And you agreed to heed the great call without bothering to try to understand it. The hour had come when you must moult, when you must rise into the sky.

The barnyard duck had no notion that his little head was big enough to contain oceans, continents, skies; but of a sudden here he was beating his wings, despising corn, despising worms, battling to become a wild duck.

There is a day of the year when the eels must go down to the Sargasso Sea, and come what may, no one can prevent them. On that day they spit upon their ease, their tranquillity, their tepid waters. Off they go over ploughed fields, pricked by the hedges and skinned by the stones, in search of the river that leads to the abyss.

Even so did you feel yourself swept away by that inward migration about which no one had ever said a word to you. You were ready for a sort of bridal that was a mystery to you, but in which you had to participate. 'Do we or don't we? We do.' You went up to the front in a war that at bottom meant little to you. You took to the road as spontaneously as that silvery people shining in the fields on its way to the sea, or that black triangle in the sky.

What were you after? Last night you almost reached your goal. What was it you discovered in yourself that was so ready to burst from its cocoon? At daybreak your comrades were full of complaint: tell me, of what had they been defrauded? What had they discovered in themselves that was about to show itself, and that now they wept for?

What, Sergeant, were the visions that governed your destiny and justified your risking your life in this adventure? Your life, your only treasure! We have to live a long time before we become men. Very slowly do we plait the braid of friendships and affections. We learn slowly. We compose our creation slowly. And if we die too early we are in a sense cheated out of our share. We have to live a long time to fulfil ourselves.

But you, by the grace of an ordeal in the night which stripped you of all that was not intrinsic, you discovered a mysterious creature born of yourself. Great was this creature, and never shall you forget him. And he is yourself. You have had the sudden sense of fulfilling yourself in the instant of discovery, and you have learned suddenly that the future is now less necessary for the accumulation of treasures. That creature within you who opened his wings is not bound by ties to perishable things; he agrees to die for all men, to be swallowed up in something universal.

A great wind swept through you and delivered from the matrix the sleeping prince you sheltered — Man within you. You are the equal of the musician composing his music, of the physicist extending the frontier of knowledge, of all those who build the highways over which we march to deliverance. Now you are free to gamble with death. What have you now to lose?

Let us say you were happy in Barcelona: nothing more can ruin that happiness. You have reached an altitude where all loves are of the same stuff. Perhaps you suffered on earth, felt yourself alone on the planet, knew no refuge to which you might fly? What of that! Sergeant, this day you have been welcomed home by love.

6

No man can draw a free breath who does not share with other men a common and disinterested ideal. Life has taught us that love does not consist in gazing at each other but in looking outward together in the same direction. There is no comradeship except through union in the same high effort. Even in our age of material well-being this must be so, else how should we explain the happiness we feel in sharing our last crust with others in the desert? No sociologist's textbook can prevail against this fact. Every pilot who has flown to the rescue of a comrade in distress knows that all joys are vain in comparison with this one. And this, it may be, is the reason why the world today is tumbling about our ears. It is precisely because this sort of fulfilment is promised each of us by his religion, that men are inflamed today. All of us, in words that contradict each other, express at bottom the same exalted impulse. What sets us against one another is not our aims – they all come to the same thing – but our methods, which are the fruit of our varied reasoning.

Let us, then, refrain from astonishment at what men do. One man finds that his essential manhood comes alive at the sight of self-sacrifice, cooperative effort, a rigorous vision of justice, manifested in an anarchists' cellar in Barcelona. For that man there will henceforth be but one truth – the truth of the anarchists. Another, having once mounted guard over a flock of terrified little nuns kneeling in a Spanish nunnery, will thereafter know a different truth, that it is sweet to die for the Church. If, when Mermoz plunged into the Chilean Andes with victory in his heart, you had protested to him that no merchant's letter could possibly be worth risking one's life for, Mermoz would have laughed in your face. Truth is the man that was born in Mermoz when he slipped through the Andean passes.

Consider that officer of the South Moroccan Rifles who, during the war in the Rif, was in command of an outpost set down between the two mountains filled with enemy tribesmen. One day, down from the mountain to the west came a group seeking a parley. Arabs and Frenchmen were talking over their tea when of a sudden a volley rang out. The tribesmen from the other mountain were charging the post. When the commandant sought to dismiss his guests before fighting off their allies, they said to him: 'Today we are your guests. God will not allow us to desert you.' They fought beside his men, saved the post, and then climbed back into their eyrie.

But on the eve of the day when their turn had come to pounce upon the post they sent again to the commandant.

'We came to your aid the other day,' their chief said.

'True.'

'We used up three hundred of our cartridges for you.'

'Very likely.'

'It would be only just that you replace them for us.'

The commandant was an officer and a gentleman. They were given their cartridges.

Truth, for any man, is that which makes him a man. A man who has fraternized with men on this high plane, who has displayed this sportsmanship and had seen the rules of the game so nobly observed on both sides in matters of life and death, is obviously not to be mentioned in the same breath with the shabby hearty demagogue who would have expressed his fraternity with the Arabs by a great clap on the shoulders and a spate of flattering words that would have humiliated them. You might argue with the captain that all was fair in war, but if you did he would feel a certain pitying contempt for you. And he would be right.

Meanwhile, you are equally right to hate war.

If our purpose is to understand mankind and its yearnings, to grasp the essential reality of mankind, we must never set one man's truth against another's. All beliefs are demonstrably true. All men are demonstrably in the right. Anything can be demonstrated by logic. I say that that man is right who blames all the ills of the world upon hunchbacks. Let us declare war on hunchbacks – and in the twinkling of an eye all of us will hate them fanatically. All of us will join to avenge the crimes of the hunchbacks. Assuredly, hunchbacks, too, do commit crimes.

But if we are to succeed in grasping what is essential in man, we must put aside the passions that divide us and that, once they are accepted, sow in the wind a whole Koran of unassailable verities and fanaticisms. Nothing is easier than to divide men into rightists and leftists, hunchbacks and straightbacks, fascists and democrats – and these distinctions will be perfectly just. But truth, we know, is that which clarifies, not that which confuses. Truth is the language that expresses universality. Newton did not 'discover' a law that lay hidden from man like the answer to a rebus. He accomplished a creative operation. He founded a human speech which could express at one and the same time the fall of an apple and the rising of the sun. Truth is not that which is demonstrable but that which is ineluctable.

There is no profit in discussing ideologies. If all of them are logically demonstrable, then all of them must contradict one other. To agree to discuss them is tantamount to despairing of the salvation of mankind – whereas everywhere about us men manifest identical yearnings.

What all of us want is to be set free. The man who sinks his pickaxe into the ground wants that stroke to mean something. The convict's stroke is not the same as the prospector's, for the obvious reason that the prospector's stroke has meaning and the convict's stroke has none. It would be a mistake to think that the prison exists at the point where the convict's stroke is dealt. Prison is not a mere physical horror. It is using a pickaxe to no purpose that makes a prison; the horror resides in the failure to enlist all those who swing the pick in the community of mankind.

We all yearn to escape from prison.

There are two hundred million men in Europe whose existence has no meaning and who yearn to come alive. Industry has torn them from the idiom of their peasant lineage and has locked them up in those enormous ghettos that are like railway yards heaped with blackened trucks. Out of the depths of their slums these men yearn to be awakened. There are others, caught in the wheels of a thousand trades, who are forbidden to share in the joys known to a Mermoz, to a priest, to a man of science. Once it was believed that to bring these creatures to manhood it was enough to feed them, clothe them, and look to their everyday needs; but we see now that the result of this has been to turn out petty shopkeepers, village politicians, hollow technicians devoid of an inner life. Some indeed were well taught, but no one troubled to cultivate any of them. People who believe that culture consists in the capacity to remember formulae have a paltry notion of what it is. Of course any science student can tell us more about Nature and her laws than can Descartes or Newton – but what can he tell us about the human spirit?

With more or less awareness, all men feel the need to come alive. But most of the methods suggested for bringing this about are snares and delusions. Men can of course be stirred into life by being dressed up in uniforms and made to blare out chants of war. It must be confessed that this is one way for men to break bread with comrades and to find what they are seeking, which is a sense of something universal, of self-fulfilment. But of this bread men die.

It is easy to dig up wooden idols and revive ancient and more or less workable myths like Pan-Germanism or the Roman Empire. The Germans can intoxicate themselves with the intoxication of being Germans and compatriots of Beethoven. A stoker in the hold of a freighter can be made drunk with this drink. What is more difficult is to bring up a Beethoven out of the stoke-hold.

These idols, in sum, are carnivorous idols. The man who dies for the progress of science or the healing of the sick serves life in his very dying. It may be glorious to die for the expansion of territory, but modern warfare destroys what it claims to foster. The day is gone when men sent life coursing through the veins of a race by the sacrifice of a little blood. War carried on by gas and bombing is no longer war, it is a kind of bloody surgery. Each side settles down behind a concrete wall and finds nothing better to do than to send forth, night after night, squadrons of planes to bomb the guts of the other side, blow up its factories, paralyse its production, and abolish its trade. Such a war is won by him who rots last – but in the end both rot together.

In a world become a desert we thirst for comradeship. It is the savour of bread broken with comrades that makes us accept the values of war. But there are other ways than war to bring us the warmth of a race, shoulder to shoulder, towards an identical goal. War has tricked us. It is not true that hatred adds anything to the exaltation of the race.

Why should we hate one another? We all live in the same cause, are borne through life on the same planet, form the crew of the same ship. Civilizations may, indeed, compete to bring forth new syntheses, but it is monstrous that they should devour one another.

To set man free it is enough that we help one another to realize that there does exist a goal towards which all mankind is striving. Why should we not strive towards that goal together, since it is what unites us all? The surgeon pays no heed to the moanings of his patient: beyond that pain it is man he is seeking to heal. That surgeon speaks a universal language. The physicist does the same when he ponders those almost divine equations in which he seizes the whole physical universe from the atom to the nebula. Even the simple shepherd modestly watching his sheep under the stars would discover, once he understood the part he was playing, that he was something more than a servant, was a sentinel. And each sentinel among men is responsible for the whole of the empire.

It is impossible not to believe that the shepherd wants to understand. One day, on the Madrid front, I chanced upon a school that stood on a hill surrounded by a low stone wall some five hundred yards behind the trenches. A corporal was teaching botany that day. He was lecturing on the fragile organs of a poppy held in his hands. Out of the surrounding mud, and in spite of the wandering shells that dropped all about, he had drawn like a magnet an audience of stubble-bearded soldiers who squatted tailor fashion and listened with their chins in their hands to a discourse of which they understood not a word in five. Something within them had said: 'You are but brutes fresh from your caves. Go along! Catch up with humanity!' And they had hurried on their muddy clogs to overtake it.

It is only when we become conscious of our part in life, however modest, that we shall be happy. Only then will we be able to live in peace and die in peace, for only this lends meaning to life and to death.

Death is sweet when it comes in its time and in its place, when it is part of the order of things, when the old peasant of Provence, at the end of his reign, remits into the hands of his sons his parcel of goats and olive-trees in order that they in their turn transmit them to their sons. When one is part of a peasant lineage, one's death is only half a death. Each life in turn bursts like a pod and sends forth its seed.

I stood once with three peasants in the presence of their dead mother. Sorrow filled the room. For a second time, the umbilical cord had been cut. For a second time the knot had been loosed, the knot that bound one generation to another. Of a sudden the three sons had felt themselves alone on earth with everything still to be learned. The magnetic pole round which they had lived was gone; their mother's table, where they had collected on feast-days with their families, was no more. But I could see in this rupture that it was possible for life to be granted a second time. Each of these sons was now to be the head of a family, was to be a rallying point and a patriarch, until that day when each would pass on the staff of office to the brood of children now murmuring in the court-yard.

I looked at their mother, at the old peasant with the firm peaceful face, the tight lips, the human face transformed into a stone mask. I saw in it the faces of her sons. That mask had served to mould theirs. That body had served to mould the bodies of these three exemplary men who stood there as up-right as trees. And now she lay broken but at rest, a vein from which the gold had been extracted. In their turn, her sons and daughters would bring forth men from their mould. One does not die on a farm : their mother is dead, long live their mother !

Sorrowful, yes, but so simple was this image of a lineage dropping one by one its white-haired members as it made its way through time and through its metamorphoses towards a truth that was its own.

That same day, when the tocsin tolled to announce to the countryside the death of this old woman, it seemed to me not a song of despair but a discreet and tender chant of joy. In that same voice the church bell celebrated birth and death, christening and burial, the passage from one generation to the next. I was suffused with a gentle peace of soul at this sound which announced the betrothal of a poor old woman and the earth.

This was life that was handed on here from generation to generation with the slow progress of a tree's growth, but it was also fulfilment. What a mysterious ascension ! From a little bubbling lava, from a vague pulp of a star, from a living cell miraculously fertilized, we have issued forth and have bit by bit raised ourselves to the writing of cantatas and the weighing of nebulae.

This peasant mother had done more than transmit life, she had taught her sons a language, had handed on to them the lot so slowly garnered through the centuries, the spiritual patrimony of traditions, concepts, and myths that make up the whole of the difference between Newton or Shakespeare and the caveman.

What we feel when we are hungry, when we feel that hunger which drew the Spanish soldiers under fire towards that botany lesson, drew Mermoz across the South Atlantic, draws a man to a poem, is that the birth of man is not yet accomplished, that we must take stock of ourselves and our universe. We must send forth pontoons into the night. There are men unaware of this, imagining themselves wise and self-regarding because they are indifferent. But everything in the world gives the lie to their wisdom.

Comrades of the air! I call upon you to bear me witness. When have we felt ourselves happy men?

10 Conclusion

Here, in the final pages of this book, I remember again those
musty civil servants who served as our escort in the omnibus
when we set out to fly our first mails, when we prepared
ourselves to be transformed into men – we who had had
the luck to be called. Those clerks were kneaded of the same
stuff as the rest of us, but they knew not that they were
hungry.

To come to man's estate it is not necessary to get oneself
killed round Madrid, or to fly mail planes, or to struggle wearily
in the snows out of respect for the dignity of life. The man
who can see the miraculous in a poem, who can take pure joy
from music, who can break his bread with comrades, opens
his window to the same refreshing wind off the sea. He too
learns a language of men.

But too many men are left unawakened.

A few years ago, in the course of a long railway journey, I
was suddenly seized by a desire to make a tour of the little
country in which I was locked up for three days, cradled in
that rattle that is like the sound of pebbles rolled over and
over by the waves; and I got up out of my berth. At one in the
morning I went through the train in all its length. The sleeping
cars were empty. The first-class carriages were empty. They
put me in mind of the luxurious hotels on the Riviera that
open in winter for a single guest, the last representative of an
extinct fauna. A sign of bitter times.

But the third-class carriages were crowded with hundreds of
Polish workmen sent home from France. I made my way along
those passages, stepping over sprawling bodies and peering into
the carriages. In the dim glow cast by the night-lamps into
these barren and comfortless compartments I saw a confused
mass of people churned about by the swaying of the train, the

whole thing looking and smelling like a barrack-room. A whole nation returning to its native poverty seemed to sprawl there in a sea of bad dreams. Great shaven heads rolled on the cushionless benches. Men, women, and children were stirring in their sleep, tossing from left to right and back again as if attacked by all the noises and jerkings that threatened them in their oblivion. They had not found the hospitality of a sweet slumber.

Looking at them I said to myself that they had lost half their human quality. These people had been knocked about from one end of Europe to the other by the economic currents; they had been torn from their little houses in the north of France, from their tiny garden-plots, their three pots of geranium that always stood in the windows of the Polish miners' families. I saw lying beside them pots and pans, blankets, curtains, bound into bundles badly tied and swollen with hernias.

Out of all that they had caressed or loved in France, out of everything they had succeeded in taming in their four or five years in my country – the cat, the dog, the geranium – they had been able to bring away with them only a few kitchen utensils, two or three blankets, a curtain or so.

A baby lay at the breast of a mother so weary that she seemed asleep. Life was being transmitted in the shabbiness and the disorder of this journey. I looked at the father. A powerful skull as naked as a stone. A body hunched over in uncomfortable sleep, imprisoned in working clothes, all humps and hollows. The man looked like a lump of clay, like one of those sluggish and shapeless derelicts that crumple into sleep in our public markets.

And I thought: The problem does not reside in this poverty, in this filth, in this ugliness. But this same man and this same woman met one day. This man must have smiled at this woman. He may, after his work was done, have brought her flowers. Timid and awkward, perhaps he trembled lest she disdain him. And this woman, out of natural coquetry, this woman sure of her charms, perhaps took pleasure in teasing him. And this man, this man who is now no more than a machine for swinging a pick or a sledge-hammer, must have felt in his heart a delicious anguish. The mystery is that they should have become these lumps of clay. Into what terrible mould were they forced? What was it that marked them like this as if they had been put through a monstrous stamping machine? A deer, a gazelle, any animal grown old, preserves its grace. What is it that corrupts this wonderful clay of which man is kneaded?

I went on through these people whose slumber was as sinister as a den of evil. A vague noise floated in the air made up of raucous snores, obscure moanings, and the scraping of clogs as their wearers, broken on one side, sought comfort on the other. And always the muted accompaniment of those pebbles rolled over and over by the waves.

I sat down face to face with one couple. Between the man and the woman a child had hollowed himself out a place and fallen asleep. He turned in his slumber, and in the dim lamp-light I saw his face. What an adorable face! A golden fruit had been born of these two peasants. Forth from this sluggish scum had sprung this miracle of delight and grace.

I bent over the smooth brow, over those mildly pouting lips, and I said to myself: This is a musician's face. This is the child Mozart. This is a life full of beautiful promise. Little princes in legends are not different from this. Protected, sheltered, cultivated, what could not this child become?

When by mutation a new rose is born in a garden, all the gardeners rejoice. They isolate the rose, tend it, foster it. But there is no gardener for men. This little Mozart will be shaped like the rest by the common stamping machine. This little Mozart will love shoddy music in the stench of night dives. This little Mozart is condemned.

I went back to my sleeping car. I said to myself: Their fate causes these people no suffering. It is not an impulse to charity that has upset me like this. I am not weeping over an eternally open wound. Those who carry the wound do not feel it. It is the human race and not the individual that is wounded here, is outraged here. I do not believe in pity. What torments me tonight is the gardener's point of view. What torments me is not this poverty to which after all a man can accustom himself as easily as to sloth. Generations of Orientals live in filth and love it. What torments me is not the humps nor the hollows nor the ugliness. It is the sight, a little bit in all these men, of Mozart murdered.

Only the Spirit, if it breathe upon the clay, can create Man.

More about Penguins

Penguinews, which appears every month, contains
details of all the new books issued by Penguins as they
are published. From time to time it is supplemented by
Penguins in Print, which is a complete list of all books
published by Penguins which are in print. (There are well
over three thousand of these.)

A specimen copy of *Penguinews* will be sent to
you free on request, and you can become a subscriber for
the price of the postage – 4s. for a year's issues (including
the complete lists) if you live in the United Kingdom,
or 8s. if you live elsewhere. Just write to Dept EP,
Penguin Books Ltd, Harmondsworth, Middlesex, enclosing a
cheque or postal order, and your name will be added to the
mailing list.

Some other books published by Penguins are described
on the following pages.

Note : *Penguinews* and *Penguins in Print* are not
available in the U.S.A. or Canada.

The Lost World of the Kalahari

Laurens van der Post

In this enthralling book a distinguished explorer and writer describes his rediscovery of the Bushmen, outcast survivors from Stone Age Africa. Laurens van der Post was fascinated and appalled at the fate of this remarkable people, who seemed to him a reminder of our own 'legitimate beginnings'. Attacked by all the races that came after them in Africa, the last of the Bushmen have in modern times been driven deep into the Kalahari Desert. It was there, in the scorching heat of an African August, that Colonel van der Post led his famous expedition. His search for these small, hardy aboriginals, with their physical peculiarities, their cave art, and their joyful music-making, provides the author with material for a dramatic and compassionate book.

'He is even better in print than he was on TV' – J. B. Priestley in *Reynolds News*.

'No one can write more feelingly of Africa . . . an experience not to be missed' – Elspeth Huxley in the *Evening Standard*

Also available

The Heart of the Hunter

Journey into Russia

Venture to the Interior

A Short Walk in the Hindu Kush

Eric Newby

A traveller's classic, rich in humour and the unexpected.

No Englishman has visited Nuristan since 1891 – so Eric Newby and his Foreign Office friend decide to take a short walk there. This is his famous account of their ill-prepared, well-fated expedition ... their amble almost to the top of a 20,000-foot mountain ... and their strange experiences with the men and the animals of the little-known 'Country of Light'.

Not for sale in the U.S.A.

Schoolhouse in the Clouds

Edmund Hillary

Without the loyalty, liveliness and endurance of the Sherpas, Sir Edmund Hillary would never have conquered Everest. In 1963 Sir Edmund returned to the Himalayas to fulfil a long-standing promise – to give these hardy mountain peoples the water, education and medical supplies which they craved.

Much more than a mercy mission, the Schoolhouse Expedition, described and illustrated in this book, was a two-way process: in the course of it Sir Edmund and his party learned the lore of an alien and invigorating way of life – and found time, in the teeth of the monsoon rains, to attack two great unclimbed Himalayan peaks.

Not for sale in the U.S.A. or Canada

Arabian Sands
Wilfred Thesiger

In *Arabian Sands* Wilfred Thesiger records the many journeys he has made by camel through and around the parched sands of Arabia's Empty Quarter. This is among the greatest books on Arabian travel.

'Following worthily in the tradition of Burton, Doughty, Lawrence, Philby, and Thomas, it is, very likely, the book about Arabia to end all books about Arabia' – Lord Kinross in the *Daily Telegraph*

'Wilfred Thesiger is perhaps the last, and certainly one of the greatest, of the British travellers among the Arabs. ... The narrative is vividly written, with a thousand little anecdotes and touches which bring back to any who have seen these countries every scene with the colour of real life' – Sir John Glubb in the *Sunday Times*

'For all who love travel and for whom the desert preserves its mystique this splendid book, magnificently illustrated with the author's photographs, is a feast' – George Millar in the *Daily Express*

'*Arabian Sands* is that rare thing, a really great travel book' – Hammond Innes

Also available
The Marsh Arabs

Not for sale in the U.S.A.

The Kon-Tiki Expedition

Thor Heyerdahl

'One of the best adventure books ever written ... a privilege to read' – Howard Spring in *Country Life*

Kon-Tiki – which has sold more than 4,000,000 copies – was the first post-war best-seller. It is surely one of the great books of our time. The story tells how six young men, against all expert advice, sailed across the Pacific on a balsa-wood raft to test a racial theory. Somerset Maugham called it 'an incredible adventure which happens to be true' and added : 'It would be a very dull reader who did not admire and envy the courage of the six men who took part in it.' Critic after critic has endorsed his estimate of a modern saga that has never grown old.

'I have never read a more tonic story of adventure' – Raymond Mortimer in the *Sunday Times*

'An enthralling account of an experience without parallel' – Richard Hughes in the *Observer*

'A fascinating account of a bizarre and adventurous enterprise, excitingly and modestly recounted' – Malcolm Muggeridge in the *Daily Telegraph*

Also available

Aku-Aku

Not for sale in the U.S.A.

Flight to Arras

Antoine de Saint-Exupéry

Saint-Exupéry, a pioneer airman, is now also recognized as one of the finest modern French writers.

In *Flight to Arras* the author is sent on a reconnaissance flight over enemy-occupied France. The time is 1940, France is a shambles, his flight is pointless, and his chances of getting back alive are two to one against.

This is a classic war story about the futility of war. It is a picture of a defeated country and an understanding portrait of men who contribute to defeat by putting humanity above patriotism. And yet it is a deeply patriotic book – an explanation of how danger can change a man from pessimistic fatalism to all-seeing courage in a few seconds. It is a book in praise of man, of France, and of flying.

Also by Antoine de Saint-Exupéry

A Puffin Book:

The Little Prince

Not for sale in the U.S.A. or Canada